Triumphs and Tragedies of the Modern Congress

Triumphs and Tragedies of the Modern Congress

Case Studies in Legislative Leadership

Maxmillian Angerholzer III,
James Kitfield,
Christopher P. Lu, and Norman
Ornstein, Editors

Foreword by David M. Abshire

CENTER FOR THE STUDY OF THE
PRESIDENCY & CONGRESS

AN IMPRINT OF ABC-CLIO, LLC
Santa Barbara, California • Denver, Colorado • Oxford, England

About the Center for the Study of the Presidency & Congress

Established in 1965, the Center for the Study of the Presidency & Congress is a unique non-partisan, non-profit 501(c)(3) organization in Washington, D.C., that collaborates with the best minds in government, the private sector, and academia to apply strategic thinking and the lessons of history and leadership to today's most critical policy challenges.

Other CSPC publications of interest:

Presidential Studies Quarterly (ISSN 0360–4918)

A Call to Greatness: Challenging Our Next President, by David M. Abshire (Rowman & Littlefield, 2008)

Saving the Reagan Presidency, by David M. Abshire (Texas A&M University Press, 2005)

Triumphs and Tragedies of the Modern Presidency (Praeger, 2001)

Library of Congress Cataloging-in-Publication Data

Triumphs and tragedies of the modern Congress : case studies in legislative leadership / Maxmillian Angerholzer III, James Kitfield, Christopher P. Lu, and Norman Ornstein, editors.

pages cm

Includes index.

ISBN 978-1-4408-3199-7 (hardback) — ISBN 978-1-4408-3200-0 (ebook) — ISBN 978-1-4408-3335-9 (paperback) 1. United States. Congress. 2. United States. Congress—Leadership. 3. United States—Politics and government. I. Angerholzer, Maxmillian.

JK1021.T75 2014

328.73—dc23   2014021586

ISBN (hardcover): 978-1-4408-3199-7
ISBN (paperback): 978-1-4408-3335-9
EISBN: 978-1-4408-3200-0

18 17 16 15 14   1 2 3 4 5

This book is also available on the World Wide Web as an eBook.
Visit www.abc-clio.com for details.

Praeger
An Imprint of ABC-CLIO, LLC

ABC-CLIO, LLC
130 Cremona Drive, P.O. Box 1911
Santa Barbara, California 93116-1911

This book is printed on acid-free paper ∞

Manufactured in the United States of America

Contents

Foreword

In 1998, when I took the reins of the Center for the Study of the Presidency & Congress from the great Gordon Hoxie, I immediately understood that this organization sat on a wealth of powerful historical lessons for today's policy makers. As Mark Twain purportedly said, "history doesn't repeat itself, but it can rhyme." One of the first projects we embarked upon was *Triumphs and Tragedies of the Modern Presidency,* where the case study model was used to examine the Executive. Now, we turn our attention to the Congress.

During my long career in Washington, I have seen, firsthand, the highs and lows of Congress—both the members and the institution. There have been times when Congress has risen to the challenge, sought compromise over political gain, made our nation stronger, and brought us to higher ground. Other times, I have seen politics, partisanship, and rivalries delay or derail needed action.

I have seen how presidents have worked closely with Congress, developing policies and legislation that move the nation. I experienced the dysfunction when Congress and the President choose secrecy and political combat instead of the national interest.

Congress—foremost among the institutions built by our founders—is often a place of inefficiencies and idiosyncrasies. Henry Clay, arguably our first great congressional leader, is the prototype for today. Leadership, character, and strategic thinking are necessary attributes for the men and women whom we elect to represent us.

The leaders we examine in this book have exemplified these characteristics. At times they have been overcome by their shortcomings. Understanding the successes and failures of these individuals is a vital tool for today's leaders, and those of tomorrow. When it is hard to understand what impact an individual can have among a body of 535, these case studies illustrate a path forward.

Our examination of domestic and foreign policy case studies demonstrate the role of Congress in shaping both our nation and the world. Congress, in times of crisis, can quickly act. At other times, congressional deadlock and inaction seems to exacerbate the predicament. These lessons show that Congress often moves at its own pace, yet manages to rise to the challenge.

Finally, when Congress has examined the scandals that have rocked our faith in our elected officials, it has been driven by institutional prerogative, political motivations, and a quest for the truth.

At a time when perceptions of Congress and its partisanship are at their lowest, these lessons allow us—as leaders, as scholars, and as voters—to better understand how the Congress—the institution and its members—can continue to help make this nation prosperous and secure.

Ambassador David M. Abshire, PhD

Introduction

When President Dwight D. Eisenhower called for the establishment of what would become the Center for the Study of the Presidency & Congress (CSPC), the Supreme Allied Commander turned President lamented the lack of historical case studies to prepare him for civilian political leadership. As a military leader, he could pour over analyses of previous battles, deployments, and international crises, yet no similar repository of institutional memory existed for the equally complex arts of governing and legislating.

In 2000, CSPC published *Triumphs and Tragedies of the Modern Presidency,* a collection of case studies focused on the complexities of presidential leadership—a modern fulfillment of President Eisenhower's wish. With this current anthology, we now turn our attention to the Legislative Branch and the intricate dynamics of leadership, procedure, and politics involved in exercising the myriad responsibilities of the Congress.

Today, the public perception of Congress—along with many of our other political institutions—is at its nadir. Partisan sniping and legislative deadlock feed a narrative that Congress is unable to address the nation's challenges. However, as many of these case studies illustrate, partisanship and rivalry are not unique to the current political environment.

As these case studies reveal, the pace of change in Congress is sometimes very rapid. At other times it can seem glacial, especially in response to immediate challenges or fast-moving crises. However, as these case studies demonstrate, Congress more often than not has been able to find its way to reasonable solutions to the biggest challenges facing our nation. In choosing these case studies, we thus looked not only for examples that stand on their own as significant legislative accomplishments, but also for major milestones that helped shape modern America as we know it today. The stories they tell speak of leadership, compromise, and coalition building, as well as to the challenges of partisanship, unwieldy caucuses, and personal foibles.

The initial case studies serve as a virtual "Congress 101," providing the reader with an overview of the constitutional dynamics of the Legislative Branch; congressional committees and the importance of rules and procedures in determining legislative outcomes; the impact of the increasingly permanent election campaign; and one particularly strong outside force that influences Congress—lobbyists.

We next profile some of the major figures of the modern Congress. Although each of these leaders has left an indelible mark on Congress—and the country—this list is not meant to be exhaustive. Entire volumes could be filled with the stories of famous—and infamous—members of Congress. The selections we made span the 20th and early 21st centuries, and provide both partisan and bicameral balance.

In the case study of Sam Rayburn, you can see the impact of a congressional leader who eschewed the spotlight in favor of behind-the-scenes work and socialization with his colleagues. Gerald Ford's time in the House of Representatives illustrates how personal relationships and the esteem of colleagues can assist in a politician's rise to power. Tip O'Neill's major legislative accomplishments were enabled by an unusually close cooperation between a Speaker and a President, despite sharp ideological differences. The story of Dan Rostenkowski illustrates the power of committee chairmen, and the pitfalls of failing to understand changing political winds. Newt Gingrich's tenure traces an arc of revolutionary leadership, political hubris, and bipartisan reform, while the story of Tom DeLay is one of ruthless political maneuvering. Dennis Hastert's story shows how even seemingly "accidental" leaders can have a lasting impact. And Nancy Pelosi's historic rise to the Speakership is a powerful example of the changing demographics of Congress and the ability to effect change in a brief period of time.

The story of Richard Russell illuminates the Senate as it was for much of the 20th century, when rules and procedures were too often used to stymie needed reforms and national renewal. Robert Taft's case study shows how the personality of one individual can have an outsized impact on a specific policy, even when that policy is being overtaken by a changing world. Our examination of Lyndon Johnson, by one senior member of his administration, shows how a president can use not only his legislative experience, but also a national mood of sorrow, to advance a legislative agenda.

Perhaps no politician personified a political philosophy like Jesse Helms, while the story of Ted Kennedy is one of historic victories, crushing defeats, and close friendships—personal and political. The story of Sam Nunn, as told through the eyes of David M. Abshire, a former U.S. Ambassador to NATO, shows how an influential member of Congress can help drive foreign policy through shrewd action and strategic acumen. The story of Dick Lugar is not only a testament to bipartisanship and expertise in a specific area—again foreign policy—but also a cautionary tale about the risks of political moderation in a polarized era. Finally, the story of John McCain, as told by Joe Lieberman, one of his closest colleagues, is a tale of uncommon leadership and character, resident in a man with the vision of a "maverick" and an instinct for reaching across the aisle.

In examining major domestic policy accomplishments, we look at how Congress overcame significant obstacles, from within and without, to shape modern American life for the better. While the public may think that most legislation moves through the orderly process detailed in civics class and *Schoolhouse Rock* videos, many of the examples we have selected illustrate how Congress has increasingly relied on outside groups such as commissions, or the expertise of key members, to craft legislation. In some circumstances, an actively engaged public has helped move Congress to action. In others, Congress has functioned better away from the public spotlight.

While it may be hard to imagine similar progress on some of today's hot button issues—immigration, our tenuous national finances, climate change—Congress has risen to the challenge in the past. Civil rights, Medicare, Social Security reform, and tax reform are just some of the legislative milestones by which Congress has put its imprint on modern America.

For those affected by injustice or prejudice, Congress has often seemed to move too slowly, but there have also been momentous civil rights victories. Major reforms often required tenacious efforts from key leaders or a determined group of legislators. In some areas, Congress found it needed to reform itself to keep up with a changing America. In other, rarer, cases, Congress found itself able to act to stave off a crisis.

In the case studies that we have selected for foreign and security policy, we examine the role that Congress has played in shaping America's global leadership, and the changing balance between congressional and presidential power in matters of national security. Even as the Commander in Chief has become increasingly powerful through the World War II, Cold War, and post–Cold War eras—and now through the post-9/11 era—Congress has made pivotal decisions regarding security at home and abroad. As the title of this book suggests, there are tragedies as well as triumphs in the telling.

In the long run-up to World War II, for instance, with Nazi Germany conquering much of Europe and Imperial Japan ascendant in Asia, isolationists in Congress tried to impede President Roosevelt's ability to come to the aid of Great Britain, or raise an army at home. Conversely, by passing the National Security Act of 1947, Congress helped build the national security architecture that would ultimately prevail in the Cold War against the Soviet Union. In passing the Gulf of Tonkin Resolution of 1964, Congress essentially gave President Johnson a blank check for war, foreshadowing the tragic U.S. military escalation in Vietnam. Largely as a result, Congress in the 1970s passed the War Powers Act to limit a Commander in Chief's ability to use military force without congressional approval; established the Church and Pike Commissions to rein in excesses by the intelligence and law enforcement communities; and established an all-volunteer military to quell protests against the wartime draft.

With the Goldwater-Nichols Act of 1986, Congress took the lead and successfully pushed through the most sweeping reforms of the Pentagon and U.S. military since 1947. During the post–Cold War military drawdown of the 1990s, Congress also established the successful Base Realignment and Closure Commission to overcome institutional resistance to closing military bases in home districts. As bookends in the ongoing struggle for war powers between Congress and the White House, the Iraq war resolutions of 1991 and 2002 revealed just how much the balance has shifted toward the Commander in Chief in the modern era. Similarly, the Patriot Act of 2001 showed once again how power accrues to the Executive Branch in times of national crisis. The congressionally mandated "9/11 Commission," which investigated the terrorist attacks of September 11, 2001, was a modern hallmark of congressional oversight, while the Iraq Study Group of 2006 represents a failed attempt by Congress to change the President's wartime strategy.

The lessons within all these case studies can inform future national security decision making, and provide a sense of how some dynamics—partisanship, leadership, procedural matters—are impacted by foreign threats.

Finally, we conclude with an examination of Congress's role in our nation's greatest political scandals. In these case studies, we explore how the Congress investigated wrongdoing by the President and the highest officials in the White House, and how these scandals affected both the political dynamics within Congress, as well as the balance between Executive and Legislative powers.

There's no doubt that Congress has changed much over the past century, and over the past decade: fundraising has taken on greater importance; friendships across the aisle are rarer; the media landscape has become more fragmented; special interest groups have taken on a greater role; political parties have become more ideologically defined and more polarized; and the Internet has transformed the relationship between lawmakers and their constituents. Nevertheless, the lessons of history contained in this book remind us of the pivotal role played by Congress in improving the economic and social well-being of the American people and projecting American leadership around the world. If the United States is to maintain its prominent position in the future, then Congress must search for ways to overcome its divisions and confront the serious challenges facing our country.

Maxmillian Angerholzer III, Christopher
P. Lu, James Kitfield, and Norman Ornstein

SECTION I
"Congress 101"

1. An "Invitation to Struggle": Congress and the Constitution

by Norman Ornstein

One of the most striking exhibits at the National Archives is that of the original U.S. Constitution. Laid out, page-by-page, under deep layers of impregnable glass, it is stirring—and instructive. It becomes visually crystal clear what the Framers had in mind with a constitutional structure built on three separate branches. Article I, on the Legislative Branch, takes up a lot of space. Article II, on the Executive Branch, takes up much less. Article III, on the Judicial Branch, takes up almost none. The numbers of words quantify the point. Article I is 2,320 words; Article II is 1,035; and Article III is 383.

Congress is first and foremost in the Constitution, reflecting a clear understanding by the Framers of its centrality in our democracy. The first article sets out in detail the powers of Congress, its organization, and forms of election. As *Federalist No. 51* says, "In republican government, the legislative authority necessarily predominates." If that were not the clear framework, the Constitution would have been structured in a different way, either starting with the Executive or starting with the broader powers of the national government before splitting them up among the branches.

Of course, legislative supremacy does not mean legislative dictatorship. The two other branches have their own distinct powers, including the President's expansive role in war making, treaty making, and diplomacy. The Constitution also gives the other two branches considerable ability to check and balance Congress.

While the powers overlap and the checks exist, there is a bottom line, and it favors Congress. The President can veto congressional actions—but Congress, by two-thirds margins in both houses, can override the veto, and the President cannot override the override. Congress can oversee the actions of the Executive, compelling documents and testimony from its staff; except in the case of suspicion of criminal activity, the Executive cannot compel members of Congress in the same way. Since *Marbury v. Madison,* the Supreme Court can rule congressional actions unconstitutional—but Congress, outside of a quite narrow original jurisdiction for the Court, can add or subtract from much of the Court's jurisdictional purview, and can change the size of the Supreme Court. Congress funds the Executive and the courts, with some constraints on its power, and Congress funds itself.

And then there is the trump card: Congress can impeach and remove presidents, other executive officials, judges, and justices from office. Neither the President nor the Supreme Court can remove members of Congress from office; only Congress itself, via expulsion—and voters, via elections—can do that.

THE WHITE HOUSE AND CONGRESS

Congress may be the first among equals, and has the most explicit array of powers and responsibilities, but that does not mean that it rules the roost. Presidents have their own special role and legitimacy: they are chosen in nationwide elections, and with a singular imprimatur that hundreds of mostly anonymous lawmakers cannot begin to challenge. At particular moments of national strife and emergency, or when their parties control large majorities in Congress, assertive presidents can bend the Legislative Branch to their will and take steps that transform America—witness Franklin Roosevelt's First Hundred Days, Thomas Jefferson and the Louisiana Purchase, and Lyndon Johnson and the Great Society. In the era of the Cold War, historians like Arthur Schlesinger warned about an imperial presidency, with unaccountable power unleashed by the ominous threat of nuclear war. Today, many in Congress and media outlets hyperbolically warn about a dictatorial President Obama, using White House czars and executive orders to bypass the Constitution.

Those trends, and warnings, reflect to some considerable degree another key reality of the Constitution. There are separate legislative and executive powers, but the separation is not exactly clean. While the Executive Branch has the executive power, there is also a legislative role for the Vice President and President; the Vice President has a direct legislative role as President of the Senate, while the President is empowered to communicate policy priorities to Congress. War powers are divided between Legislative and Executive Branches, but in a way that in practical terms is murky and often favors the Commanders in Chief sitting in the Oval Office.

The great constitutional scholar Edward Corwin many decades ago referred to the Constitution as "an invitation to struggle." That remains the template for understanding Congress's role as established in the Constitution and Congress's relationship to the other branches. Congress has the two most consequential powers explicitly set out in the Constitution: the power to declare war and the power to tax Americans and spend their tax dollars. But presidents have often engaged in military conflicts, some lasting years and involving tens of thousands of casualties, that were not triggered by or ratified by a formal declaration of war; the Korean and Vietnam wars are the most conspicuous examples.

And the congressional power of the purse can also be countered by a clever, ruthless, and aggressive president. Congress denied funds for President Teddy Roosevelt to send the U.S. Navy around the world as a show of American strength and resolve—so Roosevelt used existing funds to send the fleet halfway around the world. He then asked Congress if they would leave our Navy there to starve, or provide the funds to bring them home.

Congress responded to the conduct of the Vietnam War—the vast expansion triggered by the Gulf of Tonkin Resolution (which congressional leaders believed President Johnson had pushed for under false pretenses), the bombing of Cambodia, and other actions Richard Nixon took without congressional approval—by passing the War Powers Resolution. The act passed even over Nixon's veto. But the War Powers Resolution has provided little additional deterrent to presidents acting militarily without initial congressional involvement; when it has been invoked with American troops already on the battlefield, Congress has not been willing to pull the plug.

Congress has also found its vaunted power of the purse countered by presidents who refuse to spend appropriated funds for laws they do not like. When Richard Nixon impounded money and refused to implement environmental and other laws passed by Congress, Congress countered with the Budget and Impoundment Control Act, which was also enacted during Ford's presidency. It created the modern budget process to give Congress more expertise and authority, but also outlawed most forms of impoundment.

THE SUPREME COURT

The tugs of war, and invitation to struggle, have not been just between Congress and the Presidency. The Supreme Court has also been a major player either in curtailing or ratifying congressional power. No decision in history was more consequential than *Marbury v. Madison,* when Chief Justice John Marshall established in 1803 the precedent of the Court ruling on the constitutionality of congressional actions. A century later, in the 1905 case of *Lochner v. New York,* the Court struck down a New York law limiting the number of hours that bakers could work, saying that it was an "unreasonable, unnecessary and arbitrary interference with the right and liberty of the individual to contract." Using *Lochner* as a precedent, the Court—over the next 30 years—invalidated a series of laws passed by Congress that tried to regulate child labor and broader working conditions, and took a dim view of Congress's power under the Commerce Clause, the section in Article I giving Congress the power to regulate commerce "among the several states."

Under pressure from the public and President Franklin Roosevelt, in 1937, the Court began to reverse course; in two cases, *NLRB v. Jones,* and *West Coast Hotel Co. v. Parrish,* a more expansive view of the government's power to regulate commerce emerged, and carried through until 2012. In the case challenging the constitutionality of the Affordable Care Act, *National Federation of Independent Businesses v. Sebelius,* the Court, in a 5–4 decision written by Chief Justice John Roberts, used a technical argument that construed an individual mandate penalty as a tax, to both uphold the law and put limits on Congress's power under the Commerce Clause. Roberts wrote:

> Construing the Commerce Clause to permit Congress to regulate individuals precisely *because* they are doing nothing would open a new and potentially vast domain to congressional authority. . . . The Framers knew the difference between doing something and doing nothing. They gave Congress the power to *regulate* commerce, not to *compel* it. Ignoring that distinction would undermine the principle that the Federal Government is a government of limited and enumerated powers.

Roberts's opinion did not return Congress to the *Lochner* era, but it signaled a new era in which the Court would be more willing to limit congressional action in an interconnected, global economy where almost any action has some relevance to interstate or foreign commerce.

CONGRESSIONAL POWER DYNAMIC

Congressional power has, not surprisingly, ebbed and flowed over the course of American history. The power and willingness to block presidents varies according to several factors. Are we in the middle of a national catastrophe or crisis—a war or depression? If so, presidents take the reins. Do we have united or divided government? With united government, Congress can have real power, but it tends to defer, when it comes to priorities, to the President, while reserving fiercely for itself the power to manage the details. (There are exceptions to this, as in Franklin Roosevelt's First Hundred Days, when the economic crisis triggered by the Great Depression enabled the President to send legislation to Congress, which was often adopted *in toto.*) In a divided government, not surprisingly, the party without the Presidency tends to assert itself inside Congress more, requiring presidents to work harder to build coalitions.

The distrust of accumulated power that is deeply rooted in the American tradition has helped shape the way in which these dynamics play out. Long-time House staffer and congressional rules expert Donald Wolfensberger has noted that divided government is normal in American political life, "Unified party government remains more the exception than the rule in the United States, primarily because the Framers' conception took deeper root than any attempts to transplant the British system on American soil."

Wolfensberger's point is well taken; the American system was set up to be different from a parliamentary system, where voters elect a government, which acts over the vociferous objections of a minority party, and the public accepts the legitimacy of the government's decisions, knowing it will have an opportunity in short order to vote to ratify or to reject the policies, retaining the majority or replacing them with the minority party.

The Constitution does not mention political parties, but parties emerged in Congress soon after the Constitution was ratified. With separate elections for the House, Senate, and White House, the Framers expected that different coalitions might emerge for different issues, after the extended debate and deliberation built into the congressional process. But the American constitutional system was not designed to work in the same way as a parliamentary system, and could not work if American parties became like parliamentary parties.

The contemporary problems of dysfunction in American national government flow, in significant part, from the fact that our parties have increasingly become homogeneous and ideologically polarized, and strategically act like parliamentary parties. This creates a challenge when there is unified party government, as in 2009–2010, and when sweeping policies are enacted not with broad coalitions, but rather by one party against the united and vehement opposition of the other, leading a sizable share of the population to view the outcomes as illegitimate. This creates an even greater challenge when there is a divided government with a parliamentary-style minority party that unites to vote "no" on most proposals, leading to gridlock.

This is not the first time the United States has faced such strains in its governing fabric. The period leading up to the Civil War, and the period around the economic crisis of the early and mid-1890s were others. The flexibility of the constitutional structure—the fact that powers are enumerated but still overlap—enabled the country to endure conflicts and governing crises and eventually return to the more typical struggles. That is what will likely happen again, without any need or impetus to change the fundamental constitutional arrangements.

◆　◆　◆　◆　◆

2. Building Blocks of Legislation: Congressional Committees and Procedures

by C. Lawrence Evans

Decades ago, Representative John Dingell (D-MI) famously quipped, "If you let me write the procedure and I let you write the substance, I'll [screw] you every time."[1] In understanding the possibilities and limits of legislative achievement in Congress, Dingell's claim about the importance of internal structures and rules is an exaggeration—but not by much.

By constitutional design, members of Congress are responsible for determining the internal structures and rules of the House and Senate, and as Dingell implied, the consequences of their structural and procedural choices are rarely trivial and almost never neutral. To be sure, the internal rules of the game help members from diverse constituencies act collectively on highly complex national issues. But they also determine how power is distributed within the House and Senate, and thus help determine who wins and who loses in the legislative game. This chapter will address two important aspects of internal congressional structure: the committee systems of the House and Senate and the rules that guide legislative decisions on the floors of the respective chambers and the impact of partisan polarization on structural politics in the contemporary Congress.

COMMITTEES: PILLARS OF EXPERTISE

The House and Senate committee systems emerged fairly early in the 19th century, and the committees of Congress have changed in number and importance over the course of American history. Within each chamber, committees are designed to provide a subset of members with the responsibility for producing the crucial first draft of legislation and taking the lead in overseeing the implementation of laws by the Executive Branch. The influence of a committee, then, is rooted in its jurisdiction, or the set of issues and programs over which it has formal authority according to the standing rules of the relevant chamber. Both the House Committee on Ways and Means and the Senate Committee on Finance, for example, have jurisdiction over the tax code, trade policy, Social Security, and Medicare, and these jurisdictional responsibilities are delineated in chamber rules.

By most accounts, committees enhance the efficiency of the lawmaking process in Congress. Members of the committee with jurisdiction over an issue tend to care the most about that policy area, which creates incentives for them to accumulate significant expertise. Committee memberships also tend to carry over from Congress to Congress, which further increases the informational advantages of committee members relative to other lawmakers. The committee systems of Congress, in short, foster a legislative division of labor that allows the two chambers to more productively respond to the multitude of complex policy challenges facing the nation.[2]

The value of committees as a source of expertise for the full body is greater in the House than in the Senate. In the smaller Senate, members tend to serve on more committees and have access to greater staff resources. Also, as representatives of states rather than less populous House districts, Senators are confronted by a more diverse set of interests and pressures from home. Even in the Senate, however, the institutional leaders and chamber experts in a policy area are disproportionately likely to serve on the committees of jurisdiction.

For example, Senator Robert Packwood (R-OR), then-chairman of the Committee on Finance, was pivotal to the passage of the landmark Tax Reform Act of 1986. And for many decades, Senator Edward Kennedy (D-MA) was an institutional leader on health reform issues in part because of his senior position on the Committee on Labor and Human Resources, which has partial jurisdiction in that area. Senators Sam Nunn (D-GA) and Richard Lugar (R-IN) were respected voices on international and national security issues in large part because of their chairmanships of the Committees on Armed Services and Foreign Relations, respectively.

In addition to serving as a source of information and expertise, committees are also a crucial means through which the House and Senate distribute power between members. The committee assignment process is characterized by constrained self-selection. Members request assignments to panels that are of particular relevance to their constituents and to their own policy interests and, for the most part, party leaders do their best to accommodate such requests.[3] As a result, the Ways and Means and Finance panels usually include members with constituencies that include energy producers and other organized interests likely to benefit from aspects of the tax code. The House and Senate Agriculture Committees, in contrast, almost entirely comprise members from farm country.

Not surprisingly, interest groups and other organized advocates tend to focus their lobbying, grassroots support, and campaign donations on members who serve on the committees with jurisdiction over their core interests.[4] Together, the assignment process and the behavior of organized interests conspire to bring the policy views and priorities of committee members closer to the entities that fall within their panel's jurisdiction.[5] For instance, the agriculture committees tend to be pro-farmer, the two tax-writing committees are especially friendly to the interests of big business, and so on.

Since the House and Senate lean heavily on their committees for policy expertise and information, the unrepresentativeness of a panel can lead to policy outcomes that disproportionately benefit organized constituency groups at the expense of the collective interests of the country as a whole. The potential for such distortions, however, is conditioned on the nature of a panel's jurisdiction.[6] If the impact of policy changes in an issue area largely affects a fairly narrow interest that is concentrated in certain geographic areas, then the bills emerging from that area are especially distorted toward special interests and away from collective goals. If the affected interests are highly organized but spread throughout the country, policy distortions are also likely, but the problem is rooted in the strategic calculations of the membership as a whole, rather than the individual members of the relevant committee. In contrast, if the effects of policy changes are broadly distributed, such as on major ideological and partisan concerns, the latent parochialism of the committee system is less consequential because members are less likely to defer to the panel of jurisdiction.

HOUSE FLOOR PROCEDURES

In both chambers of Congress, the number of potential bills, amendments, and other legislative proposals far exceeds the available institutional time. As a result, procedures that restrict access to the floor agenda are essential for the House and Senate to even function as legislative bodies. Within both chambers, it should be emphasized, floor procedures are more than politically neutral tools for the efficient processing of legislation. As is the case with committee assignments and jurisdictions, these procedures also provide certain members with disproportionate power over outcomes. This power can take two forms: one, the right to offer proposals for consideration by the full body, and, two, the right to block proposals from such consideration. Importantly, the nature of floor procedure differs substantially between the House and Senate.

The standing rules of the House stipulate that any amendments offered to legislation in committee or on the floor must be germane to the base bill. Germaneness is a complex, and often malleable, criterion, but essentially it means substantively relevant. The requirement that modifications to bills be substantively germane helps gird the policy-making role of House committees. For the most part, members can only legislate on the issues within a committee's jurisdiction by offering modifications to bills reported by that panel.

On the floor of the House, legislation tends to follow one of two main procedural tracks.[7] On the one hand, bills and resolutions that are relatively noncontroversial or minor are often considered via the "suspension calendar." Under "suspension of the rules," measures are brought to the floor (usually on Mondays or Tuesdays when the House is in session) and debate is limited to just 40 minutes, with no amendments or points of order permitted. Passage requires a two-thirds supermajority. The Speaker generally controls access to the suspension calendar, but the two-thirds requirement means that a degree of bipartisan support is necessary for measures to pass. Use of the suspension calendar has increased from the 1980s to the 2000s, accounting for about 80 percent of passed bills by 2010.

Consideration of major or controversial legislation under suspension of the rules is not generally feasible. Under such conditions, members will usually want the opportunity to offer amendments and/or a two-thirds vote in support of passage is not in the cards. As a result, most major legislation is considered via a special "rule" devised by the Committee on Rules. These special rules are bill-specific resolutions that delineate the procedures to be used for the consideration of a piece of legislation. Typically, special rules delineate when a measure will be brought to the floor and for how long, which amendments are in order, who can offer these amendments, the order in which amendments will be considered, and whether or not second-degree amendments (amendments to amendments) are permissible. On occasion, special rules are also used to waive the germaneness requirement and other aspects of the chamber's standing rules that might constrain the operating autonomy of the leadership or other backers of legislation. Although formally crafted within the House Rules Committee, special rules must receive majority support on the floor to have any force.

Prior to the 1970s, the Rules Committee functioned with considerable autonomy from party leaders within the chamber. In the 1940s and 1950s, for example, the panel was often dominated by a conservative coalition of Southern Democrats and Republicans. Progressive legislation dealing with labor or civil rights issues periodically was reported by the standing committees of jurisdiction, only to be blocked from floor consideration because a rightward-leaning Rules panel refused to provide the measure with a rule.

As part of a wave of internal reforms in the 1970s, Democrats provided the Speaker with the authority to appoint all Democratic members of the Rules Committee, and Republicans soon followed suit by granting their party leaders the same authority. These changes in the Rules Committee selection process transformed the panel into an extension of the leadership, with the majority leadership exercising effective control. In the contemporary House, the majority leadership's control over the Rules Committee—and how legislation is considered on the floor—is now the lynchpin of party power.[8]

The move from a semiautonomous to a party-dominated Rules Committee coincided with a shift from special rules that were relatively open—that is, allowing many amendments—to rules that were increasingly restrictive. Prior to the late 1980s, most bills were brought to the floor without significant restrictions on amendments. Ever since then, however, rules have been increasingly restrictive, so that by the 2000s, roughly 80 percent of the rules emanating from the Rules panel were restrictive.[9]

To be sure, part of the reason for the rise of restrictive floor procedures in the House was efficiency and the need to reduce uncertainty on the floor. The number of amendments offered on the floor of the House increased substantially because of rules changes—for example, facilitating the use of recorded votes on floor amendments—and broader changes in the political environment of Congress—for example, the increased scope of government brought on by the 1960s "Great Society" programs and an accompanying expansion in the number and importance of interests groups in Washington. The House leadership came to rely on restrictive floor procedures to make the legislative agenda more predictable and to conserve scarce floor time.[10]

But highly restrictive floor procedures—combined with the transfer of control over the Rules Committee to the House leadership—also had consequences for the distribution of power within the chamber, and thus the content of legislation. In the contemporary House, the majority leadership uses its control over the Rules Committee and floor procedure more generally to promote adoption of the party's policy agenda and to limit—or even block—consideration of alternatives emanating from the partisan minority.

There are aspects of floor procedure, of course, that constrain somewhat the majority party's monopoly control over the agenda. As mentioned, the special rules that are produced by the Rules Committee still need majority support on the floor, and thus there are incentives for House leaders not to push their procedural prerogatives too far. But rules votes are also loyalty votes, and leaders of both parties expect their fellow partisans to toe the party line. There can be repercussions for members who regularly vote against the party on procedural matters, such as difficulty getting their bills scheduled for action, fewer opportunities for more preferred committee assignments, and fewer party campaign donations.

Another procedural check on majority party agenda control is the "discharge rule," which allows rank-and-file members to bring a bill directly before the full chamber if 218 signatures—a majority of the House—can be secured for a petition discharging the matter from committee. In addition, since 1995 the minority party in the House has been guaranteed under House rules the right to offer a "motion to recommit" with instructions prior to votes on the final passage of legislation. The motion to recommit provides the minority party with an opportunity to offer an amendment immediately before the vote on passage, which in theory can undercut the majority party's control over the agenda. As is the case with votes on special rules, however, the House majority leadership can pressure rank-and-file members of their party not to sign a discharge petition or to vote for minority motions to recommit. Not surprisingly, few bills are actually discharged out of committee and motions to recommit seldom pass on the floor.

SENATE FLOOR PROCEDURES

Floor procedures in the Senate differ from those of the House in important ways. For one, there is no general germaneness requirement in the standing rules of the Senate. On the floor, individual Senators are free to essentially "change the legislative topic" by offering amendments on subjects very different from the content of the bill under consideration. The lack of a germaneness rule serves to empower individual Senators and constrain the authority of committees and leaders.

In sharp contrast to the House, the procedures of the Senate give the majority party only limited control over the floor agenda. There is nothing analogous to the House Rules Committee in the Senate.[11] Indeed, the Senate Majority Leader's agenda prerogatives mostly take the form of priority recognition rights on the floor. In other words, the Majority Leader is recognized first if more than one member is asking for the right to speak. Rather than use special rules to structure floor action on major bills, in the Senate the leadership attempts to manage floor operations via unanimous consent agreements, which any Senator can block. Indeed, the passage of major legislation may require the adoption of dozens or even hundreds of discrete unanimous consent requests relating to the order and timing of amendments, who has permission to speak and for how long, and so on.

Most important, unlike the House, the Senate standing rules lack a motion on the previous question, which is the parliamentary procedure that legislatures generally use to end debate and move to a vote. As a result, any Senator can take the floor and filibuster, that is, engage in extended debate and other dilatory tactics aimed at putting off or blocking resolution of a matter. Indeed, any debatable motion in the chamber is potentially open to a filibuster.

Prior to 1917, there was no procedural vehicle for ending a filibuster. Since the adoption of Senate Rule XXII that year, a supermajority of Senators has been able to invoke cloture, and after brief debate postcloture, secure a vote on the affected question. Rule XXII has been modified through the years. In the contemporary chamber, 60 votes are required to invoke cloture, and deliberations postcloture are limited to 30 hours and only those amendments that are germane and pending. As a result of the scarcity of floor time, especially as recesses and other deadlines near, filibusters of even fairly consensual proposals can kill the targeted initiative.[12] And throughout Senate history, the consideration of major legislative initiatives with substantial bipartisan support often has been shaped by actual and threatened filibusters. The critical hurdle to passage of the landmark Civil Rights Acts of 1957 and 1964, for example, was overcoming filibusters led by prominent Southerners such as Senator Richard Russell (D-GA). (See "Richard Russell Jr.: Patriarch of the Senate," Chapter 13.)

PARTISAN POLARIZATION

Over the past four decades, the House and the Senate increasingly have become polarized along partisan lines. Prior to the 1970s, Democrats tended toward the left of the ideological distribution and Republicans to the right, but there were dozens of members in the ideological overlap between the two parties. As a result of the civil rights revolution of the 1960s, conservative Southerners shifted their allegiance from the Democratic to the Republican Party, which helped sort the two congressional parties more cleanly along ideological lines. In the 1980s, the deeply ideological program of the Reagan Administration further polarized the two parties on Capitol Hill. And modern communication and campaign fund-raising strategies enabled party elites to better mobilize and respond to their respective activist bases. As a result, by the 1990s and 2000s, partisan polarization within the Congress had reached historically high levels. The intense partisanship of the contemporary era has affected the policy-making role of committees and the usage and impact of floor procedures in important ways.[13]

Especially in the House, for instance, power has shifted from the standing committees to the majority leadership. Following the GOP's victory in the midterm elections of 1994 and the assumption of majority status, incoming Speaker Newt Gingrich (R-GA) shepherded through reforms that limited the power of committee chairs relative to the party leadership. (See "Newt Gingrich: The Partisan Revolutionary," Chapter 9)

Now, if a bill is at all important to the party agenda, its content is largely determined by partisan imperatives, rather than by members of the committee of jurisdiction acting to further the interests of important constituencies back home.

In this more partisan era, major legislation is also normally considered via a highly structured rule in which at most a few amendments are in order and the time available for debate is sharply limited. Speaker Dennis Hastert (R-IL) articulated what became known as the "Hastert Rule"—only legislation supported by a majority of the majority party would be allowed on the floor.[14] The guideline has been an informal rule of thumb for decades, but became a widely recognized norm during the 2000s as ideological differences between the two parties became especially pronounced.

In the late 1990s and early 2000s, Republican leaders repeatedly blocked floor action on proposals to reform the nation's campaign finance laws. Although these bills typically were supported by a majority of members, most Republicans were in opposition. The landmark McCain-Feingold law was adopted in large part because of credible threats to discharge the measure to the floor if GOP leaders attempted to block consideration by the full House. During the 113th Congress (2013–2014), there were a few widely publicized violations of the Hastert norm on major bills, but these were exceptions to a widely accepted practice.

Finally, in the increasingly polarized Senates of the 1990s and 2000s, the filibuster has emerged as perhaps the central tool that members of the minority party used to stymie the policy program of the majority party. Filibusters and cloture motions became more common during the 1970s and 1980s, as individual Senators attempted to use the tactic to promote their personal agendas. But as partisan polarization became more pronounced in the 1990s and 2000s, the incidence of dilatory behavior likewise grew to historic levels. In 1989–1990, for example, 38 motions for cloture were filed, there were 24 votes on cloture, and cloture was invoked on 11 occasions. In 2011–2012, in contrast, fully 115 motions for cloture were filed, there were 73 votes on cloture, and cloture was invoked 41 times.[15]

Importantly, in contrast to previous decades, the filibusters of the 1990s and 2000s were largely partisan fights in which the minority party used the dilatory potential of Senate rules to block the policy agenda of the majority party. Except for a brief period in 2009, the size of the majority party in the chamber has not reached the 60 votes necessary to invoke cloture without some support from members of the minority party. By the 2000s, partisan polarization had thus produced what many observers came to call "The Sixty Vote Senate."[16]

The partisan use of filibusters on judicial nominations has especially ran-kled Senate majorities. In 2013, faced with sustained obstructionism by the minority Republicans on nominations from the Barack Obama Administra-tion, Senate Democrats used a parliamentary maneuver called "the nuclear option" to eliminate filibusters on all nominees except those to the U.S. Supreme Court. This procedural change likely will impede the ability of Sen-ate minorities to block presidential appointments, but it did not extend to legislation. In other words, members of the minority party retained their abil-ity to block bills and resolutions that do not receive formal protection from filibusters under chamber rules (e.g., certain budget and trade measures). As partisan polarization continues or even deepens on Capitol Hill, an interest-ing question will be whether or not future Senate majorities once again make use of the nuclear option to extend these filibuster curbs to Supreme Court nominations and even legislation.

The bottom line? Over congressional history, House members and Sena-tors have developed committee structures and floor procedures that serve to further the collective interests of their respective chambers. Along with pro-moting the efficient consideration of legislation, however, these structures and procedures significantly affect the balance of power. In the contemporary House, committees and procedures primarily are used by the majority party to advance measures that are important to that party's legislative and elec-toral agendas, and to block measures championed by the partisan minority. In the modern Senate, the majority's control over chairmanships and other salient aspects of the committee process help that party advance its agenda somewhat. But procedures within the Senate also constrain the ability of the majority party to advance its policy program to a vote and final passage. As a result of committees and floor procedure, then, partisan majorities within the House are empowered, while in the Senate they are highly constrained. And as the chapters of this volume demonstrate, the consequences for legislative achievement can be profound.

◆   ◆   ◆   ◆   ◆

3. Zero-Sum Governing: The Permanent Campaign

by Norman Ornstein

The term "permanent campaign" was popularized by Sidney Blumenthal in 1982, but the phenomenon goes back much further. What Blumenthal referred to was the end of any sense of seasons in the political/policy arena in America—the notion of a season of campaigning, followed by a transition, and then a season of governing. That cycle has been replaced by all campaigning, all the time—what Hugh Heclo defined as "a *nonstop* process seeking to manipulate sources of public approval to engage in the act of governing itself."[1] Indeed, Theodore White's classic *The Making of a President* alludes to the highly sophisticated and systematic polling that was already supreme in the 1960 campaign.

But it took a bit longer for the permanent campaign to dominate in Congress. During the 1970s and 1980s, when I would go to "issue retreats" conducted by lawmakers of both parties, members would be joined at the table by staff and a few outsiders; by the 1990s, the staff tended to be relegated to seats behind the table, supplanted by pollsters and political consultants. In the 1970s, one would see the pollsters and consultants only for a six-month period leading up to the election, after which they would go off for 18 months and do polling or public relations for commercial clients; by the late 1980s, the pollsters and consultants were there throughout the two-year cycle—on staff or doing year-round consultancies.

What brought about the change? Heclo mentions several factors:

- The decline of political parties in recruiting candidates and generating broader coalitions, even as parties grew more ideological and distinctive, becoming better at fund-raising and constructing campaign messages that attacked the other party.
- The rise of a more open and extensive system of interest-group politics, making politicians more subject to pressures from groups and more obliged to engage in perpetual campaigning, and creating a new pool of candidates who were more policy oriented and less pragmatically tied to political parties.
- The emergence of new communications technologies, making available instantaneous communications to voters, but also creating a cacophony of messages. That made crafting powerful messages that could cut

through the noise more desirable—and attacks on opponents and sharp and pungent campaign slogans came to trump boring stories about policy accomplishments or nuances.

- The parallel emergence of new campaign technologies, making continuous polling and sophisticated public relations irresistibly attractive to politicians, and adding to the incentive to focus on issues and policies that polled well and worked politically, including those that drove wedges between rival politicians and their potential voters.

- The need for political money, driven by the increased costs of reaching voters across new media and communications platforms, to pay for pollsters and consultants, and to raise the money in the first place.

- The growing stakes involved with activist government, involving more special interests in the lobbying and political fund-raising process, and raising the stakes in elections that decided not only the number of seats held by the parties, but also the control of congressional chambers.

CHANGES IN CONGRESS

For Congress itself, there are additional factors fueling the permanent campaign. One is that with two-year terms in the House, members are particularly susceptible to the siren song of nonstop campaigning. A second is the advent of jet travel from Washington across the country, making it much more feasible for lawmakers to go back to their districts every weekend, no matter the distance from the Capitol. That in turn made it easier for lawmakers to keep their families back home, loosening their ties to colleagues, including those from the other party, thus making it easier to demonize them. Another is a set of reforms in the 1970s that made Congress more transparent—especially transforming unrecorded votes on most amendments to recorded ones— making it easier to hit lawmakers for controversial votes and to engineer votes designed for political gain more than for policy amendment.

There have been other crucial changes in Congress in recent decades. The dramatic changes in regional politics, which began in the 1960s, caused a "sorting out" of the parties, moving them from being big tents with disparate memberships to becoming narrower bands of ideological conferees. Moderate and liberal Republicans virtually disappeared, while moderate and conservative Democrats were sharply reduced in number. The parties became more polarized, adding to the stakes of majority control.

As Thomas Mann and I point out in *It's Even Worse than It Looks*,[2] Newt Gingrich began exploiting these phenomena almost from the moment of his election to Congress in 1978, planting the seeds for a Republican majority in the House. By polarizing and tribalizing Congress, creating greater partisan animosity, and campaigning relentlessly against a corrupt Democratic Congress, Gingrich was able to achieve his goal in 1994. He thereby ushered in a new era in Congress; after 40 consecutive years of Democratic hegemony in the House, we saw highly competitive elections regularly with majority control each time within reach for the minority. With the stakes so high—dramatically different agendas for the two parties, and marginal changes in a handful of seats potentially making the difference between majority and minority status—building coalitions across party lines to make policy became less and less desirable, while dramatizing differences and demonizing the other side became more and more attractive.

The combination of the proliferation of safe seats in general elections, the rise of primaries in campaigns for House and Senate seats, and new channels for big and often anonymous donations of money through outside groups like the Club for Growth has pressured lawmakers to move further toward the extreme, and discouraged them from voting for compromises that make them targets of ideologically driven hits.

ZERO-SUM GOVERNING

It would be a mistake to overly romanticize the era when there was a separation between campaigning and governing. Much of the policy-making process was conducted outside of public view and without public input, while there was plenty of input from a small and select group of lobbyists and well-heeled special interests. A long era of one-party dominance led to complacency, condescension toward the minority, and corruption and carelessness in the management of Congress. The seniority system also insulated the most powerful members of Congress from their colleagues' views and needs, and from broader public concerns. There was ample corruption—financial and otherwise—again largely out of public view. The openness and transparency that has been brought about by recent reforms has much to commend it, and was long overdue.

But there is little doubt that the costs of the permanent campaign are deep and broad. The separation between campaigning and governing reflected some fundamental principles. Campaigning is a zero-sum game—there is a winner and a loser, and nothing in between. It is no coincidence that campaigns often use the metaphors of war. Governing in the American political system, on the other hand, is an additive process—it requires building coalitions, usually broad coalitions, and any significant changes in policy require broad leadership consensus to build a broad public sense of legitimacy. In the earlier era, lawmakers referred to colleagues from the other side of the aisle as "adversaries," not enemies. An adversary one day can be an ally the next. In the permanent campaign, those on the other side are always the enemy, and cooperating with them is akin to collaboration—to sleeping with the enemy.

At the same time, the permanent campaign is costly. Lawmakers now must raise money not just for themselves, but for the team—and leadership positions, like committee chairmanships or ranking positions, are often allocated on the basis of money-raising prowess. Less time is spent legislating or deliberating, and more and more is devoted to "call time"—racing off the Capitol grounds to call donors to raise money. The time spent on fundraising is itself debilitating, but the process—pandering to wealthy donors or corporations with their own policy agendas—also corrupts the policy process.

Agenda-setting is also affected profoundly and adversely by the permanent campaign. Major national issues that should be the central focal points for congressional leaders looking to build consensus for action—including the basics of taxing and spending, immigration, and climate change—often take second fiddle to wedge issues. These divisive issues can be social ones like abortion and guns, or symbolic ones like votes to repeal Obamacare that have no chance of success, but are used as electioneering markers. And debate and deliberation, the hallmarks of a functional legislative process in Congress, are dropped in favor of position taking, political attacks, and harsh rhetoric.

One consequence of today's politics, where attack ads are increasingly harsh, is a coarsened political culture. With social media now amplifying the new communications technologies identified in 2000 by Heclo, and with the impact of money on politics amplified and distorted further in the aftermath of the Supreme Court's *Citizens United* decision and its progeny, public alienation, cynicism, and distaste for politics and political institutions have reached new highs, even as approval of Congress has plummeted to new lows. The decreasing ability of Congress to focus on solving broad problems that affect American competitiveness in a global economy and address new threats outside our borders as well as deep challenges close to home, combined with public alienation and anger at politics and politicians, have created a depressing dynamic in Washington. Many of the remaining problem-solving politicians in Congress have decided to leave voluntarily rather than face bitter, negative campaigns in order to return to an institution that is focused less and less on solving big problems. The more negative that atmosphere becomes, the more amenable it is to ideologues and demagogues who can exploit anger and frustration.

COUNTERING THE PERMANENT CAMPAIGN

What can be done to alter this negative cycle? Many of the factors that have created the permanent campaign are not going to be reversed or slowed down. We will not be able to stop the advent of new communications and campaign technologies and techniques. Campaign costs will continue to rise. But there are steps to consider. One is to try, even in the absence of a Supreme Court that is sensitive to the consequences of its decisions, to alter the destructive dynamics of political money in campaigns. Public money via multiple matching funds for smaller donations, as is done in New York City, could make it easier for politicians to raise money without some of the corrosive effects of the current fund-raising dynamic. And a ban on leadership Political Action Committees (PACs) used to leverage influence inside Congress in ways that devalue policy making and overvalue fundraising, would be a big help.

Efforts to enlarge the electorate—ideally, via the Australian system of mandatory attendance at the polls—would reduce the role of consultants who focus on turning out one's own partisan base while suppressing that of the other party, by the use of wedge issues, inflammatory rhetoric, and the politics of fear. In Australia, where politicians know both bases will be at the polls, the focus turns to the persuadable voters in the middle, altering the issues discussed and debated and the tone used. But in the absence of such a sweeping change, there are other ways to enhance turnout beyond ideological activists, including open primaries, preference voting, and weekend voting.

Incentives for lawmakers to spend more time in Washington might provide more time for debate and deliberation, more time for interacting with colleagues, and more of an incentive to move their families to Washington and spend weekends there, with opportunities to see colleagues of both parties socially. One idea worth considering is enforcing a different schedule for lawmakers of three weeks in Washington and one week off each month, with the three weeks in which Congress is in session from 9 A.M. on Monday to 5 P.M. on Friday being devoid of fundraising.

More broadly, it would help to change the culture in ways that discourage outrageous characterizations and comments, devalue harshly negative campaigns, and put a premium on problem solving. But the reality is that the permanent campaign is likely with us—permanently. At best we can adapt to it and keep its destructive capacity in check.

◆ ◆ ◆ ◆ ◆

4. The Influence Business: Lobbying in Washington

by Lee Drutman

Lobbyists are often cast as the villains of modern Washington. On the campaign trail and back home in their districts, politicians pour rhetorical scorn on the lobbyists and the special interests who are said to be running Washington, and they promise to counter the lobbyists' nefarious influence. But lobbyists have become integral—perhaps indispensable—players in the legislative and policy-making process. When these members of Congress get back to their Washington offices, they and their staff sit down with lobbyists to craft policy and discuss issues. Often, upon leaving the Hill, members of Congress and their staff become lobbyists themselves, earning an income far more lucrative than their previous government salaries.

In 2012, Washington lobbying was a $3.3 billion industry, but the true amount of lobbying activity is probably double that amount. Lobbyists are intimately involved in the policy process, from agenda-setting to policy formulation to policy implementation. Most legislative activity or agency rules are the product of widespread consultation with lobbyists, who often possess the greatest level of expertise on an issue.

This chapter will provide a brief overview of who lobbyists represent, what they do, how influential they are, and how this has changed over the years. Lobbyists represent a remarkably wide array of political interests, and engage in an impressively wide variety of tactics. Some of these interests and some of these tactics are certainly more influential than others. Still, the fact that lobbyists primarily represent business interests means that policy making in Washington is almost certainly biased toward the priorities and perspectives of business interests.

A DOMINANT BUSINESS LOBBY

In 2012, the $3.31 billion that was reported to have been spent on lobbying was a decline from $3.55 billion in 2010. But it is still a significant increase from $1.82 billion just 10 years earlier (in constant 2012 dollars).

While the data on lobbying expenditures only go back to 1998, the growth in lobbying activity has been consistent for decades. For example, between 1981 and 2006, the number of organizations listed in the *Washington Representatives* lobbying directory more than doubled, from 6,681 to 13,777.

As measured by the number of organizations, the fastest-growing lobbies in Washington have been the education lobby, the health lobby, and the state and local government lobby. But the business lobby still remains the dominant group.

Certainly, it is true that many interests are represented in Washington. Unions have lobbyists. Local governments and universities have lobbyists. Identity groups and civil rights groups and groups advocating for the eradication of various diseases have lobbyists. In 2012, a total of 9,323 unique organizations spent *something* on lobbying. But fewer than half (4,041) spent more than $100,000. The top 5 percent of organizations (462 groups), meanwhile, accounted for 59 percent of spending on lobbying. The top 200 groups (barely 2 percent of all organizations) accounted for 44 percent of all spending. Of these top 200 spending groups in 2012, 144 were individual corporations, 37 were trade associations, and 2 were business associations. That's 172 out of 200, or 86 percent, that represent business.

Indeed, more than three-quarters of the money spent on lobbying has consistently gone toward representing business interests. In 2012, 3,587 individual corporations reported a combined $1.84 billion in lobbying expenditures. In other words, corporations accounted for 56 percent of *all* the money spent on lobbying in 2012. If we include an additional $553 million in spending by trade associations plus $175 million in spending by business-wide associations, we get $2.57 billion in combined spending. That adds up to *78 percent* of all the money spent on lobbying in 2012 coming from business interests.

THE QUIET COLLABORATORS

In the public mind, the image of lobbying is one of booze-soaked steak dinners, cigars, and chummy backrooms where members of Congress happily write bills to give tax breaks to corporate lobbyists. The reality is different.

First, it is important to understand that there are different types of lobbyists. Some lobbyists work exclusively for one organization or company as "in-house" lobbyists. Other lobbyists are employed by Washington, D.C. lobbying firms, and represent multiple clients at any given time on a contract basis. Typically, organizations with a more permanent presence in Washington have full-time lobbyists on staff, while often contracting with lobbying firms for additional advocacy support. Typically, organizations with a limited or temporary political issue will prefer the flexibility of a contract lobbyist.

Lobbying primarily involves dogged persistence and persuasion. Much of the work involves making variations on the same arguments, over and over again, to an ever-changing cast of decision makers. Much of it involves constant monitoring: waiting for opportunities and staying vigilant against threats. Often it involves working with allies, building coalitions, and developing strategic plans.

Richard Hall and Alan Deardorff capture this basic approach to lobbying in their "lobbying as legislative subsidy" model. They describe lobbyists working closely with congressional allies, helping them to research and develop legislation, and then building support for that legislation both inside and outside of Congress. Hall and Deardorff argue that, "the proximate political objective of this strategy is not to change legislators' minds but to assist natural allies in achieving their own, coincident objectives."[1]

Developing and enacting policy, after all, is a time-consuming, labor-intensive activity. Since legislative staffers are overburdened and sometimes lack expertise in a specific policy area, legislators and their staffs often rely on interest groups for help. Interest groups, meanwhile, know that the key to success is identifying and then fortifying their potential "champions." This means that legislators who are interested in enacting policy gravitate toward issues where they can get help from lobbyists to advance their agenda.

Much lobbying is also just basic information provision, and several scholars have argued that most influential lobbyists are those who do the best job of providing timely policy expertise. In an analysis of Enron's political e-mails, Daniel J. Hopkins and I found that Enron's representatives spent much time making energy policy arguments on their merits, and that perhaps Enron's greatest resource was "its monopoly on policy-relevant information about electricity, natural gas, and communications markets, information that policy makers could not easily obtain elsewhere."[2] In recent surveys, a majority of staffers have described lobbyists as "necessary to the process" and as either "collaborators," "educators," and or "partners." As Patton Boggs lobbyist Nicholas Allard argues, lobbyists assist staffers "by sifting information and noise, putting information into a coherent framework, and by challenging or checking facts on impossibly short time deadlines."[3]

Lobbying is also a matter of personal connections, and well-connected lobbyists earn premiums, especially when their former bosses are in positions of power. Those who have spent substantial time in government know people. They have friends in high places. They know how these people think, what they respond to, and what they don't like. They know how to package policies, how and when to approach people, and what to tell them. They also go to the cocktail parties and events where they can hear the latest scuttlebutt about what's going to happen when and how. In short, as Bruce E. Cain and I have written that the value of a congressional staffer to a lobbying firm is likely to be a function of their knowledge of congressional procedure, their personal contacts, and policy expertise related to bills that come before Congress.[4]

Many lobbying groups also engage in grassroots activity, mobilizing constituents to contact their members of Congress. In 2008, the Congressional Management Foundation (CMF) estimated that 44 percent of Americans had communicated with Congress at some point in the previous five years, and that Congress received almost 200 million communications in 2004 (90 percent through e-mail), as compared with 50 million in 1995. In a 2010 CMF survey, the majority of staff (57 percent) said e-mail and the Internet made legislators more responsive to their constituents and 88 percent responded that e-mail had the potential to influence their boss if he or she were undecided. But as Kenneth Goldstein has shown, most constituent mobilization is not organic, but rather is stimulated by lobbying groups.[5]

Lobbyists and the organizations they represent also make campaign contributions. The general consensus both in Washington and in the political science literature is that campaign contributions buy access, but do not guarantee outcomes. One lobbyist described them as "respect for the process."[6] Scholars have conducted at least 40 studies trying to link Political Action Committee (PAC) contributions to roll call votes. Steve Ansolabehere and colleagues, summing up the studies, conclude: "Overall, PAC contributions show relatively few effects on voting behavior. In three out of four instances, campaign contributions had no statistically significant effects on legislation or had the 'wrong' sign—suggesting that more contributions lead to less support."[7] More likely, campaign money has an effect that is further upstream. The conversations that politicians have with their funders help to shape their thinking on issues, putting some ideas on the agenda, and taking other ideas off the agenda.

Certainly, the practice of lobbying has become more sophisticated over the years. Lobbyists have become better at messaging, and at developing lobbying approaches that look more and more like political campaigns, complete with issue advertising, a media strategy, active coalition building, and sophisticated grassroots strategies. But the core activities of lobbying—working with allies to develop and build support for legislation and delivering persuasive information targeted to the political and policy needs of congressional offices—have remained the same.

The big change over time is in the amount of lobbying (there has been much more of it), and how this has changed the political environment (it has become harder to accomplish *anything*).

MANIPULATING THE POLICY MACHINE

In the most comprehensive survey of lobbying and policy outcomes, Baumgartner found no correlation between resources and likelihood of policy success. One reason is that it is just really hard to change the status quo.[7] And usually, lobbying efforts on one side of an issue are countered by lobbying efforts on the other side. Additionally, when issues enter the public debate, public opinion takes on greater importance and can be more difficult to change.

In short, political influence is not a vending machine, in which the insertion of money reliably produces a desired outcome. The more accurate metaphor is that political influence is a vending machine that works somewhat randomly, occasionally distributing desired outputs. On occasion, the vending machine can be shaken and cajoled to produce outcomes by experienced users. But sometimes no amount of shaking can make a difference. Yet, the more one plays at the vending machine, the more one hires experienced hands to manipulate it, the more likely one is to get something out of it.

A classic example of influence is a lobbyist who slips a narrow tax loophole in an omnibus bill. Nobody reads the entire bill because it is very long and highly technical, and so nobody notices the loophole until it is signed into law. Opportunities to accomplish this, however, are not predictable. Yet they do happen. In 2005, a presidential panel noted that following the Tax Reform Act of 1986, "there has been nearly constant tinkering—more than 100 different acts of Congress have made nearly 15,000 changes to the tax code" (p. 16). The report's authors noted: "Each one of these changes had a sponsor, and each had a rationale to defend it. Each one was passed by Congress and signed into law. Some of us saw this firsthand, having served in the U.S. Congress for a combined 71 years, including 36 years on the tax-writing committees. Others saw the changes from different perspectives—teaching, interpreting, and even administering the tax code."[8]

The organizations that can take advantage of these opportunities often have lobbyists who are plugged in enough to know when these opportunities arise, and who have long-standing relationships with congressional offices that are built on trust and friendship. This means that when the congressional office has a chance to slip an amendment into a large bill, that congressional office will be receptive to that organization's request.

One of the consequences of the increasingly competitive lobbying environment on Capitol Hill is that it is harder and harder to pass anything. More than 20 years ago, in the 92nd Congress (1971–1972), Congress passed 607 public bills, spanning a total of 2,330 pages, about 3.8 pages per bill. In the 111th Congress (2009–2010), Congress passed just 383 bills, but those bills spanned 7,617 pages, an average of 19.9 pages per bill, an all-time record. As one lobbyist noted, "Now, less legislation is being passed, but it's more complicated, and the average bill is bigger, more expensive, with more strings attached, the process is more like making sausage than it used to be."[9]

As bills get larger, this creates more opportunities for well-connected lobbyists to insert small provisions without attracting attention. Larger bills are also sign of more complex policy, and more complex policy is a result of all this expanding lobbying. The more lobbyists there are to represent more interests, the more provisions and subprovisions find their way into the final legislation.

Growing policy complexity puts lobbyists in a more powerful position, because increasingly lobbyists are the policy experts, while congressional staffers struggle to get up to speed. While there is far more lobbying now than ever, congressional staffing has remained stable for more than two decades, and staff in key policy positions have actually declined. The consequence, as Lorelei Kelly explains it, is that "many contemporary and urgent questions before our legislators require nuance, genuine deliberation and expert judgment. Congress, however, is missing adequate means for this purpose and depends on outdated and in some cases antiquated systems of information referral, sorting, communicating, and convening" (p. 1).[10] All this gives lobbying a centrality in the policy process. And since most lobbying spending is on behalf of business interests, this puts business in a central policy position. But because the policy process is so unpredictable, none of this easily translates into predictable influence. Still, as the old adage in Washington is "if you're not at the table, you're probably on the menu," it helps to have lobbyists who are at the table. And the more tables your lobbyists attend and the more they get to win the trust of the hosts, the more likely they might occasionally get to plan the menu.

INDISPENSABLE PLAYERS

Modern lobbying is tactically varied, and there is no consistent relationship between the amount of lobbying and the likelihood of policy success. The biggest change in lobbying over time is that there is more of it now than ever before, and that it is more sophisticated. But because the lobbying environment is more crowded, any given lobbying activity is almost certainly less influential.

Yet, the changing policy environment also privileges lobbyists. Because it is harder to accomplish policy changes, the cost of entry is higher. Gone are the days when a single public interest advocate with a good idea whose time had come could effectively make the rounds in Washington and see his idea adopted into law. Now policy changes require massive investments, which means that only those interests that can devote substantial resources to the process have a shot at meaningful influence. This means primarily business interests.

Going forward, the challenge for lobbyists is what role they will play in a gridlocked Washington in which members of Congress are often more interested in appealing to a narrow slice of their constituents in order to avoid a primary challenge than they are in solving big policy problems. The 112th Congress (2011–2012), which passed only 283 laws, was the least productive in decades and was marked by partisan skirmishes that have only intensified since then. In such a polarized environment, the value of lobbyists becomes less clear.

Nevertheless, at some point in the not-so-distant future, Washington will likely emerge from this period of gridlock and resume the normal legislative process. Lobbyists often like to say that without their involvement in the policy process, Washington could not function. They are almost certainly correct.

BIBLIOGRAPHY

Allard, Nicholas W. "Lobbying Is an Honorable Profession: The Right to Petition and the Competition to Be Right." *Stanford Law and Policy Review* 19, no. 1 (2008): 23–68.

Ansolabehere, Stephen, John M. de De Figueiredo, and James M. Snyder. "Why Is There So Little Money in U.S. Politics?" *The Journal of Economic Perspectives* 17, no. 1 (2003): 105–30. http://www.jstor.org/stable/3216842.

Bertrand, Marianne, Matilde Bombardini, and Francesco Trebbi. "Is It Whom You Know or What You Know? An Empirical Assessment of the Lobbying Process." *NBER Working Paper Series* no. 16765 (February 2011): 1–37. http://www.nber.org/papers/w16765.

Blanesi Vidal, Jordi, Mirko Draca, and Christian Fons-Rosen. "Revolving Door Lobbyists." *American Economic Review* 102, no. 7 (December 2012): 3731–48. doi:10.1257/aer.102.7.3731. http://www.aeaweb.org/articles.php?doi=10.1257/aer.102.7.3731.

Drutman, Lee, and Bruce E. Cain. "Congressional Staff and the Revolving Door: The Impact of Regulatory Change." *Election Law Journal* 13, no. 1 (March 2014): 27–44.

Drutman, Lee, and Daniel J. Hopkins. "The Inside View: Using the Enron E-Mail Archive to Understand Corporate Political Attention." *Legislative Studies Quarterly* 38, no. 1 (February 17, 2013): 5–30. doi:10.1111/lsq .12001. http://doi.wiley.com/10.1111/lsq.12001.

Esterling, Kevin M. *The Political Economy of Expertise: Information and Efficiency in American National Politics.* Ann Arbor: University of Michigan Press, 2004. http://www.loc.gov/catdir/toc/ecip0417/2004008127 .html.

Goldstein, Kenneth M. *Interest Groups, Lobbying, and Participation in America.* New York: Cambridge University Press, 1999. http://books.google .com/books?id=raPgCM53hUsC.

Hall, Richard L., and Alan V. Deardorff. "Lobbying as Legislative Subsidy." *American Political Science Review* 100, no. 1 (2006): 69–84.

Heinz, John P. *The Hollow Core: Private Interests in National Policy Making.* Cambridge, MA: Harvard University Press, 1993.

Kelly, Lorelei. *Congress' Wicked Problem: Seeking Knowledge inside the Information Tsunami.* Washington, DC: New America Foundation, 2012.

LaPira, Timothy M., and Herschel F. Thomas. "Just How Many Newt Gingrich's Are There on K Street? Estimating the True Size and Shape of Washington's Revolving Door." *SSRN Electronic Journal* (April 2, 2013). doi:10.2139/ssrn.2241671. http://papers.ssrn.com/abstract=22 41671.

Policy Council. "The Changing of the Guard: 2007 State of the Industry for Lobbying and Advocacy," 2007.

President's Advisory Panel on Federal Tax Reform. "Simple, Fair, and Pro-Growth: Proposals to Fix America's Tax System," 2005.

Schlozman, Kay Lehman, Sidney Verba, and Henry E. Brady. *The Unheavenly Chorus: Unequal Political Voice and the Broken Promise of American Democracy.* Princeton University Press, 2012. http://www.amazon.com/ dp/0691154848.

Schuman, Daniel. "Keeping Congress Competent: Staff Pay, Turnover, and What It Means for Democracy," 2010.

Schuman, Daniel, and Alisha Green. "When It Comes to Pay, All Feds Aren't Created Equal," 2012.

Wright, John R. *Interest Groups and Congress: Lobbying, Contributions, and Influence.* Boston: Allyn and Bacon, 1996.

◆ ◆ ◆ ◆ ◆

The Individuals Who Shaped the Modern Congress

5. Sam Rayburn: The Power of Persuasion

by Anthony Champagne

Born Samuel Taliaferro Rayburn on January 6, 1882, the former Texas Representative is originally from Kingston, Tennessee. In 1887, Rayburn moved to Texas where he attended East Texas Normal College (now Texas A&M University) and the University of Texas. By 1908, Rayburn had been admitted to the bar and he began practicing in Texas. From 1907 to 1913, Rayburn was a member of the State house of representatives; he was a speaker during his last two years in the house. Elected as a Democrat to the 63rd Congress in 1913, Rayburn commenced his congressional service that lasted 25 consecutive Congresses. His positions during his time in Congress included speaker, minority leader, and chairman of the Committee on Interstate and Foreign Commerce.

One of Rayburn's triumphs in his career was the strategic management and balance he achieved between the Northern and Southern wings of the Democratic Party in the House. The major influence Rayburn exercised over the New Deal and important laws including the Emergency Railroad Transportation Act and the Stock Exchange Act further portray his energy and impact in behind-the-scenes policy making.

Upon his death in 1961, Sam Rayburn was not only the longest-serving Speaker of the U.S. House of Representatives in history, but he was also the longest-serving member of the House of Representatives. Rayburn served in the House in an era when the House leadership had little formal power—power was largely in the hands of committee chairmen. Yet, Rayburn wielded great power over his colleagues because of seniority, geography, and relationships.

By the early 1950s, Rayburn was an institution, and he adroitly used his senior status as a political asset: As authors D. B. Hardeman and Donald Bacon recount in *Rayburn: A Biography*, "When he began a speech with the phrase, 'As I said forty years ago on the floor of this House . . .,' colleagues stopped and listened: a man of history and vast experience was giving them his candid judgment."[1]

Rayburn was a Southerner at a time when the South was the strongest Democratic region in the country. The Texas congressional delegation was overwhelmingly Democratic and contained a number of committee chairmen.

In wielding his power as Speaker, Rayburn also relied on friendships with key members of Congress, personal persuasion, his ability to influence committee appointments, and his ability to advance or retard careers of members. Early in his House career, Rayburn was a protégé to powerful members like John Nance Garner; later in his career, Rayburn returned the favor and was a mentor to future House leaders.

Born in 1882 in the Clinch River valley of Tennessee, Rayburn and his family moved to Fannin County, Texas, in 1887. The family was a large one, with 11 children on a cotton farm. Later in life, Rayburn claimed that he "missed being a tenant farmer by a gnat's whisker."[2] His father was a Confederate veteran who encouraged Sam to attend East Texas Normal College. After completing college, Rayburn briefly taught school and then ran for a Texas House seat. He served in the Texas House of Representatives from 1907 to 1913, the last two years as Speaker. Rayburn was a protégé of Joseph Weldon Bailey, a U.S. Senator and former Representative from a district that included Fannin County. Through his ties to Bailey, Rayburn was able to become Speaker of the Texas House, and used his power to carve the congressional district that he represented from 1913 until his death in 1961.

Once in the U.S. House of Representatives, Rayburn became a protégé of John Nance Garner, a Representative from South Texas elected to the House in 1902 and who had political ties with Joseph Bailey. Garner was a member of the U.S. House Committee on Ways and Means when the Democratic members of the committee served as the "Committee on Committees." He helped Rayburn obtain a seat on the U.S. House Committee on Interstate and Foreign Commerce, his only committee during his lengthy tenure in Congress. Rayburn continued to benefit from his close relationship to Garner, who became Minority Leader in the 71st Congress, Speaker in the 72nd, and Vice President from 1933 to 1941. One distinctive aspect of the House of Representatives during much of the 20th century was the importance of mentor-protégé relationships where senior members advanced the careers of junior members who served as their lieutenants in the House. As Rayburn gained seniority, he became a mentor to many members of the House who went on to leadership positions, including President Lyndon Johnson; former Speakers of the House Carl Albert and Jim Wright; Hale Boggs, House Majority Leader; and Richard Bolling, Chairman of the U.S. House Committee on Rules.

With Democratic control of the House in the 72nd Congress, Rayburn became Chair of the Committee on Interstate and Foreign Commerce, where he was a workhorse for Franklin Roosevelt's New Deal. His committee was responsible for key legislation dealing with regulation of the securities industry, utility-holding companies, communications, and rural electrification. With support from Vice President Garner, Rayburn became Majority Leader in the 75th Congress, and then Speaker in the 76th Congress. He would serve as Speaker longer than anyone else in congressional history, from 1940 until his death in 1961 (with the exception of the 80th and 83rd Congresses, during which he served as Minority Leader).

In 1951, Rayburn's protégé, Lyndon Johnson, became Democratic Whip in the Senate, and in 1953 served as the Democratic Minority Leader in a closely divided Senate. Johnson became Democratic Majority Leader in 1955, holding that position until he became vice president in 1961. The close personal relationship with Johnson and the similarity in their political values and perceptions of Texas's interests enhanced both Rayburn's and Johnson's influence in their respective houses.

Geography was both a source of Rayburn's strength and a constant challenge that had to be managed. The South was dominant in the House's power structure because of "the power of the committee chairmen, the seniority rule, the dominance of the Democratic Party in House elections since 1932, and the fact that the safest Democratic House districts were in the southern states."[3] However, Rayburn also had influence in the Northern wing of the Democratic Party, and had been close to Franklin Roosevelt and Harry Truman. Although a known segregationist, he was quiet and mild about segregation in contrast to many Southerners in the House. From the late 1940s and into the 1950s, he was probably the only senior House member who was acceptable in the top Democratic leadership to both Southern and Northern Democrats. In 1946, Representative J. Percy Priest (D-TN) claimed that without Rayburn at the helm, the Democrats in the House would "be torn apart internally."[4]

Nevertheless, geography posed several major problems for Rayburn while in leadership. For instance, he was a leader of the Democratic Party in the House, though he represented a state which, while overwhelmingly Democratic during his lifetime, was far more conservative than the national party. Rayburn also faced major opposition in several Democratic primaries. The greatest political threat he faced after gaining leadership in the House was in 1944, when conservatives mounted an effective radio campaign against him. Rayburn was attacked for being a Socialist and pro-black. He was so threatened that, in order to campaign in his district, he abandoned

plans to attend the 1944 Democratic convention where there was a possibility that he might receive the vice presidential nomination. He won with
55 percent of the vote.[5]

In the 1950s, Rayburn faced opposition at the state level from conservative Texas governor Allan Shivers, who threatened to redistrict Rayburn
out of office. Rayburn's power was so great, however, that the redistricting
threat proved vacuous. In 1958, his district had slightly over 216,000 people,
compared to an average population of a congressional district in Texas at the
time of over 435,000.[6] By the time Rayburn died, he had a grossly malappor-
tioned district that was nevertheless exactly the type of district he wanted—a
rural district of small towns and small farmers.

The oil industry was the dominant part of Texas's economy—at the time
of Rayburn's death Texas produced 38 percent of the country's oil, had
about half the country's oil reserves, and employed one out of 11 Texas
workers.[7] Texas had numerous wealthy oilmen with views hostile to national
Democrats. Rayburn was able to ward off opposition from most of them,
actually gain support from many of them, and at the same time benefit the
Texas economy by providing tax benefits to the oil industry. The most important of those benefits was the oil depletion allowance, which provided oil
producers with 27.5 percent of their income tax free. Rayburn made sure that
Congressmen hostile to the oil depletion allowance did not get on the Ways
and Means Committee.[8]

As Speaker, Rayburn faced two other related problems. One was the Conservative Coalition—an alignment of conservative Democrats and Republicans that tried to prevent the passage of progressive Democratic legislation.
The other problem was that the Speaker did not control the House Committee on Rules, and a coalition of conservative Democrats and Republicans
on that committee became a barrier to floor consideration of progressive
legislation. Because the Speaker possessed little formal power during Rayburn's career, Rayburn was forced to rely on his powers of persuasion and
his relationships in order to accomplish his aims. Finally, in frustration with
the Rules Committee's unwillingness to cooperate with the new Kennedy
Administration, Rayburn engaged in a battle that expanded the size of the
Rules Committee, reducing its ability to block New Frontier proposals.

Upon his death in November 1961, a *New York Times* obituary summed
up Rayburn's career: "Mr. Rayburn will go down in history as one of the
strong Speakers, but also as a parliamentary leader who relied mainly on persuasion and almost never on raw power to achieve his aims."[9]

◆　◆　◆　◆　◆

6. Gerald Ford: A Politician without Enemies

by Richard Reeves

The former President's full name is Gerald Rudolph Ford Jr. and he was born on July 14, 1913, in Omaha, Nebraska. He graduated from University of Michigan in 1935 and from Yale University Law School in 1941. Ford was admitted to the bar the same year he graduated. From 1942 to 1946, Ford served in the U.S. Navy. From the 1949 to 1973, Ford served 13 consecutive Congresses as a Republican in the House. The end of his congressional career marked the beginning of his role as U.S. Vice President. The Vice Presidency was secured with the President's nomination, followed by congressional confirmation. And on April 9, 1974, Ford became fortieth U.S. President following Nixon's resignation. Ford served as President until 1977. He died on December 26, 2006.

Ford is the only President and Vice President that was not elected by the American people. His credibility was severely tainted by two major incidents, the conditional amnesty program he created for evaders of the draft and deserters during the Vietnam War, and a pardon of Nixon's offenses.

By October 1973, the United States was staggered by the cumulative body blows of the late 1960s and early 1970s. Many of the institutions that grounded Americans' faith in their country and government were shaking. The last U.S. combat troops were returning in defeat from Vietnam, where more than 58,000 soldiers lost their lives in a war that bitterly divided the nation. The 1968 assassinations of Martin Luther King and Robert Kennedy—along with race riots, antiwar protests, and the cultural wars that would scar an entire generation—were still fresh wounds. Additionally, the shadow cast by the Watergate scandal was threatening to engulf even the White House and the presidency.

When an already embattled President Richard Nixon sought the advice of congressional leaders for a replacement for Vice President Spiro Agnew, who had resigned in disgrace, the name that was offered almost in unison was not that of Congress's most flamboyant politician, gifted legislator, or dazzling orator. Rather, it was a man known primarily for his honesty, integrity, and steadfastness, values that the American public had begun to doubt in their leaders. So on November 27, the Senate voted 92–3 to confirm Gerald Ford (R-MI) as the next vice president. Before another year had passed, Ford would become the only person to become president without ever having been voted into executive office.

ASCENSION TO THE VICE PRESIDENCY

On October 10, 1973, Vice President Spiro Agnew resigned from office during the course of an investigation into bribes he took as Baltimore County Executive and Governor of Maryland. President Richard Nixon—himself under tremendous political and legal pressure because of the growing Watergate scandal—became the first president to invoke the recently passed Twenty-Fifth Amendment, which allowed the President to nominate a replacement Vice President, who would be confirmed by majority of the House and Senate.

Nixon's first choice to replace Agnew was John Connally, a former Democratic governor of Texas who had become a Republican five months before while serving as Nixon's Secretary of the Treasury. When Nixon dispatched aides to discuss Connally's nomination with leaders of the Democratic-controlled Senate and House, those leaders told him the Texan could not be confirmed in either house. Democrats considered him a turncoat, and Republicans did not trust their new, fellow Republican. The Speaker of the House, Carl Albert, an Oklahoma Democrat, said: "If the President wants to know who would be the first choice of the House, it would be Jerry Ford." Later in the day, the President called Albert, as well as Mike Mansfield (D-MT), the Senate Majority Leader, asking him if the Senate would confirm Ford. "Yes," answered Mansfield. "Ford would be a good choice."

A MAN OF INTEGRITY

Gerald Rudolph Ford was first elected to the House from the Grand Rapids area of Michigan in 1948. His tenure was longer than it was distinguished, but he was a loyal moderate conservative, a stolid fellow, and well liked by colleagues on both sides of the aisle, though he had few significant accomplishments. He worked hard, told the truth as much as any politician can, kept his word, and was ambitious—he hoped one day to be Speaker—but he was never considered assertive.

Asked once about the most exciting thing that happened during his service as a Lieutenant Commander in the Navy during World War II, he answered that he came out on deck of his carrier during a storm and was knocked off his feet, sliding across the ship's runways, and being saved by the nets on the sides of the deck. Ford had volunteered for sea duty aboard the USS *Monterey* aircraft carrier during World War II, and served onboard during many combat actions in the Pacific Theater in 1943 and 1944. That naval service earned Ford the Asiatic-Pacific Campaign Medal with nine engagement stars, the Philippine Liberation Medal with two bronze stars for Leyte and Mindoro, and the American Campaign and World War II Victory Medals.

Ford's life changed the day after New Year's in 1963. A group of "young Turk" Republican congressmen was determined to try to unseat their party's seemingly arrogant and lazy leader, 62-year-old Charles Halleck (R-IN). Led by Charles Goodell (R-NY), who was 36, and Robert Griffin (R-MI), 39, they approached Ford, 49, and tried to persuade him to challenge Halleck as the 88th Congress convened and organized. Ford said he did not believe Halleck could be defeated.

"What if we went after Hoeven?" said Goodell, referring to 67-year-old Charles Hoeven (R-IA), the chairman of the House Republican Conference and third-ranking of the 176 Republicans in the House minority. The Conference had met only once during the past two years. Ford said yes to that and defeated Hoeven 86–78 in a secret vote.

"It wasn't that everyone was wildly enthusiastic about Jerry," said Goodell, "It was just that most Republicans liked and respected him. He didn't have enemies."

As conference chairman, Ford did little to distinguish himself, but he was already in the leadership when the Republicans, with Senator Barry Goldwater of Arizona as their presidential candidate, were crushed in the 1964 elections. In the two months before Congress organized at the beginning of 1965, Goodell and Griffin, joined by other younger members, including both Donald Rumsfeld (R-IL) and John Anderson (R-IL), approached Ford again about running against Halleck for party leadership. This time, Ford agreed, and he won 73–67. While the young Turks were doing his campaigning for him, Ford took three separate vacations. "I did it because I had nothing to lose," he told me. "I could have kept my House seat, and I was careful not to get anyone mad at me."

Ford's ascension is further evidence of a theme, commented on by perceptive foreigners studying the Congress in the 19th century, first Alexis de Tocqueville in 1830 and later Lord James Bryce in 1888, who wrote: "[T]he methods and habits of Congress, and indeed of political life generally, seem to give fewer opportunities for personal distinction, fewer modes in which a man may commend himself to his countrymen by eminent capacity in thought, in speech, or in administration . . . [E]minent men make more enemies, and give those enemies more assailable points, than obscure men do."

A POLITICIAN WITHOUT ENEMIES

As the Minority Leader for eight years, Ford faced a majority that often had twice as many members as his caucus. He was able to deliver 85 to 95 percent of his members in opposition to President Johnson's "Great Society" legislation, but was unable to prevent its passage. However, in the area of foreign policy, Ford and his fellow House Republicans provided important support to Johnson for the ongoing war in Vietnam. Ironically, when he finally questioned Johnson's foreign policy leadership, President Johnson mocked him, saying "he played too much football without a helmet."[1]

Ford was also able to deliver the overwhelming majority of the Republican caucus during the Nixon presidency, this time in support of White House decisions. Although the numbers were a little less than Halleck's overall leadership percentages, Ford was far more popular than his predecessor because he did everything he could to help his colleagues, making 238 speeches and fund-raising appearances for them in a single election year. He also played a significant role in the bipartisan passage of some of Nixon's signature domestic initiatives, including the National Environmental Policy Act, the Tax Reform Act of 1969, and the 1972 revenue sharing program for state and local governments.

"He kept us together," said another Republican from Michigan, Representative Guy Vander Jagt. "He didn't do it with intellectual brilliance, persuasion or pressure. He kept us together with his personality. We did it for Jerry!"

Then, in 1973, the life of a Congressman who had stayed away from the public limelight was turned upside down. Just as Ford was approached by younger congressmen in the 1960s to assume a leadership role, history tapped him in 1973 to become the vice president. In August 1974, when President Nixon resigned because of the Watergate scandal, Ford, the man without enemies, became the 38th president of the United States, the first unelected president.

In his first address to the nation upon taking the oath of office as president, Ford stated: "My fellow Americans, our long national nightmare is over. Our Constitution works; our great Republic is a government of laws and not of men."

◆ ◆ ◆ ◆ ◆

7. Thomas "Tip" O'Neill: New Deal Champion

by John A. Farrell

Thomas Philip O'Neill Jr. was born on December 9, 1912 in Cambridge, Massachusetts. O'Neill graduated from Boston College in 1936. From 1936 to 1952, O'Neill served in the Massachusetts House of Representatives. From 1953 to 1987, O'Neill served in Congress as a Democrat in the House, and his congressional service lasted through 17 Congresses. His positions included chair for the Select Committee on Campaign Expenditures, majority whip, majority leader, and speaker. He died on January 5, 1994.

    O'Neill has long been remembered as a staunch liberal unafraid to voice his opinion that many times reflected widespread sentiment amongst his colleagues. He vocally opposed the Vietnam War, publicly asked President Nixon to resign following the Watergate scandal, and often criticized President Reagan's administration. Needless to say, O'Neill gained approval and respect among Democrats.

Speaker Thomas P. O'Neill Jr.'s favorite bit of scripture was the Sermon on the Mount. Its precepts were dear to his heart. But what made him such an effective leader is found in Ecclesiastes, not Matthew. For all the splendid political gifts that Tip O'Neill possessed—and there were many, and they were surely splendid—the most sublime was timing.

O'Neill's career is studded with pivotal moments when he sensed change, recognized opportunity, and won a wager on the future: the campaign of 1948 that led to his election as the first Democratic Speaker of the Massachusetts House; his break with Lyndon Johnson over the Vietnam War in 1967, which made him a hero of the New Left and helped propel him into the House leadership; his choreography of Richard Nixon's impeachment in 1973 and 1974; and, most notably, his calibrated resistance to Ronald Reagan's conservative revolution in 1981.

"Speaker O'Neill's legendary sense of loyalty . . . was no dull or wooden conformity," said the Reverend J. Donald Monan, S.J., then the President of Boston College, in his eulogy at O'Neill's funeral in 1994. "It has been a creative fidelity to values pledged in his youth that he kept relevant to a world of constant change by dint of effort and imagination."[1]

Indeed, O'Neill's greatest flop was a singular occasion when his creative fidelity failed him—when dull conformity to decaying Democratic doctrine fed Jimmy Carter's domestic woes, and led to their party's disaster in the

1980 election. The Republicans ran a cruel and effective television commercial that year, portraying O'Neill as a fat, clownish figure whose gas-guzzling car runs out of fuel. Led by the charismatic Reagan, the GOP took the White House and the Senate and picked up 33 seats in the House.

"The House will become the national Democratic Party, to the extent that it exists," *The Washington Post* noted. The new national spokesman for that party was a shambling old cigar-smoking pol, coming off a bad season. Reagan's aides could not suppress their glee. Reagan's brash new budget director David Stockman would recall that O'Neill "with his massive corpulence and scarlet, varicose nose, was the Hogarthian embodiment of the superstate he had labored so long to maintain."[2]

BIDING HIS TIME

O'Neill was the son of an Irish American ward heeler from the working class neighborhoods of North Cambridge, Massachusetts. From the exalted position of superintendent of sewers, Tom Senior had ruled a little world of precinct captains armed primarily with Christmas baskets and patronage jobs. Both O'Neills had preached that "all politics is local." With an election of a Republican President, the younger O'Neill bet that Democrats and independents would desert Reagan when they saw what Republican policies—and Federal Reserve Board Chairman Paul Volcker's unflagging campaign against inflation—did to their communities.

But there is a time to lose, and a time to win; a time to be silent, and a time to speak. Before he could win, the Speaker had to lose.

O'Neill concluded, immediately, that he would not use his parliamentary powers to obstruct Reagan's economic program. It was a crucial decision, the key to all that followed. "We're going to cooperate with the president. It's America first and party second," O'Neill said in November 1980. "We're going to give 'em enough rope. They can use it either to herd cattle or make a mistake."[3]

Why give the new Republican administration loose rein? O'Neill and his advisers were closely watching Volcker, because they foresaw the economic hardship ahead. If the Speaker refused to bring Reagan's program up for a vote and the country slid into recession, then the President would have a precious excuse, and the Democratic Party would get the blame. O'Neill needed to make sure that Reagan "owned" the coming hard times.

Moreover, the Speaker's overriding imperative was to retain Democratic control of the House. If Republicans had control of both congressional chambers and the presidency, then the "Reagan Revolution" might indeed succeed, and huge chunks of the Democratic Party's legacy—the New Deal and Great Society legislation so dear to O'Neill's heart—would be dumped in the dustbin of history. To maintain his hold on the Speaker's gavel, O'Neill had to keep a group of some 40 "boll weevils" in the party and help them weather the upcoming election in 1982. These conservative Democrats came mostly from Sun Belt districts that had been carried by Reagan, where the voters were enthralled with the President, especially after he endured a March 1981 assassination attempt. O'Neill had to give them the option of voting for Reagan's tax and budget cuts.

In addition, though it may seem quaint in a hyper-partisan era, O'Neill was a Cold War patriot, and he worried about the office of the presidency. America had lurched through five blighted presidencies: Kennedy, Johnson, Nixon, Ford, and Carter. Now along came Reagan, facing perilous times, with a mandate for a new beginning. Even if he could swing it (a questionable prospect, given the ebbing powers of the Speaker in the television age and the threat of retaliation by the voters), O'Neill shied away from a scorched earth strategy. He would bicker, haggle, nag and gripe. He would call on Democrats to stay united, and to reject Reagan's proposals. He would fight like a wounded bear to protect the legacy programs of the New Deal and the Great Society, but O'Neill would not purposely wreck another presidency. He honored Reagan's mandate, that much, at least.

So was born the strategy. Necessity became a virtue. The Democrats would give Reagan the political rope, betting that the President would hang himself.

RISKY STRATEGY

As it turned out, it was a fine long-term strategy. Volcker was unwavering in his effort to wring inflation from the American economy, and interest rates soared to 20 percent, stifling growth. The 1981–1982 Recession brought the highest unemployment rate—10.8 percent—since the Great Depression. O'Neill had not blocked the President's program, as a result Reagan owned the subsequent economic misery. As factories closed and workers lost their livelihoods, "Reaganomics" got the blame, not Democrats.

In the near term, however, O'Neill had consigned himself to a world of hurt. Someone had to play Horatius, the famed Roman soldier who held the Tiber River Bridge against an army of Etruscans, giving his comrades time to rally and regroup. The role fell to O'Neill. Like Horatius, he succeeded. Like Horatius, he also bled.

"That sonofabitch rolled us. God, did Reagan ever," House Majority Leader Jim Wright recalled. "If you quote me, I didn't say sonofabitch—I said that charming old thespian rolled us. But God, did he ever." In a series of votes in the summer of 1981, Reagan's Republicans joined with dozens of conservative Democrats to pass whopping tax cuts, and cutbacks in many federal programs. There were calls in the Democratic caucus for new leadership, and there were murmurs of mutiny.[4]

"This is only the first skirmish in the war. The war is the election of 1982," O'Neill told his panicky troops. He knew his way around a racetrack. "A horse that runs fast doesn't always run long," he said.

Slowly, events turned in their favor. The conservative "supply side" economic theory resulted in massive budget deficits. O'Neill polished his performance for television, the medium by which Reagan waged political war. The then-sturdy journalistic imperative to always "get the other side," combined with the media's love of conflict, gave O'Neill a platform like no previous House Speaker. The man who played the inside game so well learned how to reach out beyond the Beltway and mold public opinion. "An old dog can learn new tricks," O'Neill vowed.

Then David Stockman—a two-term House Republican from Michigan who resigned from Congress to accept Reagan's appointment to be Director of the Office of Management and Budget—took a knife to Social Security. For all of Reagan's rhetoric about swollen, wasteful government, there just was not enough low-hanging fruit in the federal budget that could be pared to pay for his tax cuts—not for a President who also insisted on greatly increasing defense spending. Entitlement accounts were the necessary bill-payer. Stockman's initial proposals were relatively modest: changes to minimum payments, cost-of-living adjustments, and the size of Social Security checks sent to beneficiaries who chose early retirement.

However, seniors howled in protest. "Someone planning to retire in nine months who thought he was going to be getting $650 per month would now be getting $450," said Stockman, recalling the flap about the early retirement benefits. "The cut was tough—but the lack of warning was devastating."[5]

The Speaker seized on these changes to Social Security. "This was right from O'Neill, right from the gut," his aide, Kirk O'Donnell would recall.[6]

"I have a statement on the Social Security," O'Neill announced to the press. "A lot of people approaching that age have either already retired on pensions or have made irreversible plans to retire very soon. . . . I consider it a breach of faith to renege on that promise," he said. "It is a rotten thing to do."[7]

During the summer and fall of 1981, O'Neill kept the pressure on. "This is a callous, right-wing administration committed to repealing the Great

Society, the New Frontier, the Fair Deal and the New Deal," he charged. "It has made a target of the politically weak, the poor, the working people." He called Reagan names: tightwad, scrooge.[8]

"O'Neill took Social Security and just drove it home ruthlessly, and in some respects dishonestly, but with great effectiveness," Newt Gingrich, then a Republican back bencher, recalled. In late September, Reagan caved. In a letter to the Speaker, he renounced the cuts in Social Security that Stockman had promoted, and called for the creation of a bipartisan commission to preserve—not dismantle—the underfunded system.[9]

POLITICAL COMEBACK

The rout was complete on Election Day 1982. Republican strategists suggested, in an inelegant fund-raising letter during the fall election, that Social Security be transformed into a voluntary pension system. The Democrats pounced again. "They used it against us and killed us with it," James A. Baker, Reagan's chief of staff, recalled. "Absolutely killed us."[10] The Democrats picked up 26 seats, and O'Neill had saved the House. "Everybody's favorite scapegoat doesn't look so bad anymore," *The Washington Post* decided.[11]

Winning is one thing, knowing what to do with victory is another. As the economy came out of the 14-month recession and Reagan prepared to run for reelection, Baker and his colleagues saw the need to defuse Social Security as a campaign issue. A bipartisan commission chaired by Alan Greenspan gave them a forum, and O'Neill recognized the opportunity. The Democrats had won some tax and spending victories in the wake of the 1982 election, but cementing Social Security for coming generations would signify—to Republicans and to history—that America's evolution as a modern social welfare state was irreversible.

The deal struck between Reagan and O'Neill was the simplest of compromises: a 50–50 split of benefit cuts and new taxes. Cost of living hikes were pared back, the retirement age was extended, and the benefits for wealthier recipients were subjected to the federal income tax. O'Neill had regrets about hiking the age of retirement—he thought it unfair to blue-collar and manual laborers—but accepted the bitter pill as part of the deal.

The April 1983 signing ceremony brought a formal end to the Reagan Revolution. In his second term, Reagan would turn to foreign affairs and, with the exception of a revenue-neutral tax reform, invest little political capital in domestic policy. O'Neill's resistance to Reagan in 1981 and 1982,

Stockman later concluded, had slammed shut the brief window for radical change. The President did get big hikes in defense spending, and the 1981 tax cuts, which set a low "new normal" for income tax rates that would last for decades. The muscle, sinew, and guts of the liberal welfare state lived on and so, even, did a lot of the fat.

SAVING THE NEW DEAL

In their first 30 months in office, Reagan and Stockman had chopped $110 billion from the baseline levels of Jimmy Carter's final budget, cutting back on the growth of programs like Medicare, school lunches, food stamps, federal pensions, and college loans. Projected federal spending was reduced by about 7 percent, but the authorizing legislation remained intact. Very few programs—no cabinet departments and none of the jewels of the New Deal or the Great Society—were eliminated.[12]

"O'Neill led a strategic retreat that turned into a successful offensive," O'Donnell recalled. "In the process he probably saved the New Deal welfare state. In the final analysis it is the laws that make the difference. Reagan was able to de-fund some programs, but he wasn't able to de-authorize them . . . (And) unless you get the laws off the books you do not dismantle the New Deal state."[13]

In 1994, Gingrich would take the House from the Democrats, and launch his own revolution. It too, faltered. "There should be no doubt about what experience has demonstrated: The specific ideas necessary to make radical cuts in modern American government consistently fail the test of public acceptability," Richard Darman, a former Reagan aide, concluded.[14]

O'Neill was not a flawless leader; he would never have been in such a fix in 1981 if he had been. Later in his presidency, Reagan outmaneuvered the Speaker in their clashes over the U.S. military interventions in Lebanon, Grenada, and Nicaragua. Although he was bruised in these minor dustups, O'Neill should be credited for giving his unflagging support to the American-aided resistance to the Soviet occupation of Afghanistan and to the President's early dealings with the new Soviet leader, Mikhail Gorbachev—two triumphs of U.S. foreign policy in the Reagan era.

The Speaker displayed more dull conformity when resisting "neo-liberalism," the reform and modernization of the Democratic Party by a new generation of leaders that would lead to its success in the 1990s and the early 21st century. Yet he recognized the changes in American media and politics that were transforming lawmakers into political entrepreneurs. With a strategy of "inclusion," he gave them their turn in the spotlight, as Chairmen and Subcommittee Chairmen and members of an array of task forces, ad hoc panels and super committees. He escaped the disastrous fates of his successors—Wright, Foley, and Gingrich—and left office on his own terms, to a chorus of huzzahs: an American Kutuzov, who preached time and patience, patience and time.

◆ ◆ ◆ ◆ ◆

8. Dan Rostenkowski: The Deal-Maker

by Richard Cohen

Daniel David Rostenkowski was born in Chicago, Illinois, on January 2, 1928. Rostenkowski graduated from St. John's Military Academy in 1946. From 1946 to 1948, Rostenkowski served in the U.S. Army Infantry in Korea. Rostenkowski served in the Illinois State House of Representatives in 1952 for the 68th General Assembly. He was a member of the State senate from 1954 to 1956. Beginning in 1952, Rostenkowski served as delegate every four years at the Illinois State Democratic convention. For the Democratic National Conventions, he served as delegate every four years from 1960 to 1976. On January 3, 1959, Rostenkowski was elected as a Democrat for the House; his congressional service continued for 17 consecutive Congresses, ending in 1995. From the Ninety-seventh Congress onward, Rostenkowski served as a chairman for the Committee on Ways and Means, Joint Committee on Taxation. He died on August 11, 2010.

Rostenkowski was a shrewd negotiator leading the way for congressional tax policy. Unfortunately, Rostenkowski's legacy has been tainted by the corruption charges that led him to prison in the mid-1990s. Rostenkowski was pardoned by President Clinton in 2000.

In 1983, U.S. House Committee on Ways and Means Chairman Dan Rostenkowski (D-IL) took on the largely thankless task of leading House Democrats in an effort to prevent the imminent insolvency of Social Security. At the time, the challenge was daunting. In 1981, when top aides to President Ronald Reagan had overplayed their hand in seeking changes to the retirement system, Democrats responded by battering Republicans for their supposed harsh treatment of senior citizens, and successfully exploited the issue in the 1982 campaign. To find a solution, Reagan created a high-level commission to unveil recommendations after the election.

Working the back rooms, Rostenkowski seized control of the effort, welcoming the chance to stop the partisan gamesmanship on both sides of the issue. As chairman of the House's tax-writing panel, he also wanted a more direct hand in shaping the response, and thus quietly negotiated with his committee's Republicans on a plan to raise taxes on workers and impose cutbacks on beneficiaries—especially more wealthy retirees. Rostenkowski then dispatched his top aides to craft the details of a possible deal with their White House counterparts.

An agreement was reached, but it quickly ran into opposition from other Democrats who particularly objected to a provision that gradually increased the retirement age from 65 to 67—the lynchpin for the system's long-term financial solvency. Rostenkowski broke the deadlock with a House vote on the retirement age. Even though House Democrats voted against the increase 188 to 76, Rostenkowski and his lieutenants prevailed with Republican support. "I was a pragmatist," he said years later. "I tried to get what I felt was possible. . . . The liberals never knew when to take the ball" to make a score.[1]

Rostenkowski's old-style deal-making skills made the sometimes gruff and domineering lawmaker something of a congressional dinosaur. His background in urban "machine" politics and his eagerness to be at the center of legislative bargaining that often led to backroom deals, are traits that have largely disappeared from Capitol Hill. Rostenkowski enjoyed working across the aisle, especially when it meant haggling with Presidents from the other party.

His was a results-oriented approach to political deal-making, with the objective always the "ink on parchment" of legislation. During more than 13 years as chairman of what he proudly called "the Cadillac committee" of Congress, Rostenkowski continually sought and often found common ground on the big issues of the day—from taxes and trade, to health care and welfare. During that time, Rostenkowski largely disdained the growing tendency of leaders in both parties to engage in media spin and partisan point scoring. Rostenkowski cared less about political posturing, and more about results. It is no accident that Congress in the next three decades showed little interest in further reforms to safeguard Social Security, which for good reason has been termed the "third rail" of American politics.

At the same time, the long narrative of Rostenkowski's career offers plenty of cautionary tales. His instincts to always look for a comfortable middle ground at times translated into an aversion to taking on more deep-seated policy challenges. The profound political and legal setbacks at the end of his career also suggest that Rostenkowski had failed to adapt to changing times, and largely lost touch with his constituents in Chicago and the prevailing national mood.

CHICAGO MACHINE POLITICS

Rostenkowski got an early start in politics, and the lessons he learned as a young Chicago pol shaped the arc of his career. With a boost from his father Joe Rostenkowski, a local alderman, the 30-year-old Dan won the endorsement of Mayor Richard J. Daley and other local bosses for an open seat in Congress in 1958. From the start of his apprenticeship representing the heavily Polish neighborhoods on Chicago's northwest side, Dan showed an abiding respect for seniority and an eagerness to learn from the old-timers—in Chicago and in Congress. He served as Daley's eyes and ears in Washington, gradually climbing up the influence ladder.

Rostenkowski's respect for hierarchy sometimes landed him in trouble. At Daley's instruction, he presided over the tumultuous 1968 Democratic convention in Chicago, for instance, quickly clashing with Democratic reformers who, energized by protests against the Vietnam War and domestic unrest, challenged the power centers in Chicago. Rostenkowski's performance at the convention was considered an embarrassment by soon-to-be House Speaker Carl Albert (D-OK)

Rostenkowski's slow, methodical rise to the pinnacles of power in Washington was marked by two key developments. In 1976, he became a close ally to Representative Jim Wright (D-TX), backing his campaign to become House Majority Leader over more liberal opponents. Wright won by a single vote. Rostenkowski also became a reliable friend of "Tip" O'Neill (D-MA), another big-city insider who was chosen as Speaker that year. While Rostenkowski was not known for crafting new policies, he had a well-tuned ear for the needs of his more senior mentors, and an uncanny ability to craft deals. O'Neill reportedly told a student classroom that he couldn't "read the House" himself, but added, "I've got a friend who knows how to do it, so he does it for me. Danny Rostenkowski. Of Illinois."[2] Meanwhile, Rostenkowski continued to gain influence on the Ways and Means Committee, where the long-standing bipartisan alliances and seniority control had been crumbling.

Rostenkowski's opportunity to become "boss" came in 1981, when he took over as Ways and Means chairman—and notably turned down an offer to become part of the House Democratic leadership. It was a difficult time for the party. Ronald Reagan had just won a landslide presidential election, and Republicans had taken control of the Senate. Reagan and the rest of the GOP had run on a pledge to slash taxes, and they moved quickly to fulfill that goal. That left House Democrats on the defensive and Rostenkowski manning the barricades, trying to fend off Republicans intent on advancing Reagan's fiscal revolution. Ever the deal-maker, Rostenkowski the committee chairman engaged in a bidding war with Reagan allies, adding costly tax breaks for some constituents to the deal, but ultimately failing to exert Democratic control over the tax bill.

The tax-cut battle showed that "he couldn't win by opposing Ronald Reagan," said Rostenkowski's long-time spokesman Jim Jaffe. "He was a legislative engineer who wanted to get the job done. Getting 218 votes was his focus." That approach helped to explain his decision to serve as a partner with Reagan to enact comprehensive tax reform in 1986. "Rostenkowski realized that there was greater enthusiasm for Reagan's approach. So, he jumped on that bandwagon," Jaffe added. Their collaboration began with the chairman's nationally broadcast endorsement that immediately followed Reagan's call for tax changes, and included the chairman's public appeal to "write Rosty." More than a year of closed-door meetings and tough bargaining followed before the bill was enacted. (See "Bygone Partisanship: The Tax Reform Act of 1986," Chapter 28.)

THE ULTIMATE PRAGMATIST

Despite occasional grumbling from party leaders and the rank and file, Rostenkowski called most of the shots for House Democrats on matters of taxes and budgets. Characteristically, his wheeling and dealing focused on legislative outcomes, rather than partisan impact or his own personal fortunes. "Danny was the ultimate pragmatist," said Representative Bill Gradison of Ohio, a long-time Ways and Means Republican member. "He was not an ideologue."

After the hard-won lessons of the tax bill battles, Rostenkowski benefited in many ways from Republican control of the White House during his first 12 years as chairman. He styled himself as something of an equal in dealing with Reagan, and together they cut deals that might have been more difficult to conclude if Rostenkowski had been working with a president from his own party. That was evident in House Democrats' prior and subsequent struggles with Jimmy Carter and Bill Clinton, even though they had a roughly two-thirds majority at the start of each presidency.

Rostenkowski's penchant for cutting backroom deals with Republican administrations arguably came back to haunt him in 1988, however, when he backed the legislation to provide insurance coverage for Medicare recipients suffering catastrophic illnesses. The legislation to cover some costs of long-term care was initially a notable success; despite its lame-duck status, the Reagan Administration's proposal garnered overwhelming bipartisan support. Yet soon after the relatively quiet enactment of the legislation, grassroots opposition grew from both liberal groups who wanted more comprehensive coverage, and conservatives who objected to the increased Medicare premiums—especially for the wealthy.

Rostenkowski dismissed the criticism and did little to rebut the attacks as they grew in intensity. A tipping point came in August 1989 when Rostenkowski was targeted by angry protesters outside a senior citizens center on Milwaukee Avenue in the heart of his Chicago district. Broadcast cameras filmed Rostenkowski desperately running to escape the melee.

The political impact was devastating to Rostenkowski. His friend Bill Daley—son and brother of the Chicago mayors—said that the incident fueled criticism that Rostenkowski was "out of touch."[3] Weeks after that protest, Congress caved to the critics and health care advocates threw in the towel. President George H.W. Bush—the chairman's long-time pal—signed a repeal of the law. Rostenkowski never fully shook the embarrassing episode, and the impression it created that he was growing out of touch with his constituents.

A year later, Rostenkowski's bipartisan approach suffered another setback. Months-long deliberations by top White House officials and congressional leaders had produced a deficit-reduction package with a careful balance of tax hikes and spending cuts; the Ways and Means chairman hailed his initiative as the "Rostenkowski challenge." But the package came under unexpected second-guessing from both the Left and Right, and the House delivered a stinging setback. Even though Democrats quickly approved a more liberal alternative, which Bush signed, the dispiriting experience left a bitter taste for Rostenkowski and his committee allies.

PASSING OF AN ERA

Those policy and legislative setbacks were soon followed by more personally distressing problems for Rostenkowski. Following a lengthy investigation by the U.S. Attorney's office into criminality and mismanagement at the House Post Office, the prosecutors turned their attention to a series of improper transactions by Rostenkowski on his payroll and other House expenditures. Individually, most were examples of petty corruption that would not have been scrutinized when Rostenkowski entered politics in the 1950s. But in a new era, these incidents, taken collectively, became the focus of a withering two-year investigation into his personal life and finances.

A May 1994 indictment forced Rostenkowski to step down from his seat of power as chairman of the Ways and Means Committee, and resulted in his being defeated for reelection in November by an unknown Republican, Michael Flanagan—who went on to serve only one term in the House before being defeated in 1996 by an up-and-coming Illinois Democratic politician, Rod Blagojevich. In 1996, Rostenkowski pleaded guilty to reduced charges, and he served more than a year at the Federal Correctional Institute in Oxford, Wisconsin—which he later termed his "Oxford education." It was a humiliating end to a lengthy and substantive public career. The crimes—which were, at once, tragic and pitiful—reflected what his friends described as his stubborn unwillingness to adapt to changing legal and political standards. "The road curved, but he kept driving straight," said former Representative Dennis Eckart (D-OH).

The road to getting things done in Washington continued to curve in ways that, in retrospect, made Rostenkowski's departure seem like the passing of an era in American politics, both in terms of style and substance. Congress has largely abandoned the consensus-building approach to doing business that was his calling card. Instead, lawmakers today are more likely to line up on opposite sides of an issue and fight to a stalemate. President Bill Clinton's grand ambitions for health care reform died without House floor votes, for instance, something that would have been hard to imagine if a House leader of Rostenkowski's stature and deal-making prowess still wielded a gavel. For the first time in 40 years, Republicans won control of both the House and Senate in 1994. Speaker Newt Gingrich (R-GA) centralized House legislative operations in his office, and the outsized influence and productivity of the Ways and Means Committee faded.

After his release from prison, Rostenkowski stayed busy as a business consultant and he made occasional media appearances. When President Barack Obama—another graduate of Chicago politics—finally led Democrats to enact historic health care changes, Rostenkowski's name was hardly mentioned. He died five months later, in August 2010. In the end, Rostenkowski's accomplishments earned less credit than they deserved and, perhaps not surprisingly, his shortcomings received more criticism than they warranted. And yet it was his very disdain for public opinion that allowed Dan Rostenkowski to step up to the plate time and again, take his swings, and occasionally knock a big deal out of the park.

◆   ◆   ◆   ◆   ◆

9. Newt Gingrich:
The Partisan Revolutionary

by Linda Killian

Newton Leroy Gingrich was born in Harrisburg, Pennsylvania on June 17, 1943. He graduated from Emory University in 1965 and from Tulane University in 1968 (M.A.) and 1971 (Ph.D.). From 1970 to 1978, Gingrich worked as a teacher at West Georgia College. In 1979, Gingrich was elected as a Georgia Republican for the House in the Ninety-sixth Congress. He remained in the House for nine succeeding Congresses. In the later years of his congressional career he took up the position of minority whip and speaker. He unsuccessfully campaigned for the Republican presidential nomination in 2012. Since September 2013, Gingrich has been cohosting a political-debate show called Crossfire *on CNN.*

Gingrich has largely been credited for the Republican Party's control over Congress after the 1994 midterm elections. Ever since then, Gingrich has lost much of his popularity. He was blamed for partial government shutdowns in 1995 and he was the first speaker in the House to be reprimanded for ethics violations in 1997. His presidential campaign was short-lived, from May 2011 to May 2012.

Newt Gingrich (R-GA) led congressional Republicans to victory in 1994, becoming one of the most powerful, controversial, and consequential House Speakers in history. And yet, nothing about the inauspicious beginnings of Gingrich's political career suggested the monumental impact he would ultimately have on U.S. politics. A history teacher at West Georgia College who served as a campaign worker for liberal Republican Nelson Rockefeller's 1968 presidential campaign, Gingrich first ran unsuccessfully for Congress in 1974 at the age of 31. His second effort in 1976 was also unsuccessful, but on his third try in 1978, Gingrich finally won election to Georgia's Sixth Congressional District.

As fate would have it, the timing of Gingrich's arrival in the House coincided with the launch of C-SPAN, the cable network that went on the air in March 1979 broadcasting live sessions of the U.S. Congress. Gingrich, ambitious and full of ideas about how to advance both the Republican Party and his own career, quickly realized that C-SPAN could be a valuable communications tool, providing a tremendous platform for an unknown junior minority member of the House. Gingrich took advantage of the C-SPAN cameras to make speeches from the floor during the evening hours after the House had finished its business. During a time known as "special orders," when members were permitted to speak for up to an hour on any topic, Gingrich took to the airwaves.

In 1989, just after being elected House Minority Whip, Gingrich appeared on C-SPAN for an interview and talked about how he had successfully used special orders speeches. Gingrich said many House members failed to understand the power of C-SPAN's audience. "I don't care how empty the House is," Gingrich said. During a special orders speech, "there are 400,000 to 500,000 people watching at any given minute, and that means the biggest audience of your career for most members."

FROM BACKBENCHER TO MOVEMENT LEADER

Gingrich enlisted the help of a dozen junior GOP House members in his effort and in 1983 they named themselves the Conservative Opportunity Society. They gave incessant late-night speeches attacking the Democrats. In just a one-month period in the spring of 1984 Gingrich and other members of the Conservative Opportunity Society spoke on the House floor for almost 30 hours.

In May 1984, during one of those special orders speeches, Gingrich charged Democrats with supporting communist propaganda and hurting America with their foreign policy agenda. In retaliation, House Speaker "Tip" O'Neill (D-MA) ordered the House cameras to pan the empty House floor. A few days later Gingrich and O'Neill engaged in a heated floor debate. Gingrich charged the Democrats with conducting "McCarthyism of the left," and O'Neill countered that Gingrich was attacking the Democrats' patriotism.

He said the Democrats were not being unpatriotic, just "blind to reality. . . . It is perfectly American to be wrong and to have bad judgment," Gingrich thundered on the House floor.

O'Neill, who left the Speaker's chair and went down to the floor of the House to speak, roared at Gingrich: "You deliberately stood in that well before an empty House and challenged these people and you challenged their Americanism, and it's the lowest thing that I've ever seen in my 32 years in Congress." The exchange was widely reported and shown on network television giving Gingrich more visibility than he ever had before.

"I am now a famous person," the delighted Gingrich declared. In taking on O'Neill, Gingrich was elevated from a lowly GOP backbencher to someone who could go toe to toe with the House Speaker, and conservatives loved it. "If you're not in *The Washington Post* every day, you might as well not exist," Gingrich would later tell *Newsweek*.

Gingrich's entire strategy for gaining media attention and advancing his political agenda was based on confrontation. He understood that a take-no-prisoner, slash-and-burn attack on the Democrats was the best way to win. He was willing to pay the price of that strategy, which predictably was an increasingly toxic political environment in Washington, D.C.

POLITICS OF PERSONAL DESTRUCTION

Next, Gingrich leveled a series of ethics charges against Jim Wright, a Texas Democrat who had succeeded O'Neill as Speaker, and in 1989 he successfully forced Wright's resignation. Taking down the Speaker of the House greatly increased Gingrich's standing within the Republican ranks, and that same year he defeated a more senior, moderate Republican to win the minority whip position.

In 1992, Gingrich was forced to move to a new congressional district and face a primary challenge because of a Democratic redistricting plan. Gingrich only narrowly managed to defeat a GOP challenger by less than a thousand votes and he went on to win the general election. His primary opponent had attempted to leverage a scandal concerning a large number of bounced checks from the House bank. In a deft bit of political Jiu-Jitsu, Gingrich used the same attack on Democrats two years later, highlighting the House banking scandal as a symbol of an out-of-control Democratic Congress. It was neither the first nor last time Gingrich would attack others for digressions for which he was also guilty.

Gingrich made it clear to House Minority Leader Bob Michel (R-IL), whose style he argued was too accommodating to the Democrats, that it was time to retire. Gingrich and his team began raising money and recruiting candidates around the country to run against House Democratic incumbents. Along with then-House Republican Conference Chairman Dick Armey (R-TX), Gingrich and fellow Republicans devised a set of goals centered on popular conservative principles, including tax cuts, balancing the budget, reductions in federal spending, and a strong national defense. The entire package was dubbed the "Contract with America."

Gingrich's confrontational style and political acumen paid off in the 1994 midterm election, when he led Republicans to one of the most historic victories in congressional history. Seventy-three Republican freshmen were elected, a net 52-seat gain that gave the GOP control of the House of Representatives for the first time in more than 40 years. Remarkably, no Republican incumbent lost that year.

Gingrich started referring to the election as the "Republican Revolution." Although polling showed that while voters did favor balancing the budget and cutting government waste, they opposed the more drastic measures that Gingrich and his conservative supporters were advocating—for example, proposals to eliminate the Commerce, Energy, and Education departments and many programs for the poor.

A LOOMING SHOWDOWN

Unfortunately, the momentum coming out of the 1994 elections did not translate into immediate results. During the first 100 days of the 104th Congress, House Republicans succeeded in getting only two of their Contract with America items passed by the Senate and signed into law by President Clinton: a provision applying federal labor laws to Congress and a curb on unfunded mandates to the states. The 73 GOP House freshmen, who called themselves "True Believers," were impatient to go much further and drastically cut government spending as a way to balance the budget. They were constantly challenging Gingrich and other GOP leaders.

No Republican had ever served in the majority before, including Gingrich, and controlling the freshmen and holding the Republican Conference together proved to be a monumental challenge. Gingrich centralized power in the Speaker's office, and ensured loyalty and obedience by doling out committee assignments and fund-raising help. Gingrich decided which Republicans would receive key committee chairmanships, often bypassing the most senior members for closer allies.

Throughout the summer and early fall of 1994, Gingrich and his team moved forward in proposing severe budget cuts primarily to programs that affected the poor and middle class like school lunches and Medicare, at the same time leaving corporate subsidies and tax breaks for the wealthy off the table.

Indeed, it was the Republican proposal for Medicare reform that set the stage for the budget showdown between the Republicans and President Bill Clinton; a high-stakes political brawl that would forever define the 104th Congress and Gingrich.

Gingrich and Clinton, both Southerners and brilliant political tacticians who were somewhat lacking in self-control and humility, were fascinating political rivals. Though similar in many ways, Gingrich lacked Clinton's rhetorical and public relations prowess. Clinton had charisma, political acumen, and a natural ability to exude concern and caring—"feeling Americans' pain"—while Gingrich often appeared angry and thin skinned.

NEWT GINGRICH: THE PARTISAN REVOLUTIONARY

In the first of many tactical blunders, Gingrich totally underestimated how big an issue the Republican Medicare reform plan would become, and the significant advantage it would provide Clinton and the Democrats during the budget showdown. Instead of the debate centering on balancing the budget, the Democrats were able to shift the focus to Republicans who wanted to pay for tax cuts for the wealthy on the backs of the poor and the elderly.

In late October and early November 1995, congressional Republicans passed their budget and Medicare reform plans. In response the GOP, freshmen insisted they were willing to shut down the government if Bill Clinton did not sign on. Gingrich wrongly assumed that Clinton would back down, which proved to be the biggest miscalculation of his political career.

GOVERNMENT SHUTDOWN

Gingrich and the Republicans, who reportedly did not conduct a public poll on a potential government shutdown, were eager for a fight with Clinton and were convinced that the American people would take their side. But Clinton and his team had done ample polling and knew that standing up to the Republicans, especially over Medicare, would be a political success for him.

On November 13, 1995, Clinton vetoed the Republican budget and at midnight the government officially shut down. As a result, half the federal workforce was sent home.

Two days later, Gingrich made a political misstep, which damaged his public and political credibility. In a breakfast meeting with reporters, Gingrich complained about his treatment aboard Air Force One while attending the funeral of slain Israeli Prime Minister Yitzhak Rabin. Gingrich commented that he and Senate Majority Leader Bob Dole (R-KS) were forced to sit and exit from the back of the plane. Additionally, President Clinton barely talked to them during the entirety of the trip. The "snub," asserted Gingrich, was "part of why you ended up with us sending down a tougher continuing resolution" which led to the presidential veto and the government shutdown.

The remarks, which received immediate and widespread national media attention, came off as childish and reinforced the problem Republicans faced with Gingrich as their front man. The *New York Daily News* featured a now-famous cartoon on its front page of Gingrich in diapers with the headline "Cry Baby: He closed down the government because Clinton made him sit at back of plane."

The image of Gingrich as a crybaby, trying to exact revenge on the President and shutting down the government because of an imagined slight, was something that caught the American people's attention. From that moment, the tide began to turn against the Republicans.

HUBRIS BEFORE THE FALL

On December 6, 1995, as Clinton was vetoing a Republican budget for the second time and forcing another shutdown, Gingrich was informed by the U.S. House Committee on Ethics that after a 15-month investigation they had determined he violated House rules, and possibly federal law, by accepting tax-deductible donations to finance a college course sponsored by a private foundation.

Barely a year earlier, at the beginning of the 104th Congress, Gingrich had seemed to be everywhere at once, holding news conferences, doing interviews, making inflammatory off-the-cuff statements, and appearing on television. But in the wake of the government shutdowns, his comments about his seat on Air Force One and the ethics charges, many Republicans were hearing from their constituents that he needed to tone it down. "Tell Newt to shut up," one Republican said he heard back home.

In just one year, Gingrich had been transformed from a larger-than-life national political figure and the head of a movement, into a seriously wounded leader. His low approval ratings in national polls reflected the public's uneasiness with his personal style.

Many of the freshmen who he had helped get elected considered Gingrich a brilliant political strategist, but also arrogant, difficult, aloof, and undisciplined. Freshman David Weldon (R-FL) expressed the general sentiment in an interview with *The Washington Post:* "The revolution . . . transcends Newt Gingrich. He may have gotten the movement started, he may have been the engineer who got the train rolling, but now the train doesn't need him to run down the tracks. It's more powerful than him."

In the end, the budget standoff with Clinton resulted in two government shutdowns that cost the federal government more than $2 billion, and the Republicans, especially Gingrich, had almost nothing to show for their effort.

The rest of the 104th Congress featured compromises with the President on issues like welfare reform and a minimum wage increase that both Clinton and the freshmen could use to get reelected, along with passage of the Defense of Marriage Act which appealed to conservative supporters.

THE REVOLUTION DEVOURS ITS OWN

The Republicans held onto the House majority in 1996 but lost seats, and President Clinton rolled to reelection. Gingrich, somewhat chastened, talked about trying to find "common ground" with Clinton in postelection interviews and said he wanted to avoid "symbolic fights that are divisive."

In the election's aftermath, many House Republicans saw Gingrich as a liability and talked about replacing him as Speaker. Addressing the House after narrowly retaining the Speakership, Gingrich acknowledged that he had caused most of his own problems. "To the degree I was too brash, too self-confident, or too pushy, I apologize. To whatever degree and in any way that I brought controversy or inappropriate attention to the House, I apologize."

A few weeks later, the House would vote 395–28 to follow the recommendation of the Ethics Committee and reprimand Gingrich, requiring him to pay a $300,000 penalty for ethics violations involving contributions and his political activities. It was the first time in the history of the House that a sitting Speaker had been formally disciplined for ethical lapses.

Many members of the Class of 1994 had lost faith in Gingrich's judgment, management, truthfulness, and his ability to pursue their conservative agenda. A group of them started meeting regularly to talk about the possibility of trying to overthrow Gingrich. In the summer of 1997, they drafted a resolution that could be offered on the House floor to force a vote on whether Gingrich should be replaced as Speaker.

Other Republican leaders, aware of the group's efforts and interested in Gingrich's job, fanned the flames of discontent. But the dissidents couldn't agree on a course of action or who should be Gingrich's successor. Finally, House Majority Leader Dick Armey, convinced he would not be chosen to replace Gingrich, informed Gingrich of the plot against him. Although the coup fizzled, the discontent remained. In the 1998 election, Republicans narrowly held onto control of the House but suffered a net loss of five seats. The finger of blame again pointed at Gingrich.

Gingrich had pushed for impeachment proceedings against Bill Clinton over the sex scandal involving White House intern Monica Lewinsky and predicted it would help Republicans pick up seats in the election. But at the same time he was criticizing Clinton's misbehavior in virtually every speech, the married Gingrich had been carrying on an affair with a House staffer more than 20 years his junior (who would later become his third wife.)

Many Republicans feared they could not hold onto control of the House with Gingrich at the helm, and a formal challenge was mounted against him. Gingrich announced shortly after the 1998 election that he would leave both the Speakership and Congress, choosing to jump before he could be pushed.

Gingrich resigned the Speakership at the beginning of 1999, becoming only the third House Speaker in U.S. history to do so after Wright, whom he had toppled, and Henry Clay, who did so for personal reasons.

After leaving the Speakership, Gingrich used his political expertise and undiminished popularity with some conservative Republicans to launch an extremely lucrative consulting business and communications firm. He also mounted an ill-fated run for the GOP presidential nomination in 2012, which peaked with a 12-point victory in the South Carolina primary.

There is no doubt that Gingrich deserves credit for the 1994 victory that brought Republicans control of the House of Representatives for the first time in decades, and that legacy would far outlast Gingrich's Speaker-ship. Republicans would maintain control of the House for 16 of the next 20 years, with only a four-year interruption from 2006 to 2010. However, the substantive goals of balancing the budget and shrinking the size of government that was the rallying cry of the Republican Revolution remain unattained. During George W. Bush's two-term presidency, much of which was backed by a Republican Congress, the GOP delivered tax cuts but also significantly increased federal spending resulting in a ballooning deficit.

Gingrich will go down as one of the most significant American political figures in the second half of the 20th century. But the lasting legacy of his leadership and rise to power is less about substance, more about style and tone. Perhaps more than any other political leader in the past 50 years, Gingrich bears responsibility for the dismal state of our current politics. Much of the negativity, extreme partisanship, and dysfunctional polarization that characterize politics today can be traced back to the improbable rise of this ambitious and sharp-elbowed history professor. Newt Gingrich scaled the heights of political power in America, only to be felled by hubris and scandal.

◆ ◆ ◆ ◆ ◆

10. Tom DeLay: Power and Hubris

by Jan Reid

Born Thomas Dale DeLay on April 8, 1947, the former Texas Representative was born in Laredo. He graduated from University of Houston in 1970. He was a business owner and served as a member of his state's House of Representatives from 1979 to 1984. DeLay served as a Republican in 11 consecutive Congresses from 1985 to 2006; he resigned on June 9, 2006 after being indicted in 2005. Two congressional positions DeLay assumed were majority whip and majority leader. Nicknamed 'The Hammer' for his control over the House, DeLay was considered persistent and bold during his congressional service until 2004 when his reputation suffered severely.

From September to October 2004, the House Ethics Committee admonished DeLay on three counts, offering support to a candidate in exchange for a Medicare vote, appearing to link political donations to legislative favor and seeking out to the Federal Aviation Administration for intervention in a domestic political dispute. In September 2005, DeLay was indicted for allegedly conspiring to violate political fundraising law in his home state. In October 2005, DeLay turned himself in after being indicted for conspiring to launder money and money laundering. DeLay's reputation was further stained in 2010 with the allegations that he attempted to sway Texas elections with corporate money for candidates. In September 2013, a three-judge panel overturned the conviction that would have sent DeLay to prison for three years.

Tom DeLay became the most effective and powerful Texan in Congress since Lyndon Johnson. How did he become de facto leader of the House of Representatives, and what precipitated his downfall? Three events frame DeLay's narrative: the election of Ronald Reagan as president in 1980; the "Contract with America" in 1994 that helped Republicans gain a majority in the House for the first time in decades; and the House's impeachment of President Bill Clinton in 1998. In the end—as so often happens in Washington—hubris brought DeLay down.

After college, a young Tom DeLay took a job with a Houston pest control company. He started his own exterminator's service in Sugar Land, a Houston suburb, but he felt his business was strangled by the Environmental Protection Agency's (EPA) ban of a poison effective in killing fire ants. He launched his political career as a foe of the EPA and of all government regulation.

DeLay won a seat in the Texas House in 1978, where colleagues cheerfully nicknamed him "Tom De-Reg." Showing a penchant for good timing, DeLay announced his race for an open seat in Congress in 1983. President Reagan's rout of Walter Mondale the next year swept into office a large GOP House class that, along with DeLay, included former academics Newt Gingrich, from the Atlanta suburbs, and Dick Armey, from the Dallas suburbs.

At first, DeLay did little more in Congress than rail against the National Endowment for the Arts, and socialize. DeLay claimed to knock down 10 to 12 martinis a night. A concerned colleague, Frank Wolf (R-VA), gave him a videotaped sermon by the evangelist James Dobson called *Where's Dad?* The sermon's relevance to DeLay's own life served as an epiphany, dropping him to his knees, weeping, and bringing him back to the Southern Baptist faith of his youth. Born again, DeLay was now prepared to work his way up the hard way.

DeLay's district included a major NASA facility and a string of refineries and chemical plants owned by companies like Monsanto and Dow, and he took good care of those constituents. In 1988, Wyoming's Dick Cheney (R-WY), the Republican House whip, remarked at the GOP national convention that DeLay had an uncanny gift for counting votes; Cheney told DeLay that he wanted him as his deputy whip. But then the new president, George H. W. Bush, appointed Cheney as his secretary of defense, which was a critical setback for DeLay.

The day Cheney resigned his seat in Congress, Bob Walker (R-PA), one of the House firebrands, convinced Gingrich to run for GOP whip. DeLay managed the race of Ed Madigan (R-IL), who was the choice of the Minority Leader, Illinois's Bob Michel (R-IL). Gingrich edged Madigan by an 87–85 vote, and he did not forget DeLay's opposition.

DeLay made enough peace with Gingrich to help craft the Contract with America, supplying the antiregulation component at the request of its principal author Dick Armey. The electorate's 1994 repudiation of President Bill Clinton gave Republicans a majority of seats in the House for the first time since 1952, and catapulted the Class of 1984 into leadership positions. Gingrich vaulted to the Speaker's chair, and Armey moved up as Majority Leader. DeLay ran for House whip, opposed by Gingrich's comrade Bob Walker. One GOP rival derided DeLay as a House "concierge," who arranged golf tee-off times for members and got them free concert tickets. But DeLay had also created a political action committee (PAC) that he used to raise funds to lavish on the campaigns of grateful GOP incumbents. His grasp of the role of money in the Gingrich revolution enabled him to defeat Walker with surprising ease.

RISING NATIONAL PROFILE

DeLay first gained national attention when he let *Washington Post* reporters observe him crafting an antiregulatory initiative called Project Relief. The stunned reporters described a crowd of business lobbyists packing into his quarters to help write the bill. DeLay boasted: "We're going to fund only those programs we want to fund. We're in charge. We don't have to negotiate with the Senate. We don't have to negotiate with the Democrats." To further his antiregulatory crusade, DeLay attached dozens of riders to bills in order to dismantle the EPA. When asked if he would keep any federal regulation intact, DeLay replied, "Not that I can think of."

The pugnacious DeLay was furious when Gingrich eventually reached an agreement with Senate Majority Leader Bob Dole (R-KS) to end the budget impasse that led to the 1995 and 1996 government shutdowns. As the Republican presidential nominee in 1996, Dole recognized that the unpopular government shutdowns would play to the advantage of Bill Clinton, who won reelection handily that year. Whatever colleagues thought about the bare-knuckle tactics that won him the moniker "The Hammer," however, DeLay was an effective whip. In the 104th Congress, his record on the floor of passed bills versus defeated bills was an incredible 300–3.

Outraged that President Clinton had won reelection, DeLay and New York Representative Bill Paxon (R-NY) blamed Gingrich in part. They saw him as a wobbling and distracted leader, beset with financial and personal scandals. In July 1996, they enlisted Dick Armey and an Ohio representative of future note, John Boehner (R-OH), in a planned coup to oust Gingrich as Speaker. But a reporter for *The Hill* newspaper found out, and the plotters ducked for cover, trying to get their stories straight. The finger-pointing and political fallout from the failed coup shredded the public perception that DeLay and Armey were friends. In a House corridor, DeLay reportedly shouted curses at Armey and grabbed him by his necktie. Current House Speaker Boehner is the only one of the four who continues to hold elective office.

When the Republicans lost House seats in 1998, Gingrich agreed with DeLay that impeaching President Clinton over his affair with White House intern Monica Lewinsky would help the GOP politically. "This is going to be the most important thing I do in my political career," DeLay said at the time. He made his whip's suite into a war room that stoked the impeachment frenzy. At one point, he told a *Texas Monthly* reporter, "Looks like the coffin's nailed shut." Shortly thereafter, however, it was not Bill Clinton, but Bob Livingston (R-LA), Gingrich's designated replacement as House Speaker, who was forced to step down over disclosures of his own infidelity. The Senate easily acquitted President Clinton in the impeachment trial.

HUBRIS BEFORE THE FALL

With the ascension of Dennis Hastert (R-IL) as House Speaker, DeLay continued to wield vast power, and in 2003, he became Majority Leader. He was even willing to defy his own party's President. In 2001, when President George W. Bush asked the House to cease blocking a low-income tax credit, DeLay simply replied, "Ain't going to happen."

DeLay used his power to reward interests close to him. He worked to create the "K Street Project," which strong-armed lobbyists to hire only Republicans. DeLay also received generous support from lobbyist Jack Abramoff to take action that would benefit his clients, including the Northern Mariana Islands and several Native American tribes. As a result, DeLay treated the American protectorate of the Northern Marianas Islands almost like a personal fiefdom, protecting textile mills that paid indentured Asian women $3.05 an hour. He also tried to force on the islanders a power plant built by Texas-based Enron, even as that company was imploding in disgrace. Two of DeLay's former aides would end up pleading guilty to charges stemming from the Justice Department's investigation into Jack Abramoff.

DeLay's downfall would come not in Washington, D.C., however, but rather in Austin, where he pressured Texas legislators to adopt redistricting maps provided by him to maximize Republican electoral victories. In September 2002, an aide sent a check for $190,000, raised in part from corporate donors, to the Republican National Committee. Along with the check, the aide provided the names of seven GOP candidates between whom those funds were to be divided. Twenty-one days later, the Republican National Committee distributed those funds to the candidates, to the penny.

Corporate donations being illegal in Texas, a Travis County grand jury indicted DeLay and two aides for money laundering in September 2005. The felony charge forced DeLay to step down from his leadership post, and the next year he declined to run for reelection to Congress.

DeLay was convicted in 2010, and sentenced to three years in prison, though he remained out on bond. In 2013, a Texas court of criminal appeals reversed his conviction, and DeLay traveled to Washington, D.C., to revisit the old haunts where he had once wielded such power. Time had passed DeLay by, and "the Hammer" no longer seemed such a fearsome figure.

In October 2013, DeLay spoke to a Tea Party gathering near Dallas, offering to lead a spiritual crusade to shut down all federal government not specified in the Constitution. DeLay told the crowd, "It's time for a revolution. I am not advocating for revolution in the streets. But if that's what it takes." In fact, DeLay had already been at the forefront of a revolution two decades earlier. His take-no-prisoners style of partisanship and his refusal to compromise across the political aisle continue to characterize relations in the U.S. House of Representatives to this day.

◆ ◆ ◆ ◆ ◆

11. Dennis Hastert: The Accidental Speaker

by Michael Dorning

John Dennis Hastert was born on January 2, 1942 in Aurora, Illinois. The former Illinois Representative graduated from Wheaton College in 1964 and from Northern Illinois University in 1967. He worked as a teacher, athletic coach, and business owner before joining the Illinois House of Representatives from 1980 to 1986. Hastert served as a Republican in the House in 11 consecutive Congresses from 1987 to 2007; he resigned in 2007 after 20 years in office. He was the speaker for the 106th through 109th Congresses, making him the longest-serving Republican speaker.

Hastert has been credited with the creation—and later, violation—of the "Hastert rule," advising the House speaker to bring legislation to the floor only when the majority supports it. That "rule" originated when he pulled out a bill from the House floor that would create the Director of National Intelligence position in 2004; the bill was later brought on the floor and passed. This majority support "guideline" is not necessarily a positive notion to be remembered by, given it sets Hastert up for blame when government shutdowns come into play.

Even Dennis Hastert was surprised when he became Speaker. On the day House Republicans turned to him, Hastert had an appointment scheduled the following day with a headhunter. A new party leader was rising, and Hastert sensed his own political star declining. He thought it time to start figuring out options for life after Congress.

That would wait. By the end of a tumultuous day, "the Accidental Speaker," as he was quickly dubbed, was on his way to becoming the Republican Party's longest-serving Speaker of the House. He emerged from the relatively junior leadership post of Chief Deputy Whip on December 19, 1998, the day the House voted to approve articles of impeachment against President Bill Clinton, a polarizing political moment made more chaotic by an announcement shortly before the roll call. The Republicans' designated Speaker, Representative Robert "Bob" Livingston (R-LA), unexpectedly resigned in response to revelations that he had engaged in an extramarital affair. Amid the disarray that followed, the Republican caucus coalesced within hours around Hastert as a replacement.

Many House Republicans had already tired of the fitful leadership of the prior Speaker, Newt Gingrich, who only a month earlier had announced he would not seek another term following a loss of seats in the midterm elections. A visionary who led the Republican takeover of the House after four decades in the minority, Gingrich's provocative public pronouncements and fund-raising scandals made him an easy bogeyman for Democrats. Negative public opinion of Gingrich was a liability so strong that in 1996 Democrats even tried to weaken Republican presidential candidate Senator Bob Dole (R-KS) by tying him to Gingrich.

An unassuming former high school wrestling coach steeped in the nuts-and-bolts job of counting votes for the party leadership, Hastert was a stark contrast to Gingrich and Livingston. There was no hint of scandal about him. Few people outside of Congress had even heard of him before he became Speaker. He avoided the media limelight and the rhetorical combat on which Gingrich thrived. Unlike his predecessor, Hastert also harbored no ambition of a higher office. In a 2003 speech on his approach to leadership, he said one of his guiding rules was "to focus on the House and nothing but the House. . . . You don't find me spending too much time on television shows, or giving big speeches." Democrats never succeeded in vilifying Hastert and instead concentrated fire on House Majority Whip (then-Majority Leader) Tom DeLay (R-TX), who shared Gingrich's penchant for hard-edged rhetoric.

Hastert provided low-key, steady legislative leadership that focused on the near-term goals of his party, and later the priorities of Republican President George W. Bush, under whom he served for six years. Hastert reduced some of the centralization of authority achieved under Gingrich, and returned more discretion to committee chairs. He held together a fractious party divided among conservatives and moderates, often through patient courtship, personal relationships, and attentiveness to individual members' political needs.

Hastert came to the Speakership with credibility with both moderates and conservatives, as a protégé of the mild-mannered former Minority Leader Robert "Bob" Michel (R-IL) and an ally of conservatives like Gingrich and DeLay.

Initially he had little room for error. During Hastert's first two years as Speaker, he had to work with a majority so slender that he could not afford to lose more than five members on a party-line vote.

UNITING REPUBLICANS

Among Hastert's chief achievements during those first two years as party leader, while Democrat Bill Clinton was still President, was unifying congressional Republicans around a $792 billion tax-cut plan, and reinforcing the party's tax-cutting identity going into the 2000 elections. With pleas for personal loyalty, and a compromise that made tax cuts dependent on a continued budget surplus, he won over moderates. Congress passed the bill, which Clinton vetoed. Hastert and the Republicans then passed popular individual pieces of the bill such as a repeal of the estate tax and a reduction of the tax code's so-called marriage penalty, drawing more vetoes. The tax-cuts pushed by Hastert became a centerpiece of Bush's first-term agenda.

Once the White House had passed into Republican hands with Bush's election, Hastert turned his attention to passing the new President's legislative program. In November 2003, facing opposition from Democrats and Republican fiscal conservatives, Hastert secured passage of a Bush-backed Medicare prescription drug benefit by holding open the roll call for three hours into the early morning while he and other Republican leaders rounded up enough support.

As Speaker, he laid out what came to be known as the "Hastert Rule," using his prerogative over legislation to advance only those bills supported by the majority of his party caucus. In his 2003 speech on leadership, he said one of his guiding principles was "to please the majority of your majority . . . The job of Speaker is not to expedite legislation that runs counter to the wishes of the majority of his majority." In keeping with that philosophy, Republicans didn't allow Democrats any role in drafting the Medicare prescription drug legislation.

Years afterward, as successor John Boehner invoked the rule to stymie legislation such as immigration reform, gun control, and a funding resolution that would have averted a 16-day partial government shutdown, Hastert denied ever applying such a policy. In an October 2013 interview with the *National Journal,* he called the rule "a misnomer" and instead described a much more prosaic principle: "the 'Hastert Rule,' really, was: If you don't have 218 votes, you didn't bring the bill to the floor."

Even before Hastert became Speaker, the House had moved toward more party-line control. Gone were the days under Democrat Tip O'Neill when Southern Democrats joined Republicans to pass pieces of President Ronald Reagan's agenda over the opposition of most Democrats. Even so, Hastert showed more flexibility than his immediate predecessor, with the House passing 12 measures not backed by a majority of Republicans during his eight years of leadership, versus four measures over four years under Gingrich (according to a list compiled by *The New York Times*).

Nevertheless, Hastert or his spokesmen publicly cited the "majority of the majority" rule as his reason for delay or inaction on key pieces of legislation during his leadership. In 2003, he initially blocked a vote on intelligence reform legislation that the 9/11 Commission, and the Bush Administration supported, despite sufficient votes for passage if he relied mostly on Democrats. He later allowed a vote after objections from key Republicans were addressed. (See "Reforming National Intelligence: The 9/11 Commission," Chapter 48.)

Likewise, in 2006, Hastert blocked a vote on immigration reform, a major Bush priority, even though the measure had passed the Senate and there was widely reported to be enough Democratic support to pass the House.

DISPENSING PORK

Hastert's handling of immigration reform contrasted with the way the North American Free Trade Agreement was handled in 1993 by then–Democratic Speaker Tom Foley—another Speaker handed a priority piece of legislation from a President of his own party that was opposed by a majority of his caucus. Foley brought the Clinton-backed trade agreement to the floor anyway, and won passage by relying on Republican votes.

Yet the Hastert Rule was an effective tool for maintaining party cohesion. Another was attention to members' home-district political needs. Congressional earmarks—line-item pork-barrel projects tucked into appropriations bills at the request of individual members—exploded under his leadership. The pork projects surged from $12 billion in 1999, the year Hastert was elected Speaker, to an all-time high of $29 billion in 2006, the final year of his Speakership, according to Citizens against Government Waste. The advocacy group began tracking the spending in 1991.

Hastert was also keenly aware of the importance of fund-raising to party unity, traveling extensively to raise money for individual members. He bitterly opposed the 2002 McCain-Feingold campaign finance law that banned "soft-money" contributions that had been a major source of funding for party campaign organizations. He argued that the law would undermine party leaders and shift power to interest groups that could channel money directly into elections. The campaign finance law only came to a vote through a "discharge petition," a rarely employed parliamentary maneuver in which a majority of House members sign a petition to override the Speaker and force a vote on a measure. (See "Before Money Was Speech: Campaign Finance Reform," Chapter 34.) Hastert continued to oppose the measure even after it passed Congress, unsuccessfully urging Bush to veto the bill.

Corruption scandals marred Hastert's final two-year term as Speaker. Though he was not personally implicated in any wrongdoing, the scandals painted an unsavory portrait of the culture prevailing in the Republican-controlled Congress and weakened the Speaker. Lobbyist Jack Abramoff, for instance, was convicted of winning favors for clients by showering members of Congress with gifts, free travel, and campaign contributions. Republican Representative Mark Foley resigned just a little over a month before the 2006 midterm election following reports that he had sent sexually suggestive messages to underage male former House pages.

The scandals broke as Americans were already turning against President George W. Bush, who began his second term with a failed effort to privatize Social Security. Bush's popularity also suffered as a result of the mishandled federal response to Hurricane Katrina in 2005 and the increasingly unpopular war in Iraq. The combination had a caustic effect on the Republican brand, and the 2006 midterm elections dislodged House Republicans from the majority after 12 years in control. Hastert declined to serve as Minority Leader and resigned from Congress a year afterward.

On the final day of the 2006 Republican Congress, a House committee released a report on Foley that criticized Hastert's office for failing to respond to warnings of the Congressman's conduct. The report supplied an ironic bookend to his Speakership, with a sex scandal contributing to his departure just as an earlier sex scandal had thrust him into leadership. But those flashes of notoriety were the exception to Hastert Rule. During the years in between, he operated mostly out of the public eye, employing a quiet pragmatism that brought Republicans a measure of calm after the stormy Gingrich years, and allowed him to narrow internal ideological divisions within the party that would widen dramatically once Republicans returned to power in the House in 2010.

♦ ♦ ♦ ♦ ♦

12. Nancy Pelosi: The Pioneer

by Elaine S. Povich

Born Nancy D'Alessandro in Baltimore, Maryland on March 26, 1940, the Representative from California has been in Congress since 1987. Pelosi graduated from Trinity College in 1962. From 1981 to 1983, Pelosi served as chair to the California State Democratic Party. From 1985 to 1986, Pelosi was finance chairman to the Democratic Senatorial Campaign Committee. On June 2, 1987 she was elected to the One-hundredth Congress in a special election, filling the vacancy of Representative Burton who had died early that year. Pelosi has retained her seat as a Democrat in the House since then. Her positions in Congress have been minority whip, minority leader, and speaker.

Pelosi was difficult on the George W. Bush Administration and helpful to the Obama administration, as she helped garner support for the 2009 stimulus package and health care reform. Unfortunately, the growing unpopularity of Obama's stimulus package and Affordable Care Act consequentially affected Pelosi's popularity. Pelosi became a target of attacks by the Tea Party.

Nancy Pelosi (D-CA) always used this motto with her children: "proper preparation prevents poor performance." Never was that slogan more appropriate than in her dogged, tenacious struggle to win passage of the Affordable Care Act in the U.S. House of Representatives in 2010.

In signing the bill into law, President Barack Obama singled out Pelosi for her heroic efforts in cobbling together a majority to enact the landmark legislation; he was right to give her a large share of the credit.

As House Speaker in January 2010, Pelosi watched with dismay, along with other Democrats, as Scott Brown (R-MA) won Ted Kennedy's (D-MA) open Senate seat in Massachusetts, depriving Democrats of their 60-vote supermajority in the Senate.

Faced with a changed political dynamic, Obama contemplated giving up on his signature health care bill, suggesting instead that it be broken into smaller pieces rather than the one sweeping measure as he had proposed earlier. "Kiddie care," scoffed Pelosi. She wasn't having any of it.

BORN TO POLITICS

While others in her party wrung their hands, Pelosi dug in. It was something she had done all her life. Never the most gifted public speaker, Pelosi relied on organizational skills learned under the guidance of her father, which helped her propel to high office. When her father, Thomas D'Alessandro Sr., was mayor of Baltimore from 1947 to 1959, all of his children were taught firsthand about constituent service. They kept the "file" of favors asked and granted. Pelosi excelled at it. She aced out all of her older brothers until it became her job. It was her first lesson on political organizing.

Later, in California, long before she became a candidate, she was an organizer for political causes. Before that, she was an organizer for her five children—lining them up, assembly-line style, to fix their own lunches on the way out the door for school. Bread, spread, sandwich filling, fruit, drink, paper bag—all set in order—a system that was efficient and, yes, organized.

Years later, before she could begin organizing a push to pass a comprehensive health reform bill, she had to convince her fellow Democrats, and maybe even the President himself, that it was worth the fight. She button-holed everyone she could think of. She cajoled, she argued, and she planned. Along with Senate Majority Leader Harry Reid (D-NV), she prevailed on Democrats in Congress to press ahead with a broader and more comprehensive approach.

The House and Senate had passed different versions of the health care bill. The House would not take the Senate's version, nor would the Senate take the House's. They would both have to be rewritten. It was a daunting task, but one that Pelosi was ready and willing to take on.

"We will go through the gate," she said at a news conference on January 28, 2010. "If the gate is closed, we will go over the fence. If the fence is too high, we will pole vault in. If that doesn't work, we will parachute in. But we are going to get health care reform passed."

The parliamentary strategy for the House was set. It involved passing the Senate bill, but with a number of modifications and changes to help ease passage. Nonetheless, there were dozens of Democrats undecided—reports said there were 68 of them. Usually, the list of wavering members would be doled out among different members of the leadership. Not this time. Pelosi decided to talk to them all.

She put her skills to work selling Obamacare and even provided her members with a handy list of talking points aimed at winning public support for the law. Pelosi encouraged Democrats to flood their districts with highlights of how the law would help different constituents—seniors, young people, and women in particular. She also provided a district-by-district rundown of provisions in the law for each area of the country, which gave Democrats a blueprint for discussing the law.

In the end, 219 House Democrats voted for the bill and only 34 voted against. No Republicans supported it, but the Democratic majority was enough. It was thus fitting that when Obama signed the bill, with Pelosi standing near him, he called her "one of the best Speakers the House of Representatives has ever had."

That momentous day proved to be the high point of her short tenure as Speaker. In the midterm elections in the fall of 2010, Democrats lost the House, and Pelosi lost the Speakership, partially due to worries about Obamacare, as well as the sluggish economy. Her barrier-breaking days as the first woman Speaker of the House were over.

A TENACIOUS RISE

In many ways, her tenacity in winning passage of the Affordable Care Act and her tireless selling of the law mirrored the approach she had taken rising to the highest position in the U.S. House of Representatives in January 2007. Years earlier, after Pelosi first became House Minority Leader, a reporter asked why she hadn't lent her stylish touch to her new leadership office, nor hung any pictures on the walls. She quipped back, "I don't intend to be here that long." Yet in the four years prior to assuming the Speakership, she made the most of the minority position.

The climb to the Speaker's rostrum began more than a decade before, beginning with Pelosi seeking to become the whip and then Minority Leader. The whip race was the key. Once she achieved that post, the Minority Leader and Speakership were relatively easy. While the whip position is nominally about counting votes and party discipline, it is also about being the "face" of the party. Before Pelosi mounted her challenge, she knew that the "face" of both the parties in Congress had always been male.

When Pelosi first started thinking about running for whip in 1998, Democrats were in the minority, but Pelosi was optimistic that they could wrest control of the House in the elections of 2000 or 2002, and she wanted to help lead that charge.

Two rivals caught wind of the Pelosi moves and weren't happy. Representative Steny Hoyer (D-MD), chairman of the House Democratic Caucus, one step below whip, believed he should move up. The other whip candidate, John Lewis (D-GA), who was a deputy whip, was equally miffed by Pelosi's running start at the job. He thought it was time for an African American in the leadership. Those sentiments did not deter her—in fact, they made her work harder.

By the time the 2000 elections arrived, Lewis had dropped out and Hoyer lagged behind Pelosi in fund-raising, $1.5 million to $3.9 million. Democrats gained seats but were still in the minority. In typical fashion, Pelosi didn't stop long to lick wounds. She kept organizing. Then, House Minority Whip David Bonior of Michigan was caught in redistricting and left the House to run for governor. The whip race was on again.

Pelosi used every tactic she could think of, even enlisting unlikely support. One day during Congress's summer recess, months before the whip election would take place, Cal Dooley (D-CA) stopped by his office to check messages. Rifling through the usual slips of paper, one jumped out at him: Ernest Gallo, the famed California winemaker. Though Dooley was a loyal member of the House's "Wine Caucus"—composed of members who have wine manufacturers in their states—the Congressman had never talked to Gallo. He called back.

Gallo wanted to talk about Pelosi and argued that electing a whip from California would be good for both of them. Dooley, more conservative than

Pelosi, had close ties with Hoyer. But how could he say no to Gallo, the elder statesman of the American wine industry and a man important to Dooley's constituents in California?

He told Gallo he'd think about it; the closest he could come to tipping his hand on the secret ballot. As summer turned into fall, Congress was back in session and Pelosi and Hoyer kept piling up the votes. Hoyer said he had 100 commitments; Pelosi said she had 120. Since there were only 215 House Democrats, there was clearly some amount of bluffing by the candidates, as well as members making commitments to both of them.

Behind closed doors, Hoyer gave a speech quoting Adlai Stevenson and Robert F. Kennedy and his soaring rhetoric brought applause. Ever the nuts-and-bolts, detail-oriented legislator, rather than an orator, Pelosi opted to let veteran John Murtha (D-PA) give her nominating speech. She won, 118–95, and was elected whip.

In 2003, Pelosi became Minority Leader and then set her sights on helping her party win back control of the House, which would allow her to be the Speaker. That challenge wasn't easy. First of all, no woman had done it before. While the House, and the nation, seemed ready for a woman Speaker, Pelosi didn't win her colleagues' support because of her gender. But, he won their support because of her shrewd playing of Congress's inside game and her tireless work at fund-raising and organizing. She had shown the importance yet again of "proper preparation."

Pelosi also had the advantage of opposing the war in Iraq from the beginning, and while that might not have been a popular position in 2002, she was on the right side of that argument by the time her ascension to Speaker seemed a possibility. In June of 2006, some 2,500 troops had been killed in the Iraq War, 18,000 had been wounded, and the cost had risen to $400 billion. While some Democratic leaders continued to support the war, Pelosi tagged it as a "failed policy."

The elections of 2006 would prove her right, at least politically. On January 3, 2007, Nancy Pelosi was sworn in as Speaker, attaining the highest office a woman had ever held in the United States. When Republicans recaptured the House majority in 2010, many observers, including quite a few in her own party, expected Pelosi to step down from the leadership. But they obviously didn't know her well. In January 2011, she ran and was elected easily as Minority Leader. Nancy Pelosi had never stepped away from a challenge in her long career, and she wasn't about to begin.

◆ ◆ ◆ ◆ ◆

13. Richard Russell Jr.: Patriarch of the Senate

by Sheryl B. Vogt

Richard Russell Jr., who served as Georgia's Representative, Governor, and Senator, was born on November 2, 1897 in Winder, Georgia. Russell graduated from University of Georgia with a Bachelor of Laws Degree in 1918. In 1920, after one year of practicing law, Russell became the youngest member elected to the Georgia House of Representatives where he served from 1921–1931. As a state representative, he worked to improve Georgia's highways and supported Georgia's public education system, and was elected Speaker pro tempore in 1923 and 1925 then Speaker of the House from 1927–1931. He was elected Georgia's youngest 20th-century Governor in 1931 and served until elected Senator from Georgia in 1933. Russell's congressional career ended when he died on January 21, 1971. While in Congress, Russell served on the Appropriations Committee, Armed Services Committee, Committee of Immigration, Committee on Manufactures, and was elected President pro tempore of the Senate in the 91st and 92nd Congresses. Russell was also appointed by President Johnson to the President's Commission on the Assassination of John F. Kennedy in 1963.

Russell prided himself as an advocate of white southern values who repeatedly led efforts to block civil rights legislation and championed state's rights. Russell was undoubtedly an influential Southern Democratic voice in the Senate until his death. Some also remember him for his failed Democratic nomination to the Presidency in 1952.

Richard B. Russell Jr. was the consummate Senator's Senator "whose knowledge and reverence of the United States Senate as an institution was so deep that even his colleagues who opposed him on the issues, or had conflicting philosophies of government, had a level of respect for him that bordered on reverence."[1] During his 38 years in the U.S. Senate, Russell became such an integral part of the institution that today one of the three Senate office buildings is named after him, as was a nuclear-powered submarine, federal courthouse, and a state highway. Yet, despite this recognition by his former colleagues and his unparalleled record of strengthening the national defense and working for the people of Georgia, Russell's legacy is tarnished by decades spent blocking civil rights legislation.

In a small town outside Winder, Georgia, Russell grew up in a family of modest means, though his father was well known throughout the state from his numerous political campaigns. Russell's parents had high expectations for their children and encouraged them all to be ambitious, learned, and industrious. While never an exceptional student, Russell was an avid reader in many fields who favored history and developed an uncommon memory. Russell set his course based on the direction given by his father to all seven sons: "All of them could not be brilliant, all of them could not be successful, but all of them could be honorable."[2]

In his contribution to a 1937 family round-robin letter, Russell expressed pride in his nieces and nephews "and hope that their parents will overlook no opportunities to instill in them the principle of the old French expression, *noblesse oblige* [that to whom much is given, much is required], which I first ran across when in about the fifth grade." Having grown up modestly in a household of 13 children, Russell grew to value a strong intellect, a charitable heart, and a frugal disposition.[3] When away at school, Russell followed his mother's example of counting items to and from the laundry, and adhered to his father's instructions to pay debts in a timely manner. Later, he was known for his Spartan lifestyle and attention to savings. Yet, within his family Russell was a generous patriarch who mentored and assisted nieces and nephews financially. These character traits forged in childhood remained strong in Russell's adult life. He never lost sight of his duty to work for the future good of his people, and gave 50 years of his life to public service.

EARLY POLITICAL LIFE

Winning a seat in the Georgia House of Representatives at the age of 22, Russell was among the youngest legislators in the 198-person body. He advanced quickly during ten years in the legislature, spending the last four as Speaker. His ascent was aided by his ability to cultivate key supporters, develop political strategy, and make progress on popular issues. Like his father, Russell believed that a political leader must be absolutely honest, straightforward, and fair to all people and points of view. He inspired the confidence and respect of others and was known for his dependability.

In the legislature, Russell advocated building and improving highways, supporting public education, and reducing the influence of special interest groups in order to develop a fiscally responsible, pay-as-you-go budget. He continued this agenda in 1930 as Georgia's youngest Governor in the 20th century. He completed a comprehensive reorganization of state government by slashing the number of agencies from 102 to 17, and he reduced state expenditures by 20 percent. Along the way he balanced the budget and honored

$2.8 million in delinquent obligations without cutting the salaries of state workers other than his own—by $3,950.

In Georgia, Russell honed the leadership skills that would serve him so well in Washington. According to Zell Miller, who would also serve as both Governor and Senator, Russell "was open, he was honest in his dealings, he was always fair and civil to both sides in an argument, and once he had given his word he stood by it without equivocation. He was a genuine representative of the people who shunned political labels and special interests, and he was scrupulous about doing his homework on the issues, so that when he spoke, it was from personal understanding."[4]

In 1933, Russell came to the U.S. Senate and earned a seat—virtually unprecedented for a freshman—on the powerful Appropriations Committee, where he played a role in all legislation considered by the Senate. Russell quickly became chairman of its subcommittee on agriculture, a post he retained throughout his career. Russell marked his first Senate decade by ensuring passage of New Deal programs, and indeed, he was more active in debate and sponsoring legislation during this period than the rest of his 38 years there. Following congressional reorganization in 1947, he continued on Appropriations and the newly formed Armed Services Committee.

Russell parlayed his leadership techniques into a power base unlike any other in the U.S. Congress. Knowledge, he believed, was power, and he usually had more than most. He made it a point to know all the rules, regulations, precedents, history, customs, and traditions of the U.S. Senate. Believing in the power and relevance of history, he brought its lessons to bear in considering policy-making decisions.[5] For the next 25 years, Russell labored predominantly behind the scenes to influence the legislative process, modifying and maneuvering when necessary, always dealing impartially, and focusing on the core issues and problems the legislation was meant to solve.

MENTOR AND PATRIARCH

As important as committee assignments and traits, Russell's standing in the Senate was built on the strong relationships he had with his colleagues. Regardless of party or seniority, he was a friend of all.[6] Russell was generous in sharing his wisdom and insight with new senators regardless of their political affiliation. According to Senator Ted Stevens, "When we came to the Senate, we were the recipients of the attention of Senator Russell, and we were guided by the Senators that he had so well instilled with the love of this institution. As they took us under their wing, as Senator Russell had done to them, they counseled us in our first years in the Senate. It is something for all of us to remember that he worked primarily to assure that this nation remained strong . . . he was very bipartisan . . . I'm very serious about saying he took time with young Senators to explain his understanding of defense and why it was so necessary to keep such a firm foundation."[7] In a 1953 talk to freshman members of the U.S. House, Russell said, "People will measure us by honest and patriotic service."[8] This was a standard that he personally met and encouraged in his colleagues.

The committees Russell chaired were models of bipartisanship. Among his best friends were the ranking Republicans on these committees, such as Senator Leverett Saltonstall (R-MA) on Armed Services and Senator Milton Young (R-ND) on Appropriations. Liking to work in committee, he was able to arrange compromises that satisfied conflicting interests.[9] Senator Hiram Fong (R-HI) recalled Russell's welcoming him to Appropriations: "One learns more about the government in one year on the Appropriations Committee than he can in many years anywhere else." He also noted that Russell was admired for his impartiality and conduct of the committee.[10]

Senator Carl T. Curtis (R-NE) related that Russell "could exert his leadership without being present. He could pick out the important from the unimportant and see what was involved in the proposition . . . he was never a tool of the lobbyists . . . he was his own man."[11] Senator Samuel J. Ervin Jr. (D-NC) remembered Russell as "one of those rare individuals who would never settle on the truth to serve the political hour. He would not sacrifice his fundamental convictions concerning what would be best for the United States . . ."[12] Senator Clifford P. Hansen (R-WY) said that he could depend upon Russell's wisdom and judgment in areas in which he had no knowledge and experience himself, and that he knew others in his party felt the same. "They would count on him because he had really grown above party . . . if anyone could speak for the nation . . . we in the Senate felt that Dick Russell would and did."[13]

While Russell often avoided speaking on the floor, he was a brilliant debater. Perhaps his closest friend, John C. Stennis (D-MS) related that "he was quick in repartee . . . devastating in debate . . . he could certainly leave an adversary obliterated" without resorting to personal attack. "His speeches were full of logic and his rhetoric was good; his sentences were rounded and complete and solid substance all the way . . . he rested his oars on going to the merit and prevailed through logic as the weight of his argument."[14]

A MIXED LEGACY

Describing his personal political philosophy, Russell noted that in times of crisis, such as the Great Depression, he was a liberal who believed that government action was necessary. In good times, he was a conservative who saw no need to tinker with the system. In a snapshot, Russell's Senate career was dominated by his unpopular stand against civil rights legislation, his role as the architect of America's national security after World War II, and his dedication in serving his constituency and nation. A fair assessment of his legacy must include a balanced view of the positive and the negative.

Russell's command of the Senate's parliamentary rules and precedents was used most effectively to block the passage of civil rights legislation for three decades. Without his standing and influence in the Senate, meaningful civil rights legislation might have passed 20 years earlier.

A defender of white southern traditions and values, Russell believed in white supremacy and had "lived all of his formative years under a system of strict segregation that was seemingly sanctioned by the highest court in the land."[15] Yet, unlike many Southern politicians of his era, Russell did not promote hatred or acts of violence in order to defend these beliefs.

Russell began contesting civil rights legislation as early as 1935, when an antilynching bill was introduced in Congress. By 1938, he led the Southern Bloc in resisting such federal legislation "based on his constitutional arguments that policies such as operation of schools, public accommodations, and similar matters were reserved for the states and not within the province of the federal government."[16] By continually blocking passage of a cloture rule in the Senate, Russell preserved unlimited debate as a method for halting or weakening civil rights legislation.

By 1964, however, American society and the U.S. Senate itself had changed dramatically, and the strongest civil rights bill up to that time passed overwhelmingly. Once the Civil Rights Act of 1964 became law, Russell urged compliance "as good citizens"[17] and counseled against any violence or forcible resistance; he was the only opponent of the bill to do so. On July 22, 1964, Lyndon Johnson wrote Russell that his statement "was significant . . . and in keeping with your personal code."[18]

In the area of national security, Russell believed after World War II that America's best defense was a military power so strong that no other nation could challenge it successfully. Russell was not eager to place America in the role of world policeman, yet he had little faith in international peacekeeping forces.

As the United States and the Soviet Union squared off, Russell strongly supported a military buildup, for which he insisted on civilian oversight or control. As chair of the Armed Services Committee, he started its Military Preparedness Subcommittee. He was a leader in establishing the Atomic Energy Commission, setting up an independent Central Intelligence Agency, and placing space exploration and development in the hands of both civilians and the military.

A stalwart nationalist, Russell favored military force only when America's interests were directly threatened. During the Cuban Missile Crisis of 1962, he advocated military action in what he saw as a direct Communist threat to the nation. Upholding the Monroe Doctrine, in this case, was of vital interest to the nation and its hemisphere.

In 1954, he spoke out against American military support of the French in Vietnam, and as the war in Vietnam escalated in the 1960s, Russell still could not see a compelling reason for America's involvement. Russell believed deeply in the Presidency, so he found himself supporting four administrations as America descended into the quagmire. While he advised the presidents to "go in and win—or get out," he discovered that the United States could neither prevail with full-scale military power nor find diplomatic solutions. However, once the flag was committed, so was Russell. Though frustrated by policy and critical of war tactics, he did all he could to support U.S. troops by assuring that they had the best equipment and supplies and by monitoring defense appropriations.

Russell steadfastly fought against rapid deployment, believing that the United States would always find reason to intervene in other nations' conflicts once its military had the ability to engage quickly in some far-flung battle. On June 25, 1969, the Senate passed the National Commitments Resolution, which Russell, along with Senator J. W. Fulbright, was instrumental in drafting. The resolution reasserted the Senate's right to be a participant in the making of commitments by the United States.

Firmly believing that he was elected to represent and work for Georgia's interest in Washington, not Washington's interest in Georgia, Russell worked to bring economic opportunities to his home state. He successfully secured 15 military installations and over 25 research facilities—including the Centers for Disease Control and the Russell Agricultural Research Center—most of which still are major employers of Georgians, contribute to the state's economy, and are beneficial to all Americans. Personally, Russell, who had supported use of farm surpluses to upgrade school lunches since 1935, thought his most important legislative contribution was to author and secure passage of the School Lunch Program in 1946. He also helped establish the forerunner of the food stamp program and was a consistent supporter of federal aid to education. Fittingly, Russell ended his Senate career as President pro tempore, making him third in line of presidential succession. And Secretary of State Dean Rusk called Russell the most powerful and influential man in Washington for a period of about 20 years, second only to the President.

Russell's legacy, however, includes his unyielding opposition to civil rights legislation—a stand that was costly to the nation and to Russell personally. It derailed his quest for the Presidency in 1952, often diverted him from other legislative and appointed business, and ultimately weakened his health. In the end, Russell's legacy is thus mixed, perhaps as complicated and complex as the man himself. An undisputed patriarch of the Senate, he remained a product of his generation and did not rise above the context of the times in which he lived to remove barriers that held black and white Americans captive in the tragedies of the past.

♦　♦　♦　♦　♦

14. Robert A. Taft: Mr. Republican

by James Patterson

Robert Alphonso Taft, son of President William H. Taft, was born in Cincinnati, Ohio on September 8, 1889. Taft graduated from Yale University in 1910 and Harvard University Law School in 1913. He returned to Cincinnati to practice law. Rejected by the Army for poor eyesight, Taft spent World War I working as assistant counsel for the U.S. Food and Drug Administration and as counsel for the American Relief Association in Paris. He was elected to the Ohio House of Representatives in 1921, became the Republican majority leader in 1926, and served as member of the Ohio Senate from 1931–1932. In 1938, Robert A. Taft was elected as a Republican to the U.S. Senate. During his time as Senator, Taft served as Co-Chairman on the Committee on the Economic Report, Chairman of the Committee on Labor and Public Welfare, and served on the Republican Policy Committee. Taft's senatorial career ended when he died in 1953.

Taft was a well-known critic of President Roosevelt and a staunch isolationist who fought against increasing military appropriations and any measure that could force the United States into war. The Senator was firmly opposed to "big government," measures he viewed as anti-business, and devoted his time to curtailing the power of the labor unions. He sponsored the Taft-Hartley Act, which restricted strikes and prohibited Unions from donating directly to campaigns. Sen. Taft is remembered for being a powerful anti-Union Republican who fought against liberalism but is also remembered for being an unsuccessful presidential candidate in 1940, 1948, and 1952.

When Robert A. Taft of Ohio entered the Senate in January 1939, he was already well known as the son of former President William Howard Taft, and he quickly joined a small but vociferous band of Republicans who contested many of President Franklin D. Roosevelt's (FDR) social and economic policies. Blunt and outspoken, he aroused the ire of Democrats—and some moderate Republicans—many of whom perceived him as a cerebral but harsh and overly conservative partisan. It was said that Taft possessed the "best mind in the Senate—until he made it up." In fact, Taft was a serious and extraordinarily diligent man. These strengths, together with a reputation for integrity, made him such a leading figure in his party that he became known as "Mr. Republican," and Taft is now regarded as one of the most significant U.S. Senators of the 20th century.

In 1939, and with few exceptions during his entire time in the Senate, Taft was an especially vocal foe of Big Government. Though he accepted some New Deal initiatives such as Social Security, he became a leader of an informal and tenacious conservative coalition of Republicans and Democrats who fought against high levels of federal spending and what they considered to be arbitrary regulation of business. As he exclaimed in 1939, "the whole history of America reveals a system based on individual opportunity, individual initiative, individual freedom to earn one's living in one's own way, and to conduct manufacturing, commerce, agriculture or other business; on rugged individualism, if you please, which it has become so fashionable to deride." Many New Dealers, he complained, "have no concern whatever for individual freedom. They are collectivists like Marx and Lenin and Mussolini."

FDR's internationalist foreign policies, which increasingly sought ways to resist the advance of fascist powers, also alarmed Taft, who emerged as a champion of isolationism. Like his friend and one-time mentor, former President Herbert Hoover, he believed that the United States should increase its defenses, especially its air power, but avoid entangling foreign alliances. He therefore opposed military conscription and most other Roosevelt administration efforts aimed at preparing the country for a possible war against Adolf Hitler and Nazi Germany. "We should be prepared to defend our own shores," he declared, "but we should not undertake to defend the ideals of democracy in foreign countries." FDR, he charged, was "trying to stir up prejudice against this country or that, and "at all costs take the minds of the people off their troubles at home." Rejecting presidential domination of foreign affairs, he added that "there are some who say that politics should stop at the water's edge . . . I do not at all agree. . . . There is no principle of subjection to the Executive in foreign policy. Only Hitler would assert that."

RISING IN THE SENATE

It was a sign of Taft's meteoric rise in national politics and public unease over war in Europe that he became a leading contender for the Republican presidential nomination in 1940. At the GOP convention in June he was the second leading vote getter—behind New York City District Attorney Thomas Dewey—on the first two ballots. But the rise of Hitler, who had already forced France to surrender, left Great Britain as the only major power blocking fascist domination of Europe. Deeply alarmed, Republican internationalists rallied behind a dark-horse outsider, Wendell Willkie, who swept to the nomination on the sixth ballot.

The struggle exposed what was to become a long-term split within the GOP. This division pitted a predominantly internationalist, moderate Eastern Bloc against a more isolationist and conservative wing that was strong in the Midwest and parts of the West. Taft persisted in 1940–1941 in criticizing FDR's domestic and foreign policies, including lend-lease aid to Britain. "Even the collapse of England," he wrote a friend in January 1941, "is to be preferred to participation for the rest of our lives in foreign affairs."

During World War II Taft continued to receive the admiration of conservative Republicans, and after narrowly winning reelection in 1944, he became the undisputed leader of the Senate's bipartisan conservative coalition. The reporter Allen Drury, who covered the chamber at the time, observed in his diary that Taft "continues to impress me as one of the strongest and ablest members here, one of the men who acts consistently as though they think what is being done here really matters to the welfare of the country."

When Republicans rallied to capture majorities in the House and Senate after the elections of 1946, Taft's influence in the Senate reached new heights. The 80th Congress of 1947–1948 featured fierce conservative battles against the administration of President Harry Truman. Taft, heading the U.S. Senate Committee on Labor and Public Welfare, as well as a GOP "steering committee," proved himself to be moderate on some domestic issues, favoring federal aid for public education as well as greater funding for public housing. (Annoyed, Senator John Bricker (R-OH), Taft's colleague from Ohio, quipped, "I hear the Socialists have gotten to Bob Taft.")

In other areas, however, "Mr. Republican" led anti-administration battles in the Senate. The GOP majorities passed income tax cuts, only to see them vetoed by the President. In 1947, they approved a Labor Management Act, widely known as the Taft-Hartley Act. This hotly contested measure became law only after Taft led fellow conservatives in overturning a presidential veto. The "slave labor bill," as many union leaders branded it, banned a number of "unfair" labor practices, including secondary boycotts and closed shops, and called upon union leaders to sign affidavits stating that they were not communists. One especially contested clause, Section 14 (b), authorized states to pass so-called right-to-work laws, which outlawed union shops that required workers to join a union shortly after being hired. From then on, Taft received praise for his skilled leadership of the bill, but also encountered unrelenting hostility from leaders of organized labor.

The GOP was far less united in matters concerning foreign policy. Led by Senator Arthur Vandenberg (R-MI), many Republicans on Capitol Hill supported Truman's internationalist measures aimed at assisting war-torn Western Europe and standing firm against communism in the Cold War. An ardent defender of individual liberty, Taft detested communism, but he argued that the Soviet Union posed no military threat to Western Europe. For this reason, and because he sought to reduce federal spending, he tried to cut funding for the Marshall Plan's economic aid to Europe. Bolstered by Vandenberg and other (mostly Eastern) Republicans, Democrats won these battles.

A TRUMAN FOIL

In 1948, Taft again sought the GOP presidential nomination, and as in 1940, he trailed only one foe on the first two ballots: Governor Dewey of New York. But many delegates, believing that his colorless public persona detracted from his vote-getting appeal, were cool to his candidacy. Dewey, supported strongly by Eastern internationalists and moderates, captured the nomination on the third ballot.

Voters in 1948 not only defeated Dewey, but they also returned Democratic majorities to the House and Senate. Taft, collaborating with Democratic senators, secured passage of a bill expanding public housing. Otherwise, he continued to attack Truman's liberal domestic and internationalist foreign policies. When Truman sought Senate ratification of a North Atlantic Treaty Organization (NATO), Taft opposed him, arguing that the Soviets did not intend to invade Western Europe, and that NATO would serve to provoke them. He added, "I am as much against communist aggression as anyone . . . but we can't let them scare us into bankruptcy and the surrender of all liberty. . . ."

In 1949–1950, the Cold War hardened dangerously. By midsummer of 1950, the Soviets had successfully tested atomic weapons. Communist forces had triumphed in China, and the United States had sent troops to counter what was widely perceived to be Soviet-inspired communist aggression in Korea. Meanwhile, Senator Joseph McCarthy (R-WI) and the House Committee on

Un-American Activities were whipping up a scurrilous "Red Scare" against supposed communist subversion. In this hotly partisan atmosphere, Taft sought reelection for a third term as Senator. He knew that a resounding victory would place him in good position to win—at last—a GOP presidential nomination.

The aggressiveness of GOP challenges, combined with American military setbacks in Korea and heightened domestic fears of communism, combined to make 1950 a Republican year. Taft was easily reelected for a third term. In the process, however, some of his positions came under sustained attack. Seeming to contradict his stance against substantial American economic or military aid to contest communism in Europe, Taft called for greater military assistance to Nationalist Chinese forces in Asia. Instead of trying to rein in McCarthy's irresponsible behavior—and as the most powerful GOP Senator he could have made a strong effort to do so—Taft responded passively, and on one occasion rose to praise McCarthy as a "fighting Marine."

Taft consistently denounced Truman's liberal domestic policies, referring to these (including the President's quest for national health insurance) as "Socialist hand-out programs." He also took special aim at the Far Eastern Division of the State Department, which he charged was dominated by a "left-wing group" that was "willing to turn China over to the communists." In 1951, when Truman fired his top general in Korea, Douglas MacArthur, Taft conceded that the President had the right to take this action as Commander in Chief. Taft also championed MacArthur's ideas, however, which called for unleashing Nationalist Chinese troops to fight in China or Korea, and bombing Chinese rail lines.

Beginning in mid-1951, Taft devoted increasing time and energy to another quest for the GOP presidential nomination the following year. As in the past, he generated fierce loyalty from the conservative Republican base, especially in the Midwest. But Gen. Dwight Eisenhower, afraid that a President Taft would endanger NATO, yielded to the entreaties of internationalist Republicans—Dewey, Taft's long-time rival, was among them—left his post as commander of NATO in Europe, and entered the race against Taft. As a World War II hero, "Ike" was a highly popular figure, and at the GOP's tumultuous national convention in July 1952 he won a decisive roll call over disputed convention delegates, going on to win the nomination on the first ballot.

Angered by what he and his allies called the "stealing" of delegates by Ike's forces, Taft seemed unwilling to lend his support—and therefore that of many of his conservative backers—to Eisenhower. In September, however, he went to New York City to meet Eisenhower at his headquarters at Morningside Heights. The result was a statement in which Eisenhower agreed that the fundamental issue of the campaign was "liberty against the creeping socialism in every domestic field." Many of Eisenhower's supporters were appalled, referring to the statement as Ike's "Surrender at Morningside Heights."

Eisenhower's willingness to appease the Taft forces, however, was not so surprising. In fact, on some domestic issues such as public housing and federal aid to education, Eisenhower was more conservative than his defeated rival. And the rapprochement with Taft, which papered over party divisions, probably helped Eisenhower in the November election. As expected, Eisenhower decisively outpolled his Democratic opponent Adlai Stevenson, and the GOP regained control of both houses—for the first time since the 1948 election.

A CONSERVATIVE ICON

Taft surprised many people by agreeing to serve as Senate Majority Leader. It was the first time he had formally held the post. Moreover, it soon became apparent that he and Eisenhower were striking up a compatible personal—and golfing—relationship, thereby enabling the President, who knew little about domestic issues, to work his way through complicated controversies on Capitol Hill.

For Taft, the ending of his political career—and life—was quick and unexpected. In the spring of 1953, Taft contracted cancer, and he died on July 31. With his passing, Senate Republicans lost a leader who was conservative to the core, yet who had proved able and willing to compromise in order to assist a more moderate Republican president.

Honors came later to Taft. Senator John F. Kennedy (D-MA) included him as one of the heroes of his book, *Profiles in Courage,* because of Taft's criticism of the post–World War II Nuremburg Trials. Kennedy also headed a bipartisan committee that named Taft as one of five men to be inducted into a Senate Hall of Fame in 1959. The others were Daniel Webster, John Calhoun, Henry Clay, and Robert La Follette. These five, the committee said, "left a permanent mark on our nation's history and brought distinction to the Senate."

Crowning the tributes paid to Taft was the dedication of a 100-foot tower housing a 27-bell carillon. Though private donations financed the building of the tower, the gift of choice public land next to the Capitol for the memorial was a telling tribute. Such was his reputation, that unanimous votes of both houses in 1955 approved the memorial.

◆　◆　◆　◆　◆

15. Lyndon B. Johnson: Presidential Legislator

by Joseph A. Califano Jr.

President Lyndon B. Johnson was born on August 27, 1908 in Stonewall, Texas. He graduated from Southwest Texas State Teachers College at San Marcos (now Texas State University-San Marcos) in 1930. After graduation, Johnson taught high school from 1928–1931, served as secretary to Representative Richard M. Kleberg from 1931–1935, and served as State director of the Texas National Youth Administration from 1935–1937. Johnson was elected to the U.S. House of Representatives in 1937, and held the seat for five successive Congresses. During World War II, Johnson was the first member of Congress to enlist and served in the Navy as a Lieutenant Commander, earning a silver star for his service. Elected to the Senate from 1948–1961, Johnson served as Democratic Whip, Minority Leader, and Majority Leader. Johnson also served as Chairman of the Special Committee on the Senate Reception Room, and the Special Committee on Astronautics and Space, Committee on Aeronautical and Space Sciences. In 1960 Johnson was elected Vice President. The assassination of President Kennedy marked the beginning of Johnson's presidency in 1963. He died in 1973.

Johnson is generally seen in a positive light for enacting the Civil Rights Act of 1964 and a tax cut that Kennedy promoted. Johnson is also recognized for winning the 1964 re-election with 61 percent of the vote, the widest popular vote margin in American history. His legacy includes social advancements, changes in the federal government's roles in domestic affairs, The Great Society, and advancements in the space exploration program. Johnson did not run for re-election in 1968.

In examining the great progressive legislative eras of the last century—the times of Theodore Roosevelt, Franklin D. Roosevelt, and Lyndon B. Johnson—it is tempting to focus on the unique characteristics of these remarkable leaders who served in the White House, but a focus solely on the men themselves risks losing sight of lessons for future Presidents and Congresses. This is especially true of the historians and political commentators dazzled by LBJ's extraordinary mastery of the U.S. House and Senate, as he persuaded three Congresses to enact his sweeping Great Society agenda, which included hundreds of bills dealing with civil rights, health, education, poverty, culture, consumer rights, and the environment, and which established the Corporation for Public Broadcasting that created public radio and television.

Yet there is much for future Presidents and Congresses to learn, perhaps most importantly that we are a Presidential Nation—and that is why the key to legislatively productive Congresses is presidential leadership. No President in the last century understood this better than Lyndon B. Johnson, and no President more effectively meshed the events of his time with his knowledge of the Congress to achieve his legislative goals.

LBJ became President as a result of the assassination of John F. Kennedy. Johnson capitalized on that tragedy by convincing Congress to enact programs that advanced virtually every idea Democratic liberals had hatched since the days of Harry S. Truman—and then some. Whether stated outright or offered as subliminal exhortation, LBJ's mantra, especially in 1964, was "Let's do this for President Kennedy." Indeed, that January, before his first State of the Union message, Johnson persuaded the Congress to create a cultural center in the nation's capital. Although this was something the House and Senate had resisted giving the predominately black city of Washington, D.C., for two decades, Johnson convinced the Congress to take action by naming the center the John F. Kennedy Center for the Performing Arts.

Johnson also understood the importance of sequencing legislative initiatives to enhance their chances of passage. In 1963, when President Kennedy and his brother, Attorney General Robert Kennedy, were working on a bill to outlaw segregation in public places, LBJ urged them not to submit the bill to Congress until the Senate had passed all the appropriations bills and a tax reduction bill. Johnson argued that otherwise Southern Democrats would kill any civil rights bill by filibuster because most senators facing reelection in 1964 would insist that such legislation be tabled so they could pass appropriations bills (which usually include pet pork projects) and reduce taxes before facing their voters. Robert Kennedy disagreed and sent the bill to the Senate where, as Johnson had predicted, it never even reached the floor.

As President in 1964, Johnson first pressed the Senate to pass all appropriations bills and the Administration's bill to cut taxes. Richard Russell (D-GA), the Georgia Senator and shrewd and powerful leader of the segregationist Southern Bloc, who also understood the importance of sequencing, told his fellow Southern senators, "We could beat Kennedy, but we'll never beat Lyndon." (See "Richard Russell Jr.: Patriarch of the Senate," Chapter 13.)

CIVIL RIGHTS CHAMPION

On the issue of civil rights, which had been stymied for decades by Southern Democrats, LBJ went to work especially with Republican Minority Leader Senator Everett Dirksen (R-IL). Johnson spent hours privately with Dirksen, usually over drinks at the White House (at the President's direction an ounce and a half of bourbon in each Dirksen drink, half an ounce of scotch in each LBJ drink). Eventually, Dirksen agreed to help break the filibuster, and the Senate passed the 1964 Civil Rights Act, which outlawed segregation in public places and discrimination in employment.

LBJ knew that maintaining a close relationship between a Democratic President and Republican Senate Minority Leader, and persuading Congress from the Oval Office, were 24/7 jobs. No opportunity could be passed up. So in November 1964, when Dirksen called LBJ to congratulate him on his 61 to 39 percent landslide victory over his Republican opponent, Barry Goldwater (R-AZ), Johnson was armed for legislative bear.

Dirksen mentioned that he needed to undergo surgery at the Army's Walter Reed Hospital, but he didn't want to schedule the operation right away if the President intended to meet with the congressional leadership. After telling Dirksen to have the surgery, LBJ said, "Isn't it wonderful, that you and I get all this medical care from the government. We can do the same thing for our senior citizens if we pass Medicare."

Dirksen chuckled and said, "Now, Mr. President." But before he could finish his sentence, Johnson mentioned that he was going to send a Voting Rights Act to Congress and hoped he would have Dirksen's support, which was again essential to break the inevitable filibuster by Southern Democrats. When Dirksen doubted he could go along with such a bill, LBJ said, "Everett, if you come with me on this bill, one hundred years from now there'll only be two people they'll remember from the state of Illinois: Abraham Lincoln and Everett Dirksen."

LBJ knew that voting rights legislation would be extremely difficult to enact and that he needed to get the nation behind it and mobilize public pressure on Congress. On January 14, 1965, he discussed his upcoming legislative agenda with Martin Luther King Jr. and said nothing would be as effective for King's people as getting "all of them voting."

King didn't need to remind the President that in the five Southern states Johnson failed to carry in the 1964 election, less than 40 percent of the blacks were registered to vote, but he did anyway. Johnson stressed that the bill was "not just for Negroes. It is for equality for all, that every person has a right to vote," and that's how he urged King to talk about the voting rights legislation. LBJ then gave King an assignment: "If you can find the worst condition that you run into in Alabama, Mississippi, or Louisiana or South Carolina . . . and get it on radio, get it on television, get it in the pulpits, get it . . . every place you can, then pretty soon the fellow who didn't do anything but drive a tractor would say well that is not right, that is not fair. . . . Then that will help us up here [in getting the Voting Rights Act passed] in the end."

Out of this presidential full court press came King's famous march from Selma to Montgomery, Alabama. In Dallas County, where Selma was located, most of the county's 30,000 voting age residents were black, but of the 10,000 registered voters, only 335 were black.

When the march began in early March 1965, it was scarred by Bloody Sunday, when 90 marchers were beaten, and again days later when a minister from Boston, was killed. Six days after Bloody Sunday, on March 13, Johnson met with Alabama Governor George Wallace at the White House. When Wallace said he could not protect the marchers, Johnson told the Alabama Governor to "stop bullshitting me." LBJ said he would protect them because there was a federal court order allowing them to march. He made certain the confrontational meeting with Wallace was widely publicized.

With the stage set, two days later Johnson addressed a joint session of Congress in prime time to urge passage of Voting Rights legislation he proposed that evening. In the speech he said, "I speak tonight for the dignity of man and the destiny of democracy," as he punctuated his remarks with the phrase, "We shall overcome." According to civil rights leader (and later Congressman) John Lewis, Martin Luther King cried when he watched on television the President of the United States invoke the anthem of the civil rights movement. A freshly inspired King led the renewed march with hope and energy, and LBJ federalized the Alabama National Guard to protect the marchers.

In Washington, LBJ directed Attorney General Nicholas Katzenbach to work with Dirksen and allow Dirksen to write the bill with him. "Let him draft the language," Johnson said, "as long as it achieves our goals. Then it will become his bill."

With Dirksen breaking the filibuster, the Voting Rights Act passed the Senate and was signed into law by LBJ on August 6, 1965. At the signing, LBJ announced that the government would file suit in Mississippi the next day to have the state's poll tax declared unconstitutional, and that the following week, he would take action in at least 15 counties in the South to enforce the new law.

As LBJ sat down to sign the legislation, everyone expected him to give the first pen to Martin Luther King Jr. Instead, he turned around and handed it to Dirksen, noting that without Dirksen's support the bill would never have become law.

OPPORTUNITY IN TRAGEDY

Timing and tenacity is another lesson for Presidents who want Congress to pass controversial legislation. In early 1966, Johnson proposed legislation to prohibit discrimination in housing. The proposal was met with stinging opposition from both sides of the aisle in the Senate and House. But Johnson kept quietly plugging away, negotiating with individual senators, and finally in 1968 the Senate passed a bill. There was still no hope in the House. The liberal chair of the House Judiciary Committee, Emanuel Celler (D-NY), was from the Crown Heights district in Brooklyn—where blacks were moving into overwhelmingly Jewish neighborhoods. Celler was not about to let his committee report out a fair housing bill.

The morning after King was assassinated in April 1968, LBJ said to me, "Out of this awful tragedy, we're going to get our fair housing bill." He instructed me to draft a letter, which he sent to House Speaker John Mc-Cormack (D-MA), and he wrote a personal note to the Minority Leader Gerald Ford (R-MI). Johnson pressed them privately and publicly to have the House pass the Senate bill. It could be taken up on the House floor without going through the U.S. House Committee on the Judiciary, thus relieving Celler of responsibility for reporting the bill out.

Johnson also sought to find something positive in the tragedy of Robert Kennedy's assassination. LBJ had proposed a tough gun control bill in early 1966 but had not been able to get any action in the Senate. His bill would require licensing of all gun owners and registration of all guns, prohibit sales to minors and across state lines, and ban the importation of the cheap handguns known as "Saturday Night Specials." On the U.S. Senate Committee on the Judiciary, Joseph Tydings (D-MD), a close Kennedy friend, wanted a different bill. LBJ said we had "only a week or ten days" to get his own bill out of committee before the National Rifle Association (NRA) rounded up the votes to kill it. Tydings did not agree and pressed for consideration of another bill. The NRA swooped down, got the committee to kill the licensing and registration provisions, and only the remainder of the Johnson bill passed—prohibiting sales to minors and certain others, establishing the licensing of firearms sellers, mandating serial numbers on firearms, and prohibiting the import of "Saturday Night Specials" and other easily concealable handguns.

Knowledge of Congress is an enormous asset to any president. In 1967 and early 1968, the chair of the U.S. House Committee on Ways and Means, Wilbur Mills (D-AR), was demanding sharp cuts in Great Society Programs as the price for his support of a bill increasing taxes. Eventually LBJ agreed

to $6 billion in cuts, and Mills agreed to move the tax bill. Johnson was con-
vinced that Congress would never cut that much from his programs, and he
was right. When Congress could not even cut $4 billion, LBJ refused to make
any further reductions. The Congress has acted, he said, and I will abide by
its decision.

LBJ was of course a master of dealing with Congress, but he did have
some important tools. The congressional leadership in those days had much
more power over members, and the President was critical to fund-raising
for many members of Congress. Today, members have more power to raise
most of their own campaign funds because there are many more federal laws
that deep-pocketed individuals and institutions want to pass, kill, or amend.
Nevertheless, the bully pulpit has never been louder than it is for a President today, and that provides enormous power to shape events and pressure
Congress.

There are important lessons from the Johnson Presidency: making the
most of every opportunity, even those that come out of tragedy; being tenacious; giving key congressional leaders attention and letting them take credit
for legislation; enlisting outside forces to help persuade Congress to act; and
being attentive to the vulnerabilities of key members like committee chairs.

Sure, LBJ had an extraordinary grasp of the "price" of members, and he
benefitted greatly from having served in both the House and Senate (the latter as Senate Majority Leader). But there is still much to learn from how he
worked with Congress that would benefit a future President that is devoted
to the Triumphs of Modern Congresses.

◆ ◆ ◆ ◆ ◆

16. Jesse Helms: The
Unapologetic Conservative

by David B. Frisk

*Jesse Helms was born in Monroe, North Carolina on October 18, 1921. He
attended Wingate College and Wake Forest College both for a year before dropping out to become a journalist, first as a sports proofreader with the* Raleigh
News and Observer *and later as Editor of the* Raleigh Times. *After serving
in the Navy during World War II, he worked at a Roanoke Rapids radio station and then as Editor of the* Raleigh Times. *He later served as administrative assistant to U.S. Senators Willis Smith and Alton Lennon; as Executive*

Director of the North Carolina Bankers Association; on the City Council; and as Executive Vice President, news editor, and Viewpoint Editorial voice of the WRAL radio station where he spoke against "left-leaning policies." 1972 branded Helms as the first popularly elected Republican Senator from North Carolina in nearly 70 years. During his congressional career, he served as Chair of the Committee on Agriculture, Nutrition, and Forestry, and the Committee on Foreign Relations. While serving on the Foreign Relations Committee he worked to reduce the debt the United States owed to the UN, on reforms to the State Department, and fought against appointments of Liberal ambassadorial nominees. Helms died on July 4, 2008.

Jesse Helms is North Carolina's longest-serving Republican politician at the national level, serving for 37 years. Senator Helms, was known for a conservative and sometimes controversial stance on issues such as social programs, communism, and blocking ratification of the UN Treaty Against Genocide. Among his controversial views were his opinions regarding civil rights and race relation, such as opposing a Martin Luther King Jr. holiday.

After a tumultuous 1960s defined largely by antiwar protests, civil rights marches, and the cultural wars, Jesse Helms entered the U.S. Senate in 1972 determined to oppose Democrats who had advanced the liberal causes of the preceding decade. He wanted to change those results, not just serve his state, North Carolina, or a few parochial interests. During his first campaign in 1972, Helms promised to "resist with all the strength I can muster the destructive tactics" of Senators Ted Kennedy (D-MA), George McGovern (D-SD), and the whole "wrecking crew" he saw "dominating" the Senate.[1] Characteristically, he cited these senators and two others, recent presidential candidates Hubert Humphrey (D-MN) and Edmund Muskie (D-ME), by name. In his 30-year career, Helms (R-NC) would rarely pull punches.

During his long tenure in the U.S. Senate, Helms never won more than 56 percent of the vote. But the Democrats never beat him. That points to a central theme of his career: the voters who liked Senator Helms tended to love him, and some of those who disliked or disagreed with him admired his sincerity and candor. As the *Almanac of American Politics* once noted, "no American politician is more controversial, beloved in some quarters and hated in others, than Jesse Helms."

Although Helms constantly made trouble—often alone—for the liberals and for anyone who preferred a less contentious politics, his "loner" quality is sometimes exaggerated. Despite his loyalty to the besieged President Nixon during the Watergate scandal, for instance, Helms had a good relationship with his home state colleague, Democrat Sam Ervin, one of the

Senate's most senior members and an acknowledged constitutional expert, who chaired its Watergate committee in 1973. After Ervin retired the following year, Helms stayed in friendly and collegial touch with him. He worked closely with an even more conservative Democrat, James Allen (D-AL), an expert on the Senate rules. Allen had been using his superior knowledge to obstruct or modify liberal bills that were bound to pass. He was able to get results without seniority, without coalition building, and without favor trading. In particular, Allen tirelessly proposed amendments. Few passed, but in return for dropping these time-eaters, a frustrated Majority Leader Mike Mansfield (D-MT) would sometimes weaken or delay a bill. The newly sworn-in Helms asked a welcoming Allen to teach him the chamber's rules, and Allen did so with intensive twice-weekly sessions. Helms also learned the often arcane procedures of the Senate by taking on the drudgery of presiding over its routine business as often as possible.[2]

Helms also worked to unify his fellow conservative Republicans for action. After arriving in the Senate, Helms had quickly noticed that they "worked independently" of each other, looking "weak and ineffectual," while the liberals "planned their offensives and knew how to get what they wanted." Therefore, Helms and another freshman Senator, James Buckley (R-NY), set up the Republican Steering Committee in 1973, a group that lasted as a valuable coordinating body for Senate conservatives. Although he didn't initially chair the committee, it soon became known as "the Helms gang." Within less than a year, its meetings sometimes drew an attendance of two dozen—more than half of the Republican caucus.[3]

CHAMPIONING CONSERVATIVE CAUSES

Much of Helms's agenda involved the hotter social issues: abortion, school prayer, and busing. He often forced senators to vote on his amendments understanding that they wouldn't pass, but believing his liberal colleagues should be held publicly accountable for rejecting them. These recorded votes—plus ratification of the Panama Canal Treaty despite strong opposition from Helms and most other conservatives—likely contributed to the defeat of many liberal Democrats in 1978 and especially 1980. That gave the incoming President Reagan the great advantage of a Republican Senate majority.

Helms helped to lay the foundation for more conservative policies in other ways. He did much to call attention to what the Right and a few allies saw as the urgent need to revive the intense anticommunism of the early Cold War. In 1975, he teamed up with the Democratic foreign policy hardliner

Henry "Scoop" Jackson (D-WA) to insist that President Ford recognize with a White House visit the greatest moral witness against the Soviet regime, the exiled Russian dissident writer Alexander Solzhenitsyn. Ford and U.S. Secretary of State Henry Kissinger refused—leading Jackson to charge, and Helms to agree, that they were "cowering with fear of the Soviet reaction." The two senators brought Solzhenitsyn to the Capitol building instead.[4] The following year, Helms was the leading force behind the Republican National Convention's adoption of the anti-détente "Morality in Foreign Policy" plank, which rejected much of the Nixon-Ford-Kissinger legacy, even as the convention narrowly nominated Ford in tepid preference to Reagan. The convention also—again much influenced by Helms—first adopted what became the party's seemingly permanent antiabortion stance.

Within the Senate, Helms extended his reach in 1979 when he joined the U.S. Senate Committee on Foreign Relations along with three other Republicans, including his later sometime adversary Richard Lugar (R-IN). The new GOP members were substantially more conservative than the four Republicans who had left the Committee, and they began to change its liberal reputation. Senior Republican members had previously taken a passive role on Foreign Relations—for instance, not even insisting on the full staff resources to which recent reforms entitled them. Indeed, there hadn't actually been a distinct Republican staff—a situation liberal Republicans Charles Percy (R-IL) and Jacob Javits (R-NY) thought acceptable. Helms and others prevailed and were successful in establishing a minority staff.[5]

The influence he accrued, like that of many ideological leaders, owed much to his willing sacrifices. Helms was hard working, focused, stubborn, and thick-skinned. He had little interest in Washington social events, attending only those related to North Carolina or to strengthening conservatives' impact. "I don't care what *The New York Times* says about me," he told a new aide who wished to answer a negative editorial. "And nobody I care about cares what *The New York Times* says about me." The young man "came to understand that I answer first to my Creator, then to my conscience."

Helms understood that compromise on mere preferences was a necessity in the Senate, since it showed that "you can engage with other people." But when principles were at stake, the conflict and pressure resulting from a serious commitment to them were simply "the price of doing business."[6] Helms's affiliation with a national conservative campaign and operation called the Congressional Club—while indicating his determination to expand the Right's power as well as its voice—didn't distract him much from Senate work. By the 1980s, according to historian William Link, the main Helms biographer, he was "a reluctant candidate" in the sense that he "hated asking for money and political support." As a Congressional Club operative said, he was more of a "policy wonk."[7]

Helms's willingness to dig noisily into what some would call the weeds, and others the guts, of the governmental process caused irritation throughout Washington. It could also get results. Shortly after Reagan's easy reelection and Helms's own difficult reelection in 1984, Helms was upset by Secretary of State George Shultz's apparent plans to remove various conservatives from the State Department. The following June, 23 senators met with Reagan for over an hour to press this concern. Several days later, Helms—again with colleagues' support—wrote Shultz to demand a meeting, while threatening to place holds on more than two dozen nominees, an unusual move from a senator of the same party as the President. From the Secretary and "the underlings who run that department," he wrote Senate Majority Leader Robert Dole (R-KS), "I have endured doubletalk, delays, and obviously deliberate confusion." Helms did manage to get six ideologically satisfactory conservatives named to the State Department.

In many other struggles involving the Executive Branch, his results were smaller. But he wasn't easily deterred. "If they think they are going to wear me down, let them try," Helms said later in 1985, during a battle with foreign aid officials and State Department lawyers over population control programs in China. "If they want to continue to play games, they are going to have games."[8]

His willingness to challenge the administration of a president supported by nearly all conservatives, including himself, added to the already large respect for Helms among leading activists on the Right. By the latter half of the 1980s, his first biographer wrote, many movement conservatives "felt betrayed by the way Reagan had dealt with the realities of the world. But while Reagan may have let them down, Helms had not." He persistently raised issues—usually with a resonance among grassroots conservatives even if they seemed minor—that most of his colleagues didn't know about, cared little about, or wouldn't take the lead on. "If he represented any part of the Bill of Rights above all others, it was . . . the right 'to petition the government for a redress of grievances.'"[9]

In domestic policy, he more than earned his reputation as an aggressive Moral Majoritarian. He attacked graphic AIDS prevention publications that, in his opinion, promoted gay sex, and he went after the National Endowment for the Arts sponsorship, with public funds, of an artist's graphic homosexual images. Among Helms's tough tactics against the NEA funding was insistence that the media and Senate colleagues actually view the items in question, and the point wasn't just verbal: he sent pictures around and made them available in his office. Helms also opposed the Ryan White Act of 1990 that provided $2.9 million in its first year for AIDS treatment and education, saying such funding shouldn't exceed federal spending on cancer or diabetes. He further contended that AIDS hysteria and gay activism would tend to reduce funding for these other diseases.[10]

The claim that Helms was a racist—based partly on his 16-day filibuster opposing creation of the Martin Luther King national holiday (on grounds of personal character and connections with a few communists) and opposition to the Voting Rights Act extension in 1982 (on constitutional grounds)—is debatable. But Helms did express hostility toward gays, not just gay causes. After President-Elect Clinton announced an intention to lift the ban on gays in the military, Helms told the *Charlotte Observer* he had "no respect for homosexuals—for perverts." His fight against the growing campaign for acceptance of open homosexuality continued with opposition to Clinton's efforts to nominate gays to significant offices. Helms alleged that one, Roberta Achtenberg, had "tried to bully" the Boy Scouts of America as a San Francisco county supervisor. He warned that she was "not your garden-variety lesbian." Helms seemed to lament that for the first time in history, "a lesbian has been nominated by a President . . . for a top job in the U.S. Government."[11]

Insensitive comments, on a wide variety of issues, sometimes made Helms's actual arguments easier to dismiss. But a less familiar part of the Helms story is the scoffing arrogance that was common among his opponents, especially liberal interest groups, in denying that he played any useful or honorable role. Also less noted are attitudes he sometimes ran into among appointed officials which could have offended any senator. When Winston Lord was named by Reagan as ambassador to China, one of Helms's questions was why, given some recent opportunity, he hadn't condemned massacres by the communist Chinese when they invaded Tibet more than 30 years before. It wasn't his job, Lord replied, "to sit here and engage in a litany of insults" against another country. This episode can be seen as a case of Helms's passion for anticommunist litmus tests, however ineffectual these might seem in policy terms, or of contempt for the diplomatic culture so alien to his own career. But given Lord's wording, it can also be viewed as an example of diplomatic callousness toward human rights concerns.

A LEADING VOICE ON FOREIGN POLICY

The Democrats' recapture of the Senate in 1986 brought Helms the chance to reassert his senior rank on Foreign Relations, which he had given up after the 1984 election by fulfilling a promise to North Carolinians that he would take the chairmanship of the U.S. Senate Committee on Agriculture. In addition, Foreign Relations now had, in Claiborne Pell (D-RI), a weak though genial chairman with a limited agenda.

The situation allowed ranking Republican Helms to play a larger role than he might have otherwise. By 1992, he was doing this with a revamped staff. Early that year, he fired nine aides on the minority side of the Foreign Relations Committee who he thought had become incompetent and had failed to do their jobs, including the staff director Jim Lucier, a Helms loyalist. In addition to the festering interpersonal trouble among GOP aides, according to biographer Link, there was "the fact that Helms was moving into a different, post-Cold War world," a situation that "made Lucier's hard-hitting polemics less relevant." Before long the new hires won praise from Democrats, who saw them as an improvement. *U.S. News & World Report* said Helms "may be mellowing."[12]

With the Republicans back in control of the Senate during the second half of the 1990s, Helms used his Foreign Relations chairmanship to pursue organizational reforms and to oppose what he considered unverifiable or otherwise dangerous arms control agreements (including the Comprehensive Test Ban Treaty for nuclear weapons, rejected by the Senate in 1999). In explaining his reorganization plan for foreign affairs agencies in 1995, Helms said they maintained too many "worn-out programs" unsuited to the post–Cold War environment, and that they had, over the years, "spun off into a constellation of money-absorbing, incoherent satellites" each with "its own entrenched, growing bureaucracies and . . . bureaucratic interests."

With no action on his reforms despite Clinton's stated acceptance of some of them in principle, Helms played his familiar hardball. He suspended business meetings of his committee, froze some 400 upcoming promotions at the State Department, and blocked various trade agreements.[13] Ultimately the plan was adopted. In order to get that result, Helms had to drop his obstruction of the Chemical Weapons Convention in 1997—a treaty that he had already gotten Clinton to amend heavily. Helms was especially proud of bringing the U.S. Information Agency and the Arms Control and Disarmament Agency under State Department control, and thus, he argued, making these agencies more responsible to the President.[14]

After his retirement in 2003, by which time he was 81 and in poor health, Helms saw as his greatest legislative accomplishment a more robust "advise and consent" role for the Senate in shaping treaties. This goal, although far from the hot-button votes on abortion and school prayer he had championed a generation before, was part of what might be called his constitutionalist populism: a conviction that neither Supreme Court decisions nor supposedly expert bureaucratic judgment should stop the Legislative Branch from asserting itself as the people's representative. "We got a right to ask questions in any number we want to," Helms told Secretary of State–designate Warren Christopher at a confirmation hearing in 1993, when the veteran diplomat said he hoped the Senator's written queries to him would be relevant. "We were elected," Helms explained. "You have not been elected."[15]

◆　◆　◆　◆　◆

17. Edward "Ted" Kennedy: A Liberal Lion

by Susan Milligan

Edward "Ted" Kennedy was born in Boston, Massachusetts on February 22, 1932. He graduated from Milton Academy in 1950, served in the U.S. Army from 1951–1953, graduated from Harvard College in 1956, graduated from the International Law School at The Hague in 1958, and graduated from the University of Virginia Law School in 1959. Kennedy later served as special assistant attorney of Suffolk County in 1961. He campaigned for his brother John F. Kennedy in the 1960 presidential election. In 1962, Kennedy was elected to John F. Kennedy's former Senate seat, a position he occupied for 47 consecutive years. During his distinguished career, he served as the Chairman for the Committee on the Judiciary, the Committee on Labor and Human Resources, as Chairman of the Committee on Health, Education, Labor, and Pensions, the Senate Armed Services Committee, the Congressional Joint Economic Committee, and as Democratic Whip from 1969–1971. He campaigned unsuccessfully for the Democratic Nomination for President in 1980. Sen. Kennedy died in 2009.

Sen. Kennedy is the third longest serving Senator in congressional history. Nicknamed the "Lion of the Senate," he was known for his opposition of the Vietnam War. Senator Kennedy is also remembered for authoring legislation to improve health care and promote AIDS research including the 1996 Health Insurance Portability and Accountability Act and the 1997 Children's Health Act. Sen. Kennedy was awarded the Presidential Medal of Freedom shortly before his death.

Senator Edward M. Kennedy was a true legend of the U.S. Senate, one of the few lawmakers in recent years whose personal fame and notoriety rivaled that of the institution in which he served. A hero to the left, Kennedy was a relentless advocate for a liberal agenda ranging from raising the minimum wage to providing universal health care and expanding rights for minorities, women, and the disabled. To conservatives, Kennedy was a symbol of all that had gone wrong in Washington, with a reckless personal life and an equally undisciplined regard for public monies Kennedy wanted to spend on social programs. By the time he died of a brain tumor in 2009, though, the 77-year-old Kennedy was widely recognized as a lion of the institution, having not only amassed a lengthy legislative record (authoring more than 2,500 bills), but also earning a reputation among colleagues in both parties as a consummate deal-maker and the chamber's most effective Senator.[1] When Kennedy was buried at Arlington Cemetery, near his brothers, an important part of the old Senate died, too: the personal relationships and cross-party dealing that kept the legislative machinery running.

Of all the myriad issues Ted Kennedy juggled during his 46 years in the Senate, health care was a constant. It was "the cause of my life," Kennedy said at the last Democratic National Convention he would attend, in 2008.[2] He had been an early and passionate advocate for a national health care system, authoring a bill in 1971 to create a single-payer system.[3] At the time, the brash, young Senator from Massachusetts was competing with President Nixon, who had offered a plan that built upon employer-provided health insurance, while providing premium support for the needy. Neither proposal became law, and Kennedy learned an important lesson that would drive his approach to legislating on health care in later years: work with the other party, compromise if necessary, and don't let an idea fail because its execution is flawed.

Much later, Kennedy would muse that one of his biggest regrets was that he did not sign onto the Nixon plan when he had the chance. It was "pay or play," Kennedy noted, using the shorthand for a plan with an employer mandate, and Kennedy wanted straight-up-national health care. In retrospect, Kennedy wished he had signed on and worked to pass it, fixing details later as needed.[4] Instead, a sweeping health care plan would not be passed out of a full congressional committee until 1994—and that effort, spearheaded by then First Lady Hillary Rodham Clinton, failed.[5]

Determined not to make that mistake again, Kennedy worked piecemeal on health legislation—always making sure to involve a key player in the other party. In 1994, Kennedy teamed up with Senator Nancy Kassebaum (R-KS) to pass the Health Insurance Portability and Accountability Act, designed to protect patients' health care privacy and help them hang onto their insurance once they leave a job.[6] He worked with Senator Orrin Hatch (R-UT), who came to be good friends with Kennedy, on the 1997 State Children's Health Insurance Program to provide coverage for low-income kids.[7]

That partnership would define Kennedy's unusual ability to build relationships on the Hill, especially with political opponents. Hatch, a Mormon and conservative who stood in opposition to Kennedy in almost every sense, said he had come to Washington to fight Ted Kennedy—not just the Democrats, or even liberals, but Kennedy himself. To Hatch's conservative Western constituents Kennedy was shorthand for government heavy-handedness and personal excess. But Hatch also realized that he could not get anything done on the Labor Committee without dealing with Kennedy.[8]

The Massachusetts Senator wooed Hatch carefully, once sending his senior aide, Nick Littlefield, to sing for Hatch (himself an amateur songwriter) in his office. It was a tactic Kennedy would use with other lawmakers, teasingly offering premium cigars (in a discreet manila envelope) to Representative Jack Brooks (R-TX) during immigration negotiations, or sending shamrock-shaped cookies to U.S. House Committee on Ways and Means Chairman Bill Thomas (R-CA) to soften him up. The Senator knew how to use his family name and fame, inviting colleagues and activists to his home, leaving them both a bit starstruck and charmed by the hominess of Kennedy's memento-filled house.[9]

A SHADOW OF SCANDAL

The formidable legislative record that Kennedy compiled—and the genuine friendships he developed across party lines—were often overshadowed by the publicity and rumors that his personal life generated. The 1969 Chappaquiddick incident derailed his presidential ambitions, after a female traveling companion of the then-married Kennedy drowned when a car he was driving went over a bridge.[10] In 1991, Kennedy again found himself at the center of scandal when his nephew was accused of rape at the family compound in Palm Beach.[11]

Ironically, it was his friend Orrin Hatch—now sincerely fond of his political polar opposite—who sat Kennedy down and told him to get his act together.[12] And Kennedy did just that: he courted Victoria Reggie, an old family friend he ran into at a dinner party, and in 1992, they married. And that relationship seemed to change Kennedy, who threw himself into his Senate work and created a social life built around his new bride, his colleagues, and his beloved dogs (who sometimes would accompany the Senator to White House visits with Bush).

By 2003, Kennedy had become one of the Senate's most ardent negotiators. And even though Republicans controlled the White House and both chambers of Congress, Kennedy realized he had another opportunity to expand health coverage: prescription drug coverage for people on Medicare.

Kennedy started out with an unlikely ally in President George W. Bush. Bush, who pledged in his 2000 campaign to do something about the onerous burden on seniors needing prescription drugs, and was eager—especially given the lingering controversy over the disputed 2000 presidential election—to get it done before his reelection went into full gear.[13] The two men had worked together on No Child Left Behind, a measure that brought unprecedented federal involvement in establishing elementary and secondary education standards. And while the relationship between the two had soured after Kennedy's vehement opposition to the invasion of Iraq earlier in 2003, both Bush and Kennedy were pragmatic enough to realize they needed each other to pass the prescription drug bill.[14]

Kennedy's first barrier in getting the prescription drug package approved was his own caucus. Democrats disliked the so-called doughnut hole—the range of pharmaceutical spending seniors would have to pay for themselves until federal subsidies kicked back in. For his part, Kennedy knew 2003 was a rare moment. When will we have another president, especially a Republican president, willing to spend $400 billion (a number that would rise to more than $500 billion over 10 years) to fund the biggest expansion of a federal entitlement program in decades? Kennedy asked his Democratic colleagues. Let's just get a framework in place, and we can fix the details later, he pleaded.[15]

The Senate did pass a bill that summer. But the House made some changes, including introducing a private-sector element to Medicare that Kennedy feared would eventually weaken the program as a guaranteed government benefit. In a controversial action that would serve as a rallying point for Democrats claiming congressional rules abuses, the House vote was kept open for three hours while Republican leaders lobbied colleagues on the floor. Kennedy sought unsuccessfully to kill the measure as written when it came back to the Senate.[16]

But Kennedy's early lesson—that it's better to pass a big piece of legislation when the political will exists, then tweak it later on—proved true. In July 2008, weakened by his terminal illness, Kennedy made a surprise appearance on the Senate floor to cast a critical vote to avert cuts in Medicare payments to doctors, a fix Kennedy had long sought. As colleagues in both parties cheered and clapped, Kennedy lifted his arms and said, "aye."[17]

Even from his sickbed, Kennedy monitored the progress of the Affordable Care Act, a measure modeled after the Massachusetts law that Kennedy helped negotiate with then-GOP Governor Mitt Romney. Kennedy did not survive to see the passage of the law (which included the closing of the "doughnut hole" as well). After the vote, though, Patrick Kennedy visited his father's grave at Arlington and left a sign by the flowers: "Dad, the unfinished business is done."[18]

◆　◆　◆　◆　◆

18. Sam Nunn: Strategic Leadership

by David M. Abshire

Samuel Augustus Nunn was born in Macon, Georgia on September 8, 1938. He attended the Georgia Institute of Technology (today Georgia Tech) from 1956–1959, and served on active duty for the United States Coast Guard from 1959–1960. Nunn graduated from Emory University in 1961, received a Law degree in 1962 and was admitted to the Georgia bar that same year. He served in the House Armed Services Committee and in the U.S. Coast Guard Reserves from 1960–68. He was elected to the Georgia House of Representatives in 1968 and served until 1972 when he won the U.S. Senate seat for Georgia. Nunn won the seat after Senator Russell died. Nunn was Senator for three consecutive terms, ending his service in 1997. During his 24-year career in the Senate, he served as the Chairman of the Armed Services Committee, the Intelligence Committee, the Small Business Committee, and the Senate Select Committee on Secret Military Assistance to Iran and the Nicaraguan Opposition. From 1997 to 2003, he worked as a partner for King & Spalding Law Firm in Atlanta. He is co-chairman and CEO of the Nuclear Threat Initiative and a professor at the Sam Nunn School of International Affairs at Georgia Institute of Technology. He serves on many boards (e.g., Coca Cola and GE) and is a Georgia Trustee.

Nunn's congressional legacy is shaped by his work in foreign policy and the proliferation of weapons of mass destruction. He advocated increased engagement with the Soviet Union and helped draft the Nunn-Lugar Act (1991), which offered the Soviet Union incentives in exchange for dismantling nuclear weapons programs.

A key component of a successful strategy is to manipulate and leverage resources in a way that maximizes their impact on potential opponents. That kind of grand strategic design is hard to achieve in Congress, where the authorization and appropriation processes weave through various committees and subcommittees, and multiple players with different agendas compete for influence. Therefore it takes a very powerful conceptualist and team builder to bring strategic coherence to that process, and to put his or her mark on the final outcome. Sam Nunn is just such a strategic leader.

I saw firsthand the powerful intellectual leadership of Senator Sam Nunn (D-GA) in the 1980s and 1990s, when I headed the Center for Strategic and International Studies (CSIS). However, Senator Nunn's importance as a strategic leader was never better demonstrated than during my appointment as NATO Ambassador in the early 1980s. It was then where he played a prominent role in the defense transformation that helped end the Cold War.

During my first year at NATO, I confronted a paradox. On the one hand, we had just accomplished a major victory with the Allies collaborating in the deployment of intermediate-range nuclear force (INF) missiles in Europe to counter the Soviet deployment of SS-20 nuclear missiles targeting NATO countries. On the other hand, nuclear issues had so preoccupied NATO headquarters and the U.S. Departments of State and Defense that no one was focused on the growing problem of conventional forces. This in spite of the fact that Supreme Allied Commander Gen. Bernard Rodgers had recently warned that if NATO was attacked by the Soviet-led Warsaw Pact, the Western alliance would run out of ammunition in only a matter of days.

At the time Europe was still deep in recession. Combined with the success of the INF deployment, this created a psychological dynamic in Europe where the defense of the continent was assumed to rest almost exclusively on the strength of the nuclear deterrent, and not on conventional forces.

While the economic recession weighed heavily on European alliance members, the challenge of convincing them to invest in conventional defenses had in fact plagued NATO since the 1950s. In 1978, the Carter administration made a concerted effort to rectify this issue when it pushed hard for, and won, the approval of NATO's Long Term Defense Program (LTDP). Unfortunately, the allies failed to live up to their 1978 pledges to spend more on defense. Average defense spending fell well below the promised annual 3 percent increase in defense spending in real terms. No ally was near the required 30-day supply of conventional munitions. In addition, allies were supposed to build essential facilities to base six U.S. divisions and 1,500 tactical aircraft, reinforcements that the United States promised to furnish within 10 days if war broke out. In fact, however, the European allies had only provided approximately 20 percent of the basing facilities, and no aircraft shelters.

All of this stood in stark contrast to significant increases in U.S. defense spending beginning in 1979.

DETERIORATING DETERRENCE

It was in this setting that Senator Nunn visited me in Brussels in 1983, on the occasion of a CSIS conference. Senator Nunn was one of many noted defense experts, who worked very closely with CSIS regarding its work on military reform. The CSIS presenter, Tom Callahan, dramatized just how much of the U.S. investment in the defense of Europe was going into redundant weapon systems, rather than into repairing gaping cracks in the common defense. Of course, weapons duplication might have been popular with the defense companies, but the bottom line for the United States was an egregious misuse of scarce defense resources. The NATO allies were investing four times that of the Warsaw Pact, and yet NATO remained vulnerable.

Senator Nunn had always been considered a friend of NATO, opposing any defense legislation calling for U.S. troop-withdrawals from Europe. That was soon to change. Nunn's growing frustration became apparent during a private luncheon I hosted, for him, members of Congress, and the NATO ambassadors. Nunn expressed great disappointment in the attitude of some of the most important NATO officials and ambassadors, up to and including the secretary general. They demonstrated little concern about the deficient state of NATO's conventional defenses, or the extent to which NATO was coming to overwhelmingly rely on the strategic nuclear deterrent and the concept of "mutually assured destruction" (MAD).

Originally NATO had relied on a strategy of "flexible response," which allowed for the potential use of tactical nuclear strikes against invading Warsaw Pact forces if NATO proved unable to repel such an assault by conventional means. However, this strategy was truly viable only as long as the United States maintained nuclear superiority. Once the Soviet Union had achieved nuclear parity by the 1970s, the flexible response strategy was fatally undermined because the Soviets might plausibly retaliate against the U.S. homeland for the use of tactical nuclear weapons in Europe. The demise of flexible response led to a de facto overreliance on "mutually assured destruction"; now a war between NATO and Warsaw Pact nations, including a Soviet invasion with conventional forces, could quickly escalate to a devastating nuclear exchange against population centers across Europe, the Soviet Union, and North America.

In the following months, I worked hard with my NATO staff, the Departments of State and Defense, and with my European counterparts to push for improvements in conventional forces as a way to bolster the alliance's shaky deterrent posture vis-à-vis the Warsaw Pact. In November, I gave a major speech at the Atlantic Treaty Association in Rome, where I called for a better return on defense investment through an improved resource strategy. The following month, during the Defense Ministers Meeting, German Defense Minister Manfred Woerner cited the speech and endorsed my call for a new NATO "resource strategy" and improved armaments cooperation. Woerner introduced a "Conceptual Military Framework," which would incorporate a long-term perspective and a more comprehensive strategy to sell programs to parliament and to improve military performance. The Conceptual Military Framework was approved, and while this was a significant success, it would prove to be too little too late to avert an impending transatlantic crisis.

ENTER THE STRATEGIST

I received a call from Senator Nunn around this time. He was encouraged by a growing recognition that the conventional forces problem needed to be fixed. He remained unconvinced, however, that the necessary follow-through would occur. Nunn intended to assist me with my NATO reform efforts, so to speak, by adding a provision to the defense-funding bill that would decrease U.S. troop levels in Europe unless the allies took action to improve their conventional capabilities. His view was that if U.S. conventional forces in Europe were just a tripwire to a nuclear chain reaction and an escalating exchange of nuclear weapons, then we did not need to maintain such a large troop commitment to NATO. I responded that such an amendment would be devastating at that particular time. Nunn's retort was that of the wily strategist: I need not worry because the amendment would not actually pass, he assured me, but it would frighten the alliance members into funding conventional forces. To reassure me, Nunn suggested that I send him a letter stating my disapproval, which he would include in his comments.

Nunn moved forward with his troop-withdrawal amendment, which would have removed 90,000 U.S. troops by 1990. However, his amendment also provided a way for the NATO allies to avoid the troop withdrawal by fulfilling their previous agreement to increase their defense funding by 3 percent annually, in real terms, or by meeting benchmarks for forces to which they also had previously committed.

I warned my fellow NATO ambassadors about the growing support in Congress for the troop-withdrawal amendment and the urgent need for us to show more NATO progress. Support for the amendment was indeed growing. The White House legislative office estimated it would have 75 Senate votes and began to talk about not actively opposing the amendment. I urged Nunn to offer his amendment as a warning, but to not call it up for a vote. At the same time, I also began phoning senators I knew, explaining that if this amendment passed in the wake of the INF deployment—and with the arrival of the new NATO Secretary General Peter Carrington—it would be disastrous.

The fight against the amendment was led by U.S. Senate Committee on Armed Services Chairman John Tower (R-TX). He pointed out that "nobody [would] regard this as a signal; they [would] regard it as bullying."[1] Nunn responded that in the event of war he simply could not look American troops in the eye on the eve of deploying and say, "Fellows, you are going over there and about the time you arrive the allies are going to run out of ammunition."[2]

Fortunately for NATO, Senator Bill Cohen (R-ME) proposed an alternative amendment that required regular reporting on NATO's progress rather than an automatic troop withdrawal. The vote margin was very narrow, but President Ronald Reagan stepped in with the needed phone calls, and the more flexible Cohen amendment passed. However, while there was great relief in Europe, many senators who voted against Nunn offered him their support for reintroducing a similar amendment the following year should NATO fail to respond.

GETTING NATO'S ATTENTION

The new NATO Secretary General Peter Carrington fully understood that we remained at risk of a transatlantic rift that could fracture the alliance. I took him to visit Senator Nunn in his Senate office. He told Nunn with a deft touch, "Senator, I am with you. Not your method, mind you, but your end, your objective." The two established an immediate rapport. Over the ensuing months, Carrington worked hard to help marshal the alliance to fully fund the critical facilities identified by Senator Nunn. That was the first hard evidence that Nunn's threat of troop-withdrawals was having the desired constructive impact.

Nunn returned to Brussels for briefings at NATO on the advancements that had been made. He was greatly impressed with the efforts to obtain a better return on defense investment, and even questioned why the Pentagon could not put in place a similar framework. Nunn then confided in me that he planned to set aside his troop-withdrawal amendment that year and instead put forth a positive incentive amendment. At the time, many still thought

Nunn might proceed with a second troop-withdrawal amendment, and he wanted to keep it that way to maintain the pressure on NATO for continued progress.

Our office began to work in secret with Nunn's staff on a positive-incentive amendment. With Nunn's consent, we collaborated with Deputy Secretary of Defense William Howard Taft IV, the chairman of the newly created NATO Armaments Cooperation Committee. There were two essential components to the new amendment. The first provided for $200 million per year for five years, which could only be spent by the services within the framework of cooperative arms development projects between the United States and its NATO allies. The second component allocated $50 million for side-by-side comparative testing of U.S. and European weapons systems. This legislation brought about a new level of cooperation between the United States and other NATO members, as well between the Congress and the Administration.

Senators John Warner (R-VA) and Bill Roth (R-DE) joined with Nunn in sponsoring this historic Nunn Amendment. I followed Nunn's advice to forge an alliance with Senator Ted Stevens (R-AK), and following a visit to NATO, Stevens became an important advocate on the U.S. Senate Committee on Appropriations.

I can recall during a Defense Ministers Meeting in Brussels, Secretary of Defense Caspar Weinberger leaning over to me to whisper, "You wait and see, Nunn is going to let you down." Ironically, it was about that time that my colleague Dennis Kloske walked over with a printout of the major speech that Nunn had just given on the floor of the Senate, detailing the successes of NATO. He not only commended this new era of transatlantic cooperation, he also went on to say that the Pentagon, and its leadership, could learn a great deal from NATO's new strategic approach. With the right strategic guidance an alliance of 16 nations had banded together behind a resource strategy that made the whole of their collective defense greater than the sum of its parts.

Throughout Europe, the two Nunn amendments became known as the "good" and "bad" amendments, but both were essential. The first without the second would have been a disaster, but the first acted as an essential catalyst in Europe. The second was born out of a collaborative process, fostering a creativity seldom seen in the governmental process. This helped breathe new life into the NATO alliance, and a new sense of direction. It was an unusual example of congressional and NATO partnership.

The partnership between NATO and the Congress continued to flourish with the creation of an official Senate advisory group to the Geneva arms-control delegation. With Senator Ted Stevens as its chairman, the group began regular visits to NATO, and its member's capitals, in what he called the "new Senate partnership" with the alliance.

Senator Nunn's strategic leadership was key in focusing government and public attention, both in the United States and in Europe, on the critical need to strengthen NATO's conventional forces, thereby reducing the risk of nuclear war. He served as a catalyst, through both of his amendments, in marshalling a cooperative effort to transform NATO's preparedness, and in doing so helped to bring about the end of the Cold War. In the 1990s, as new challenges arose in the post–Cold War order, he continued to lead the military reform movement in Congress. By the time Nunn retired from Congress in 1997, he had bestowed an enduring legacy to the Senate Armed Services Committee, the Congress, and the North Atlantic Alliance. Nunn's legacy was built on a determination to always "think anew and act anew," and to be truly strategic.

◆ ◆ ◆ ◆ ◆

19. Richard G. Lugar: Statesman of the Senate

by John T. Shaw

Richard Green Lugar was born in Indianapolis, Indiana on April 4, 1932. He graduated from Denison University in 1954 and from Pembroke College at Oxford as a Rhodes Scholar. Since receiving his master's degree, Lugar has helped manage his family's food machinery manufacturing business in Indianapolis; today he manages the corn, soybean, and tree farm. He served in the Navy from 1957–1960. Lugar was member of the Indianapolis Board of School Commissioners from 1964–1967. The following year, Lugar was elected and served for two consecutive terms as Mayor of Indianapolis until 1975. As mayor, he served two terms as the Vice Chair of the Commission, President of the National League of Cities, and three terms on the U.S. Advisory Commission on Intergovernmental Relations. In 1974, Lugar failed to win a seat as United States Senator, but was successful in 1976 and served as a Republican Senator from Indiana for six consecutive terms. During his long career in Congress, Sen. Lugar served on the Senate Foreign Relations Committee, Committee on Agriculture, Nutrition, and Forestry, and was Chair of the Republican Senatorial Campaign Committee. Senator Lugar left office 2013 after failing to win reelection. He was awarded the Presidential Medal of Freedom in 2013.

Lugar is known for his active role in promoting federal farm reforms, research advancements, and increased export opportunities. The Nunn-Lugar Act, which dismantles weapons of mass destruction around the world, is a hallmark of Lugar's congressional career. To date, the Nunn-Lugar Act has helped dismantle over 7,200 weapons of mass destruction worldwide.

Richard G. Lugar entered the Senate in January of 1977 as an ambitious former mayor of Indianapolis and departed the upper chamber in January of 2013 as a global statesman. Soft-spoken, deliberate, and purposeful, Lugar worked for 36 years with presidents and lawmakers from both parties to tackle difficult problems.

The two-time chairman of the U.S. Senate Committee on Foreign Relations racked up major accomplishments in foreign policy: promoting arms control, combating the spread of weapons of mass destruction, crafting forward leaning energy policies, confronting the global food crisis, and striving to make the machinery of American foreign policy run more effectively. Although he was a proud and loyal Republican, Lugar worked closely with Democratic lawmakers such as Sam Nunn (D-GA), Joe Biden (D-DE), Barack Obama (D-IL), and John Kerry (D-MA). Lugar cooperated with both Democratic and Republican administrations to advance the national interest, but his commitment to bipartisanship ultimately exacted a heavy political price.

Lugar made an impact on American foreign policy soon after becoming chairman of the Senate Foreign Relations Committee. In 1986, his leadership on legislation imposing economic and political sanctions on South Africa marked a turning point in the U.S. response to apartheid and represented one of Lugar's finest moments in the Senate. That same year, Lugar also helped convince the Reagan administration to recognize Corazon Aquino as the winner of the disputed presidential election in the Philippines against incumbent Ferdinand Marcos.

ARMS CONTROL CHAMPION

Without a doubt, Lugar's landmark legislative accomplishment was the Nunn-Lugar Cooperative Threat Reduction Act, which partnered him with Democratic Senator Sam Nunn on a plan to secure and dismantle weapons of mass destruction in the Soviet Union as it was collapsing in 1991. Facing an indifferent administration and opposition from many in Congress, the two senators cobbled together an emergency program that was acceptable to a wary President George H.W. Bush and skeptical lawmakers.

The Nunn-Lugar program evolved over 20 years into a global initiative to control the spread of weapons of mass destruction. It provided American funding and expertise to help the countries of the former Soviet Union and elsewhere safeguard and dismantle their stockpiles of nuclear, chemical, and biological weapons, as well as related materials and delivery systems. The program helped remove all strategic nuclear warheads from Ukraine, Kazakhstan, and Belarus. Lugar proudly observed that the Nunn-Lugar program eliminated more nuclear weapons than the combined arsenals of France, China, and the United Kingdom.

While Nunn played a central role in developing the program, he retired from the Senate in January of 1997. For the next 15 years, Lugar was the program's chief advocate and innovator on Capitol Hill. The Nunn-Lugar program spawned related initiatives in the United States and around the world, and is a striking example of the successful pursuit of enlightened self-interest by the United States. Analysts have described the program as a historic achievement worthy of being referred to in the same breath as the Marshall Plan. For their efforts, Nunn and Lugar were both nominated for the Nobel Peace Prize.

Lugar also played a major role in helping to secure Senate approval of major arms-control treaties, including START I, the Intermediate Nuclear Forces Agreement, and the Chemical Weapons Convention. His advocacy for New START in 2010 was a masterful display of statesmanship. Convinced that the treaty was in the national interest, Lugar worked with President Barack Obama to secure its ratification even as many of his Republican colleagues stood against it. Lugar carefully helped assemble a comprehensive record about the treaty, highlighting its importance and acknowledging its imperfections. At a critical moment at the end of 2010 when Senate Minority Whip Jon Kyl (R-AZ) tried to delay consideration of the treaty as a way of killing it, Lugar resisted his stalling tactics and helped propel the treaty through the Senate.

A BROAD PORTFOLIO

Lugar's legislative legacy also includes major contributions to energy law. He initiated a biofuels research program to reduce American dependence on foreign oil, and fought to boost fuel efficiency standards in cars and trucks. He even committed the ultimate political heresy and proposed increasing the federal gas tax to reduce the consumption of oil in the United States.

The Senator from Indiana was likewise a staunch champion of free trade, arguing that trade is the engine of growth and employment. He supported the North American Free Trade Agreement—even when it was controversial at home—and was a lead author of the African Growth and Opportunity Act, even when it was little noticed back in Indiana. Lugar successfully championed the U.S.-India Civilian Nuclear Agreement, which remains controversial in nonproliferation circles, even as it helped forge a new American relationship with India. During his Senate service Lugar also did the essential but unglamorous spadework of making American foreign policy function. He served as a presidential envoy to Libya, a key election observer in the Philippines and Ukraine, and a congressional observer to arms-control talks in Geneva. Lugar took Congress's oversight responsibilities seriously as well, conducting studies of America's foreign assistance programs, the global food crisis, long-term energy challenges, and the Law of the Sea treaty. Because of his expertise in international affairs, Lugar often served as Congress's de facto foreign minister. He was one of the first American lawmakers that foreign diplomats asked to meet when visiting the United States. He proved a gracious and informed host to hundreds of envoys, and a strong supporter of American diplomats and embassies.

For all of Lugar's achievements, however, there are aspects of his record that deserve greater scrutiny. Even some of the Senator's strongest supporters believe that he should have been more forceful in challenging the Bush administration in the run-up to the Iraq War. In the fall of 2002 and the winter of 2003, Lugar was concerned the Administration had not fully thought through the impending war in Iraq. During hearings by the Senate Foreign Relations Committee before the war began, Lugar raised hard and prescient questions. But when the Bush administration failed to provide persuasive answers about how Iraq would be governed after a U.S. invasion, Lugar opted not to challenge the White House publicly. And while Lugar warned for years that the Administration and Congress needed to pay more attention to the war in Afghanistan, he supported an Iraq invasion, which clearly distracted Washington's attention from struggles in its "other war."

POLITICAL DEFEAT

Lugar's Senate career ended in a crushing political defeat in 2012. Facing his first Republican primary challenge since 1976, Lugar ran an uncertain campaign against a Tea Party–endorsed opponent, Richard Mourdock. Lugar initially moved sharply to the right to defuse Mourdock's challenge, but clearly appeared uncomfortable on that terrain. By primary day, he was running as a conservative Republican willing to work with people of goodwill from either party to solve problems. Lugar was also hampered by the perception that he spent more time solving problems overseas than in his home state.

Mourdock defeated Lugar by a lopsided margin and later lost the general election to Democrat Joe Donnelly. Lugar offered a gracious concession speech on primary night, but also released a separate searing statement, charging that Mourdock's embrace of "an unrelenting partisan mindset is irreconcilable with my philosophy of governance and my experience of what brings results for Hoosiers in the Senate." Seven months later, Lugar delivered a conciliatory farewell address on the Senate floor in which he urged lawmakers to work cooperatively for the national good rather than continue bitter partisan battles.

Since leaving the Senate in January 2013, Lugar has maintained a busy and productive life. His interest in national security policy continues with the Lugar Center, which educates the public, policy makers, and future leaders on three of his passions: controlling weapons of mass destruction, enhancing global food security, and reforming foreign assistance programs in the United States.

Through his Senate service, Lugar has left an indelible mark on American foreign policy. Senate historian Don Ritchie believes Lugar will be remembered in the same league as foreign policy giants William Fulbright, Arthur Vandenberg, and Scoop Jackson. "When it comes to shaping foreign policy, Lugar is near the top of the class," Ritchie argues. "You would be hard pressed to find many senators who have been more influential on America foreign policy over the last quarter century than Senator Lugar."

◆　◆　◆　◆　◆

20. John McCain: The Happy Warrior

by Joe Lieberman

John Sidney McCain III was born on August 29, 1936 at the Coco Solo Naval Station in the Panama Canal Zone. He graduated from United States Naval Academy in 1958 and joined the U.S. Navy the same year. He graduated from flight school in 1960 and shortly after volunteered for combat duty after the outbreak of the Vietnam War. On October 26, 1967, his plane was shot down by enemy fire during a bombing raid over Hanoi and was taken as a prisoner of war. He spent the next five and a half years in prison camps, being repeatedly

tortured and beaten, until his release on March 14, 1973. He earned the Sil-
ver Star, Legion of Merit, Purple Heart, and Distinguished Flying Cross for
his service. Unfortunately, McCain's wartime injuries prevented him from
advancing further in the Navy. In 1976, McCain was appointed as the
Navy's liaison to the Senate and served in that role until 1981. He was elected
as a Republican from Arizona to the U.S. House of Representatives in 1982
and was re-elected in 1984. In 1986, McCain was elected to the U.S. Sen-
ate where he has served for five consecutive terms. During Senator McCain's
congressional career, he has served as Chairman of the Committee on Indian
Affairs, and the Committee on Commerce, Science, and Transportation. John
McCain continues to serve as a Senator from Arizona.

He made two attempts to become President of the United States. In 2000
McCain was unsuccessful in receiving the Republican presidential nomina-
tion, and in 2008 he lost to the then-Democratic candidate Obama. McCain
is known throughout his Senate career as being a "Maverick," speaking out
against policies from both sides of the aisle that he stood against. His legacy also
includes his successful efforts to reform the campaign finance system.

One of the great pleasures of my 24 years in the Senate was working with
and forming a personal friendship with Senator John S. McCain of Arizona.
I learned a lot from John about life and legislating.

To begin to understand him, you have to know that John is an avid reader
and student of history. He learns and grows from what he reads. One of his
greatest heroes is President Theodore Roosevelt, who in a speech on "Citizenship in a Republic" on April 23, 1910, famously declared:

It is not the critic who counts; not the man who points out how the
strong man stumbles, or where the doer of deeds could have done
them better. The credit belongs to the man who is actually in the arena,
whose face is marred by dust and sweat and blood; who strives valiantly;
who errs, who comes short again and again, because there is no effort
without error and shortcoming . . . [Credit goes to he] who does actually strive to do the deeds; who knows great enthusiasms, the great
devotions; who spends himself in a worthy cause; who at best knows in
the end the triumph of high achievement, and who at worst, if he fails,
at least fails while daring greatly. . . .

These words reflect a quality that I believe is central to John McCain's
legislative record of accomplishment—his willingness to fight the good
fight, no matter the risks. That willingness has become increasingly rare and
increasingly important in recent years as Congress has become so much more

politically and ideologically divided and its members so reluctant to upset their core constituencies. Congress has become risk averse. But unless members of Congress are willing to take political risks, they will never solve the biggest problems our nation faces because the solutions to those problems will never please everyone. It takes risk-takers, and John McCain remains one of the greatest.

As those who know him well can attest, he is fundamentally a happy warrior. In fact, he is happiest when he is fighting for a cause that, as he says, "is larger than himself."

Memorable examples of John's relishing the good fight are the many speeches he has made on the Senate floor calling out his "pork list" of egregious congressional earmarks—identifying their congressional sponsors and their intended beneficiaries. "Making them famous," as he calls it, and making him unpopular among his colleagues in Congress. But that hasn't stopped him from doing what he thought was right. John's attention to government inefficiency and the misuse of taxpayer dollars laid the foundation for the earmark moratorium in Congress, and proves that you can be effective in Congress if you are willing to take on a good fight—including one that is unpopular with your colleagues.

But John also knows when to stop fighting and start working to find common ground so that Congress and our country can get things done. John has been a bipartisan bridge builder at a time when most others have been unable or unwilling to do so. He is a champion for the integrity of our institutions of government and for a style of politics that is transparent and accountable. He coauthored historic bipartisan legislation that aimed to reform our campaign financing system. He has also been protective of the continued relevance of the authorizing committees, in particular, the Armed Services Committee, vis-à-vis encroachment by the appropriators. As a result, the defense authorization bill always gets through Senate floor debate, one of the very few authorizing bills that regularly does anymore, and it does so with bipartisan support.

A GLOBAL FREEDOM FIGHTER

John has worked hard and produced much for Arizona, but he also understands that America's security and prosperity depend on our principled leadership in the world. He's fought for freedom, for justice, for the right to life, liberty, and the pursuit of happiness wherever in the world those universal ideals have been denied. For example, he's been the leading advocate for America's support for the Syrian moderate opposition in its war for a just and democratic future for the Syrian people. Indeed, he was an early supporter of the Arab Spring because he believed that the best antidote to Islamic extremism and the terror it breeds is self-government and respect for the human dignity. He's fought for the freedom of people in Bosnia, Kosovo, Burma, North Korea, Russia, China, Eastern Europe, Iran, and places in between, traveling just about every congressional recess to meet both with world leaders and dissidents in some of the toughest places in the world.

He has also denounced the deterioration of the rule of law and the expansion of unchecked state power wherever it exists, including powerful countries like Russia. John's op-ed in *Pravda.ru,* directly and candidly addressing the Russian people in response to an op-ed by Vladimir Putin in *The New York Times,* and classic John—no pulled-punches and all heart. As I can tell you in detail from our travels around the world together, John has earned the respect of world leaders and the gratitude of people struggling against tyranny whose names he will never know; but they know his name and appreciate his leadership.

In Vietnam, he forgave old enemies and helped heal the deep wounds of war by, for example, leading the effort to normalize relations with Vietnam along with his fellow veteran John Kerry.

In Iraq, his was the first, most persistent, and most persuasive voice to call for a counterinsurgency strategy, and a troop surge to execute it, in Iraq. He insisted that detainees captured in the fight against terrorism receive treatment consistent with the values of the great nation that held them prisoner.

John McCain's willingness to fight the good fight extends beyond legislation into congressional oversight, and here he has had some of his greatest accomplishments. About 10 years ago, when Republicans regained the Senate majority, a reporter asked John how he felt assuming the chairmanship of the Commerce Committee and its broad oversight jurisdiction. He answered, with a very McCainesque turn of phrase, "The Commerce Committee, I'm telling you, is like being a mosquito in a nudist colony—you pick the issue you want and go after it. That's commerce. Hell, what's not commerce?" That's John.

Sometimes, what starts as John simply asking questions in keeping with Congress's constitutional oversight prerogative, turns into an accomplishment and a legacy. For example, his inquiries in 2001 about an arcane appropriations provision that let the Air Force sole source a $30 billion contract to Boeing to procure aerial refueling tankers ultimately uncovered evidence that led to the imprisonment of Boeing's financial officer and a top Air Force official on public corruption charges. His investigation of allegations of misconduct by several Native American tribes against flamboyant GOP lobbyist

Jack Abramoff and his public relations partner, which included what *Vanity Fair* called "five gory, highly publicized [hearings] in 2004 and 2005," similarly led to 17 convictions, including the imprisonment of a member of Congress and a senior White House administration official for public corruption. As *Roll Call* noted at the time, that investigation "set a standard for what congressional oversight should be, but often isn't."

The worthy causes—the good fights—that John has taken on. Recall Teddy Roosevelt's admonition to always "remember what a legislative body is. It is a body whose first duty is to act, not to talk. The talking comes in merely as an adjunct to the acting."

For John, as befits a happy warrior, there is value in the fight without regard to victory or spoils. Just fight long enough, hard enough and when the stars align right, you will win. In the annals of congressional history, John has separated himself from those who Teddy Roosevelt described as "cold and timid souls who neither know victory nor defeat" because, unlike John McCain, they never dared to try. He has tried and tried. Sometimes he has failed, but many times on the big issues of his day John McCain has succeeded. As a result, Congress is a better institution and America is a much better country.

◆ ◆ ◆ ◆ ◆

SECTION III

Congress and Domestic Policy

21. Regulating Sunrise and Sunset: The Long Arm of the Commerce Clause

by Susan Sullivan Lagon

Since the New Deal era, Congress has relied often on the Commerce Clause—"To regulate Commerce with foreign nations, and among the several states, and with the Indian tribes"[1]—for constitutional justification to enact broad-reaching statutes. With a few notable exceptions, the Supreme Court has upheld the expansive use of the Commerce Clause to address a wide array of topics: crop acreage allowances, racial discrimination in public accommodations, the length of railway trains, and medicinal marijuana—among others.[2] This case study examines one transformative use of the Commerce Clause that touches the life of every American, young or old.

Picture this scenario: an ambitious Democrat with a professorial persona is elected President and brings with him Democratic majorities in both chambers of Congress. He is determined to pass a bill his party considered long overdue, a bill that would affect every citizen and have far-reaching consequences for years to come.

The bill is controversial. Research conducted by both public and private sector researchers produces conflicting claims about its costs and benefits. The bill sparks intense debate between impassioned supporters and equally ardent foes about the proper role of the federal government. It generates vigorous lobbying from an unusually diverse collection of powerful interest groups; in fact, given the breadth of the legislation, it is difficult to find a group that does not weigh in on the issue.

Ultimately, the President narrowly prevails and signs the bill into law, and the President's party subsequently loses dozens of seats and control of the U.S. House and Senate. Although he manages to get reelected to a second term himself and Democrats retain control of the Senate, the President complains that a willful minority is ignoring the election results and obstructing the will of the majority.

A vocal faction in the newly installed House majority remains steadfastly opposed to the law and persists in attempting to repeal it, provoking the President's promise of a veto. Meanwhile, its defenders insist that once the law becomes fully operational it will grow in popularity, but public opinion is ambivalent at best. Implementation of the policy is a major undertaking and the President acknowledges that some confusion during the transition is inevitable.

A former government official who had worked on the policy's implementation later called it "the most persistent political controversy in American history."[3] Another commentator pronounced it "the greatest continuing fraud ever perpetrated on the American people," and labeled it "America's greatest shame."[4] Others were disappointed that the law did not go far enough and vowed to press for its expansion.

What law could possibly elicit such a strong reaction? The Affordable Care Act passed by Congress in 2010? No. The scenario above describes the institution of Daylight Saving Time (DST) in 1918. A century later, debate continues about the propriety, utility, and legitimacy of the semiannual requirement for clocks to "spring forward, fall back."

ORIGINS OF DAYLIGHT SAVING TIME

Known at the time as the Calder Act after its Senate sponsor, Senator William Musgrave Calder (R-NY), the Standard Time Act[5] was passed at the request of President Woodrow Wilson during World War I. The House bill, sponsored by Kansas City Representative William P. Borland (D-MO) passed before Calder's bill cleared the Senate. Borland's party affiliation and personal friendship with Speaker Champ Clark, a fellow Missouri Democrat, may have helped.[6]

The Standard Time Act officially recognized four one-hour-wide time zones in the continental U.S. based on a system the railroads had been using since 1883. Rather than using "sun time" to set town hall clocks to noon when the sun was at its highest point overhead, railroads began operating on "standard time" to keep trains running on schedule. The system had proven workable and widely accepted even though a number of doubters urged that local clocks remain on "God's time."[7]

Far more inflammatory than formalizing time zones was the statute's mandate that clocks be adjusted to provide an additional hour of daylight each evening for seven months. The rationale was that reducing domestic demand for electric lighting would conserve coal needed for the war effort. Germany had begun using DST in 1916, and Wilson appealed to Congress to allow the United States to reap the same fuel-saving benefits that the enemy enjoyed. While the Standard Time Act was a legitimate application of the Commerce Clause, World War I and the President's characterization of the law as patriotic duty provided the impetus for its passage. Commercial reasons also played a role, but Congress passed the DST provision with the understanding that it was a temporary emergency measure brought on by the war.

The idea of adjusting clocks during the warmer months to save energy is often attributed to Benjamin Franklin. He wrote a letter that appeared in the *Journal of Paris* in 1784 in which he calculated that Parisians were burning 127 million candles unnecessarily each year. The letter was a satirical look at Parisians' penchant for sleeping in late, and Franklin proposed a tax "on every window that is provided with shutters to keep out the light of the sun."[8]

DST in the United States owes more to English architect—and avid golfer—William Willett than to Benjamin Franklin. Like Franklin, Willett was disturbed by his fellow city-dwellers' early morning torpor. In 1907, he wrote a pamphlet that circulated in London pitching the idea not for commerce, but for leisure: "Now, if some of the hours of wasted sunlight could be withdrawn from the beginning and added to the end of the day, how many advantages would be gained by all, and in particular those who spend it in the open air, when light permits them to do so, whatever time they have at their command after the duties of the day have been discharged."[9] He suggested that clocks be changed at 2:00 A.M. because there were few trains running at that hour, so timetables would need minimal alteration. Willett's plan was realized after his death when Britain enacted the Summer Time Act of 1916, shortly after Germany had established DST.[10]

A Cincinnati businessman named E. H. Murdoch was impressed with Willett's idea and even met with President William Howard Taft at the White House in 1909 to discuss it, but nothing more came of it.[11] Willett's health and recreation angle, however, was not lost on DST proponents, who tried to gain the support of members who were concerned with social welfare. Senator Calder echoed Willett's view:

> This is not a question of accommodating the golfer or the tennis player or the baseball fan or the automobilists . . . but it is something for the benefit of teeming millions who work in the factories, the offices, the stores. Under [DST] they are at home early in the evening and have the opportunity to be around home and play with their children and to enjoy some part of spring, summer, and fall with their families.[12]

Of course, there may have been a commercial motive in addition to concern for the general welfare or pure altruism. John K. Tener, President of the National League of Professional Base Ball Clubs, enthused, "The proposition should recommend itself to all [especially] those red-blooded Americans who are interested in outdoor sports . . . and who appreciate how necessary it is to the nation's moral worth that its leisure hours be spent in outdoor, healthful recreation."[13]

The National Daylight Saving Association painted idyllic scenes of outdoor family picnics, people tending their "victory gardens" each evening, sedentary office workers taking a swim or playing tennis on their way home from work, reduced incidences of headaches and eyestrain, factory workers having fewer industrial accidents, and everyone being more relaxed simply by breathing more fresh air while outdoors.[14] Physicians touted DST's potential health benefits such as reducing eyestrain and encouraging exercise to prevent disease, which was of particular concern given troop movement in and out of war-torn Europe.[15] Unfortunately, extra daylight proved no match for the Spanish flu outbreak that same year.

BUSINESS VERSUS AGRICULTURE

The biggest beneficiary of DST, however, was the business community. Unions suspected business of trying to squeeze an extra hour of labor out of workers, but the real motivation for business came from increased sales of goods, not production. People were using their "extra" hour of daylight not just for recreation, but for shopping. During DST, the New York Stock Exchange had an extra hour's overlap with the London Market. Tourism boards and recreational businesses thrived. DST was supporting the economy, not just the war effort.

Squarely on the other side of the DST debate were almost all agricultural interests, many of whom considered adjusting their clocks as unnatural as it was unfair. When DST took effect in 1918, approximately 30 percent of the population made its living on the nation's 6.5 million farms.[16] DST effectively "robbed" them of an hour of morning sunlight in exchange for an hour of evening sunlight. Their days were still governed by the sun: For ranchers who raised livestock, their animals needed feeding (or milking) in the dark, and farmers who grew hay had to wait an extra hour for the morning dew to burn off.[17] Their hired hands worked an hour less but still left at the same time at the end of the workday.

Westerners were also critical of DST, in part because Western states tended to be more rural, but also because their time zones covered wider expanses of territory. The considerable difference between "sun time" and standard time within the same zone was even greater under DST. American Indian tribes, explicitly mentioned in the Commerce Clause, ridiculed DST. Upon being told the reason for DST, one member of a tribe reportedly quipped, "Only the government would believe that you could cut a foot off the top of a blanket, sew it to the bottom, and have a longer blanket."[18]

Even as proponents of DST touted the positive impacts on business, opponents found evidence of negative impacts. Utility companies were not able to collect as much revenue since people used less electricity. Urban workers with early shifts were concerned about walking to work in the dark. Theaters needed to be dark to show movies, and the extra hour of daylight made it more difficult to dispel the day's heat in the summer. More time outdoors also meant less time indoors at music halls, bowling alleys, billiard halls, and even church meetings.[19]

Less than a year-and-a-half after it was enacted, DST was repealed.[20] The Treaty of Versailles that marked the end of World War I had been signed just a few weeks before, the war was officially over, and Congress felt the farmers' pressure. Some DST opponents had grudgingly complied with the law, but by now they felt they had "done their bit" for the war and were ready to revert to the *status quo ante*.

President Wilson vetoed the repeal legislation, but Congress overrode his veto, reflecting just how unpopular DST had become, at least in some quarters. Notably, of the 44 bills that Wilson vetoed in office, only 6—including the repeal of DST—were overridden.[21]

Following the repeal of DST, some states and cities chose to retain it. But growing resentment of "big business" for profiting—literally—at the expense of others had led to a markedly hostile attitude toward DST. At a hearing on repeal, the Secretary of the U.S. Chamber of Commerce angrily testified, "Mr. Chairman, I do not think that the interests of business which have been referred to this afternoon in a derogatory tone, as swivel-chair interests, should be disregarded in this matter."[22]

DST's constitutionality was never challenged, but the Supreme Court did hear a case that involved its repeal. Although the national DST law was no longer in effect, several states enacted their own DST statutes, including Massachusetts. Predictably, the Massachusetts law was challenged as a violation of federal law by the Massachusetts Grange, a mother whose children had to get up an hour earlier and therefore lost an hour's sleep, a school district afraid of forfeiting state aid for its schools, and a landowner whose property straddled the New Hampshire border who claimed that "to adjust himself to two standards cause[d] him worry and pecuniary loss."[23] Writing for the majority, Justice Oliver Wendell Holmes was unpersuaded and saw no conflict between the nation reverting to standard time while Massachusetts chose to retain DST. Congress had been free to use the Commerce Clause to install and remove DST nationwide, and Massachusetts could accomplish the same goal within its borders by exercising the police powers reserved under the Tenth Amendment.

CONGRESS MANAGING TIME

Since introducing DST in 1918 and repealing it in 1919, Congress has intervened another half dozen times. In 1942, DST returned in response to

World War II and the need to conserve coal and oil, but was again repealed at the end of the war in 1945. In 1966, Congress enacted the Uniform Time Act to end confusion resulting from states and cities following their own notions of DST.[24] For example, 23 different start and end dates were used in Iowa alone, and five weeks a year, Boston, New York, and Philadelphia were not on the same time as Washington, D.C., Baltimore, and Cleveland.[25]

The 1966 law did not require states to follow DST, but if they did, they had to adhere to uniform dates set by Congress. Some saw even that as excessive government meddling. Georgia State Senator Bobby Rowan warned his colleagues, "Not since Biblical times has there been a man who could change sunrise and sunset, but the bureaucrats are attempting to do it."[26] Other criticisms were downright bizarre, such as the sinister aspects of DST expressed by Hugh A. Vail, representing a group from rural Iowa:

A child gets up in the morning under daylight time and cries because he has lost an hour of sleep. A parent has to whip him to get him to go to school. Maybe he has had breakfast and maybe not. He whines all day. When he comes home, his parents give him aspirin. We are living in a drug age. The school-children are so busted that they have to have drugs. Then when Communism comes along, what are we going to do?

In 1973, Congress temporarily extended DST from six months to eight months in response to the OPEC oil embargo. The Department of Transportation found that adding March and April saved the equivalent of 10,000 barrels of oil each day.[27] The trial extension ended in 1975. The next revision came in 1986, when DST was extended by a month (lasting from the first Sunday in April to the last Sunday in October) to the delight of the golf and barbecue industries, which estimated that the change would yield $400 million and $200 million in revenues, respectively.[28]

Finally in 2005, as part of a larger energy bill, Congress bumped the start date for DST to the second Sunday in March and the end date to the first Sunday in November. Representatives Fred Upton (R-MI) and Ed Markey (D-MA), both of whom championed the change, asserted that the change could save 100,000 barrels of oil a day and reduce electricity consumption by one percent. Opponents responded that the estimates overstated savings and that people would drive their cars to activities during the extra daylight hours, so the energy savings would be minimal.

Moving the end date by just a week into November also conveniently accommodated Halloween trick-or-treaters. That idea was advanced as a safety measure by Senator Mike Enzi (R-WY), who had introduced a separate bill in previous Congresses at the request of first and second graders at an elementary school in Sheridan, Wyoming.[29] Candy manufacturers, not surprisingly, were very pleased. Across the country, parent groups, many of whom used to oppose DST, welcomed the extra daylight in the evenings for organized youth sports.

But as usual, reaction to the change was strong and mixed. While many Americans enjoyed the extra sunshine, airlines and utility companies argued that the change would cost them millions of dollars to change flight schedules and recalibrate automatic meters. Religious groups that pray at daybreak were worried about being late to work, and parochial schools without public transportation worried about children going to school in the dark.[30] Psychologists noted more sleep disorders as the body's circadian rhythms try to adjust to waking up in darkness, and studies found an increased risk of heart attacks, traffic accidents, and injuries among miners and construction workers in the first few days following the change to DST.[31]

Just as Oliver Wendell Holmes had written in 1926, states are still free to opt out of DST, and Arizona—the state whose flag, fittingly, depicts the sun setting in the western sky—and Hawaii do so, as did Indiana until 2005.[32] The Navajo Nation, which is partly in Arizona, observes DST, but the Hopi Nation (which is surrounded by the Navajo like a doughnut hole) does not.[33] States seeking to change time zones can submit a request to the Department of Transportation, which decides whether the proposed change is in "the convenience of commerce."[34]

A century after the first invocation of DST, debate on the issue endures, with advocates on both sides of the issue armed with ever more sophisticated research. Will Congress step in yet again in the name of commerce to make further changes? Might it make DST year-round, or decide that it has outlived its usefulness? Only time will tell.

◆ ◆ ◆ ◆ ◆

22. In Roosevelt's Shadow: The New Deal Congress

by Patrick Maney

Overshadowed from the start by Franklin D. Roosevelt (FDR), Congress has never received the billing it deserves for its role in the New Deal. The image still persists of Roosevelt and his brain trust bending a pliant Congress to their will, especially during the dramatic first months of his administration. As one of FDR's biographers put it: "Bills originating in the White House were passed almost daily. This was presidential power without precedent—FDR could dream up an idea, something that had never been tried, and set the huge machinery of government in motion to implement it." In another account, Roosevelt "proposed, and proposed, and proposed again," while Congress "scampered in panic to approve those proposals as fast as it could."[1] Commentators routinely talk of "Roosevelt's New Deal" or say that FDR "gave us Social Security."

Though an appealingly simple narrative, that's simply not the way it happened. The enduring accomplishments of Roosevelt's presidency came about because of the efforts of many people—Roosevelt and his advisers, of course, but also well-organized interest groups, grassroots activists, and key legislators. But of all the participants in the New Deal, it was Congress, and not the President, that took the lead in initiating and shaping most of the foundational legislation. That was true not only during the First Hundred Days, but throughout Roosevelt's first term. No history of the New Deal is thus complete unless it takes into account the pivotal role of Congress. And even after 1936, when Roosevelt assumed more of the legislative initiative, Congress remained a vital force.

A SEASONED CONGRESS

At least since Reconstruction, Congress has been a perennial target of public ridicule and scorn and a favorite subject for American humorists. Mark Twain wrote: "It could probably be shown by facts and figures that there is no distinctly native American criminal class except Congress." Some 40 years later, Will Rogers quipped that Americans had "come to feel the same when Congress is in session as we do when the baby gets hold of a hammer. It's just a question of how much damage he can do with it before we can take it away from him."

Whether such unflattering characterizations are justified or not today, they certainly did not apply to the 73rd U.S. Congress, which convened in March 1933, or to the successive Congresses that were in session during the Roosevelt Administration. To be sure, no legislators of the stature of Daniel Webster, Henry Clay, or John C. Calhoun sat in Congress during the New Deal. But its members did include persons of uncommon intelligence, high-mindedness, and creativity, such as Senators Hugo Black (D-AL), Bronson Cutting (R-NM), Robert M. La Follette Jr. (R-WI), George W. Norris (R-NE), and Robert F. Wagner (D-NY), and Representatives David J. Lewis (D-MD), Maury Maverick (D-TX), and Sam Rayburn (D-TX).

When Roosevelt convened Congress into special session in March 1933, fellow Democrats controlled both houses for the first time since 1919. Almost to a man, the Democratic leaders of Congress were longtime veterans of Capitol Hill. In the Senate, four Southerners—with a combined 105 years of service—comprised the leadership: Vice President, President of the Senate, and former Speaker of the House, respectively John Nance Garner (D-TX), Majority Leader Joseph T. Robinson (D-AR), Byron "Pat" Harrison (D-MS), and James F. Byrnes (D-SC). In the House, the Democratic Speaker Henry T. Rainey of Illinois had first been elected during Theodore Roosevelt's first term. House Majority Leader Joseph W. Byrns (D-TN) was a 24-year veteran. In both houses, the leaders were facilitators rather than innovators. The drafting of bills was relegated to more issue-oriented colleagues such as Wagner and La Follette in the Senate, and David Lewis and Sam Rayburn in the House. But if the leaders did not write legislation, they did everything else. They scheduled debates, negotiated compromises, and mustered votes for final passage. In both houses, Southern Democrats dominated most of the key committee chairmanships, and as long as the issue of race did not arise, they supported the New Deal.

The Republicans, meanwhile, lacked both the numbers and the will to mount an effective challenge to the early New Deal. That's partly because several progressive Senate Republicans, including La Follette, Norris, and Bronson Cutting (R-NM) had campaigned for Roosevelt in 1932 and later drafted key legislation. The Republican Minority Leader Charles L. McNary (R-OR), a veteran of the farm relief battles of the 1920s, privately conceded that he enjoyed working with Roosevelt more than he had with fellow Republican Herbert Hoover. House Republicans were less accommodating, but even they shied from wholesale resistance to the Administration.

Before Roosevelt took the oath of office, Congress had paved the way for government action by documenting the extent of the economic crisis. A series of dramatic Senate hearings left no doubt that the Depression was deep, national in scope, and—contrary to the claims of President Herbert Hoover—beyond the capacity of states and localities to manage. Then, when Roosevelt called for "action and action now" in his stirring inaugural address, Congress responded to the challenge.

Of the 15 major pieces of legislation that became law during Roosevelt's celebrated First Hundred Days in office, all but two or three originated in Congress and many, such as the Federal Emergency Relief Act and the bill creating the Tennessee Valley Authority (TVA), had legislative histories long predating Roosevelt's election. And, contrary to popular belief, some of the most enduring measures of the New Deal were initially opposed by Roosevelt. Few agencies became better known or more closely identified with Roosevelt, for instance, than the Federal Deposit Insurance Corporation (FDIC). But when Senator Arthur Vandenberg (R-MI) and Representative Henry Steagall

(D-AL) first proposed creating a federal agency to insure bank deposits, Roosevelt thought it bordered on what economists call "moral hazard." To bail out all banks, no matter how good or bad, he insisted, would encourage sloppy and dishonest banking practices. Yet after it became clear that Congress intended to create the FDIC with or without his support, Roosevelt endorsed the measure.

The President was also initially indifferent to Senator Robert Wagner's proposal to create a National Labor Relations Board as a means of encouraging collective bargaining. Only after the bill cleared the Senate and appeared almost certain to pass the House did Roosevelt lend his support. U.S. Secretary of Labor Frances Perkins recalled that the President "never lifted a finger" for the landmark legislation. "All the credit for it belongs to Wagner," she said.[2]

Congress also used its investigative power both to prod the Administration and to build public support for congressional initiatives. In 1933, the U.S. Senate Committee on Banking and Currency's exposure of malfeasance on Wall Street led to the separation of investment from commercial banking and government regulation of the stock market. A four-year probe of antiunion practices by the U.S. Senate Committee on Education and Labor's special Civil Liberties Committee spurred the growth of organized labor during the 1930s, while Gerald Nye's (R-ND) U.S. Senate Special Committee on Investigation of the Munitions Industry's controversial investigation into the origins of U.S. entry into World War I reinforced isolationism in the years before Pearl Harbor.

To recognize the impact of Congress during this period of time is not meant to shunt Roosevelt to the wings. With the possible exception of Woodrow Wilson, Roosevelt involved himself in lawmaking more directly than any of his predecessors. He helped coordinate legislative activity, backing some measures, and opposing or modifying others. His speeches and fireside chats mobilized public support for the New Deal and articulated its rationale. He dispensed patronage and public works to build support for bills he wanted, and vetoed those he didn't want. But if Roosevelt played a more active part in legislative affairs than had his predecessors, he was less active than most of his successors, several of whom carved out legislative roles for themselves that were larger than FDR ever dreamed of, to include Lyndon Johnson and Bill Clinton.

Nor was all congressional influence positive. The devil lay in the details, and the details of some legislative initiatives denied aid to those who needed it most. White Southern Democrats saw to it that domestic and farmworkers— most of whom were black—were excluded from coverage under the pioneering Social Security Act. Congressional insistence on maximum state participation in the operation of federal programs, like the Agricultural

Adjustment Act and Aid to Dependent Children, also gave whites a free hand to withhold benefits from blacks. Then there were initiatives FDR might have taken, such as support for national health insurance, antilynching legislation, and immigration reform, but for the opposition of powerful legislators.

WARTIME SHIFT IN POWER

World War II brought a sharp downturn in Congress's fortunes. During the 1930s, power had already begun to shift from the Legislative to the Executive Branch, although not nearly to the extent many have supposed. But the war greatly accelerated the trend. After Pearl Harbor, Roosevelt requested and received from Congress sweeping authority to mobilize the nation for war. He assumed additional powers that he said were inherent in his role as Commander in Chief.

In addition to a real power shift, Congress suffered a severe loss of prestige. Although Congress may not have gotten all of the credit it deserved for the New Deal, as late as 1939 it enjoyed a favorable public approval rating almost identical to Roosevelt's. After Pearl Harbor, however, Congress became the whipping boy for the accumulating frustrations of wartime. Influential commentators began to question Congress's legitimacy as a coequal branch of government. "The ignorance and provincialism of Congress," wrote distinguished journalist Raymond Clapper, "render it incapable of meeting the needs of modern government." Historian Henry Steele Commager defended the presidential ascendancy over Congress by claiming that "democracy apparently flourishes when the Executive is strong, languishes when it is weak."[3] One scholar even exempted the Presidency, though not Congress, from Lord Acton's famous dictum that power corrupts and absolute power corrupts absolutely. "The Presidency," Clinton Rossiter wrote, "is a standing reproach to those petty doctrinaires who insist that executive power is inherently undemocratic" and "no less a reproach to those easy generalizers who think that Lord Acton had the very last word on the corrupting influence of power."[4]

The presidency was in, the Congress out. After the war, the history of the New Deal was rewritten to accord with the new preference. College students in the 1950s and 1960s learned of FDR's legislative prowess, but not much about Congress's role. *The New York Times'* reporter, R. W. "Johnny" Apple, who studied history at Princeton and Columbia, recalled being taught that "Roosevelt and the Brains Trust and not the young legislators . . . had most of the responsibility" for the New Deal.[5] It's not surprising that Washington reporters in the post-Roosevelt era, including Apple, made FDR the standard by which they measured his successors, even going so far as to use Roosevelt's

First Hundred Days as a benchmark to assess the early performance of our new presidents. The irony, of course, is that not even Roosevelt performed the Rooseveltian feats that commentators credited him with.

From time to time historians might note, as Arthur M. Schlesinger Jr. did, that Congress "played a vital and consistently underestimated role in shaping the New Deal" or, in William E. Leuchtenburg's words, that FDR's "success with Congress has often been exaggerated." But such insights never made their way into the nation's historical consciousness. And in truth, most Roosevelt scholars, including Schlesinger and Leuchtenburg, didn't have it in their hearts to call attention to Congress's contributions to the New Deal. Their sympathies lay with Roosevelt, and they were mainly interested in telling the story of his commanding leadership. Congress became an afterthought.[6]

Note: This essay is adapted from the author's "The Forgotten New Deal Congress, 1933–1945," in *The American Congress: The Building of Democracy*, ed. Julian E. Zelizer (Boston: Houghton Mifflin, 2004): 446–73.

◆ ◆ ◆ ◆ ◆

23. Dawn of a New Era: Building the Modern Congress

by Ross K. Baker

The first ceremonial act in the construction of a building is often the laying of the cornerstone that contains a capsule filled with tokens of the time and era. However, the precise beginnings of political institutions, unlike the buildings that house them, are often shrouded in the mists of history. It is doubly difficult to place a date on which an institution of long standing became "modern." Assigning a date—even an imprecise or a rolling date—is diabolically difficult for some straightforward reasons.

The U.S. House of Representatives and the U.S. Senate evolved differently. In the case of the Senate, one could argue that modernity came with the installation of John Worth Kern (D-IN) in 1913 as the first party floor leader recognized as such. An equally strong case could be made that the Senate became the institution we know of today when newly chosen Democratic Minority Leader Lyndon B. Johnson (D-TX) prevailed upon the party's Steering Committee in January 1953 to place low-seniority senators, some of them liberals, on key committees from which they had previously been barred by the ironclad custom of seniority.

In the House, 1910 might be seen as the dawn of modernity. That year, the dictatorial Speaker Joseph G. Cannon (R-IL) was deposed by a vote of Democrats and Republican progressives, and the principle of seniority was established as the path to committee leadership, as opposed to the whim of party leaders. A protracted surge of modernization also came in the early and mid-1970s, when Democratic insurgents mounted a series of challenges to the venerable conservatives of their party who enjoyed a virtual monopoly on committee chairmanships, paradoxically produced by the reforms of 1910.

But a more contemporary turning point in the history of the institution was the 1994 election, which reduced House Democrats to the minority for the first time since 1955. The Republican takeover ushered in a period of profound institutional change including, for the Republicans at least, a downgrading of the importance in seniority in the selection of chairs of the standing committees and the enhanced power of party leaders to influence those appointments.

It should not be surprising that the onset of what passes for modernity in the Senate began six decades ago in relatively ancient history, while major institutional change in the House is of far more modern vintage. This is, of course, emblematic of the differences between the two chambers, with the House being subject not only to more dramatic policy swings election to election, but also to more fundamental alterations of the ground rules by which the chamber operates.

One example of this disparity was the "reform" of the filibuster in 1975 when the requirement for cloture was eased from two-thirds of those voting to three-fifths, while the requirement for a two-thirds' majority for rules changes remained in place. No reform in the history of Congress had so little practical effect as this change. Indeed, the frequency of the use of the filibuster increased markedly in the years following 1975 even as the threshold for cloture was lowered. In 2013, its use was curtailed when Majority Leader Harry Reid invoked the so-called nuclear option with a rules change on a simple majority vote of the Senate. The change set a simple majority as the threshold for the confirmation of Executive Branch nominees and judges below the level of Supreme Court. Sixty votes continued to be the hurdle for ordinary legislation and confirmation of Supreme Court justices. Reid acted out of frustration at the use of filibusters by Republicans, one of the symptoms of political polarization.

THE ERA OF POLARIZATION

While the House and Senate have each evolved in different ways—and at different speeds—there is one feature in the modern era that is common to both: polarization. Thus, for all the many milestones that have occurred in Congress over the past century, including bipartisan efforts to reform the institutions in 1946 and 1970, denominating the dawn of the modern Congress as the onset of polarization is a reasonable, though melancholy, conclusion.

Whatever internal changes have occurred in each body over the years, the House and Senate operate within the larger universe of American politics. Indeed, the fractious spirit in contemporary politics is reflected in both the greater disposition of presidents to assert unilateral powers in the face of congressional opposition, and the internal realignment of the parties into homogeneous and mutually antagonistic political denominations. Without the polarization and relentless conflict that characterize our politics, the filibuster could not be used as frequently as it is currently used, and the informal but equally restrictive "Hastert Rule" in the House would not be so effective (under which the Speaker of the House only brings to the floor legislation that is supported by a majority of his or her own caucus, thus requiring no votes from the minority party for passage).

The rise in polarization is also evident in the ongoing debate about returning to "regular order"—the established customs and practices by which Congress does its work. Allowing for the fact that the term "regular order" is exasperatingly elusive and often used in self-serving ways, most people understand the concept to approximate the old legislative process, how-a-bill-becomes-law model of committee action followed by floor debate. In reality, complaints about regular order are often about what the other guy is not doing that he should be doing. Not surprisingly, minority parties typically complain that the majority is usurping power and vow to restore regular order when they retake power, only to backslide into the same practices they previously criticized.

The modern movement away from "regular order" can be traced to the rediscovery of the unanimous consent agreement in the Senate by Majority Leader Lyndon Johnson in 1955. Although the rule had been on the books since the mid-19th century it was rarely used and, if employed, it was typically at the end of a session when the legislation had been thoroughly discussed. These "time agreements" shifted decision making away from committees and toward party leadership. The practical effect was to curtail substantive floor debate. But, as Robert Caro has pointed out, "Majority Leader Lyndon Johnson may have been limiting debate on the Senate floor; he was not eliminating speeches. He wanted speeches and he wanted plenty of them."

The abandonment of regular order has taken several forms. One is the writing of legislation by party leaders and leadership staff in negotiations that are often kept secret from the rank-and-file of both parties. The call for a return to regular order was one of the first utterances of John Boehner after he assumed the Speakership in 2011. Within just a few months of Boehner's call for regular order, he was deep in negotiations with President Barack Obama on the "grand bargain" to reduce the deficit. A similar departure from regular order is the resort to "omnibus" bills which, because they cross many committee jurisdictions, are crafted by party leaders and their staffs.

Yet another manifestation of the departure from regular order has been the emergence of bipartisan "gangs" of senators. In the Senate, recent years have seen "the Gang of 14" whose compromise proposal on judicial nominees in 2005 fended off the unleashing of a "nuclear option" to change Senate rules such that a simple majority could end filibusters, rather than the two-thirds provided for in Senate rules. This was followed by the "Gang of Six" in 2011 that proposed deficit reduction with a combination of revenue increases and entitlement cuts and was materially responsible for the collapse of the Obama-Boehner "grand bargain." Next came the "Gang of Eight" that produced a bipartisan compromise on immigration reform in 2013.

All of these examples of what Barbara Sinclair calls "unorthodox lawmaking" are a product of the age of political polarization in Congress which is, in turn, the result of an American public deeply divided over many issues. The modern Congress, then, is an institution of virtually intractable political discord for which there is but one remedy. And it is a remedy that resides, uniquely, in the hands of the American people and cannot be applied in the absence of their initiative. That corrective is an election which gives to one of the parties a solid majority in both houses. In an ideal world, the return of bipartisan cooperation would come about as the result of the rediversification of both parties to resemble the grand coalitions of years past. That pathway out of polarization seems far less likely than another "wave election" that reorders the composition of both houses of Congress.

◆ ◆ ◆ ◆ ◆

24. Defeating Jim Crow: The 1965 Voting Rights Act

by Kareem U. Crayton

A common misconception about the legislative process is that enacting new laws is the norm. In fact, the usual result of a bill being introduced is failure. Indeed, fewer than 5 percent of all proposed bills in a session ever reach the President's desk.[1] The institution's procedural rules, veto points, and time limits all present impediments for establishing new laws. Major legislation faces an even greater challenge, since opposing political interests are also working to scuttle it. Every enacted law thus has a unique story that distinguishes it from the multitude of proposed bills that never emerge from the process.

The story behind the signing of the Voting Rights Act (VRA) on August 6, 1965, involved a remarkable effort to build a national consensus to reform the political system in the American South. In a span of merely five months, Congress marshaled enough support to outlaw a nearly century-old practice in many Southern states of effectively denying the right to vote based upon race. This "triumph for freedom," as President Lyndon B. Johnson described it, would not have been possible without the confluence of a number of factors at opportune moments in time.

BLOODY TURNING POINT

One cannot understand the tremendous public pressure on Congress to take action without reviewing the horrific events of March 25, 1965.[2] The typically slow and plodding progress of creating national legislation accelerated dramatically due to the courage of ordinary Americans whose sacrifice prompted an official response. On what became known as "Bloody Sunday," the country witnessed a phalanx of Alabama police officers confronting a peaceful voting rights march across the Edmund Pettus Bridge in Selma, Alabama.

The evening network news showed brutal scenes of attack dogs, tear gas, and nightsticks being unleashed on people whose only offense was protesting a system that unlawfully denied the ballot to black citizens.[3] Dallas County (where Selma is located) resembled those Southern communities where the political impact of the Jim Crow segregation system on the democratic process was most severe. Black adults were a majority of Dallas County's adult population, yet less than 10 percent of blacks were registered to vote due to the county's racially restrictive laws and practices.[4] Protests, court litigation, and legislative efforts had not managed to undo this system for most of the 20th century, so civil rights groups resorted to organizing a voting rights march to Montgomery, the state capital.[5] The stunningly cruel use of state force to stop the march shocked the conscience of the American public and their elected representatives.

As important as the sacrifice of civil rights activists was to the passage of the VRA, however, leaders in Washington, D.C., also had to move this issue to the top of the policy agenda. Even an outraged electorate needs political leaders who can translate public fervor into actionable legislation, which depends upon careful planning and salesmanship. In contrast to his predecessor in the White House, Lyndon Johnson was especially well-equipped in both respects to address this issue in 1965. (See "Lyndon B. Johnson: Presidential Legislator," Chapter 15.)

During the Kennedy Administration the civil rights agenda had led to several crises in the South, including school desegregation standoffs in places like Oxford, Mississippi, and Tuscaloosa, Alabama.[6] Often, these flash-points yielded quiet negotiations with segregationists whose support was crucial to Kennedy's reelection effort. During the same period, civil rights bills had stalled in Congress partly due to tepid support from the White House, even after episodes of violence that included the killing of civil rights workers in Mississippi and the attacks on Freedom Riders.

By the time he assumed the presidency, Lyndon B. Johnson had developed a record as an ally of the Southern Democrats, along with an unparalleled mastery of the legislative process. Having been elected to the White House in a 1964 landslide, Johnson could convey the necessity of a voting rights bill with both conviction and credibility to his former colleagues in Congress and to the nation as a whole.[7]

Johnson expertly wielded a key power of the presidency—the power to persuade—in a nationally televised speech before a special joint session of Congress.[8] He spoke passionately about the shared moral outrage over Selma, noting that the marchers were calling the nation to address a deep wrong that offended human rights and the democratic system. Selma demonstrated that the violent resistance by Southern segregationists had to be confronted and brought to an end. In making his position clear, Johnson essentially initiated a national conversation on the issue of a voting rights bill directed at the South. And the President's direction to Congress was to commence the consideration of his proposal immediately.

Behind the scenes, Johnson helped to focus the legislative process, directing his Attorney General—in no uncertain terms—to develop the toughest possible remedial system available.[9] Following decades of failed efforts, the President was now prepared to organize federal power to bring a clear and certain end to the era of race discrimination in the South's political system. To crush the resolve of those who had staunchly defended Jim Crow, Johnson added that this law's true goal was even broader—overcoming the legacy of bigotry and injustice. The President even added a line from the protestors to leave no doubt about his level of commitment to the task at hand: "And we shall overcome."[10]

CONFRONTING THE "DIXIECRATS"

The original version of the bill contained both permanent and temporary provisions. The permanent provisions Sections 2 and 3 restate the mandates of the Fifteenth Amendment, affirming that neither states nor Congress can "deny or abridge the right of any citizen of the United States to vote on account of race or color."[11] Section 3 of the Act empowers federal district courts to impose the criminal penalties for certain violations of the statute. Both of these sections apply to any state or local jurisdiction nationwide that is found to have violated the Fifteenth Amendment.

The temporary sections, by contrast, specifically responded to the South's sustained efforts to evade federal antidiscrimination mandates. To identify the states with especially closed political systems, the Justice Department developed a triggering formula that determined the scope of special coverage. Any state that used a test or qualification device for voting and had registered less than half of its voting age population as of November 1964 would be subject to Sections 5 through 9. In places where this formula applied, Section 4 suspended the use of certain qualification devices that registrars arbitrarily applied to prevent blacks from voting.

To prevent what President Johnson described as ingenious state attempts to avoid compliance, Section 5 froze election laws in covered states. Enacting further changes "in any voting qualification or prerequisite to voting, or standard, practice, or procedure with respect to voting" required approval, or "pre-clearance," from the Justice Department.[12] Sections 6 through 8 of the Act borrowed the idea of appointing federal registrars and observers from the previous Civil Rights Acts. In appropriate circumstances, federal examiners and poll watchers could be deployed to a state to ensure that fair election procedures were followed.

As a formal matter, however, a president can only propose his ideas to Congress. The chief executive's will to enact new laws is only as effective as his ability to persuade and influence a majority of the members in the Legislative Branch. The primary challenge in enacting the VRA was navigating the bill through an institution populated with powerful members who represented constituencies that enforced a whites-only political regime. With the black population largely fenced out of the political process in their districts, Southern white Democrats were able to thrive advocating a segregationist agenda. These Dixiecrats comprised one of the most long-standing voting blocs in Congress, allowing its members to gain powerful posts in the leadership ranks. Their seniority also gained them important gatekeeping roles in the legislative process. Not surprisingly, the level of their opposition threatened the success of the voting rights bill.

In the Senate, the Southern opponents of the bill were some of the chamber's most senior members, including Richard Russell of Georgia and Russell Long of Louisiana. In the House of Representatives, Rules Committee

Chairman Howard Smith of Virginia railed against the proposal as an unconstitutional vendetta against the Southern states. Notwithstanding their opposition, the bill moved forward on the momentum started by President Johnson. While they might have taken more radical steps to derail the bill, the Dixiecrats opposing the bill mostly limited their energy to speaking against it in committee and during floor debates.

One might have expected a more grand and concerted strategy to block one of the most significant and sweeping federal mandates of the 20th century, but President Johnson's electoral landslide had brought in more liberal Democratic members of Congress who represented districts outside of the South. In the House alone, more than 37 new Democrats were elected on the President's coattails. With a greater share of the caucus, the allies of the President were disinclined to tolerate an organized strategy of delay. In the wake of their defeat on the Civil Rights Act in 1964 (which had the support of some Republicans), most Dixiecrats recognized that a sustained filibuster a year later could not withstand the groundswell of support behind the voting rights bill.

This is not to say that the Dixiecrats simply accepted the VRA was a foregone conclusion. Key legislators in this bloc had to be convinced to limit their attacks on this bill, using reasons beyond the moral conviction in Johnson's speech and in the marchers' message. Among the most astute tactics that the White House employed to this end was tailoring the geographic reach of the VRA's special preclearance provision to avoid the strong opposition of certain gatekeepers. For example, the original targeting formula fashioned for Section 5 excluded the states of Texas (home of the President), Arkansas (represented by Senator J. William Fulbright), and addressed fewer than half the counties in North Carolina (home to Judiciary Committee Chairman Sam Ervin). These concessions helped to build additional support as the bill continued on the path toward enactment.

The legislative coalition that moved the bill toward final passage exemplifies how bipartisanship and regionalism can shape the dynamics for enactment. With the imagery of the Selma attacks still fresh in memory and informing public opinion, non-Southern legislators (particularly in urban areas) recognized that the VRA reflected the strong federal action endorsed by their constituents of all races. Representing major cities like Chicago, Detroit, and New York, African American Congressmen were quite able to convey the burdens of the Jim Crow system on behalf of their constituents, many who were themselves migrants from the South. Pivotal members like John Conyers, William Dawson, and Adam Clayton Powell played a primary role in advocating the bill's adoption. Their efforts were joined by the white liberal Democrats in the House who arrived in 1965.

Coordinated support from Republican members also proved a crucial part of the coalition. In fact, lobbying from the public and the White House even wrestled "yes" votes from a few moderate white Southerners in states like Tennessee (which also escaped preclearance coverage). Taken together, this broad legislative coalition demonstrated that the VRA was the embodiment of a national consensus. The final bill received 79 votes in the Senate and 328 votes in the House of Representatives.

TECTONIC ELECTORAL SHIFT

The immediate impact of the law's adoption was dramatic. In the few years after the VRA was enacted, registration and voting among blacks across the South rose rapidly. With the aid of federal examiners and poll workers, black registration and participation rates in the states covered by Section 5 soon approached the rates for white voters. And Southern communities like Dallas County soon began utilizing this newfound power by promoting and later electing black political candidates as well.[13] Noting all of these advancements, Congress has gradually expanded the VRA's reach to improve legal protections for voters in the Latino, Native American, and Asian American communities.

A secondary effect of the law is the hastened realignment in the partisan politics of white voters in the South. Even before 1965, Southern states were increasingly replacing conservative Democrats with Republican challengers in Congress. As more black Southerners registered and joined the Democratic Party, more white Southerners were choosing to exit—many of them in favor of the Republican Party.[14] The tectonic electoral shift of this era created the blueprint for today's national GOP, which finds its stronghold in the Southern states. Excepting the distinct pockets of black majority counties and cities that remain zones of Democratic strength, the state politics of the contemporary South is now dominated by Republican candidates, voters, and policy interests.[15]

Passage of the VRA offers three lessons about the legislative process. First, the legislation was directly attributable to the public outcry about the denial of voting rights. Frustrations that grew in the Kennedy era led to moments that exposed the brutality of the Jim Crow political system. Citizen activism catalyzed activity in Washington, D.C., with politicians pursuing an accelerated timeline for action. Not only did the confrontation on the Edmund Pettus Bridge focus Congress, but it also dissuaded an otherwise potent Dixiecrat wing from meddling with or wrecking the legislative effort.

Second, black political power was a crucial tool of the supporters in Congress. While the majority of blacks lived in states where they could not vote, members of Congress who relied on the support of black voters outside of the South were sensitive to public reactions to the Selma Crisis. The public pressure moved not only black Congressmen who had long advocated for federal protections, but it also led liberal and moderate whites in the Democratic caucus to support the bill. Alongside Republicans who also embraced the moral principles espoused in the Fifteenth Amendment, these Democrats helped to form a multiregional and bipartisan majority that reflected an emerging national consensus about voting rights.

Finally, there is also a lesson in this tale about leadership. This transformative moment occurred in large measure because President Johnson knew how to utilize his power to obtain his preferred outcome. His effective management of the bill depended upon his familiarity with the institutional and partisan pressure points in Congress, knowledge that he developed from his years in the Senate. His expertise helped orchestrate the deals that increased the bill's margin of support. Without the assent of at least a few of Congress's crucial gatekeepers, the crown jewel of civil rights laws might have never seen the light of day.

♦ ♦ ♦ ♦ ♦

25. Great Society Milestones: Medicare and Medicaid

by Marilyn Moon

The 1960s proved to be a time of great opportunity for the passage of social legislation. The prosperity of the early half of the decade, empathy for the agenda of an assassinated president, and a large Democratic majority elected to Congress in 1964 all combined to make possible legislation that had languished for years. Yet, even the most ardent supporters of expanding health care were surprised by the breadth of the Medicare and Medicaid programs that passed in 1965.

The creation of a Medicare program for persons over age 65 was the culmination of efforts that trace their roots back to President Harry Truman. The concept of public health insurance enjoyed a history of bipartisan political support. For example, Earl Warren, the Republican Governor of California, proposed compulsory health insurance for the state in 1945.[1] But, public provision of health insurance was not popular during the administration of Dwight Eisenhower—employer-provided insurance continued to expand, and health care costs remained low. And, Republican opposition coupled with the vociferous objections of the American Medical Association (AMA) ended legislative initiatives through the 1950s.

Yet the issue never died. A number of influential leaders in the field of social insurance, including Robert Ball, I. S. Falk, Wilbur Cohen, and Union Leader Nelson Cruikshank, developed a bill that was introduced by Representative Aime Forand (D-RI) in 1957. Well-publicized hearings were held, and the bill, although it failed to pass, represented the rallying point for later Democratic proposals.[2] In 1959, President Eisenhower's Secretary of Health, Education, and Welfare (HEW), Arthur Flemming, released a report on options for providing hospital insurance to Social Security beneficiaries.

HEALTH CARE "HAVES" AND "HAVE NOTS"

By 1960, the United States was separating into two camps: the health care "haves" and "have nots," with the elderly constituting a disproportionate share of the "have nots." Coverage of workers through their employers was becoming increasingly common. By contrast, prior to the passage of the Medicare program, a little over half of all seniors had health insurance.[3] Generally, coverage could be obtained through former employers or from groups such as the American Association of Retired Persons (AARP). Some public support for low-income older Americans was available in the form of Medical Assistance to the Aged (MAA), which began in 1958, but states had been slow to expand the program. Nor were the needy confined just to those with low incomes. Private insurers had shown a reluctance to cover the elderly, so, for many people, insurance was unavailable at any price. As with the uninsured population that spurred the 2010 Affordable Care Act, the problem was both of affordability and availability.

Thus, in this environment, covering senior citizens was a logical starting point for government action. The elderly also were viewed as the most sympathetic population to initially cover. After supporting such legislation in the U.S. Senate, John F. Kennedy pledged in his presidential campaign to offer legislation for health insurance for the aged. Within a month of taking office, President Kennedy delivered to Congress a message calling for such legislation. Bills introduced by Representative Cecil King (D-CA) and Senator Clinton Anderson (D-NM) became the focus of debate throughout the early 1960s.[4] But President Kennedy was thwarted in his efforts.

Not until after Kennedy's assassination did sympathy and support grow for his proposal. The 1964 elections created a lopsided victory for the Democrats in Congress, thus setting the stage for action. The 1965 Medicare legislation represented one of the major planks of President Lyndon Johnson's Great Society, drawing heavily from the earlier proposals. More than five years of strong economic growth also contributed to a sense that the country could afford to take such a step to improve access to care for older Americans.

CONFLICT AND COMPROMISE

An influential player in the passage of these landmark health care laws was Representative Wilbur Mills (D-AR). As the Chairman of the House Ways and Means Committee, Mills was in a commanding position, but initially he was not inclined to act; before the 1964 election he did not have enough votes in the House to pass the legislation, and Mills was not a legislator who took on lost causes. But President Johnson's landslide victory suggested that some health care legislation was inevitable, so Mills took control of the process. Suspense then centered on what shape the plan would take.

Sensing that stonewalling was unlikely to work, opponents began to develop options to limit the scope of health care legislation. For example, the AMA, which had been strongly opposed, lobbied actively for an approach to limit eligibility to the elderly poor to minimize the impact of a public plan. The Republicans embraced this AMA alternative.

Supporters of Medicare viewed such a means-tested approach as dangerous. One of the reasons for focusing on the elderly, in fact, had been to avoid creating a means-tested program. Universal coverage offered an approach that had proven extremely popular with Social Security, and supporters felt this was crucial for Medicare as well. They stressed that the program was social insurance, with universal coverage paid for by broad-based taxes. They also argued that so many elderly were poor that it would not be worthwhile to means test the benefits. The debate over means testing assumed a broader significance, since both sides recognized that this issue would dramatically affect the public's perception of the plan and influence future policy moves in health care. Remnants of this debate still arise today when changes to Medicare are debated.[5]

The breadth of services to be covered also became an issue. The King-Anderson bill, which was the starting point for the legislative proposals in 1962, applied to all persons aged 65 or older, but it was limited to hospital insurance. Proponents of social insurance believed that further benefits could be added later if the public accepted the concept of national insurance for hospital services. Supporters also worried about the costs of the initial undertaking.

Somewhat surprisingly, advocates of expanding coverage came from both sides of the political spectrum. Liberal backers wanted fully comprehensive care. For example, the Forand bill introduced in 1957 had been expansive in its scope. But the major proponents of broader coverage were the conservatives. The AMA/Republican strategy was to argue that it was better to comprehensively cover the elderly poor than to only partially cover everyone. Consequently, their alternative bill was much more inclusive in terms of covered services.

The twin issues of eligibility and coverage threatened to stalemate the entire process. For months, the different parties wrangled and threatened to divide the interest groups lining up for and against various approaches. The AMA and the unions expended enormous sums to influence both public opinion and Congress. In retrospect, the interest groups for the elderly who are thought of as key players today had little influence on these debates. The AARP—which had a membership of more than 10 million in 1964— kept a conspicuously low profile. The AARP testified in 1959 in support of a public-private partnership in which Social Security would serve only as a premium-collecting entity to foster private insurance, which would help the organization sell its own Colonial Penn policies. Only the newly created National Council of Senior Citizens, which was effectively a subsidiary of the AFL-CIO, prominently spoke out for seniors.[6]

SURPRISE HEALTH CARE EXPANSION

When the dust settled, the outcome stunned nearly all observers. Mills's final package went beyond what either side had proposed. His solution to the impasse over competing approaches was to establish two programs: Medicare and Medicaid. Medicare would cover all those over 65, and would be divided into two parts: Part A, Hospital Insurance (which was essentially the original Democratic option introduced in the Kennedy years) and Part B, Supplementary Medical Insurance (a voluntary, but subsidized, insurance plan to cover primarily physician services). Thus, a more comprehensive benefit package was proposed, but with only Part A treated in the same way as Social Security.

The final structure of Medicare, with its large variety of benefits and complicated cost sharing, resulted from the negotiations between the House and the Senate. In particular, Senator Russell Long (D-LA) insisted on changes to add further catastrophic protections, creating a complicated structure of hospital benefits. Part B drew from a proposal from Representative John Byrnes (R-WI),[7] and thus ensured that Republicans had an impact on the final legislation, although perhaps not the impact most Republicans were counting on. Rather than providing a substitute or alternative, their proposal was combined with the Democrats' plan and resulted in a much larger and more comprehensive piece of legislation.

INSURING THE POOR

Medicaid was the big surprise. A new program targeted to low-income persons of all ages who were participating in other welfare programs, Medicaid was much broader in scope than what many believed would come out of the legislation. Medicaid reflected President Johnson's interest in antipoverty policies. It was also quite different than Medicare, creating a joint federal-state program that was consistent with welfare policies of the time that allowed states to determine the level of generosity of the program. The concern expressed by the AMA and the Republicans that those with the lowest incomes needed extra protection became part of the justification for an expanded scope of Medicare benefits, and for the creation of the Medicaid program.

The rules established to govern Medicare intentionally did little to disrupt or change the way health care was practiced or financed in the United States. Claims processing and payment rates were structured to resemble the private sector, and the statutes specifically assured free choice of provider and no interference in the routine practice of medicine. But even though the early emphasis was on ensuring that Medicare would be considered as part of mainstream medical care, there was a concern that the AMA might sink the program. The organization's ominous warnings about dangerous moves toward socialized medicine carried the implicit threat that physicians might shun patients enrolled in either of these new programs. Indeed, in an article in *The New York Times* of August 12, 1965, the Association of American Physicians and Surgeons called for a boycott of Medicare.

Another critical part of the new Medicare program, which is now often overlooked, was the requirement for hospitals to take all comers if they wanted to participate in Medicare—that meant racial integration of hospitals that had long held out against efforts to end racial discrimination. President Johnson's strong push for civil rights was thus reflected in Medicare, and it helped to speed integration of hospitals. At the time, this provision was controversial, and a number of steps were put in place for the initial rollout of Medicare in 1966, including placing National Guard troops on alert to quell any potential unrest. Fortunately, those fears were never realized.[8]

Looking back it's interesting to note how little attention was paid to Medicaid at the time; President Johnson gave a number of speeches concerning Medicare but rarely mentioned Medicaid. All of the focus was on Medicare and how it would work. For example, one prominent letter to the Secretary of HEW by the President spelled out key implementation measures, and the only allusion to Medicaid was insistence that the appropriate cooperative agreements were in place with the states. Medicaid was not even mentioned by name.

POPULAR AND EXPENSIVE REFORMS

Medicare—and to a lesser extent, Medicaid—proved remarkably popular from the beginning. Large numbers of the elderly enrolled, and use of services expanded rapidly. There was no noticeable boycott by health care providers. By May 31, 1966, 17.6 million elderly persons had enrolled in the optional Part B plan—out of approximately 19 million who were eligible. Medicare also led to a major increase in the elderly's use of medical care. For example, hospital discharges averaged 190 per 1,000 elderly persons in 1964, and grew to 350 per 1,000 by 1973.[9] The proportion of the elderly using physician services jumped from 68 percent to 76 percent between 1963 and 1970.[10]

Medicaid's history has also been one of growth, but its progress has been less consistent because it depended upon the willingness of states to partner with the federal government. A number of states retained very restrictive policies toward the poor, and payment levels to providers were held well below private rates. Certain Medicaid benefits are federally mandated; beyond that, the states decide whether to cover additional services and additional beneficiaries. The extensive efforts to make Medicare a part of the mainstream medical care system from the beginning did not apply to Medicaid. Consequently, access of the poor to care has always lagged behind that for the elderly.

As costs of health care escalated into the 1970s, the costs of the Medicaid and Medicare programs grew much faster than anticipated, raising concerns about the long-term affordability of both programs. Indeed, critics at the time warned of the danger of increasing health care costs—criticism that proved well founded. These issues are also very much a part of today's debates over the future of the two programs.

It is tempting to look to Medicare and Medicaid for lessons that can be applied to the 2010 Affordable Care Act. Both pieces of legislation were controversial and faced questions about their ultimate affordability and acceptability to the public. Today Medicare and Medicaid are often criticized for their size and some of their characteristics, but it is rare for any politician or pundit to suggest total repeal; however, that was not the case in the earliest days of the programs. While they enjoyed some bipartisan support, Medicare and Medicaid still faced fierce opposition on the part of many Republicans. The Republican opposition was not nearly as vociferous after Medicare and Medicaid became law, but it is also the case that Medicare failed to usher in an era of universal health care coverage for all Americans that some supporters originally envisioned.

Before 1965, supporters of a public health insurance program for seniors were not able to secure its passage; after a short period of goodwill that brought about sweeping domestic legislation under President Johnson, the window of opportunity closed again. Over time, both Medicare and Medicaid have been expanded and have proven immensely popular overall, but there have been few times since 1965 when another sweeping change in health care policy seemed possible. Indeed, many observers of the Affordable Care Act have noted that its structure is designed to change our health care system in a much more conservative and incremental fashion than what was undertaken in 1965.

◆ ◆ ◆ ◆ ◆

26. The Power of the Purse: Rethinking Runaway Debt and a Broken Budgeting Process

by Jason J. Fichtner

Since the founding of the country there have been political battles over the budget. Yet, the seeds of today's current budget dysfunction were sown with the passage of the Congressional Budget and Impoundment Control Act of 1974. While various amendments to the 1974 Budget Act have attempted to improve the budgeting process, Congress's attempts to fix the dysfunction have produced only temporary solutions, and the budget battles get worse and worse. The 1974 legislation sought to promote "regular order" to authorize and appropriate spending for the federal government. Forty years later, the new normal appears to be budgeting through crisis and brinkmanship, where deals are only passed at the last minute (or after) and with great political and economic cost.

Is the federal budget process broken? Washington has given many observers, at home and around the world, good reason to think so. In October 2013, for the first time in almost two decades, the federal government partially shut down for 16 days. As a result of the shutdown, approximately 800,000 federal employees were furloughed. To add insult to injury, Congress also failed to raise the government's ability to borrow money. The so-called debt ceiling was instead used as a negotiation tool by a Republican majority in the U.S. House of Representatives in an attempt to force a Democratic President to defund his signature health care legislation.

As alarming as the recent breakdown in governance has been, the broader picture is even more alarming. Over the past several years, Congress has all but abandoned the existing budget process. Both chambers have failed to regularly pass—or in some cases, even to write—their respective budget resolutions, which set the overall framework for spending levels and revenue targets. Without budget resolutions passed by the House and Senate, the two chambers cannot form a conference committee, where selected members meet to work out the differences between budget resolutions. In fact, the last budget conference that took place through regular order was in 2009, for the 2010 fiscal year budget resolution, and that's because Democrats held the majority of both the House and Senate. Among other problems, Congress's regular failure to produce a budget conference report has made it unable to utilize "reconciliation"—a procedure that makes it easier to pass changes to mandatory programs and tax law.

Proper budgeting is about making trade-offs between competing wants and limited resources, and it requires planning, setting priorities, and making difficult decisions. But the current budget process no longer appears capable of dealing with today's heightened political partisanship, especially when there is split political control of Congress. Because there is no legal penalty for failing to follow the current budget process, there is no mechanism to force compliance or compromise. Instead, partisan bickering and brinkmanship has become the norm.

Just since 2011 there have been four budget crises: April 2011, when Republicans threatened to shut down the government unless Democrats agreed to small spending cuts; August 2011, when Republicans threatened not to raise the debt ceiling; December 2012, when various tax and spending provisions were set to expire at the end of the year, creating the so-called fiscal cliff crisis; and October 2013, when the government did shut down due to Congress's inability to pass a budget, coupled with another fight over the debt ceiling. Although the bipartisan budget agreement reached in December 2013 is a step in the right direction, it remains to be seen whether this might signal a return to regular order, or whether it is simply an aberration.

THE POWER OF THE PURSE:
THE BUDGET ACT OF 1974

The Constitution sets forth that Congress has the power to raise taxes and authorize the borrowing of money. It states: "No money shall be drawn from the Treasury, but in Consequence of Appropriations made by Law." In other words, Congress has the "power of the purse" to control the federal government's spending. Congress has also used the power of the purse as a means to curb Executive Branch power.

The current federal budget process is framed by the Congressional Budget and Impoundment Control Act of 1974, which came about in part because of a political power struggle between the Legislative and Executive Branches. Through a process called "impoundment," President Nixon refused to spend approximately $12 billion that Congress had authorized and appropriated for 1973–1974. With the White House in a weakened position due to the Watergate scandal, Congress was able to pass and persuade President Nixon to sign the 1974 Budget Act, which placed more centralized power over the budget process in the hands of Congress. While the 1974 Budget Act has been amended several times, it remains the fundamental framework in place today.[1]

Both branches have wrestled for control of the budget process since the founding of the country, as the checks and balances inherent in the Constitution provided that all spending bills must originate in Congress, but the Executive Branch is tasked with carrying out laws and administering the budget. By shifting primary control of the federal budget to Congress, the 1974 Budget Act created a process whereby all 535 Members of Congress have a say in the budget, putting a premium on the art of negotiation and compromise.

The 1974 Budget Act created the Congressional Budget Office and a Budget Committee in both the House of Representatives and in the Senate, and moved the start of the fiscal year from June 1 to October 1—presumably to give Congress and the President more time to work on budget negotiations. The 1974 Budget Act also set up a timeline for the budget process. The President kicks off the process by submitting a budget to Congress on or before the first Monday in February. The President's budget sets forth the spending priorities of the President and Executive Branch agencies. In response to the President's budget, Congress must pass a budget resolution that sets revenue and spending totals for the coming fiscal year. The budget resolution is not a law, as it is not sent to the President for signature or veto. However, the budget resolution provides an important framework in which the Congress must consider all of the spending and revenue-related bills.

The budget resolution is supposed to be passed by April 15. Though there is no penalty for failing to pass a budget resolution on time, or even at all, the budget resolution provides much-needed structure for Congress to consider appropriations bills. Without a congressional budget resolution in place, the government loses much-needed structure to keep the budget process moving and the system of governance working.

After a budget resolution, Congress must then pass separate appropriations bills (currently there are 12) to fund the various activities of the government. These bills are for discretionary spending, such as defense, education, and transportation. Once the appropriations bills are passed by the House and the Senate, any disagreements are supposed to be worked out in a conference committee. The House and Senate then each vote on identical bills, which if passed are sent to the President for signature. Though Congress has traditionally considered each appropriations bill separately, recently Congress has considered omnibus appropriations, where separate appropriations bills are combined into one spending bill to smooth passage. If Congress fails to pass the 12 regular appropriations bills, or an omnibus bill, before the start of a new fiscal year, a "continuing resolution" (CR) can be passed for a specified period of time (or for the entire year) to provide continual funding for the government while budget negotiations continue.

Mandatory spending, which makes up the vast majority of the federal budget and includes interest on the national debt, Social Security, Medicare, and Medicaid, is not part of the annual budget process. The 12 appropriations bills deal with discretionary spending only. Although Congress can take up review of entitlement programs at any time, the 1974 Budget Act largely left the annual funding of mandatory spending programs unaffected and essentially set them on automatic pilot. Tax laws are also considered to be "mandatory." Thus, the funding for mandatory activities, such as Social Security, as well as tax laws, generally continues from year to year unless Congress passes legislation to change the law.

Though not formally part of the budget process, Congress often used "earmarks," or legislative provisions directing funds to be spent on specific projects, to help convince members of Congress to vote for appropriations bills. For example, in exchange for a member's vote on an appropriation bill, an earmark might be included directing spending for a road or bridge in that member's congressional district. Often derided as "congressional pork," earmarks came to be viewed as unseemly by the public; a congressional version of "you scratch my back and I'll scratch yours." Although earmarks often provide legitimate direction by Congress on where federal funds should be spent, the traditional use of earmarks has generally been banned since 2010.

A BROKEN SYSTEM

The current tensions in the budget process resulting from rising debt and an increasingly partisan Congress are creating an environment where negotiation and compromise appear to be almost impossible. The end result has been lack of a budget. For example, in 2010, and for the first time since adopting budget reform rules in 1974, both chambers of Congress separately failed to pass their own annual budget resolution, the overall budget framework used to pass annual appropriation bills. Therefore, to fund government operations for the 2011 fiscal year, Congress passed a CR allowing the government to continue spending at FY 2010 levels for several weeks. Another CR had to be passed allowing the continuation of these funding levels through March 4. In the end, the federal government's 2011 fiscal year was funded by a series of CRs maintaining funding at or near FY 2010 levels.

Ultimately, the budget negotiations initially led by House Speaker John Boehner (R-OH) and President Barack Obama resulted in the passage of the Budget Control Act of 2011,[2] but only after a very tense legislative standoff that led to the threat of a government shutdown and a debt ceiling crisis. The Budget Control Act of 2011 created the Joint Select Committee on Deficit Reduction (more popularly known as the "Super Committee"). If a plan could not be produced that would pass both chambers of Congress and be signed by the President, then a process called "sequestration" would automatically begin reducing government outlays. As a result of the inability to pass a long-term deficit reduction plan—what was once thought to be an unthinkable outcome—a sequester resulting in across-the-board spending cuts loomed at the beginning of 2013.

As the end of the 2012 calendar year approached, a new, but well foreseen, crisis presented itself. The tax cuts passed under President Bush were once again set to expire—this time at the end of 2012. Tense negotiations and political battles once again brewed as Congress and the President needed the crisis of expiring tax provisions to force a deal.

The American Taxpayer Relief Act of 2012[3] was passed not in 2012, but on January 1, 2013. The Act delayed the spending reductions set to begin January 2, 2013 from sequester to March 1, 2013. There was hope that Congress and the President could use the time to find a budget deal to avoid or modify sequestration. No such deal came about, however, and the sequester level cuts began to take place in 2013.

The budget battles of the last few years have created distrust and animosity among the political parties, and, to an extent, between the Congress and the President. The result is an increasingly partisan political environment where "budgeting" is no longer the norm. The Congress and the President were once again unable to pass regular appropriations bills for the 2014 fiscal year, which began October 1, 2013. The result was a government shutdown lasting 16 days, and yet another debt ceiling crisis.

This level of dysfunctional partisanship does not just happen overnight. And while the 1974 Budget Act set forth the framework for today's budget process, the Act is not the only reason that politicians have been unable to recently pass a budget. Part of the problem rests in how much of federal spending is devoted to mandatory spending and currently walled off from the annual budget process in the first place.

MORE MANDATORY SPENDING, LESS BUDGETING

Since the financial crisis of 2008, the federal government has vastly increased spending. In fiscal year 2007, before the recession, the federal government had a $163 billion deficit. The federal gross national debt was $9 trillion. For fiscal year 2012, the federal government had a $1.1 trillion deficit, which declined to $680 billion in fiscal year 2013. While debt held by the public was approximately $12 trillion in fiscal year 2013, or 72 percent of gross domestic product (GDP), the national gross debt, which includes bonds such as those held in the Social Security trust fund, was over $16.7 trillion in 2013, or over 100 percent of GDP.[4]

In response to the increasing federal debt, both political parties have called for reducing the deficit and slowing the growth of federal debt. From a political standpoint, many Republicans have viewed the increase in national spending and borrowing as a national crisis and have vowed to do whatever it takes to reduce federal spending, while holding down tax revenues. In general, Democrats have held that the government should continue to spend at a level above the long-term U.S. average because the needs of the country have grown as the country has grown, and further have advocated for higher tax revenues to support higher levels of government spending. The middle ground between those two positions has steadily declined, and the vastly divergent views of the two main ruling political parties have made finding a compromise difficult, if not impossible. Moreover, given the public distaste for both higher taxes and/or large cuts in social programs, there is little incentive for members of Congress to do anything other than the kick the can down the road.

The nation's addiction to deficit financing is clear when one considers the past 10 years. As a share of the economy, federal receipts from taxes have ranged from a low of 14.9 percent of GDP in 2010 to a high of 20.6 percent in 2000. On the other hand, federal outlays have ranged from 18.2 percent of GDP in 2000 to a high of 25.0 percent in 2009. The reduction in tax revenues was partly due to the tax-reform laws of 2001 and 2003, as well as the recent recession, although tax revenues are expected to increase as the economy recovers.[5]

Mandatory spending, mainly through entitlements and interest payments on the national debt, are the biggest fiscal problems facing the nation. The ability to fund discretionary spending has been made more difficult, for instance, as mandatory spending explodes and crowds out the ability of federal dollars to support discretionary spending.

In 1970, the federal government spent $900 billion (in 2011 adjusted dollars). Of that, 62 percent or $0.62 of every $1 was spent on discretionary spending. Mandatory spending was only 38 percent (31 percent for entitlement programs such as Social Security, Medicare and Medicaid; and seven percent for interest payments on the gross debt). In 2011, a whopping 56 percent of federal spending was devoted to mandatory spending, 63 percent if one includes interest on the debt, known as "servicing the debt."[6]

Meanwhile, the share of federal spending that Congress has "discretion" over has markedly decreased. While total nominal dollars might increase each year along with a larger economy, instead of having 62 cents of every dollar to fund discretionary programs as was the case in 1970, now only 37 cents is available. Imagine a pack of hungry wolves that over time finds the food source it's sharing diminish. Are the wolves likely to behave nicely and continue to share? Or are they likely to fight over the diminishing share? Again, the outcome seems self-evident.

The problems of deficit spending and a broken budgeting process are bound to only get worse as the share of funds available for discretionary spending continues to decline, and mandatory spending continues to explode. In 2050, it is estimated[7] that mandatory spending will take up 60 percent of total spending, but a whopping 82 percent when servicing the national debt is taken into account. This leaves only 18 percent of total outlays under the annual discretion of Congress and subject to the current budget process. How well will the wolves get along then?

CONCLUSION

As stressed earlier, proper budgeting requires planning, setting priorities, and making decisions—it is about making trade-offs between competing wants and limited resources. As entitlement spending grows it will crowd out discretionary spending, the very spending that Congress is supposed to budget through normal authorization and appropriation bills. Controlling the increase in the runaway growth of mandatory expenditures will require tough choices that many politicians seem unable or unwilling to make, and that the public may or may not support.

Without question, our deficits and debt need to be brought under control. Delaying the tough choices will only require even tougher and harder choices down the road. The longer we wait, the more combative and dysfunctional the U.S. political system will become. If we fail to reform the budget process, including finding a way to more frequently review and approve entitlement spending, we might in the future look back at the government shutdown of 2013 as the good old days.

◆ ◆ ◆ ◆ ◆

27. Myth and Reality of the Safety Net: The 1983 Social Security Reforms

by Rudolph G. Penner

As Congress considers once again how to make Social Security financially viable in the long run, it is instructive to look at the last time Congress undertook reform in 1983. Back then, there were also partisan battles and intense ideological differences over how to fix Social Security, but congressional leaders showed a desire to accomplish something and a willingness to compromise without either side having to completely abandon its ideological principles.

In 1983 everyone knew that reform was urgently needed. The cost of benefits began to exceed the income of Social Security's Old Age and Survivors Insurance (OASI) trust fund in the mid-1970s, and the fund was declining rapidly. By 1982 the fund balance was only one-third of its peak in 1975, and it was clear that the trust fund would soon be empty. The elderly population panicked at the thought of Social Security going "broke" and imperiling their benefits.

In a sense it was an artificial crisis in that no component of the federal government had ever actually gone "broke." The government could have continued paying full benefits even with an empty trust fund by simply transferring general revenues to the system. But such action would have radically altered the philosophy underlying Social Security.

From its beginning, benefits had been financed by dedicated revenues, the bulk of which come from the payroll tax. That created the impression among current and future beneficiaries that they paid for their benefits. Although this was not true for a majority of beneficiaries in 1983, the myth that people paid for their benefits is very powerful—it undoubtedly contributes to the strong political support for the system. It was clear to politicians that they had to fix the system without changing its fundamental characteristics.

A POLITICAL FIRESTORM

Soon after taking office in 1981, the Reagan Administration reacted to Social Security's financial problems by proposing benefit cuts that were focused on early retirees. The benefit cut for someone retiring at age 62 was to be more than 30 percent.

Reagan Administration officials gave congressional leaders little warning before making their proposal, however, and they made almost no attempt to educate the public. A political firestorm ensued, leaving President Reagan with few allies. He was strongly opposed by the American Association of Retired People, the AFL-CIO, and numerous other interest groups. There was absolutely no chance that Congress would approve his proposed reforms.

The President responded in September 1981 by creating a 15-member, bipartisan National Commission on Social Security Reform. The Commission was to report by the end of 1982—conveniently after the congressional elections. The Commission was chaired by Alan Greenspan, who had been highly respected as Chairman of the Council of Economic Advisers in the Ford Administration. Members were appointed by the President, Speaker Thomas P. "Tip" O'Neill (D-MA) of the Democratically controlled House, and Howard Baker (R-TN), Majority Leader of the Republican Senate. Each chose both Republican and Democratic members. Nine of the 15 were politicians who either were or had recently been members of the Senate or House. Their political experience was crucial to the eventual success of the commission. All members were knowledgeable about the structure of Social Security and the nature of its financial problems.

As the deliberations wore on, it appeared the Social Security Reform Commission would be an abject failure. Chairman Greenspan was especially depressed. Democrats and Republicans seemed to be as far apart as today's legislators, with the Democrats adamantly opposing benefit cuts and the Republicans opposing payroll tax increases just as passionately. The Commission requested that its deadline be extended by one month. It was given two weeks.

In early January 1983, Senator Robert Dole (R-KS), a Commission member and Chairman of the Senate Finance Committee, wrote an op-ed in *The New York Times* hinting that tax increases might play a role in solving Social Security's problems. Senator Daniel P. Moynihan (D-OK) recognized this as a crack in the Republican wall of opposition to revenue increases and immediately seized the opportunity. With doubts running high that the whole Commission could reach a compromise, a subgroup formed that included Moynihan, Dole, Robert Ball (the founding Commissioner of the Social Security system and a strong defender of scheduled benefits), and Representative Barber Conable (R-NY), the ranking member on the House Ways and Means Committee.

The subgroup began intense discussions with White House Chief of Staff James Baker, his aides Richard Darman and Kenneth Duberstein, and Office of Management and Budget Director David Stockman. They reached a compromise that essentially split the difference between Democrats and Republicans. A cost-of-living adjustment to benefits was delayed six months, saving $40 billion over the rest of the 1980s. The acceleration of an already-scheduled tax increase brought in $40 billion in extra revenues. An additional $30 billion was raised by making 50 percent of benefits taxable for middle-class and high-income recipients. It was the first time any Social Security benefits were subjected to taxation. Democrats called that a revenue increase, while Republicans called it a benefit reduction. Coverage was expanded by bringing in new federal civil servants, while state and local civil servants already in the system were prevented from withdrawing. Taxes were also raised on the self-employed, and a general revenue transfer helped pay the benefits of former military personnel.

Although a majority of the commission had been excluded from the final deliberations, they did not seem to resent it. The Commission approved the plan by a lopsided 12–3 margin. The three dissenters were conservatives who disapproved of the tax increases. The Congress quickly debated the Committee recommendations. In the Senate, the debate was expedited by an informal rule promulgated by Senator Dole stating that anyone opposing the recommendations had to come up with a solution of their own.

RAISING THE RETIREMENT AGE

Something remarkable happened during the congressional debate. Commissions are generally formed to solve national problems when Congress is perceived as lacking the courage to vote for painful solutions. Commissions of experts are thus supposed to give politicians the cover to do what needs to be done. In the end, however, the Greenspan Commission was more cautious than Congress. Its proposals did not solve Social Security's financial problems for the entire 75-year period, which was the traditional time horizon for judging the system's financial viability.

During the House debate, Representative J. J. Pickle (D-TX), Chairman of the Ways and Means Subcommittee that dealt with Social Security, added a provision that would very gradually raise the normal retirement age (NRA) from 65 to 67. It began to increase for those reaching age 62 in 2000, and would not reach 67 until 2022. This provision did more to improve the financial health of Social Security than any single recommendation of the Commission. The gradual nature of the increase in the NRA meant that no one would be affected for 17 years, thus providing plenty of time for those approaching retirement to adjust their plans. Although the Greenspan recommendations and the Pickle amendment were vigorously attacked from right and left, Congress passed the Greenspan recommendations and the Pickle amendment survived the House-Senate conference, beating out a weaker Senate proposal to increase the NRA to 66. Throughout the congressional debate, President Reagan and Speaker O'Neill remained steadfast in support of the Commission recommendations. They had quietly agreed before the Commission was formed that neither would attack the Commission proposals. Clearly the reforms would have been doomed if either Reagan or O'Neill had opposed them. According to Alan Greenspan, the Reagan-O'Neill agreement was the single most important factor leading to the success of the reforms.

Although the 1983 reforms were generally thought to keep the Social Security trust financially healthy for 75 years, it was clear that the reality fell short of that goal. The reforms led to large projected surpluses early in the 75-year period, for instance, but large deficits late in the period. Consequently, as each year went by, the 75-year time horizon lost one surplus year and gained one deficit year. All else being equal, the actuarial balance facing the fund would gradually deteriorate.

But all else did not remain equal. The financial outlook worsened for other reasons as well. The economic and demographic projections made at the time of the reforms, for instance, proved to be too optimistic. In successive trustees' reports, the estimated year that the combined Old Age Survivors and Disability Insurance (OASDI) trust funds would be depleted crept closer. In the 1983 trustee report, the estimated trust fund depletion date was 2058. By the time the 1994 trustee report was published, the year of reckoning had moved forward to 2029. Since then the estimated depletion date has swung up and down depending on the business cycle, with the 2013 trustee report estimating that the combined funds will be depleted by 2033, and the OASI fund by 2035—hence the need for yet another round of reforms.

MARSHALING POLITICAL WILL

Does the experience with the Greenspan Commission suggest that a new commission might be the answer to our current fiscal woes? We have already had the Simpson-Bowles Commission and the Domenici-Rivlin Commission, along with numerous other committees and groups suggesting fiscal reforms in general and, more specifically, Social Security reforms.

Yet, it cannot really be said that the Greenspan Commission was primarily responsible for the success of 1983 reforms. The Commission was unwieldy, and it was not until a subgroup broke off that real progress was made. Moreover, the Commission report was cautious, and failed to restore the financial health of Social Security for the entire 75-year period traditionally used by the system's trustees. It took courageous actions by the Congress to enhance the Commission report and make it much more meaningful.

Although the Commission did not provide sufficient momentum to enact the reforms, it was important in getting the ball rolling. Not only did the Commission bring together able people from diverse backgrounds who represented very different interest groups, but it also contained especially talented legislators such as Robert Dole, Daniel Moynihan, and Barber Conable. Once the Commission finally arrived at a conclusion, it thus had significant clout. But the ball had to be passed to the Congress and people like Danny Rostenkowski and J. J. Pickle. And most important, President Reagan and Speaker O'Neill had to stay out of the way as the reform ball rolled forward.

While none of the main actors were purely nonpartisan, they were certainly highly skilled. Confronted by a major problem, they were determined to fix it. They compromised without surrendering their partisan credentials. Neither side won a total ideological victory, and yet neither side suffered a total defeat. President Reagan put it well saying that "[T]he essence of bipartisanship is to give up a little to get a lot. . . . I think we've got a great deal."

Today it is once again apparent that Social Security is financially unsustainable in the long run, with current estimates predicting that the OASI trust fund will run dry in 2035. The situation is not as urgent as in 1983, however, and the reforms necessary to make the system financially viable will be much less painful if undertaken sooner rather than later. Unfortunately, it is difficult to persuade politicians to prescribe painful medicine to the voting public unless the malady is acute.

An even greater concern is that today's intense partisan and ideological battles are more paralyzing than in 1983. However, the clear lesson of the Social Security reforms of three decades ago is that at some point the politician's desire to score partisan points has to be trumped by the public servant's strong desire to accomplish difficult things on behalf of the public good.

◆　◆　◆　◆　◆

28. Bygone Bipartisanship: The Tax Reform Act of 1986

by Richard Cohen

Four months after winning reelection in a landslide, President Ronald Reagan launched a battle to overhaul federal income taxes, which he hoped would be a signature domestic accomplishment of his second term. In doing so, he formed an unlikely bipartisan alliance with U.S. House Committee on Ways and Means Chairman Dan Rostenkowski (D-IL), a product of the Chicago political machine. Then the House and Senate committee chairmen with deep understanding of the relevant issues used the considerable power of their personalities to ultimately seal the deal. The script they wrote for the dramatic passage of the Tax Reform Act of 1986 thus reads today like a drama from a bygone era.

Both men made clear at the time the important stakes involved in overhauling a tax code that helps define the relationship between citizens and their government. "No other issue goes so directly to the heart of our economic life," Reagan said in his nationally broadcast Oval Office speech on May 28, 1985. "A second American revolution for hope and opportunity is gathering force again—a peaceful revolution, but born of popular resentment against a tax system that is unwise, unwanted and unfair." In his follow-up speech from the Capitol that evening, Rostenkowski told Americans that President Reagan would find plenty of Democratic support for his objective to make the tax code "simple and fair." And he memorably requested them to "write Rosty" in Washington with their support. "The post office will get it to me."

Those opening speeches set the stage for a classic legislative showdown. With the reelection mandate that came from having won 49 states, Reagan set the agenda on a topic that deeply affected most Americans. A Democratic-controlled House and a Republican-controlled Senate responded with a year-long struggle to hammer out the specific provisions. The devil was in the details of the complex legislative horse-trading, and both sides were forced to overcome internal divisions in each party resulting from grassroots, constituent, and lobbying pressures.

Momentum was maintained by critics on both sides of the political aisle who complained that the tax code was riddled with loopholes. Regardless of their original intention, those loopholes had accumulated over time, creating an arcane and overly complex system that made business compliance difficult and undermined public support. Even the major tax cuts that Reagan successfully sought after he became President in 1981—which cut most individual taxes by 25 percent, and reduced the top rate to 50 percent of income—left those loopholes mostly intact.

Both Reagan and Rostenkowski understood the public's intense dissatisfaction with the tax code. Sizeable portions of the public believed taxes were simply too high, while others perceived inequities that too often favored the wealthy. Neither politician wanted the other political party to gain partisan advantage from seizing on that dissatisfaction, and coming to own a popular cause. So when objections from congressional Democrats or Republicans threatened the deal, the committee barons stepped in to squelch the problem with some old-fashioned head-knocking. More junior lawmakers who supported reforms were likewise encouraged in a new style of legislative entrepreneurship, and they proposed some initial outlines of the proposal.

Inevitably, neither Republicans nor Democrats were fully satisfied with all the compromises they were each forced to make to win passage. Despite intense lobbying campaigns, some powerful special-interest groups with deep pockets and long memories were also displeased about losing their often narrowly crafted tax breaks. Despite the unhappiness, however, the effort to reform the tax code demonstrated that the cynics were wrong: Washington could put partisanship aside to conduct the public's business on an issue that had a real impact on the lives of average Americans. In that way, Reagan and Rostenkowski created one of the notable feel-good moments in modern legislative history.

LONG SHOT FROM A BASKETBALL STAR

The project to reform the tax code was actually launched by first-term Senator Bill Bradley (D-NJ), who was best known as a college and professional basketball star. With an intellect honed by his studies at Princeton and Oxford, Bradley spoke with many experts and uncovered countless examples of unfairness and economic inefficiency in the Internal Revenue Code.

Bradley filed his initial proposal in 1982 with Representative Richard Gephardt (D-MO), a rising star in the House. Their plan featured three core elements premised on overall lower tax rates: elimination of numerous tax breaks and loopholes; reliance on the marketplace to allocate economic resources; and adherence to the principle that corporations and the wealthy should pay more, so that the total plan would be revenue-neutral for the Treasury. "There was something in there for both Democrats and Republicans," Bradley said years later. "Republicans wanted lower rates, and Democrats wanted fewer loopholes. And there was an agreement that together we could get both."[1]

Reagan took the next key step in his January 1984 State of the Union address to Congress, when he directed Treasury Secretary Donald Regan to prepare a plan to simplify the tax code and "make the tax base broader, so personal tax rates could come down, not go up." To the laughter of many Democrats, he gave Treasury a December 1984 deadline, which assumed his reelection and conveniently removed the specifics of tax reform as an issue in the 1984 presidential election campaign. In fact, during that campaign, Democratic presidential nominee Walter Mondale missed an opportunity to distance himself from Washington's special-interest groups when he rejected Bradley's pleas to embrace his initiative. In effect, Mondale permitted Reagan to retain his outsider appeal by seeking reelection championing tax reform against vested interests in Washington.

The Treasury plan was unveiled shortly after the election, and Reagan importantly made Treasury Secretary Regan his White House chief of staff, sending the more politically attuned James Baker to run the Treasury Department. Baker and his deputy Richard Darman, a savvy Washington insider, then tinkered with Regan's earlier plan to make it more acceptable to some key groups—notably the business community.

The Treasury plan established a blueprint for Congress to use in writing the legislation and negotiating the final deals. Leveraging their expertise and clout on tax issues, House and Senate chairmen showed deal-making skills and the requisite trust that each had built with other members. Though neither had previously shown much interest in tax reform, both Rostenkowski and his Senate counterpart Bob Packwood (R-OR) were centrists who were able to work with each other and across the aisle more generally. This dynamic created tensions in their respective caucuses, however, and Packwood had the further challenge of working with the conservative Republican in the White House.

In some ways, the two key congressional players were also studies in contrast. Rostenkowski was an old-style bargainer who rarely focused on policy details but enjoyed working the back rooms with both parties—and especially with top Executive Branch officials. As 1985 began, his chief objective was to reduce the large federal deficit. Packwood was new to his post of U.S. Senate Committee on Finance chairman, and was initially reluctant to take command of the tax overhaul, even though he was familiar with tax issues and styled himself a policy maven. Packwood also benefited from the advice and assistance of the new Senate Majority Leader Robert Dole (R-KS), who had previously chaired the Finance Committee and understood the obstacles facing tax reform.

Both chairmen deferred to Reagan on the broad outlines but took control of negotiations in their committees on the details. They quickly discovered that while the general idea of tax reform had wide support, serious objections were quickly raised when their panels delved into the specifics. Each was thus forced to maneuver a Perils-of-Pauline obstacle course, in which other committee members were reluctant to upend the status quo or make tough decisions. At several points, the chairmen faced internal revolts and were forced to step back and craft new strategies and workarounds. Failure beckoned at every obstacle, especially when each was accompanied by a drumbeat of daily news coverage that dwelled on the incremental problems, rather than the broader appeal of tax reform.[2]

BUILDING CONSENSUS

Abiding by the constitutional requirement that the House initiate tax legislation, Rostenkowski sought the support of Ways and Means members—especially Democrats—by dangling "incentives" (often parochial tax provisions) and threatening punishment of those who opposed him. Securing committee support from reluctant members required all of the negotiating skills of one of Congress's legendary deal-makers. (See "Dan Rostenkowski: The Deal-Maker," Chapter 8.)

After Representative Ronnie Flippo (D-AL) won committee approval of his amendment to expand a tax break for banks, for instance, Rostenkowski was initially stymied in seeking to reverse the vote. Following lengthy private discussions and some of Rosty's signature arm-twisting, Flippo agreed to modify his proposal so it would not apply to the nation's biggest banks. Later, Representative Raymond McGrath (R-NY) said that he would support the bill only if it protected the deductibility of state sales taxes, which was vital to his home state. Rostenkowski promised his support. Later he was forced to drop that provision in the final negotiations, with Rostenkowski telling the disappointed McGrath, "Ray, I told you I will be with you until the end. This is the end."[3]

Opposition to Packwood in the Finance Committee was at least as formidable. In a widely circulated incident, the Senate chairman took his Chief of Staff Bill Diefenderfer to lunch at a Capitol Hill bar to discuss how they could rescue tax reform from lobbyists' attacks. While consuming two pitchers of beer, they agreed on a radical shift in strategy: Packwood decided to offer a plan with sweeping removal of tax breaks, rather than continue fighting individual skirmishes on each interest group's favored provision. Under intense pressure from Reagan and public opinion, committee members set aside their hesitation and adopted Packwood's approach.

House Republicans initially revolted against the bill and delivered a stinging setback when it reached the House floor in December 1985, with some of them objecting that Democrats had not pushed for sufficient reforms. Reagan visited Capitol Hill to appeal privately for their support. He agreed that the bill crafted by the Ways and Means Committee was disappointing, including its 38 percent top rate, but he asked for their provisional support with the promise that it eventually would be strengthened.

Overriding the objections from some Democrats who had little interest in bailing out Reagan, Speaker Tip O'Neill (D-MA) said that he would permit a second House vote only if at least 50 Republicans agreed to back the measure. On the key procedural vote, with some arm-twisting by GOP leaders, 70 Republicans voted in favor. Representative Jack Kemp (R-NY), the former pro football quarterback who was a leading proponent of the 1981 tax cuts, played a vital role in securing that support.

"The way this legislation was fashioned, careening between extinction and dramatic revival, wasn't a very neat or efficient process; the dance of legislation rarely is," wrote veteran Washington journalist Albert R. Hunt. "Compared to the Tax Reform Act of 1986, a sausage factory is tidy and orderly."[4]

BIPARTISANSHIP FROM A BYGONE ERA

A House-Senate conference committee crafted the final version of the bill during several weeks of grueling backroom negotiations in the summer of 1986. In a key early move, Rostenkowski agreed to strive for the 27 percent top rate in the Senate-passed bill in exchange for Packwood's pledge to accept many of the corporate-tax loophole closings that the House had approved. After Rostenkowski demanded the removal of all Treasury Department officials from the final negotiations, the two chairmen and a few senior aides privately reached the final deals—including two tax brackets, of 15 and 28 percent.

The House and Senate approved that agreement with broad support. Before an enthusiastic crowd outside the White House, an upbeat Reagan signed the measure while surrounded by its bipartisan authors. "The journey has been long and many said we'd never make it to the end, but as usual the pessimists left one thing out of their calculation—the American people," he said.

In these legislative machinations, House and Senate chairmen—with intimate knowledge of the issues and support from their committees—wrote the final bill, not party leaders. They operated mostly outside of public view, and with minimal partisan attacks or game-playing from either side. And they built real bipartisan coalitions, with some support from lobbyists.

Whether you favor it or not, that consensus-building approach to handling major legislation stands in marked contrast to the process politically divided Congresses have adopted in recent years. These days, leaders in both parties increasingly wield the greatest influence on major legislation as opposed to committee chairmen. In many cases, the party-line approach and views of those leaders are closer to those of rank-and-file lawmakers than were the more independent Rostenkowski and Packwood. More broadly, there is little doubt that the elevation of partisan goals over policy expertise can poorly serve the public interest.

In the final analysis, the enactment of the Tax Reform Act did not play to either party's political advantage. The measure received little attention, for instance, in subsequent congressional and presidential campaigns. For that matter, its immediate economic impact was also somewhat limited. According to economic scholar Henry Aaron of the Brookings Institution, nothing happened in the three years following its enactment "to confirm either the worst fears of its opponents or the best hopes of its supporters." Investment, savings rates and employment showed modest change. Nor were the reforms encased in the Tax Reform Act particularly long lasting. Subsequent major tax legislation under Presidents Bill Clinton, George W. Bush, and Barack Obama restored tax loopholes and reversed some of the 1986 base-broadening. "Two decades later, the changes wrought by the 1986 act have proven neither revolutionary nor stable," wrote Yale University law professor Michael J. Graetz. "The 1986 act did enhance both the equity and efficiency of the income tax, but it was far from the purist cleansing of the tax code that some of its more ardent admirers implied."[6]

Enactment of the 1986 law, however, was a marker for an era when Republicans and Democrats viewed good government as good politics. Even with widespread charges of excessive partisanship lodged against both Reagan and congressional Democratic leaders at the time, each side showed that Washington could respond to public pressure and fix long-standing policy inequities.

Given the backsliding from the 1986 tax reform and the additions of loop-holes over the years, more work surely is needed to improve today's tax code to make it less complex and its enforcement by the Internal Revenue Service more evenhanded. As the tax-writing committees contemplate another round of reforms, however, they should consider the lessons of a bygone era when strong presidential leadership was met with a resolute congressional response. The result was the crafting of major legislation that improved the lives of ordinary Americans, however incrementally.

◆ ◆ ◆ ◆ ◆

29. Grand Bargain or Grand Collapse: The Case of Immigration Reform

by Muzaffar Chishti and Charles Kamasaki

Congress enacts major immigration reforms only rarely, in part because the issue inevitably evokes, in the words of former U.S. Senator Alan Simpson (R-WY), "emotion, fear, guilt, and racism."[1] The last landmark bill, the Immigration Reform and Control Act (IRCA), passed more than 25 years ago in 1986. A similarly ambitious attempt failed in 2006–2007. At a time when Congress is considering another set of sweeping immigration reforms, it's worth considering why the 1986 endeavor succeeded, and why the 2006–2007 effort did not.

THE IMMIGRATION REFORM AND CONTROL ACT OF 1986

In the 1960s and 1970s, illegal immigration, especially from Mexico, grew rapidly.[2] Ironically, policy choices made by the U.S. Congress in that period greatly contributed to the growth. Congress cut legal immigration channels for Mexicans by half and eliminated the *bracero* agricultural "guest worker" program. That program was infamous for its exploitation of Mexican work-ers, but at its height it allowed over 400,000 workers annually into the United States to fill agricultural and other seasonal jobs. Legislative attempts to staunch the unauthorized flow had failed for over three decades. An influx of Southeast Asian refugees that eventually numbered over 1.2 million dur-ing the 1970s and 1980s, and the arrival in South Florida of 140,000 Cubans in the Mariel boatlift, on top of 40,000 Haitians, added to the widespread perception that immigration was "out of control."[3]

In 1978, Congress authorized a "Blue Ribbon" Select Commission on Immigration and Refugee Policy, chaired by Father Theodore Hesburgh, President of the University of Notre Dame and former Chairman of the U.S. Commission on Civil Rights. The Select Commission was unusual: its membership included four House and Senate members and four Cabinet officers with jurisdiction over immigration matters; it vetted the issue through exhaustive research and public field hearings across the country; and Chairman Hesburgh was among the most respected personages of his generation. As a result, the Select Commission's recommendations, issued in 1981, carried considerable weight.[4]

In March 1982, Senator Alan Simpson and Representative Romano Mazzoli (D-KY)—chairmen of their bodies' respective immigration subcommittees but almost unknown inside the Beltway—introduced legislation largely reflecting the recommendations of the Select Commission. Both Simpson and Mazzoli had earned their expertise, and learned the art of compromise, during deliberations of the Select Commission and as respected state legislators before coming to Congress.

The Simpson-Mazzoli bill sought to reduce illegal immigration through a "three-legged stool" approach: heightened border enforcement; penalties on employers for knowingly hiring unauthorized workers ("employer sanctions"); and "regularization" of long-term unauthorized U.S. residents ("legalization"). The bill was largely silent on the question of legal immigration—either temporary or permanent.

The 1982 bill's prospects were uncertain. Although insiders had characterized the upper body during this period as the "Last Great Senate" for its ability to act on a bipartisan basis,[5] it had long been a graveyard for immigration reform. U.S. Senate Committee on the Judiciary Chairman James Eastland (D-MS), a cotton farmer close to agricultural interests that depended on unauthorized workers, refused to act on the issue when he chaired the committee through most of the 1970s, even after the House twice passed legislation by overwhelming margins. His successor, Edward Kennedy (D-MA), a previous supporter of immigration reform, had seemingly turned against the issue during his ill-fated 1980 presidential primary run. When Strom Thurmond (R-SC), took over the committee in 1981, he was viewed by some as a near-ideological twin of Eastland. Surprisingly, Thurmond turned out to be supportive of Simpson's efforts.[6]

The 1982 omnibus bill faced even more difficult crosscurrents in the House. To overgeneralize only slightly, most Democrats generally favored employer sanctions and legalization, and opposed guest-worker programs. Members of Congress from districts with large minority populations almost uniformly opposed employer sanctions and guest-worker programs, while supporting legalization. Moderate Republicans generally supported employer sanctions and legalization, albeit less enthusiastically than their Democratic counterparts. Conservative Democrats and Republicans, especially those from rural areas, largely opposed employer sanctions and legalization while supporting a guest-worker program. In other words, both political parties were split along ideological, geographic, and sometimes racial/ethnic lines.

Major interest groups, similarly, had conflicting policy objectives. In the business community the Chamber of Commerce opposed employer sanctions as excessive government regulation, for instance, while the Business Roundtable supported the bill as advancing the overall public interest.[7] As Select Commission executive director Lawrence Fuchs explained: "For the AFL-CIO, it was the enactment of employer sanctions and the prevention of a large-scale guest-worker program; for Mexican American leaders, it was the legalization of a substantial number of illegal aliens, the prevention of a guest-worker program, and no employer sanctions; for the restrictionists, it was employer sanctions, a cutback in legal immigration and refugee admissions, and no legalization or guest-worker program; and for the growers of perishable fruits and vegetables, it was the status quo, the continuation of de facto cheap labor immigration . . . and/or a large temporary worker program . . ."[8]

ROCKY ROAD TO PASSAGE

Owing to this swirl of conflicting, overlapping interests, the road to final passage was rocky. The Senate passed its bill quickly in 1982, but the bill died on the House floor amid a flurry of amendments in a lame duck session that year. The Senate acted again in 1983, and although the 1984 House bill squeaked through on a 216–211 vote, the bill expired in a House-Senate conference committee in the waning days of the 98th Congress. In the 99th Congress, the Senate again moved first, passing its bill in 1985.

In the House there were three final roadblocks to the bill's passage in 1986: civil rights protections against discrimination that could result from employer sanctions; costs to state and local governments from the legalization of previously unauthorized persons; and agricultural guest-worker programs to replace the previously unauthorized farm labor force. The discrimination issue was addressed through an amendment by Representative Barney Frank (D-MA), to establish a new mechanism within the Justice Department to address such claims. That provision had passed the House almost unanimously in 1984, but later attracted opposition from business groups and the Reagan Administration.

State and local governments feared that newly legalized aliens would tax their health, education, and welfare systems, in part because the legislation made this population ineligible for most federal benefits. As a result, these governments demanded "100 percent reimbursement" for such costs, which they argued could exceed $6 billion; the Reagan Administration offered a block grant capped at $1.8 billion. Technically, the failure to resolve this matter ended the 1984 conference committee, although many argued the cost issue was "camouflage" concealing other factors that brought down the bill.[9]

The guest-worker issue was the most contentious. In 1983 and again in 1985, agricultural interests led by Senator Pete Wilson (R-CA) were able to overcome Simpson's opposition and include a provision for a larger guest worker program over time. In the House, Representative Leon Panetta (D-CA), a popular and highly respected former Republican-turned Democrat, carried the amendment, which passed by a decisive margin in 1984 and seemed poised to do so again over the strenuous objections of the powerful Judiciary Committee Chairman Peter Rodino (D-NJ), who declared, "I would rather see no bill than one which could jeopardize the wages and working conditions of American workers."[10]

Despite his objections, Rodino authorized bill supporter Representative Charles Schumer (D-NY) and opponent Representative Howard Berman (D-CA) (who was long associated with farmworker interests) to negotiate a compromise with Panetta. After eight months of often marathon negotiation sessions, the three members announced a compromise in late summer 1986.[11] The resulting "Special Agricultural Worker" (SAW) program satisfied farmworker advocates by granting legal status and a path to citizenship—and thus full labor rights and protections to the workers—while protecting growers by ensuring an adequate supply of labor. With Rodino's blessing, the SAW program and other amendments requested by Hispanic Caucus Chairman Esteban Torres (D-CA), were added to the bill, which moved swiftly through committee.[12]

However, the new additions proved a bridge too far for conservative supporters, led by Representative Dan Lungren (R-CA), who joined with the bill's opponents to defeat the rule setting the terms for House floor debate. After another flurry of negotiations, the bill was revived and it passed the House. Lungren famously described the bill's revival: "It was a corpse going to the morgue, and on the way to the morgue a toe began to twitch, and we began CPR again."[13]

Behind closed doors, Simpson and Rodino negotiated a "pre-conference agreement," in Capitol Hill parlance, that was expeditiously ratified in a brief *pro forma* conference committee. The compromise cut back but preserved anti-discrimination protections, capped state-local legalization expenses at $4 billion, and maintained a slightly restricted SAW program. The bill passed the House by a 238–173 margin on October 15, with nearly half of Hispanic and Black Caucus members, who had uniformly opposed previous legislation, voting "aye."[14] The Senate followed suit two days later after lengthy opposition speeches—but tellingly no filibuster. With Reagan's signature three weeks later, the IRCA became the law of the land in 1986.

COMPREHENSIVE IMMIGRATION REFORM 2006–2007

IRCA was "an idea whose time had come" because of what political scientists identify as the three prerequisites for major reform—a "problem stream" that galvanizes action; a mature "policy stream" of accepted ideas and reforms; and "political will," often generated by policy entrepreneurs. Given that those three prerequisites also seemed in play in 2006–2007, one might have expected another successful outcome.[15] By then the problem of illegal immigration was far more serious, for instance, with the unauthorized population estimated to have grown from about 3 million when IRCA was enacted to over 10 million in 2005.

Though President George W. Bush had made immigration reform a central legislative agenda item soon after his election in 2000, the 9/11 terrorist attacks made it impossible to act on immigration until 2005. By then, a policy consensus on immigration reform had developed. Legislation by Senators John McCain (R-AZ) and Ted Kennedy (D-MA)—and a companion House bill by Representatives Jeff Flake (R-AZ) and Luis Gutierrez (D-IL)—largely reflected the recommendations of two private but bipartisan initiatives organized by the Carnegie Endowment for International Peace and the Migration Policy Institute. Thus, there was a mature "policy stream" for immigration reform.[16]

The 2005 legislation proposed tough enforcement measures, legalization of most unauthorized persons in the United States, and major reforms to the legal immigration system, including expanded skills-based visas. This legislative push was spearheaded by two of Congress's most accomplished legislators—McCain, coauthor of landmark campaign finance reform, and Kennedy, the Senate's consummate deal-maker. (See "Edward 'Ted' Kennedy: A Liberal Lion" and "John McCain: The Happy Warrior," Chapters 17 and 20, respectively.) And their efforts were supported by President Bush, fresh off a reelection victory that had garnered over 40 percent of the Hispanic vote.

Despite these advantages, comprehensive immigration reform was not to be. In December of 2005, the Republican-controlled House passed its own "enforcement only" legislation sponsored by Representative James Sensenbrenner (R-WI). The Sensenbrenner bill galvanized immigrant communities and their supporters, and, in March of 2006, triggered large protest marches across the country. Partly in response to the protests, the Senate took up its own immigration bill. In the summer of 2006, after a series of procedural maneuvers and an agreement among the sponsors to oppose "poison pill" amendments, the Senate passed the McCain-Kennedy immigration bill by a 62–36 vote, with 23 Republicans joining one independent and 38 Democrats in support of the bill.[17] By the August recess, however, the bill had become a wedge issue. Congressional town hall meetings across the country provided opportunities to organize opposition against the Senate bill. Invoking this opposition, the House declined to appoint conferees, and McCain-Kennedy died with the end of the 109th Congress.[18]

The 2006 midterm elections resulted in Democratic majorities in both Houses, seemingly implying smoother sailing for immigration reform. In May 2007, with Senator McCain seeking the Republican presidential nomination and forsaking leadership on the issue, Senator Jon Kyl (R-AZ) negotiated with Kennedy a "grand bargain" endorsed by the Bush Administration. While superficially similar to the previous McCain-Kennedy legislation, the Kyl-Kennedy bill included additional enforcement measures, a far more restrictive legalization program, a new legal immigration "point system" favoring higher-skilled immigrants while reducing family based visas, and a larger, business-friendly temporary worker program, reflecting Kyl's long-held views.

Senate floor debate began in May under an agreement to consider 30 amendments, which were quickly debated and disposed of. Partisan wrangling over the number of additional amendments to be allowed, however, led to a failed attempt by Senate Democratic leader Harry Reid (D-NV) to invoke cloture and end debate. In June, debate reopened under a second agreement authorizing a list of 26 additional amendments, most considered "poison pills." The first eight were defeated, but then a series of amendments—including enforcement provisions noxious to progressives (largely with Republican support) and one eliminating the bill's temporary worker programs viewed as essential to business (mainly with Democratic support)—were approved, fracturing the fragile coalition backing the effort. Conservative talk radio hosts damned the bill's legalization provisions as "amnesty," and the Capitol Hill phone system crashed under the weight of callers, the vast majority of whom opposed the legislation.[19]

A number of prominent Republican supporters of the bill either "tacked to the right while considering presidential runs" or avoided the issue.[20] Although President Bush remained publicly supportive of the legislation, the war in Iraq had dragged down his approval ratings, and he had little clout left to move Republican votes. Democratic Senators seeking their party's nomination were less than enthusiastic about the bill, while the party's House leaders indicated "grave concerns" about the Senate legislation.[21] With growing opposition and fractured support, a final attempt to invoke cloture on the bill failed, with 16 Democrats joining 37 Republicans to kill the bill. Although this final tally probably understates support for the bill, it was clear that the "grand bargain" had turned into a "grand collapse."[22]

HYPER-PARTISANSHIP AND BAD TIMING

In retrospect, the enactment of an immigration bill in 1986 was attributable to several factors. Its policy recommendations were blessed by a respected "blue ribbon commission" at a time when the American public's faith in such bodies was considerably higher than at present.[23] It benefitted from an extraordinary cast of "policy entrepreneurs," including sponsors Simpson, Mazzoli, and Rodino; architects of key compromises like Representatives Schumer, Panetta, Berman, and Lungren, who chose to negotiate when faced with an eleventh-hour proposal he initially found unacceptable. Senator Kennedy cooperated with Simpson in the Senate, even though obstruction would have been popular among elements of his base had he chosen to run for president again.

Crucially, House Speaker Tip O'Neill (D-MA) brought IRCA, a bill that divided the Democratic Caucus, to the floor, just as he earlier had permitted action on Reagan's 1981 budget and tax bills that were opposed by the vast majority of Democrats. Similarly, O'Neill negotiated a compromise deal on Social Security with Reagan in 1983, and enabled bipartisan tax reform to move forward in 1986. (See "Thomas 'Tip' O'Neill: New Deal Champion," Chapter 7.) Although often attacked as a partisan politician, O'Neill demonstrated enormous respect for his obligation to "allow the House to work its will" even on legislation opposed by the majority of Democrats.[24]

The willingness of interest groups to compromise was also essential as IRCA limped toward passage in the final hours of the 99th Congress.[25] And the ability of Simpson and Rodino to "pre-conference" their respective bills also played a role, representing the very kind of private deal-making discouraged in contemporary times when "transparency" is often universally accepted as a prerequisite to policy making.[26]

Finally, luck mattered as well. In 1986 the Senate had extended its adjournment date in anticipation of a potential arms control treaty with the Soviet Union that was being negotiated at the Reykjavik Summit. Although Reagan returned from the Summit with no agreement in hand, the delayed adjournment provided precious time for immigration negotiations to succeed.

Why did the "corpse" survive in 1986 and the "grand bargain" collapse in 2006–2007? Two of the common explanations for growing congressional gridlock apply here: "hyper-partisanship" and a concomitant aversion to compromise. There were also related institutional barriers, such as more frequent use of the filibuster in the Senate, and the informal "Hastert Rule" requiring that a "majority of the majority" support a bill before it can be considered on the House floor.[27] Had then-Speaker Dennis Hastert (R-IL) acted in 2006 as O'Neill had 20 years earlier and scheduled the Kennedy-McCain bill for a House vote, it might well have become law. (See "Dennis Hastert: The Accidental Speaker," Chapter 11.) Similarly, the now-routine requirement for 60 votes in the Senate was unheard of in 1986. Over nearly six years of debate on immigration reform in the 1980s, only once was a filibuster even threatened.[28] If that practice held true in 2007, immigration reform could have easily passed the Senate.

Moreover, the issue of immigration has become increasingly partisan since the 1980s.[29] With large majorities of Democrats now supporting and equally large majorities of Republicans opposing immigration reform, partisanship is an ever-growing obstacle in this arena. It is also difficult to avoid the conclusion that race played a role in killing the 2006–2007 effort. As the percentage of immigrants in the U.S. population approaches historic highs, with an ever-increasing proportion of the flow coming from Latin America and Asia and both new arrivals and subsequent generations moving into states with little tradition of immigrant settlements, immigration reform debates inevitably carry racial overtones.

But "micro" as well as "macro" factors also mattered in 2006–2007, such as ineffectual support from a Bush Administration already weakened by a failed attempt to reform Social Security and growing opposition to the Iraq War, and the vastly more effective mobilization of conservatives opposed to the bill than their proimmigration counterparts. Unfortunate timing played a role as well, inasmuch as the bill that passed the Senate in 2006 might well have passed the Democratically controlled House in 2007, but it couldn't make it out of the upper body that year, weighed down in part by the beginning of the presidential primary process.

Finally, notwithstanding the success in 1986, omnibus immigration reform legislation—like any controversial legislation with multiple moving parts—has always been difficult to enact. In the end, the difference between victory and defeat is often a matter of personalities, chance, and timing.

♦ ♦ ♦ ♦ ♦

30. Showdown over Judicial Nominations: Robert Bork

by Mark Gitenstein

In October 1987, the U.S. Senate rejected Judge Robert Bork's nomination to be a Justice on the U.S. Supreme Court. A quarter century later, political analysts and academics continue to debate the implications of Bork's defeat. To many, the Bork nomination marked a turning point for Supreme Court nominations specifically, and for political civility more generally. Bork and his allies have effectively framed his defeat as evidence that the nomination process is flawed and that only "stealth" candidates can survive. Indeed, the Bork hearings and the political battle surrounding them have even become a verb. To this day, some of my liberal friends continue to ask me: "Don't you think this was a mistake? Wasn't it wrong to 'bork' Bork?"

Having served as the Chief Counsel of the U.S. Senate Committee on the Judiciary during the Bork nomination, I have a perspective on the proceedings that perhaps is different than the conventional view. In my opinion, what brought down Robert Bork was not some illegitimate "politicization" of the nominations process but a struggle over "matters of principle." At the heart of the struggle were two radically different interpretations of what the Constitution means. Bork and his allies espoused a very narrow vision of the Bill of Rights. This vision explicitly rejected the more generous concept of "fundamental rights" espoused by the Warren Court, and in five days of testimony and decades of writing, Bork explicitly rejected many landmark Warren Court decisions.[1]

Senator Joseph Biden (D-DE), then-Chairman of the Judiciary Committee, argued forcefully with Bork about these decisions and tried to convince Democrats and Republicans alike that, if confirmed, Bork would have been the only Justice in history to espouse such a narrow view. To Bork, if a right was not explicitly written into the Constitution, it simply did not exist.[2] In my mind, that is why the Bork nomination was opposed by a majority of the American people and rejected by a vote of 58–42 on October 23, 1987.

Bork was stunned with the result and considered the hearings an "unserious" dialogue over the Constitution and what it means. He believed that all members—even then–Republican Senator Arlen Specter (R-PA)—came into the hearings with their minds made up. Having discussed the issue with Specter, and a number of moderate and conservative Democrats on the Committee before and after the hearings, I am convinced that Bork was wrong. The sad irony was that it was his five days of testimony before the Committee that convinced the senators to vote "no." His nomination was dead at the conclusion of his own testimony. Not only had critical moderates and "swing" Democrats—Senator Specter, as well as Senators Dennis DeConcini (D-AZ) and Howell Heflin (D-AL)—turned against him, but so too had public opinion.[3]

The New York Times editorialized that the hearings were "extraordinary" and agreed with Biden that a "debate of consequence and caliber" had occurred. Anthony Lewis of the *Times* explained: "[The hearings] have instructed all of us on the Court and the Constitution. They have confounded the cynical view that everyone in Washington has base political motives."

But it is legitimate to ask whether it was appropriate for Biden and the Committee to delve so deeply into Bork's judicial philosophy. Was this truly unprecedented, and did it set a new and dangerous precedent?

A HISTORICAL PERSPECTIVE

From a historical perspective, it is not unprecedented for Supreme Court nominations to fail generally, or to fail specifically on ideological grounds. Overall, 20 percent of Supreme Court nominees have failed. In fact, this was quite common in the century after our founding. There were 21 nominees rejected during this period. Indeed, the 20th century was the exception to that general rule with only seven rejections.

The question of whether it was appropriate to look into the jurisprudence of the nominee, as opposed to simply examining whether the nominee had the basic legal qualifications, was an issue that Biden carefully considered. Soon after the Bork nomination was announced, Biden delivered a speech on the Senate floor exploring the topic. Indeed, for most of his career up to that point, Biden had taken a narrow view of his responsibility as a senator, focusing primarily upon the nominee's qualifications.

In a speech on June 23, 1987, Biden laid out in detail how the framers had assumed that the substantive views of the nominee would play a role in the Senate's consideration. Indeed, in all but one of the two-dozen cases where a nominee had been rejected, the nominee's views had driven the inquiry by senators. In the very first case of a nominee being rejected, President Washington's nomination of John Rutledge in 1795, the opposition was based almost entirely on Rutledge's denunciation of the Jay Treaty.[4]

Many scholars similarly espoused the opinion that a nominee's views were fair game. Walter Dellinger, then a constitutional law professor at Duke, argued: "When a President attempts to direct the court's future course by submitting a nominee known to be committed to a particular philosophy, it should be a completely sufficient basis for a Senator's negative vote that the nominee's philosophy is one that the Senator believes would be bad for the country."[5]

In his speech, Biden cautioned that just because the Senate could consider a nominee's views—and had in the past—did not necessarily mean that it should base its decision entirely on the nominee's views. This could, if unchecked, overly politicize the process. Biden set out three circumstances in which the Senate should consider a nominee's views: one, when the President, via his nominee, attempts to remake the court in his image by considering the nominee's views; two, when the President and the Senate are deeply divided by the issues at stake before the court; and three, when the balance of the court on these issues is at stake.

Biden argued that all three circumstances applied in the case of Robert Bork. At the time that President Reagan nominated Bork, several White House aides explicitly stated that the nomination would change the direction of the Court, especially on controversial social issues. As Chairman of the Judiciary Committee, Biden had presided over debates on the politically volatile issues and the bitter battles that had ensued. Finally, there were scores of cases where Lewis Powell—who Bork was slated to replace—had been the swing vote on cases decided by a 5–4 margin.

ADVERSE CONSEQUENCES

Of course, an examination by senators of the views of judicial nominees can lead to two adverse consequences. One adverse result would be that nominees simply refrain from disclosing their views either in their prior writings or in their testimony before the Judiciary Committee. There have been a number of so-called stealth nominees before the Committee, for instance, who either refused to answer the questions or did so in a disingenuous manner. Equally problematic, the Committee could, in effect, attempt to use the hearing process to force the nominee to take positions on matters that were at the time currently before the Supreme Court. This would force the nominee to campaign for the position before the Committee.

Both of these outcomes would be troubling, and the Committee must be extremely careful in how it conducts its questioning of nominees. In the first circumstance, faced with a stealth nominee, a senator can and should vote "no" if it appears the nominee is withholding critical information. As to forcing the nominee to "position" himself on pending issues, the Chairman should instruct the nominee not to answer questions on specific pending cases and instead limit questions to broader legal theories. Most hearings since the Bork nomination have attempted to strike that balance.

However, the real solution to this dilemma is to avoid such a confrontation in the Committee altogether. One of Biden's favorite historical anecdotes came from Henry Abraham in his classic book *Justices, Presidents, and Senators*. In 1932, Senator William Borah (R-ID) was one of the most powerful figures in the Senate. He strongly supported Benjamin Cardozo for a position on the Supreme Court. President Hoover shared with Borah a list of possible candidates to replace Oliver Wendell Holmes. Cardozo was on the bottom of the list. After Hoover showed him the list, Borah responded that he must have had the list upside down. Hoover nominated Cardozo.

For Biden, the story illustrated the value of advance consultation between the Senate and the President. In advance of the Bork nomination, Biden tried to engage in those kinds of consultations with his old friend and colleague, former Senate Majority Leader Howard Baker (R-TN), who was serving as Reagan's Chief of Staff. He warned Baker and then Reagan that the Bork nomination would be a mistake. It was too divisive, according to Biden, and would make for "a long hot summer."

CONSULTATIONS AVOID CONTROVERSY

After the defeat of the Bork nomination, and another failed effort with Douglas Ginsburg, whose nomination was withdrawn after allegations arose about previous marijuana use in college, President Reagan finally resorted to consultations. In the case of Anthony Kennedy, who ultimately occupied the seat for which Bork was nominated, the President discussed the nomination with Biden before it was made. Although Biden made no commitments in the meeting in the Oval Office, he clearly sent the message that he would be easier to confirm than Bork. On February 3, 1988, Anthony Kennedy was confirmed by a 97–0 vote.

Of course, the process of nomination to the Supreme Court begins with the President. When he engages the process with an ideological choice, he will likely provoke an ideological reaction from the Senate. Not only did President Reagan understand that with the Kennedy nomination, so did

President George H.W. Bush with the nomination of David Souter, who was confirmed by a 90–9 vote.

So the final lesson of this classic interbranch struggle comes from President Woodrow Wilson, who, as an academic, was an expert on checks and balances. According to Wilson, separation of powers is not an invitation to "warfare between the branches." In circumstances like we faced in the late 1980s and indeed, that we still face today, it is essential that leaders in both branches of government act as statesmen and attempt to avoid such "warfare."

◆ ◆ ◆ ◆ ◆

31. A Republican Revolution: The 1994 Contract with America

by Linda Killian

In February 1994, House Republicans held a retreat in Salisbury, Maryland, to discuss a political agenda for the fall campaign. They agreed on a basic set of conservative principles centered on tax cuts, reductions in federal spending, and a strong national defense. Newt Gingrich (R-GA), then minority whip, and Dick Armey (R-TX), House Republican Conference Chairman, led the effort. Working with conservative interest groups, such as the Heritage Foundation, they spent the next six months further developing the platform into a set of 10 basic principles, which were test-marketed by GOP political consultants using focus groups and polling to determine how and in what order they should be presented to best appeal to voters.

The Republicans unveiled their "Contract with America" on the steps of the U.S. Capitol on September 27, 1994, as a way to nationalize the 1994 congressional elections. The policy manifesto's provisions included welfare reform, a balanced budget amendment, a 50 percent cut in the capital gains tax rate, term limits, and tort reform. But the effort by Gingrich and the Republican leaders to win a majority of House seats did not end there. They also had launched an intensive drive to recruit appealing and self-funded candidates to run for Congress against Democratic incumbents.

The plan to retake the House for Republicans had been launched by Gingrich many years earlier. In 1980, as a freshman member of the House, Gingrich had helped to organize a media-campaign event on the Capitol steps called "Governing Team Day." That event featured presidential candidate

Ronald Reagan, along with members of Congress and congressional candidates, who all promised a conservative platform if elected.

Then in 1983, Gingrich formed a group of GOP House members called the Conservative Opportunity Society, which advocated that Republicans become more partisan and less interested in compromise with the Democrats. He also used late-night partisan speeches on C-SPAN to reach conservative supporters around the country. In 1989, Gingrich managed to force the resignation of Democratic House Speaker Jim Wright (D-TX), who had succeeded Tip O'Neill as Speaker in 1987, over an ethics charge.

Gingrich's success in toppling Wright was a major career boost, and he became minority whip the same year. Gingrich quickly laid out a plan for the Republicans to take over the House majority and force the retirement of House Minority Leader Bob Michel (R-IL), whose style was seen as too accommodating to the Democrats. In 1992, despite Bill Clinton's presidential victory, Republicans picked up nine seats in the House. Gingrich continued to use attacks on the Democrats and divisive, antigovernment rhetoric to win the House majority for the Republicans and the Speakership two years later.

A WATERSHED ELECTION

The 1994 election was a watershed in American politics. Seventy-three new Republicans were elected to the House, giving the GOP control of that chamber for the first time in 40 years and ending the longest span of one-party rule in the history of Congress. Conservative political ideas about taxes and government spending emerged front and center in the American political debate and have remained there ever since.

Most of the GOP freshmen elected that year were significantly more conservative than senior Republicans in the House and Senate, and they constituted one of the most celebrated and historic classes in congressional history. Brash and irrepressible, the Class of '94 included a number of memorable characters and future national political leaders, including entertainer Sonny Bono (R-CA) and media personality Joe Scarborough (R-FL). Seven were later elected to the Senate—including Lindsey Graham (R-SC), Tom Coburn (R-OK), and Saxby Chambliss (R-GA). Three went on to serve as governors. Ray LaHood (R-IL) was named Secretary of Transportation in the Obama Administration.[1]

The freshmen of 1994 were young, with nearly 60 percent of them under the age of 45. Many of them had business backgrounds, and half of them had never previously served in any political office. As a result they often operated more on stubbornness than actual knowledge of the legislative process. Nor did they believe in compromise. They considered themselves outsiders and didn't want to get too comfortable in Washington. Many had young families who didn't move with them to the capital, and some of them even refused to rent an apartment in Washington, D.C., instead choosing to sleep on the couch in their office. They called themselves "True Believers," and they were deeply committed to balancing the budget, shrinking government, and lowering taxes. They talked about eliminating the Energy, Education, and Commerce Departments, and started referring to their election as "The Republican Revolution."

It was clearly a wave election. Not a single Republican incumbent lost in 1994, and 34 incumbent Democrats were defeated including Tom Foley (D-WA), the first sitting House Speaker to fail to win reelection since 1862.

There were several reasons for the voters' unhappiness with Democrats that year, including tax increases passed by a Democratic Congress and supported by President Bill Clinton, and a House banking scandal.

The Democrats' Deficit Reduction Act of 1993 raised the tax rate for the wealthiest Americans, repealed a cap on the Medicare payroll tax, raised the gas tax, increased the taxable portion of Social Security benefits, and increased the corporate tax rate by 1 percent. Every Republican in Congress voted against the tax increases.

The banking scandal that had unfolded over the previous several years involved overdrawn accounts of members of Congress from the House bank. Although taxpayer funds were not involved, it was a potent symbol of an out of touch and profligate Congress not living by the same rules as everyone else. The scandal was also expertly exploited by Gingrich, although he himself had bounced checks from the House bank.

CLAIMING A MANDATE

Rather than understanding that their victory was due more to voters' dissatisfaction with the Democrats than their own agenda, however, Republicans started talking about the 1994 election result as a mandate to remake government in their own conservative image. Although Gingrich repeatedly credited the Contract with America for the win, there is little evidence to back up this view. A CBS-*New York Times* poll released the week of the 1994 election showed that 71 percent of those questioned had never heard of the Contract with America; 15 percent said it would make no difference in how they voted; and only 7 percent said it would make them more likely to vote for a Republican. As in all midterm elections, turnout was low at under 40 percent, and many of the freshmen won their races by very small margins of only a few thousand votes.

The Contract did prove instrumental though in motivating core constituencies and groups like the National Rifle Association and the Christian Coalition, which donated money and mobilized conservative voters using the mantra "God, guns and gays" to describe what they believed was wrong with the country under Bill Clinton and the Democrats.

The extreme partisan polarization of the 104th Congress began even before members were sworn into office. For the previous 20 years, the orientation of all House freshmen had been held at Harvard's Kennedy School of Government. However, the GOP freshmen decided they didn't want to go to Harvard, choosing to hold their orientation at the conservative Heritage Foundation in Washington. Instead of offering sessions on how the House actually worked, the Heritage Foundation orientation concentrated on how to get the Contract with America passed, and featured panels on welfare reform and cutting taxes. Speakers included conservative partisans like Ralph Reed of the Christian Coalition, party strategist Bill Kristol, and radio personality Rush Limbaugh.

Since the Democratic freshmen had no interest in attending an ideologically focused orientation at the Heritage Foundation, there was no bipartisan orientation that year. Republican and Democratic freshmen didn't even meet each other until the 104th Congress convened, and even then rarely spoke to anyone across the aisle unless they served on the same committee. The 104th Congress marked a new level of partisanship, polarization, and discord in the House.

In addition to Gingrich, the GOP leadership team included Dick Armey (R-TX) as Majority Leader, Tom DeLay (R-TX) as Whip, and John Boehner (R-OH) as Conference Chairman. None of the Republicans in the House had ever served in the majority before.

Gingrich, a brilliant political tactician, became a strong if somewhat erratic Speaker, exercising more power than any Speaker since Joseph Cannon (R-IL), who was Speaker from 1903 to 1911. Like Cannon, Gingrich expanded the powers of the Speakership and set the agenda of the House, making committee assignments and selecting which senior Republicans would chair key committees. Instead of using seniority—which had been the traditional method of naming chairmen in the House for years—Gingrich skipped over ranking Republicans to select the chairmen of the Rules, Appropriations, Commerce, and Judiciary Committees, ensuring their loyalty and obedience in pushing the conservative agenda.

FIRST HUNDRED DAYS

The House Republicans decided to enact all of their Contract with America planks in a push during the First Hundred Days of the congressional session. There was some irony in this approach, since the strategy had been used by Franklin Roosevelt during the Great Depression to pass his New Deal programs, which became the foundation of the Democratic Party's agenda for the rest of the 20th century.

On its first day, the House stayed in session until 2:30 A.M. Republicans passed legislation that would require a three-fifths majority vote for any income tax rate hike, along with procedural measures and House rule changes abolishing several House committees, reducing the size of committee staffs, and opening all committee meetings to the public. They also voted to limit committee chairs to six-year terms, and adopted a measure that would require Congress to live under the same laws it passed for the rest of the country.

The breakneck pace required to pass all of the Contract items in three months meant that when the House was in session votes were usually scheduled from early in the morning until after 10 at night. At the end of the First Hundred Days, the Republicans had brought all 10 Contract items to the floor, but only two pieces of legislation—one applying federal labor laws to Congress and another restricting the application of unfunded federal mandates to the states—had also been passed by the Senate and signed into law by President Clinton. Due to the intervention of Republican moderates in the Senate and threatened presidential vetoes, most of the Contract items went no further than the House. The Senate, even though it was also controlled by Republicans, moderated and, in some cases, reversed what the House was trying to do.

One of the first major pieces of the Contract passed by the Republicans involved tax cuts—a $500 per child tax credit for any family making less than $200,000 in income. The Democrats opposed the idea saying the Republicans wanted to cut programs for the poor, middle class, and elderly to finance tax cuts for the rich. The Senate lowered the income level for the credit to $110,000 for a two-income household.

Some moderate House Republicans went along with the Senate change to the legislation, but most of the House freshmen opposed the compromise. Because they represented such a large voting bloc within the GOP conference, it was almost impossible to get anything passed without them. The Republicans had 231 House members in 1995, a majority plus 13 votes. In the previous Congress the Democrats had a majority cushion of 40 votes.

Despite that small margin, though, on most issues the House Republicans voted as a bloc to pass an agenda the Democrats detested.

The Republicans tended to focus their budget cuts on programs with Democratic constituencies. They called it "defunding the left." The National Endowment for the Humanities, the National Endowment for the Arts, and the Corporation for Public Broadcasting were favorite targets. Although the Republican freshmen were eager to cut funding for federal programs, many also tried to protect items important to their own districts and conservative constituencies.

House Majority Whip Tom DeLay, a Houston exterminator before being elected to Congress, was determined to gut the Environmental Protection Agency, which he called "the Gestapo of government." On national television DeLay declared, "We're only going to fund those programs we want to fund. We're in charge. We don't have to negotiate with the Senate. We don't have to negotiate with the Democrats."

DeLay launched what became known as the K Street Project, named for the Washington corridor where many lobbyists have their offices. He informed lobbyists if they wanted access to the Republicans now in charge of Congress, they needed to start giving money to their campaigns, stop giving to the Democrats, and hire GOP hill staffers for their firms. He was nicknamed "The Hammer" by the lobbyists he hit up for money.

By the end of the August recess in 1995, the Contract with America had become a distant memory as the Republicans braced for a showdown with Bill Clinton over the federal budget and their proposed spending reductions. If agreement could not be reached, government operations would not be funded after the October 1 start of the fiscal year, and the government would shut down.

SHUTTING DOWN GOVERNMENT

The Republicans were confident that if they forced a government shutdown the public would be on their side. Newt Gingrich also thought Bill Clinton and the Democrats would ultimately cave in and the conservatives would be victorious. That calculation turned out to be an extremely costly tactical mistake, leading to two government shutdowns in the fall and early winter of 1995 that came to define the 104th Congress.

Newt Gingrich became the face of the shutdown and House Republicans, and an extremely unpopular figure. When American political leaders had traveled to Israel that fall for the funeral of Israeli leader Yitzhak Rabin, Gingrich complained to reporters about having to sit at the back of the plane, and suggested that he sent a tougher budget plan to the White House because of the snub, leading directly to the government shutdown.

The *New York Daily News* ran a famous front-page cartoon of Gingrich in a diaper calling him a "Cry Baby." That image stuck with an American public that believed Gingrich had forced a government shutdown over a petty personal slight.

Clinton was able to veto the GOP budget plans and make the Republicans look unreasonable. When the dust of the 1995–1996 shutdowns had settled, House Budget Chairman John Kasich (R-OH) would observe that "When the president doesn't want to do something, you really can't make him."

The shutdowns were Newt Gingrich's Waterloo and the turning point of the 104th Congress. It was, however, a costly political lesson many Republicans would forget and another group of unyielding House Republicans would wind up repeating the same mistake when they forced another government shutdown in the fall of 2013. The outcome was the same in both cases—public disapproval over their actions and concern about future GOP electoral prospects causing the Republicans to ultimately give much more than they wanted on government spending.

In the spring of 1996 the Republicans were terrified Bill Clinton would call their hand and there would be another shutdown for which they would again be blamed. Republicans also realized they were going to have to cut a deal with the President on welfare reform if they had any hope of holding onto the House in the next election. In exchange, they agreed to do some things Clinton and the Democrats wanted, including raising the minimum wage.

Clinton and the GOP freshmen now had a common goal—getting themselves reelected—and their political fortunes were linked. Clinton's failures with a Democratic Congress during his first two years in office had created the backlash that made the 1994 election possible. But the Republican insistence on the government shutdown and perceived extremism had revived his presidency. Clinton was at his strongest when he was battling Gingrich and the freshmen. In standing up to them during the government shutdown he had found his footing, and he was ready to compromise with them to move popular legislation. As a result, Clinton won decisive margins of victory in many of the same districts where GOP freshmen were reelected in 1996.

Some Republicans still claim the 1994 shutdown was worth it because the GOP managed to hold on to their House and Senate majorities in 1996 and achieve welfare reform and a balanced budget plan. Clinton's decision to sign welfare reform was severely criticized by liberals in the Democratic Party, but it deprived GOP presidential candidate Bob Dole of an issue to use against

Clinton in the fall presidential campaign. Signing the bill in a Rose Garden ceremony, Clinton declared "we are ending welfare as we know it."

POLITICAL OVERREACH

The freshmen of 1994 had come to Washington to shake things up. They were going to chop the federal budget and rip out programs and departments by the roots. They dismissed anyone who disagreed with them and believed they had a mandate from the voters for their agenda. As it turned out, voters did want change, but not necessarily the change Republicans were offering. The public didn't want government dismantled, they just wanted it to work better. Americans liked the idea of a balanced budget and smaller, more accountable government. But in cutting government, the Republicans did not wield the ax fairly. They disproportionately cut programs which affected the poor and the elderly. They also tried to impose their social agenda on the nation, trying to lift the Democrats' ban on assault weapons, rolling back environmental regulations, imposing restrictions on abortion, and passing the Defense of Marriage Act defining marriage as between a man and a woman.

In its second year, the 104th Congress was extremely productive. But judged by their own campaign rhetoric and the goals of the Contract with America, the Republicans' achievements were limited. Had the Republicans not compromised with Bill Clinton to pass welfare reform and other legislation, many of the freshmen probably would not have been reelected.

Newt Gingrich would serve only four years as Speaker, dogged by ethics charges and replaced by his own members because of losses in the 1996 and 1998 elections. He was seen by many House Republicans as undisciplined and a lightning rod for criticism. They realized they needed a leader who could make the trains run on time and present a positive image of the party and ultimately settled on the uncontroversial Dennis Hastert (R-IL) who adopted a much lower public profile than Gingrich and who would serve from 1999 to 2007, becoming the Republican House Speaker with the longest tenure in history.

The specter of the government shutdowns hung heavy over the party for years, and Republicans continued to make budget concessions with Bill Clinton to avoid another shutdown. The GOP fervor to cut government spending receded when George Bush captured the presidency in 2000, and Republicans had control of both Congress and the White House. Like Ronald Reagan before him, Bush proposed tax cuts which overwhelmingly benefited the wealthy but did not cut spending commensurately, causing the deficit to balloon on his watch. In fact, many members of the Class of '94 became born-again believers in government spending. They were working their way up on committees, seeking higher office, raising campaign cash to insure their own reelections, and funding programs their donors and constituents wanted.

"Over time we became just like the people we replaced. We were going to change Washington and instead Washington changed us," John Shadegg (R-AZ), a 1994 GOP freshman from Arizona who served in the House for 16 years, told me. "It begins to happen literally the day you arrive."

It would take 16 years for a new crop of wild-eyed, conservative GOP freshmen to arrive in Washington in 2010, this time supported by a grassroots movement known as the Tea Party. The ideological origin of the Tea Party movement can be traced directly back to the Republican Revolution and the Class of '94. Both groups disdained compromise, wanted tax and budget cuts, and opposed the enlargement of government. And both forced a government shutdown to make their point.

It remains to be seen whether the Tea Party Republicans will learn the right lessons from the 104th Congress. After the Republican takeover in 1994, House Republicans succeeded not when they closed down the government and refused to compromise, but rather when they worked with the President and the Democrats on legislation to get things done for the American people.

◆ ◆ ◆ ◆ ◆

32. Compromise amid Bitter Partisanship: The Welfare Reform Law of 1996

by Ron Haskins

The 1996 welfare reform legislation was a triumph of bipartisan lawmaking, and serves as an instructive example of how to cut through the fog of partisanship to enact important legislation.[1] The parallels in the relationship between Congress and the President in the age of Bill Clinton during the mid-1990s, and in the age of Barack Obama beginning in 2009, are striking. Republicans controlled at least part of Congress in both cases; both Presidents Clinton and Obama were exceptionally unpopular among Republicans; and during both presidencies, a newly elected group of conservative Republicans won control of one or both houses of Congress and adopted a conservative agenda while often rejecting compromise as unprincipled. For their part,

Democrats were intensely critical of the Republican agenda and often used caustic rhetoric during debates on the floor of the House and Senate. In both eras highly partisan fights led to closure of the federal government.

Yet despite these parallels, the Clinton Administration and congressional Republicans were able to reach bipartisan compromises to balance the budget, enact the North American Free Trade Agreement (NAFTA), and pass the landmark 1996 welfare reform law. On these and other issues, the major political players of the 1990s were able to find common ground in a way that has so far eluded their contemporary counterparts.

Considered one of the major accomplishments of both the Clinton Administration and the Gingrich Speakership, the 1996 welfare reform law replaced a New Deal program that provided cash benefits primarily to single mothers with a new program that required most mothers to prepare for and find work in exchange for their benefits. The law also greatly reduced welfare for noncitizens, eliminated disability benefits for drug addicts and alcoholics, reduced food stamp benefits, strengthened the nation's child support system, and made several other important changes in welfare programs.

FOUR FACTORS TO SUCCESS

There are at least four factors that contributed to the passage of such a seminal law, with bipartisan support, in a highly partisan political environment: a historic increase in the percentage of working mothers, a healthy economy, a fundamental agreement on principles between Clinton and Republicans, and strong political leadership on both sides of the political aisle.

First, the labor force participation rate of women, including mothers with young children, had been increasing for decades. In the two decades between 1975 and 1995, the percentage of mothers with children under three with jobs increased from about 35 percent to nearly 60 percent.[2] As most mothers with young children worked and paid taxes, while other mothers with young children didn't work and drew welfare, it became difficult to defend welfare payments. This sea change in demography created a situation ripe for reform.

Second, the American economy was entering a period of growth when Bill Clinton assumed office. Unemployment fell from 7.5 percent in 1992 to 4.0 percent in 2000, and GDP expanded rapidly. Federal tax revenues grew 57 percent in real terms over the same period and the federal budget, for the first time in decades, ran a surplus from 1998 through 2001. The strong economy of the 1990s added to the momentum that Republicans were building for welfare reform. What better time to argue that able-bodied mothers on welfare should work than when the economy was generating jobs at a steady pace?[3]

Third, President Clinton and Republicans fundamentally agreed on the major principle that drove welfare reform—namely that mothers on welfare should work. Since the English Poor Laws of the 16th century, there has been great tension over the view that giving welfare to able-bodied adults may help them avoid destitution, but at the cost of reducing their motivation to work and maintain self-sufficiency.[4] Modern research has provided abundant empirical support for the view that welfare reduces the incentive to work.[5] The traditional view of Republicans is that America, following the lead of European societies, has created too many welfare benefits and lured too many adults into dependency.[6] By contrast, Democrats argued that a decent society provides for the poor, and that with all its wealth America could afford to do more.[7] If federal spending on welfare benefits is taken as a measure of which side has been winning the welfare debate, Democrats have been the clear winners. Even with the 1996 reforms, federal spending on means-tested programs has increased (in constant dollars) from $74 billion in 1968 to $746 billion in 2011, with increases nearly every year during the period.[8]

Clinton advertised himself as a New Democrat, however, and he was willing to compromise on many of the issues that separated Republicans and Democrats, including welfare.[9] During the 1992 presidential campaign, Clinton talked frequently about reforming welfare by making adults on welfare work. His catchy phrase "end welfare as we know it" was a staple during the campaign and after.[10] Although Republicans were suspicious that Clinton would deliver on his promise to reform welfare, they decided to test him.

A fourth factor in the law's passage, and perhaps the most decisive, was strong political leadership. U.S. House Minority Leader Newt Gingrich (R-GA) was an example of a strong leader who knew what he wanted to accomplish and how to marshal his forces to overcome the obstacles to getting it done. During the 1994 congressional elections, Gingrich and his lieutenants, especially Dick Armey (R-TX), mounted a fund-raising juggernaut, developed an agenda called the Contract with America that Republicans could run on, and provided extensive and effective help in the form of advice and money to Republican candidates. The Contract with America was an agenda of ten popular legislative initiatives that House Republicans pledged to enact if they won the majority.[11] Republicans captured 54 additional seats in the 1994 House elections to win the majority for the first time in four decades. They also achieved a net increase of eight seats to take over the Senate.

Strong leadership from committee and subcommittee chairmen was also essential to drafting and passing welfare reform legislation. The U.S. House Committee on Ways and Means has jurisdiction over many of the nation's major welfare programs. Arguably the top leader on welfare reform in the House during the 1990s was the late E. Clay Shaw Jr. (R-FL), who chaired the Human Resources subcommittee of Ways and Means. Shaw had been working for more than two years with the House leadership and other House members, especially Jim Talent (R-MO) of the U.S. House Committee on Education and the Workforce, which shared jurisdiction over some important aspects of welfare reform. Shaw and his colleagues on Ways and Means, including chairman of the full committee Bill Archer (R-TX), and subcommittee members Rick Santorum (R-PA) and Jim McCrery (R-LA), developed extensive expertise on welfare reform issues, especially reforms that increase work rates among mothers on welfare. Although these Republican committee leaders managed to write a bill supported by almost all Republicans in the House, and was therefore capable of passing on the House floor (which it did on March 24, 1995 by a highly partisan vote of 234–199, with only nine Democrats voting in favor), the test of their leadership was just beginning.

By January 1996, Clinton had vetoed the Republican welfare reform bill twice. Shaw and most House Republicans hoped to modify the most-recently vetoed bill and send it back to Clinton a third time. However, if that strategy was to lead to enactment, some important changes in the bill were necessary. Perhaps the single most important change was to drop the Republican-backed provision that would have turned Medicaid into a block grant program. This would have been a transformational reform, converting an open-ended entitlement program into a block grant with capped funding. Clinton said publicly—and his staff repeatedly told Republican staffers privately—that the President considered the Medicaid block grant a "poison pill" that would force him to veto the entire bill.

Shaw and a group of Republicans on the Ways and Means Committee started a quiet campaign to convince Republican House members that if the party wanted to achieve welfare reform and substitute work for entitlement, they would have to give up the Medicaid block grant. The choice for most Republicans was not difficult. By the winter of 1996, after Clinton had vetoed virtually their entire agenda, Republicans were concerned that they had little to show for having taken over the House and Senate. They needed to pass important legislation to show that they could effectively govern, and welfare reform was at the top of their list. Republicans quickly began to talk about dropping the Medicaid block grant and within a few weeks, Gingrich gave in and the block grant was dropped. Shaw often said to other Republicans that there would be no reform unless President Clinton signed the bill; in the case of the Medicaid block grant provision, Shaw and his Ways and Means colleagues removed an important barrier to an eventual Clinton signature.

REPUBLICAN DIVISIONS

As the Medicaid example shows, the fight to get welfare reform passed in 1996 also required compromise among factions within the Republican Party. Another divisive issue that threatened Republican unity on welfare reform was aggressively highlighted by former U.S. Secretary of Education Bill Bennett when he testified before the Ways and Means Committee in January 1995. He told members of the Committee that the real issue in welfare reform was nonmarital births, not work requirements. If Bennett had been a lone voice on this claim, no one would have paid any attention. But Bennett was far from alone. The Heritage Foundation, the most politically powerful conservative think tank in Washington, and its influential welfare expert Robert Rector, made the same argument.

The specific policy dispute dividing Republicans was whether to deny cash welfare and food stamps to teens under age 18 who gave birth to babies outside marriage. Jim Talent (R-MO), the most influential Republican on the Education and Workforce Committee during the welfare reform debate, introduced legislation that would put this policy in place. Ways and Means Republicans were strongly opposed, arguing that the issue that had created Republican unity was mandatory work requirements, which the American public supported. Cutting babies off cash welfare and food stamps would be seen as cruel and could alienate many Americans. Besides, President Clinton would veto any bill that contained such a tough provision, meaning that Republicans would be unable to enact welfare reform at all.

The issue festered unresolved until the last negotiating session among Republicans before the final vote on the bill in July 1996. Thanks to the productive working relationship between Shaw and Talent, Talent agreed to get Heritage to drop its insistence on this provision in exchange for an incentive grant to states designed to reduce nonmarital birth rates. The leadership of Shaw, Talent, and others had made it more likely that Clinton would sign the bill.

Most historic legislation involves numerous compromises both within and between the political parties, plus at least some level of agreement between the parties on principles. In addition to favorable demographic trends and economic conditions, President Clinton was willing to work with the Republican majority in Congress. His views on many policies, including welfare reform, were also closer to those of the Republican Party than to more traditionally liberal Democratic positions. For their part, Republicans had leaders with the expertise, experience, and standing within their party to convince others in the party to accept the compromises necessary to get a Clinton signature on their bill. On the day the compromise bill passed the House in July 1996 with the support of half the Democrats, President Clinton announced that he would sign the bill. Passage of this historic legislation had required great leaders with vision from both parties, a willingness to compromise, and the political will to reach the finish line.

◆ ◆ ◆ ◆ ◆

33. The Backfire of Unintended Consequences: The 1997 Balanced Budget Act

by Scott Lilly

On a warm and muggy August morning in 1997, invited guests gathered on the South Lawn of the White House to witness the signing of two bills that had been the central focus of White House and congressional attention since early spring. The Balanced Budget Act of 1997 (BBA) and its companion the Taxpayer Relief Act of 1997 were clearly a source of great pride to President Bill Clinton and his longtime adversary, Speaker of the House Newt Gingrich (R-GA).

Clinton told the assembled audience, "Without regard to our party or our differences . . . we were able to transform this era of challenge into an era of unparalleled possibility."[1] Gingrich echoed, "the American constitutional system works, that slowly, over time, we listened to the will of the American people, that we reached beyond parties, we reached beyond institutions, and we find ways to get things done."[2]

This legislation was indeed extraordinary from numerous perspectives. Most obviously, Clinton and the two congressional leaders, Gingrich and Senate Majority Leader Trent Lott (R-MI), were able to work past their deep personal animosities and find common ground on a range of policy matters.

Clearly all three principals believed the budget agreement was a positive from the perspective of their personal public images and political standings. Having just won reelection, Clinton believed that the agreement could create a foundation for a more bipartisan and less acrimonious relationship between the two branches of government during his second term. He was also a compulsive conciliator. Persuading an arch opponent to cut a deal of this apparent magnitude was a challenge that he found almost impossible to resist.

Gingrich hoped that the agreement would usher in a new era as well. He had entered into the negotiations at a low point in his tenure as Speaker. He had been reelected Speaker in January by less than a majority of the House, with nine members of the Republican Conference voting either present or for another candidate.[3] An ABC-*Washington Post* poll indicated that 65 percent of the public opposed his being reelected as Speaker, and shortly after his reelection Gingrich became the first Speaker to be reprimanded by the House for ethics violations.[4] Even within his own party, Gingrich was viewed as divisive and overly partisan. Thus, he hoped that a budget deal would allow him to reinvent himself as a new Newt, a statesman and conciliator—someone who would be both more appealing to the public and less of a burden to his fellow Republicans.

Senate Majority Leader Trent Lott, who had ascended to his leadership in 1996, also stood to benefit from helping broker a bipartisan compromise. His party's image had been damaged by the government shutdown in the previous Congress, and moving a major bipartisan piece of legislation would not only be good for his party, but also would help to establish him as a strong and capable floor leader and a central player in the highest levels of policy making.

BIPARTISAN MISLABELING

Notwithstanding the shared interest of these three leaders in passing a landmark piece of economic legislation, what they crafted was extraordinary in its lack of real policy import. In fact, the budgetary problem that the legislation was purported to solve had already been solved by earlier efforts at austerity and a robust economy. In May of 1996, Congressional Budget Office (CBO) had forecast a Fiscal Year 1998 deficit of $194 billion.[5] Eight months later, it had trimmed that forecast by nearly 40 percent to $120 billion, and eight months after that (shortly after BBA became law), they cut their projection again, this time by more than 50 percent to $57 billion.[6] Ultimately all of those forecasts were overly pessimistic. In the fiscal year that began only 60 days after BBA became law, the United States ran a $69 billion surplus— the first such surplus in almost three decades.[7]

How much did BBA contribute to that achievement? CBO scoring a month after the Act became law projected that the agreement would actually increase the size of the deficit in the first year by a little more than $20 billion with spending (outlays) rising that year by $11.3 billion and revenues declining by $9 billion.[8] As a result the surplus that occurred in Fiscal Year 1998 was $20 billion smaller than it might have been without the "help" of BBA.

A second problem with spinning the budget legislation as a "big deal" was its relatively tiny impact, by almost any measure. While it seemed to deal with a variety of important issues, it did so largely in trifling ways. The first four years that the law was in effect, fiscal years 1998 through 2001 (the four years that the budget actually was in balance), CBO projected the act contained total spending cuts of $90.5 billion, offset by revenue losses of $66 billion, for a combined total deficit reduction over those four years of only $24 billion.[9] That equaled only six one-hundredths of 1 percent (0.06 percent) of gross domestic product over the course of that period—little more than background noise in either fiscal or macroeconomic terms.

As modest as that may sound, most of the purported savings under the act never actually took place. While taxes were cut $242 billion over 10 years, the caps on future year discretionary spending (scored by the CBO to save $380 billion over 10 years) were ignored. In fact Congress spent significantly more than the amounts supposed to be cut.

CBO historical tables indicate that discretionary outlays in the 10 years that followed the BBA totaled $8.4 trillion instead of the $5.9 trillion projected at the time the act was signed.[10] Instead of forcing discretionary spending down by $380 billion as projected, spending thus exceeded the BBA caps by $2.1 trillion.

One reason for this increased long-term spending was that the legislation contained a variety of provisions dealing with entitlement programs. Children's Health Insurance was increased by nearly $40 billion over 10 years, Supplemental Security Income by $15 billion, food stamps by $3 billion, and Earned Income Tax Credits by $29 billion. In theory, this spending was supposed to have been more than offset by other cuts that would lead to a net reduction of $373 billion in entitlement spending over 10 years. About 80 percent of that net reduction was the result of a series of reductions made in Medicare reimbursements to health care providers. In practice, many of these supposed cost reductions were amended following their enactment. The Balanced Budget Refinement Act of 1999, for instance, restored about $17 billion in previously agreed-to reimbursement reductions.

CAREER MOMENTS: THE PRICE OF SERIOUS POLITICAL MISCALCULATION

The BBA not only failed to accomplish its economic goals, it also appears to have failed to advance the personal political agendas of the three principals. Gingrich did not strengthen his standing among his colleagues as he had hoped. Even as he was negotiating the agreement, there was growing dissent from his party's right. Christian Coalition Leader Ralph Reed told the Conservative Political Action Conference in March of 1997 that conservatives "were not elected to ride at the back of the bus. . . . We were elected to lead, we were not elected to follow, and this Republican Congress should be leading President Clinton and not the other way around."[11] Reed accused the congressional majority leaders "of timidity, of retreat and of muddle-headed moderation."

By the time the conference report reached the House floor in August, 32 Republicans voted no. Many of those who voted yes worried that the Speaker had been outmaneuvered by the President, and that the agreement would not result in the savings that it had promised. Perhaps just as important was the sense among individual members that the Speaker's support for the legislation was driven more by ego than common sense.

Interestingly, it was Gingrich, not Clinton who initially broke the agreement on discretionary spending. By the spring of 1998, the dissatisfaction on the right over BBA and its lack of real savings had become more intense. The House Budget Committee reported a resolution that cut discretionary funding considerably below the levels agreed to in the BBA. The White House quickly responded that the agreement was not only a ceiling on discretionary funding, but also a floor. Nevertheless, Gingrich directed House Appropriations Chair Robert Livingston (R-LA) to proceed with the levels contained in the House Budget Resolution in preparing the annual appropriation bills.

There was an obvious flaw to Gingrich's strategy. What if the President refused to sign appropriations at a level below the prior agreement? What if he refused to sign a continuing resolution at a level lower than the agreement? What if the reopened controversy and the threat of a veto gave the White House the leverage to force Gingrich to produce appropriations above the level of the agreement?

While such a scenario may not have seemed that plausible to the Speaker in the spring of 1998, that was exactly where he found himself and his fellow Republicans by September. Desperate to adjourn and return to their districts for the fall campaign, embattled Republicans found that they could not leave unless they avoided another government shutdown, and to do that they had to produce appropriations that the President would sign. Clinton had decided that his signature would come at a high price. Since in Clinton's view the House Republicans had violated the discretionary spending portion of the BBA agreement in the budget resolution they had passed the previous spring, he felt no obligation to abide by it himself. As the days of September passed, Members of Congress began to believe they might spend the entire campaign stuck in their Washington offices.

Finally on October 20, two weeks before the election, House Republicans sued for peace. The agreement that the White House and congressional Democrats forced them to swallow seemed to be a reversal of everything they had advocated when they were elected to the majority four years before. Further, it made a complete sham of the notion that the BBA would in any way constrain discretionary spending.

ANYTHING BUT FISCAL RESTRAINT

While CBO scored the new appropriations for fiscal year 1999 at slightly less than the amount permitted under the BBA cap, the actual amount of new spending made available was far greater.[12] Congress had agreed to an additional $21 billion in "emergency appropriations" and a $4.6 billion increase in so-called advanced year appropriations. According to CBO, the Fiscal Year 1999 appropriation bills decreased the surplus by $16.4 billion rather than increasing it by $1 billion as the BBA had promised.

Stephen Slivinski, currently the senior economist at the Goldwater Institute and previously director of budget studies at Cato Institute and senior economist at the Tax Foundation, described the deal as "in every way a rout of the very ideals that won the GOP a majority in Congress in the first place."[13]

Gingrich lost 64 Republicans on passage of the Fiscal Year 1999 Omnibus Appropriation bill. A more significant problem was the 162 Republicans who voted for the bill as the lesser of two evils, but seethed at the Speaker's tactical error that had backed the Republican conference into a corner. Perhaps angriest of all was Appropriations Committee Chairman Robert Livingston. Livingston did nothing, however, until after the 1998 midterm election.

Following the unexpected Republican loss of five House seats in an off-year election—an election that Republicans expected to dominate because of the Lewinsky scandal that had dominated the news in 1998—Livingston made his move. In a four-page letter he demanded: "In order for the majority to complete its work and demonstrate that we can properly govern, I believe it imperative that you acknowledge and agree to these suggested changes in House procedure." The most important point among the 16 which Livingston raised, was that as chairman of the Appropriations Committee he would have the powers similar to previous committee chairs, namely that he be allowed to "run the committee as I see fit and in the best interest of the Republican majority, but without being subject to the dictates of any other Member of Congress."

Two days later Gingrich announced his resignation. Reporting on the Gingrich decision, *The New York Times* noted, "For the last few years

Mr. Gingrich has feuded with party conservatives who say he is not a true conservative, that he has capitulated to President Clinton on spending issues and has not advanced conservative causes like tax cuts."[14] The BBA, which the Speaker had hoped would strengthen his position among his colleagues, had ultimately been a major factor in his undoing.

For his part, President Clinton fared better as a result of the deal. Substantively he won nothing that would help him balance the budget, but he did win a number of important legislative victories. He forced major revisions in the welfare reform law he had signed with significant reservations a year earlier. He rolled a large amount of relatively routine legislative business into the law that may have had little budget impact, but had been sought by various agencies in the Executive Branch. He pocketed an increase in the discretionary spending caps that resulted in $10 billion in additional funding for administration priorities. Although Clinton had agreed to a mechanism that appeared to force long-term cuts in discretionary programs (most scheduled to occur after he left office), those cuts were not just subject to reversal, they were in fact reversed.

But perhaps Clinton's top priority—building a foundation for future bipartisan cooperation and diluting the toxic rhetoric in national politics— was an abysmal failure, in large part because of personal failings that were exposed during the Lewinsky scandal. When the House began moving toward impeachment in 1998, it was clear how little the political environment had been affected by the bipartisan discussions Clinton had fostered under the guise of the BBA.

CENTRALIZED POWER AND THE DIMINISHING CAPABILITY OF THE LEGISLATIVE BRANCH

Beyond the impact of the BBA on federal deficits or the careers of the central players, there was also an impact on the process by which our laws are made. That impact was one part of a dramatic centralization of power that took place in the House of Representatives following Gingrich's accession to the Speakership.

About a quarter of a century before the Balanced Budget Agreement was negotiated, Nelson Polsby wrote in the *American Political Science Review* that those who study government and politics are in general agreement that: "for a political system to be viable, for it to succeed in performing tasks of authoritative resource allocation, problem solving, conflict settlement and so on in behalf of a population of any substantial size, it must be institutionalized. That is to say, organizations must be created and sustained that are specialized.

Otherwise, the political system is likely to be unstable, weak and incapable of servicing the demands or protecting the interests of its constituent groups."

Polsby went on to describe how the U.S. House of Representatives had since the beginning of the Republic become increasingly "institutionalized." This was reflected in the tenure of its members and the specialization they had achieved in the performance of their work. A powerful and effective committee system was a central aspect of that institutionalization.

The process by which the BBA was negotiated was another step toward the deinstitutionalization of Congress, and the centralization of power within the House of Representatives. In his first week in the Speakership, Gingrich eviscerated the independent power of committee chairs by forcing rules changes that limited their terms to six years, and left it to the leadership to determine what their role in Congress would be at the end of that period. He passed over senior committee members to pick their more junior colleagues to preside over them. Congressional scholar Richard Fenno described other actions: "The new Speaker abolished some committees and subcommittees, appointed the Committee Chairman, extracted loyalty pledges from committee leaders, controlled committee staff, selected committee members, created and staffed ad hoc task forces to circumvent committees, established committee priorities and time lines, and monitored committee compliance."[15]

But establishing total dominance over his committees was not enough for Gingrich in his quest to enhance to role of the Speakership. In agreeing to direct negotiations between his office and the White House, he was in effect supplanting the same committees that he already subjugated. Policy in both branches of government was to be conducted at a level well above where the expertise resided and traditionally provided a critical component of good policy.

While there had been earlier high-level summits, they traditionally included committee chairs or their designees in all parts of the formal process. Further, they were a mechanism of last resort—only used when short-circuiting the regular process was necessary to avoid dire consequences. The BBA negotiations seemed more a race to take credit for fiscal good health than an effort to treat a dire and deteriorating condition.

Since the passage of the BBA, the deinstitutionalization of Congress has continued. Committees are weak. A Speaker who once served as a committee chairman and has committed himself to the strengthening of committees has injected himself repeatedly into committee deliberations. Little that can pass as constructive oversight of the Executive Branch occurs, and the congressional schedule seems to provide fewer days in the legislative calendar for such efforts with each passing year.

The passage of the BBA was perhaps a harbinger of a legislative system that directs most policy from the top without fully taking advantage of those members and staffers with the greatest expertise on the issues. One could argue that such a concentration of power strengthens the Speakership and makes for more coherent leadership, but that did not appear to be the case with Gingrich nor his successor or the current Speaker. It may have simply seriously eroded the power of Congress as a constructive force in our system of checks and balances.

◆ ◆ ◆ ◆ ◆

34. Before Money Was Speech: Campaign Finance Reform

by Susan Milligan

Campaign finance reform has always been a delicate matter for lawmakers. It's a great campaign issue, especially for challengers who are up against the sophisticated fund-raising machines of the incumbents they seek to unseat. It's not so appealing for those same lawmakers when they have to raise money for reelection. The harsh reality is that it takes money to run political campaigns, and the money has to come from somewhere—be it individuals or political action committees. By the turn of the century, the public had grown increasingly frustrated with what it perceived as the undue influence of money in American politics. Congress felt pressure to act.

Washington at the time was gripped by fierce partisan tensions. President Bush was starting his first term after a bitter, disputed 2000 election ultimately resolved by the U.S. Supreme Court. The House was barely controlled by Republicans, whose numerical advantage hovered around a dozen seats in 2001–2002. Instead of forcing lawmakers to work across party lines, the narrow division kept everyone on edge, knowing the majority depended on just a handful of seats that could flip later that year.[1]

The Senate had been through its own emotional and political rollercoaster. Evenly divided at 50–50 after the 2000 election, the Senate was controlled by the GOP by virtue of Vice President Richard Cheney's tie-breaking vote. But in mid-2001, Senator James Jeffords (R-VT), angry over what he saw as inattention to an education program dear to him, declared himself an Independent and caucused with the Democrats, giving them a slim 51–49 majority.[2]

The two chambers were having relationship troubles as well. The 9/11 attacks in 2001 had brought a brief sense of common purpose to the Hill, but it also added to the general anxiety. House leaders in both parties were angry that the Senate decided to stay in session after the anthrax scare, while the House went into recess. It certainly didn't help that the *New York Post* carried a page-one photo of House Speaker Dennis Hastert (R-IL) and Democratic leader Richard Gephardt (D-MO) and the headline "WIMPS: The Leaders Who Ran Away from Anthrax."[3]

Into that combustible mix walked four lawmakers—a Republican and a Democrat each from both the House and Senate—who had decided to push for an historic law regulating campaign finance reform. Perhaps it was an apt sign of the times that the law that became known as McCain-Feingold lasted less than a decade before being gutted by the Supreme Court.

REFORM VERSUS SELF-PRESERVATION

Campaign finance reform tested congressional instincts for self-preservation. Scandal tends to force Congress to act, as the body did in the mid-1970s to respond to Watergate. Disclosures that former President Nixon's reelection campaign had received millions of dollars in secret donations led Congress to approve the first-ever limits on allowable donations by individuals and political action committees.[4] But lawmakers in both parties were wary of passing reforms that deprived them of the advantages of incumbency. Sitting Congressmen were in a much better position to raise campaign cash than challengers, and were sometimes able to frighten off potential opponents merely by amassing a large war chest. Financial disarmament—even if it was bilateral—was an unsettling thought for many lawmakers.

As is often the case with reform legislation, sponsors were also unable to use the usual legislative negotiating tools. In an appropriations bill, for instance, earmarks help sway wavering members of Congress who are able to show their constituents that they brought home the pork. On broader policy legislation, lawmakers hold congressional hearings, interview experts and hammer out compromises in conference committee meetings. Lawmakers might trade promises for votes to get their bills passed. But with reform—especially reform that was going to have a huge impact on the lawmakers' ability to keep their own jobs—such deal-making does not apply.

Passing campaign finance overhaul was thus going to require forceful, bipartisan leadership in both chambers of Congress. It was also going to require careful navigation of the rules peculiar to the House and the Senate, both of which are set up to make it easier to stop legislation than to pass it. And finally, any reform effort was going to depend on public events and campaign scandals to keep the pressure on Congress and the White House to change the law.

Those conditions appeared to come together in 1996, when Senator John McCain (R-AZ) teamed up with the fiercely liberal Senator Russ Feingold (D-WI) to put new limits on campaign activity and financing. On the House side, Representative Martin Meehan (D-MA) found an ally in Representative Christopher Shays (R-CT), a mild-mannered, moderate Republican who got along with colleagues in both parties. Meehan had been an architect of the Massachusetts "Clean Elections" law when he was a state legislator. When he ran for Congress in 1992, Meehan pledged not to accept contributions from political action committees—so called PAC money. The promise helped burnish his reformer image, but it also left him at a financial disadvantage: the day after he won the election, Meehan found himself $200,000 in debt. Even before he was sworn in, he knew he'd have to erase that debt and begin raising money for his reelection.[5]

Meanwhile, concerns over campaign financing had changed. With individual and PAC contribution limits in place since 1974, donors found another way to influence campaigns: soft money. While individuals could give just $1,000 to a federal candidate (for the primary, and again for the general election) and PACs could give $5,000, loopholes in the law allowed corporations, labor unions and wealthy individuals to give unlimited, unregulated amounts of money to party committees for so-called party-building activities. These included overhead and administrative costs as well as get-out-the-vote efforts, and they allowed party committees to free up "hard money" donations to give directly to candidates. In 1992, the national parties raised $86 million in soft money. By 1996, the number had shot up to $262 million. Campaign cash, it was becoming clear, was like water. Dammed in one area, it would flow out another way.[6]

Advocates were also growing increasingly troubled by so-called issue ads they felt were being used to get around existing campaign laws. Federal courts had ruled that unless an ad had one of the "magic words" that made it expressly a campaign ad ("vote for," "elect," or "defeat"), it wasn't strictly a campaign ad subject to restrictions under campaign law. So parties and organizations cleverly crafted ads—often funded with soft money—that might urge voters, for example, to "call Sen. Jones and tell him to stop supporting tax hikes." Such an ad did not strictly violate the law, and McCain, Feingold, Meehan, and Shays wanted to clamp down on the practice.

Finally, scandal entered the picture to give campaign finance reform efforts a boost. During his 1996 reelection campaign, President Clinton had come under fire for hosting big-money donors at White House coffee klatches, or letting donors spend the night in the Lincoln Bedroom. Vice President Al Gore was criticized for appearing at a Buddhist monastery event where funds were solicited. In 1997, congressional committees investigated questionable campaign finance activities, as did the Federal Election Commission and the Justice Department. The Democratic National Committee was forced to return $3 million in illegal contributions. It was a black eye for the party, but it provided the public pressure needed for change.[7]

A DIFFICULT JOURNEY

The road to reform on Capitol Hill, however, was winding and full of political potholes. On the Senate side, McCain and Feingold pushed for a measure that would ban soft money and regulate what they saw as "sham issue ads," treating them as straight-up campaign ads under the law. The bill banned "issue ads" within 30 days of a primary or caucus or within 60 days of a general election (the ads could still run, but only under the funding limit rules imposed on traditional campaign ads).

Getting a majority to support the reform measure was tough; getting the 60 votes necessary to invoke cloture and stop a filibuster was proving almost impossible. Republicans, most notably Senator Mitch McConnell (R-KY), argued that the legislation was an affront to free speech and the right of free association.[8] Senate Majority Leader Trent Lott (R-MS), concerned about the power of union money to elect Democrats, wanted a "paycheck protection" provision that would require employees in a union shop to sign a form giving the union the right to spend their dues on political activities. The standoff left the Senate with nothing in 1997. Lott was unable to get cloture on his paycheck protection amendment, while Democrats failed to break a filibuster of the entire bill.[9] Again in 1998, Democrats tried, this time with tweaks to the bill to make it more palatable to Republicans. And again, the bill's supporters failed to get enough votes for cloture.

The House, meanwhile, was journeying down its own reform track. As in the Senate, Shays and Meehan were running into procedural hurdles. In the House, it is extremely difficult to get full consideration of a bill unless leadership allows it to come to the floor. Further, legislation (unless it is presented "in suspension" of the rules, which requires a supermajority for passage) must first go through the Rules Committee. That committee is heavily weighted toward the majority party, and it determines how much time will be allowed for debate and what, if any, amendments will be allowed for a vote.[10]

House Speaker Newt Gingrich (R-GA) opposed the bill and refused to allow it to the floor for a vote. Even if Gingrich thought the measure would fail on the floor, he didn't want to put his members in the position of explaining to their constituents why they voted against it. Meehan and Shays took the extraordinary step of collecting signatures on a "discharge petition." Such a document, if it receives the signatures of 218 members (a majority of the House) allows the bill to go to the floor. When Shays and Meehan got to 200 signatures Gingrich relented, and the measure eventually passed. But without Senate action, the idea languished for several more years.[11]

The 2000 elections provided another chance. McCain ran—and lost—in the GOP primaries, but he had enhanced his national stature and continued to hammer away at campaign finance reform on the stump. In mid-2001, Democrats seized control of the Senate when Vermont Senator Jim Jeffords left the GOP and began caucusing with the Democrats, making Senator Tom Daschle (D-SD) the new majority leader. And McCain and Feingold made a renewed push. This time, the debate was real, and it was heated. Unlike other debates, in which senators would make speeches and leave the chamber, this debate had a higher quality to it. One got the sense that minds were being changed by the arguments lawmakers were presenting.

The measure was amended to bring on more votes. The "hard money" contribution limit was doubled to $2,000, and a "millionaires' amendment" was added to allow candidates up against self-financed opponents to collect contributions above the $2,000 limit. And critically, the Senate rejected an amendment that would have nullified the ban on soft money if any substantial part of the law were found unconstitutional.

McConnell, facing the reality that the law would pass, warned his colleagues on the floor: "I promise you if McCain-Feingold becomes law, there won't be a penny less spent on politics, not a penny less—in fact, a good deal more spent on politics. It just won't be spent by the parties. And even with the increase in hard money, which I think was a good idea and I voted for, there is no way that will ever make up for the soft dollars lost."[12]

Shays and Meehan again had to carefully navigate the House rules—and again had to force the measure, as they wrote it, to the floor with a discharge petition. The bill passed (with the Senate's changes) and President George W. Bush, who had been on record opposing the measure, was faced with a choice. He could veto it, and face charges in his reelection campaign that he squashed a chance to bring more integrity to the system, or he could sign it and wait to see the consequences for his party. Without fanfare or a signing ceremony, Bush put his name on the law, known as the Bipartisan Campaign Reform Act (BCRA).[13]

SUPREME COURT WEIGHS IN

The celebration by campaign finance reform advocates would be relatively brief. McConnell immediately filed a challenge to the law on First Amendment grounds. He lost, with the high court upholding BCRA in 2003.[14] But a half-decade later, the makeup of the court had changed, most notably with the appointment of John Roberts as Chief Justice. In 2008, a conservative group, Citizens United, was stopped by a federal district court from running TV ads for *Hillary: The Movie,* a film highly critical of then-Democratic primary contender Hillary Clinton. The Supreme Court heard oral arguments on the case in 2009 and at first, appeared ready to rule in favor of Citizens United, but on the narrow terms that the group had the right to advertise the film without violating BCRA restrictions on "issue ads." Roberts, however, asked that the case be reargued, and the scope of the constitutional questions broadened dramatically.[15]

In 2010, a divided court dealt a deathblow to BCRA, throwing out the provision that bans individuals, corporations, and labor unions from spending unlimited amounts of cash to influence an election. The contribution limits stayed in (as did the ban on direct contributions from corporations and unions to candidates). Independent spending—as long as it was not coordinated with a campaign—was protected as free speech, the court said.[16] It was the biggest change in campaign finance law since the 1907 Tillman Act, which banned direct contributions from corporations, and the Taft-Hartley Act of 1947, which extended the ban to labor unions.

McCain, the last of the campaign finance reform foursome still in office when the *Citizens United* ruling came down (Shays and Feingold lost reelection, while Meehan left to become chancellor of the University of Massachusetts at Lowell) was devastated. Had any of the members of the Supreme Court ever had to run for office, McCain said, the ruling would have been different. In an interview, McCain said, "How is money speech? If money is speech, then wealthy people, not low income people, will then decide who the members of Congress are and who the President of the United States is."[17]

John McCain's concerns were well founded. Overall spending for the 2012 presidential election clocked in at a record $2.34 billion, with hundreds of millions of dollars going to loosely regulated Super PACs and "social welfare" groups.[18] McCain predicted that further reform would occur only after a major scandal involving campaign finance: "This is the history of American politics. There will be a scandal. It may be foreign money, or it may be a small group of people who really poured so much money into targeted races that they made the difference, which is already happening."[19]

Even if they are armed with the public outrage generated by a major scandal, however, future reformers will face a much higher hurdle than McCain, Feingold, Shays, and Meehan had to overcome—a Supreme Court precedent that, barring a significant change in the composition of the justices on the Court, is not likely to be overturned.

Frustration over that impasse produced a rare, public rebuke of the Supreme Court by President Barack Obama, who in his 2010 State of the Union Address took direct aim at the black-robed justices seated before him. "Last week, the Supreme Court reversed a century of law to open the floodgates for special interests—including foreign corporations—to spend without limit in our elections," Obama said. "Well I don't think American elections should be bankrolled by America's most powerful interests, or worse, by foreign entities. They should be decided by the American people, and that's why I'm urging Democrats and Republicans to pass a bill that helps to right this wrong."[20]

During the rebuke, Supreme Court Justice Samuel Alito was captured by television cameras mouthing the words "not true." And the always-contentious issue of the role of money in American politics awaits its next scandal.[21]

◆ ◆ ◆ ◆ ◆

35. Federal Reform of Education: No Child Left Behind

by Patrick McGuinn

The passage of the "No Child Left Behind" law (NCLB) in 2001 was one of the signature legislative accomplishments of the George W. Bush Administration, and it inaugurated a new era of federal influence in the U.S. education system. In fact, NCLB came about because of developments in the 1990s that fundamentally challenged the old politics of education, and ultimately transformed national education policy.

Several important groups were disenchanted with the slow pace of state education reform, and began to doubt whether states would ever generate meaningful change in the absence of federal pressure. As Paul Manna has noted, reform-minded governors sought to "borrow strength" by leveraging federal authority to advance their own school reform agendas. They were joined in this effort by business groups, which were increasingly concerned about the training and productivity of American workers, and civil rights groups that hoped to use such reforms to document and close racial achievement gaps. This alliance of governors, business leaders, and civil rights groups blurred the longstanding ideological divisions over school reform, and represented a potent outside political force for change in Washington, D.C.

As it happened, change inside Washington also helped ensure that the education reform alliance would find a more receptive audience of policy makers at the federal level. The 1992 election of President Bill Clinton, a reform-minded "New Democrat" and former Education Governor, pushed Democrats to embrace a more centrist position on education, and led to the passage of two major school reform bills in 1994—Goals 2000 and the Improving America's Schools Act (IASA). Many of the reform ideas that would later form the core of NCLB—such as standards, assessments, adequate yearly progress, school report cards, and corrective action—found their first expression in the 1994 Elementary and Secondary Education Act (ESEA) reauthorization. (IASA ostensibly required states to adopt standards, assessment, and accountability policies, but it was weakly enforced and by 2002 only 16 states had fully met its requirements.)

Under the leadership of House Speaker Newt Gingrich (R-GA), Republicans in the mid-1990s actually tried to reduce federal involvement in education through a variety of means, including cutting federal spending, converting education funding into block grants or vouchers, and eliminating the Department of Education entirely. These conservative positions on education, while popular with the party's base, proved extremely unpopular with the general public, particularly with moderate swing voters. Between 1984 and 1996, polls showed that Democrats maintained a double-digit polling advantage over Republicans in terms of which party best addressed education.

The partisan education gap became increasingly costly for the GOP by the end of the 1990s as education rose to the top of the public agenda and became a decisive national electoral issue. In addition, the failure of most states to comply with the 1994 federal mandates, or to make significant progress in closing achievement gaps despite greatly increased federal and state education spending, put pressure on national policy makers to undertake more substantive education reform.

The unpopularity of the earlier Republican focus on deregulation and privatization, and the discrediting of the Democratic focus on resources and regulation, led to a new bipartisan consensus around standards, testing, and accountability. In the 2000 election, voters ranked education as the single most important issue of the election, and presidential candidates George W. Bush and Al Gore proposed remarkably similar plans for an expanded federal role in schools that became the basis for NCLB.

Clearly there was growing political support for a "grand bargain" that included increased federal education funding and greater flexibility in exchange for expanded accountability for school performance. After years of debate over whether there should even be a federal role in education, there was general agreement not only on the need for federal leadership to improve public schools, but also on the broad direction that such leadership should take. As one veteran congressional aide noted in 2001, "Most congressional Democrats and Republicans now share the belief that a major way to improve education is to raise academic standards, test schoolchildren to determine if they have mastered those standards, and take action in those schools that show lack of success in raising student achievement."[1]

A COMPASSIONATE CONSERVATIVE

By the time President Bush took office in 2001, the time was ripe for a new education policy regime. Education had been the centerpiece of Bush's campaign, and as promised, he made education the top domestic priority of his new administration. In his inaugural address, Bush remarked, "Together we will reclaim America's schools, before ignorance and apathy claim more young lives."[2]

On just his second full day in office, Bush sent to Congress an education blueprint based on his campaign proposals. The NCLB Act was the first proposal he sent to Congress, and it became the focal point of the new Congress's early deliberations. Two strategic decisions about NCLB proved crucial to how the legislative negotiations unfolded: Bush's decision to submit an outline of his education reform ideas rather than detailed legislative language; and his decision to seek a bipartisan bill rather than attempt to force a Republican bill through Congress on a narrow party-line vote.

Some Republicans argued that the party should use its narrow majorities in the House and Senate to pass a conservative bill that contained vouchers, block grants, and other controversial items, which Democrats strongly opposed. Bush declined to follow this strategy, and his pursuit of a bipartisan compromise fundamentally influenced the nature of the final legislation as well as its long-term impact on the politics of federal education policy.

Bush opted for the bipartisan approach for a number of reasons, some political, and some having to do with policy. First, while Republicans technically controlled Congress, they had a slim majority in the House, and the

Senate was so evenly divided that the GOP could not stop a Democratic filibuster.

Second, Bush had pledged to work with Democrats and foster a new spirit of bipartisanship during the campaign, and his controversial and bitterly contested victory in 2000 ensured that a partisan approach on his first and highest profile domestic issue would generate a great deal of rancor. By beginning his presidency with a bipartisan compromise on school reform, Bush could create an important symbol of his centrist "compassionate conservatism."

Finally, Bush's views on education reform were actually closer in many respects to those of New Democrats than to conservative Republicans. The Bush Administration clearly thought that the way to maximize the political and policy gains from education reform was to create an alliance with moderate Republicans and New Democrats, and then to lobby more conservative Republicans to support their new President on his first policy initiative.

When Bush introduced his education blueprint, he publicly distanced himself from the more conservative elements of his party by stating that "change will not come by disdaining or dismantling the federal role in education. Educational excellence for all is a national issue and at this moment a presidential priority."[3] At a meeting of education leaders held in Austin prior to his inauguration, Bush reached out to education leaders from both parties and made clear that he wanted to pass a bipartisan education bill. The congressional Democratic leaders on education—Senator Ted Kennedy (D-MA) and Representative George Miller (D-CA)—had gradually become convinced that it would take more than money to fix what ailed American public schools. Bush's decision to seek a bipartisan bill and Kennedy's decision to work with the Administration ensured that the final version of NCLB would represent a compromise between the Republican and Democratic visions of education reform.

Bush's second important strategic decision on education was to send only a 28-page blueprint of his reform ideas to Congress. He never actually sent legislation to Capitol Hill, opting instead to merely sketch out the general contours of ESEA reform that he supported. This approach had several advantages for Bush, although it resulted in somewhat reduced Administration influence over the final product. By publicly committing only to general principles rather than specific legislative language, Bush retained the flexibility to negotiate with all of the different players during the congressional debate. In addition, by focusing on broad goals such as accountability and flexibility, Bush could claim credit for negotiating in a bipartisan manner and for whatever legislation Congress ultimately approved.

BUILDING BIPARTISAN SUPPORT

As had been the case during the 1990s, the debate over NCLB revealed four different factions in Congress regarding federal education policy: liberal Democrats, New Democrats, conservative Republicans, and Main Street Republicans. The liberal Democratic faction wanted to preserve federal education programs and regulations and to obtain large increases in federal spending. It was adamantly opposed to vouchers and generally reluctant to support tough testing or accountability measures. Many in the conservative wing of the Republican Party, meanwhile, continued to oppose any federal influence over elementary and secondary education and viewed NCLB as a threat to local control of schools. The key difference in 2001, however, was that growing numbers of moderate Republicans and New Democrats had become increasingly concerned about the status quo and were more willing to embrace tough new federal reforms.

The evolution of John Boehner (R-OH), the conservative then-Chairman of the House Education and Workforce Committee, illustrates the extent to which Republicans had shifted their positions on the issue by 2001. Boehner had been a leading opponent of federal influence in education in the 1990s, voting to eliminate the Department of Education and remarking in 1995 that "it is clear that the current experiment of having the federal government heavily involved in education has failed."[4] After Bush's election, however, Boehner acknowledged that "I think we realized in 1996 that our message was sending the wrong signal to the American people about the direction we wanted to go in education."[5]

Boehner became one of the most vocal supporters of NCLB, and one of Bush's key allies in mobilizing Republican support for the bill. He said that "the 2000 campaign paved the way for reform, and conservatives must capitalize by implementing the president's plan . . . conservatives have yearned for an opportunity to break the status quo in federal education policy. This could be our moment. On behalf of parents and students, let's seize it."[6]

For Kennedy and other liberal Democrats who had long resisted rigorous testing and accountability measures, the decision to work with the Bush Administration was also based on both politics and policy. Republicans had a majority in the House and Senate, and there was concern that they might be able to overcome any Democratic resistance to advance a conservative education bill. As National Education Association (NEA) lobbyist Joel Packer noted, "the political environment was such that even if Democrats opposed Bush he was going to get the bill, so leading Democrats made the decision that it was best to be involved instead of opposing the whole thing (much of which New Democrats supported anyway.)"[7] In addition, discontent with the performance of the public schools had grown among the general public as well as among African Americans and Hispanic Americans,[8] two key parts of the Democratic base. Though groups like the NAACP (National Association for the Advancement of Colored People) remained wary of testing and accountability, a number of minority advocacy groups such as the Education Trust, the Black Alliance for Educational Options, and the Citizens' Commission on Civil Rights joined New Democrats in pressuring liberal Democrats to support what they saw as necessary reforms to improve the public schools.

In keeping with his pursuit of a bipartisan bill, Bush's education plan contained elements that each party could support. Democrats were pleased with Bush's call for increased federal spending and activism on education, while Republicans supported the increased flexibility given to states and the emphasis on accountability.

But the initial Bush plan also contained elements that each party opposed. Democrats quickly labeled Bush's proposals for private school vouchers a deal-breaker, and voiced opposition to his charter agreements proposals, which they criticized as a block grant that would remove important federal safeguards for disadvantaged and minority students. Bush's call for federally mandated testing, meanwhile, made many on both the left and the right wary. Despite these concerns, however, the new political dynamic created a real opening for a far-reaching reconsideration of the federal role in education. In the end, while Bush's leadership was crucial, the creation of a new federal education policy regime would not have occurred without congressional leaders from both parties reconsidering their longstanding opposition to many of the reforms contained in the bill.

Despite the Bush Administration's deep involvement with the bill and the support of leaders from both parties, the congressional deliberations were often contentious, and a number of key elements of NCLB were either defeated or only narrowly survived the legislative process. The key testing provision was saved by heavy White House lobbying and by the efforts of Boehner and Miller, in the House, and Kennedy and Judd Gregg (R-NH), in the Senate, a group that kept the centrist coalition from collapsing under pressure from the left and right. House Majority Whip Tom DeLay (R-TX), a staunch conservative, also noted at the time "that the majority of our members want to support the president, and the centerpiece of his proposal is testing."[9] The vocal public support and energetic lobbying by business groups such as the National Alliance of Business, Achieve, and the Business

Coalition for Excellence in Education (BCEE) were also crucial in defeating attempts by liberals and conservatives to water down or remove many of the legislation's standards, testing, and accountability provisions.[10] The bipartisan reform efforts also received a major boost from public opinion polls showing that NCLB was supported by more than a three-to-one margin.[11]

TOUGH TRADE-OFFS

The bill ultimately passed both chambers of Congress by wide margins; the House passed its version of NCLB on May 23, 2001 by a vote of 384–45, while the Senate passed its version on June 14, by a vote of 91–8. The conference committee was left with two primary tasks—to settle on the level of funding for the bill and to finalize the details of the bill's new accountability system.

However, by the time the conference committee convened, a number of disagreements had become public, and pressure from the left and right led some observers to question whether a compromise could attract sufficient support to pass both chambers. Educational interest groups that felt threatened by many of the bill's new testing and accountability requirements intensified their efforts to derail the legislation. At this crucial moment came the terrorist attacks of September 11, 2001. The attacks apparently created a sense in the leadership of both parties that completing work on a bipartisan education bill could reassure a jittery public by providing a symbol of a unified and functioning government.

The vote to approve the conference report of NCLB was overwhelming and bipartisan in both the House (381–41) and Senate (87–10). The final version of the legislation was a compromise bill in every sense of the word—the reforms went too far for some and not far enough for others. Given the broad and passionate policy disagreements between Democrats and Republicans during the 1980s and 1990s, however, NCLB's passage with bipartisan support was a remarkable development. Both sides made major concessions—Republicans dropped vouchers, most of their "Straight A's" block grant proposals, and their major consolidation effort. Democrats accepted extensive new federal mandates regarding teacher quality, testing, and accountability.

At the heart of the bill was a fundamental trade-off—it put in place a number of new mandates on states and school districts, but provided greater flexibility in how increased federal funds were spent.[12] The most important requirements in the new law were that states must adopt academic standards to guide their curricula and adopt a testing and accountability system that was aligned with those standards.[13] States would have to test all students in grades 3–8 every year (as well as once in high school) in math and reading beginning in the 2005–2006 school year. States were free to develop and use their own standards and tests, but every school, school district, and state would have to make student test results publicly available and disaggregated for certain groups of students including: major racial and ethnic groups; major income groups; students with a disability; students with limited English proficiency; and migrant students.

NCLB mandated that every state and school district issue report cards that detail student test scores and identify those schools that have failed to meet proficiency targets and are in need of "program improvement." NCLB explicitly required that states use this information to track their efforts to close the achievement gaps on reading and math between different racial, ethnic, and income groups. States were required to establish a timeline (with regular benchmarks) for making "adequate yearly progress" toward eliminating these gaps and moving all students to state proficiency levels within 12 years. The law's accountability provisions required states to take a number of escalating actions with schools that do not reach their performance objectives. In exchange for meeting these new federal demands, NCLB provided a significant increase in federal spending (approximately 34 percent in the first year) and new flexibility in how states could spend it.

MIXED RESULTS

NCLB represented the most significant overhaul and expansion of the federal role in education since 1965. The scope, specificity, and ambition of the law's mandates were akin to a revolution in federal education policy. For the first time, the federal government would pressure states to undertake systemic change in their education systems and hold them accountable for the academic performance of their students.

Since the passage of NCLB, states have bristled at how coercive and prescriptive the law's mandates are, and they have struggled mightily to implement them on the ground. There is also considerable evidence that states have used their broad discretion to set their own standards, tests, and proficiency levels to game the system by lowering their expectations for student achievement. NCLB forced states to change many of their educational practices, but political resistance and capacity gaps at the state level meant that these changes were often more superficial than substantive. As a result, the law did not generate as much meaningful school improvement or progress in closing student-achievement gaps as was originally hoped.

As states have struggled to meet NCLB's ambitious goals, some of the initial philosophical reservations within both parties have boiled back to the surface. Many Republicans resent the coerciveness of the new federal role, while many Democrats are concerned about the impact of standardized testing on instruction, and about the focus on schools as the problem in poor educational outcomes as opposed to broader economic and social factors. So while the passage of NCLB was a considerable bipartisan triumph from a political standpoint, whether it will ultimately be judged an effective educational reform is an open question.

♦ ♦ ♦ ♦ ♦

Congress and National Security

36. FDR versus Congressional Isolationists: The Road to World War II

by Carl Cannon

Unless they lived in the Hawaiian Islands and could see the smoldering ships and hear the bombs dropping, Americans learned their country was at war from an Associated Press bulletin that was broadcast over the radio at 2:20 P.M. on December 7, 1941. The phone lines in Hawaii were commandeered by U.S. military authorities, so the report came from the nation's capital, where William Peacock, the Washington editor of the Associated Press, was at his desk eating a peanut butter and bacon sandwich. The bureau chief was interrupted by a telephone call from White House press secretary Stephen Early. An infantryman in World War I and former AP man himself, Early got right to the point: "I have a statement from the president," he said. "The Japanese have attacked Pearl Harbor from the air."

"Flash!" Peacock yelled to his wire editor before repeating the information, which was then dispatched to the nation, interrupting football games, musical broadcasts, and the Sunday activities of a people who had hoped to avoid the deadly war enveloping the world.

In Pittsburgh, Republican Senator Gerald P. Nye, the outspoken isolationist from North Dakota was the headliner at an America First Committee rally at the city's Soldiers & Sailors Memorial Hall.

"Whose war is this?" the speakers at the rally shouted.

"Roosevelt's!" the crowd shouted back.

When a U.S. Army colonel who had been out for a walk with his wife tried to tell the rally that more than 1,100 U.S. sailors and Marines lay dead in the sunken USS *Arizona* in Hawaii, he was booed and thrown out of the hall. Nye, informed of the attack midway through his talk, kept speaking, announcing the news only near the end—while expressing skepticism.

At the White House Navy Secretary Frank Knox passed by the phalanx of reporters who gathered after hearing the news, and a murmur passed through the crowd, "How did he ever let the Navy be surprised?" they asked one another—noting that the distance between Japan and Hawaii is farther than Berlin to New York. At 8:50 P.M., Republican Senator Hiram Johnson made his way into the West Wing meeting. It could not have been an easy trip for the proud progressive from California.

"What a sight!" wrote journalist Richard Strout. "The great isolation-ist, Hiram Johnson, grim-faced, immaculately dressed, stalks across our little stone stage on the White House portico. All the ghosts of isolationism stalk with him, all the beliefs that the United States could stay out of war if it made no attack. . . . [He] walks by, refusing to comment, looking straight ahead through the crowd of reporters, who are silenced for a minute with the sense of history passing and a chapter closing."

In that moment, Franklin Delano Roosevelt had vanquished his isolationist adversaries on Capitol Hill—but at tremendous cost to them and the country. The question, even seven decades later, is how did it even come to that?

A NATIONAL AVERSION TO WAR

It's difficult to exaggerate the toll the Civil War took on the psyche of the American people. If the underlying cause of that war—ending slavery—was profound, so was the carnage on the battlefield. In a land of 34 million peo-ple, nearly 4 million men had donned the blue or the gray. When the num-bers of dead, wounded, and missing are totaled, some 1 million Americans were killed or maimed among a population one-tenth the size of the present-day United States.

The result was a near-universal abhorrence of war. The attitude crossed ideological, geographical, and generational lines, and it hardened into a national aversion to the very idea of a large standing army. Polling didn't yet exist in its present form, but savvy politicians knew the electorate's mindset. Women, who could not yet vote, were even more pacifistic in their outlook than their husbands. The reverence for "the generals" one hears in 21st cen-tury political discourse was much less in evidence. Although it is true that Presidents Ulysses S. Grant, Rutherford B. Hayes, James A. Garfield, and Chester Arthur had all been officers in the Union Army, it was also true that President Grover Cleveland had paid someone to take his place in the ranks during the Civil War, and did not suffer for it politically. Americans were also aware that Union General George G. Meade lost more men in a single day at Gettysburg than George Washington lost in eight years fighting the British—and they never wanted to see anything like it again.

This attitude continued well into the 20th century, and was greatly ampli-fied by World War I. President Woodrow Wilson, whose father was a promi-nent Presbyterian pastor and Southern sympathizer who took his family to Georgia and later served as a chaplain in the Confederate Army, famously determined that future generations of Americans would not equate his presi-dency with flag-draped coffins.

When Europe exploded 16 months into his White House tenure, Wilson made it clear that he wanted no part of the conflict. Paying homage to the rhetoric—if not the fighting spirit—of Thomas Paine, the neutrality-obsessed president dispatched peace envoys to Europe while telling Americans it was their patriotic duty to remain neutral "during these days that try men's souls."

Wilson adhered to this position long after it became impractical and even after it put Americans in grave peril. This point was underscored on May 1, 1915, when *The New York Times* carried an advertisement placed by the German government warning that anyone venturing into the seas near the British Isles was putting themselves in mortal danger. Although these were international waters, Wilson registered no protest at the German provocation. And the *Lusitania,* a British ocean liner with a manifest of nearly 2,000 passengers and crew, set sail that very morning from New York to Liverpool. Five days later, as the *Lusitania* cruised in the Irish Sea while nearing port, a German U-boat fired a torpedo striking her below the wheelhouse, setting off a secondary explosion that sunk the ship in 18 minutes, taking 1,198 souls with it—128 of them Americans. Wilson demanded reparation from the Germans, as well as an apology, and urged the Kaiser to halt indiscriminate naval warfare against noncombatant vessels—but that was all.

The national outrage over the *Lusitania*'s sinking gradually subsided, overwhelmed by American's aversion to sending its sons to the trenches. In 1916, Wilson ran for reelection as the man who had spared his nation from that fate. The Democrats' slogan that year was, "He kept us out of war."

Of course, war came for America anyway, and in its aftermath, the nation's attitude was even more bitter than after the Civil War. Some 53,000 Americans died in combat in France in World War I; another 63,000 died from other causes, most of them influenza, and 204,000 Americans were wounded. These casualties paled in comparison to those of the European powers, but as the Roaring Twenties gave way to the Great Depression a deep sense of cynicism set in. Why, Americans asked one another, were we fighting and dying in Europe in the first place? What, if anything, had been gained?

For most Americans, this was a question that answered itself. That was the country that Franklin D. Roosevelt governed in the 1930s while Germany rearmed and Japan began dreaming of an ocean empire.

WAR CLOUDS GATHER

The 1940 presidential election pitted two internationalists, Republican challenger Wendell Willkie and FDR, who had decided to break with the precedent set by George Washington (and honored by every succeeding president) to run for a third term. The rationale Roosevelt cited was the gravely deteriorating situation in Europe. That was a pretext, but not a flimsy one. As the 1940 campaign got underway in late spring, the news from Europe was about France's surrender, Germany's invasion of the Low Countries, and Britain's near-disaster at Dunkirk.

Great Britain seemed poised to fall next to the Nazi juggernaut. Among those who thought so was Joseph Kennedy, U.S. Ambassador to the Court of St. James. "The jig is up," Kennedy wrote Roosevelt. But the British had a new prime minister, a man with a different outlook. In his first days in office, Winston Churchill had acted decisively to save 340,000 British and French troops trapped between Germany's *Wehrmacht* and the sea at Dunkirk. Next, he turned to America for help.

Through his ambassador in Washington, the British government relayed a stark message to Washington. "If we go down," he said, "Hitler has a very good chance of conquering the world." Roosevelt was receptive to taking action, but he'd been waiting for a sign that Britain wouldn't capitulate the way France had. As historian David M. Kennedy has put it, Churchill was that sign. But what could Roosevelt realistically do?

Secretary of State Cordell Hull had observed that when it came to U.S. editorial opinion about Nazi Germany, widespread hostility to Hitler coexisted with a nearly unanimous view that the United States should not become entangled in European conflicts.

The newspapers were accurately reflecting this national mood. Surveys done by Gallup and *Fortune* showed that Americans simply did not believe the bloody events in Europe—or Manchuria, for that matter—were their problem. As historian James MacGregor Burns explored in *Roosevelt: The Soldier of Freedom*, isolation was as much of a mental state in this country as a cogent political philosophy.

"This was not a program or group or opinion," he wrote. "It was a mood, expressed in the simple outcry, 'No Foreign Wars!' It was a mood compounded by fear, frustration, disillusion, and cynicism," MacGregor noted. As World War II raged on the continent, this national mindset took form in a simple—some might say simplistic—conviction: Defense, yes; aid to the Allies, perhaps; but foreign wars, never.

Despite his antiwar rhetoric in the 1940 campaign, FDR himself had come to realize the danger posed by Germany, Japan, and Italy—and the peril of underestimating their threat. After nearly eight years in office, Roosevelt had a better sense of the pulse of the American people than the pollsters did. He also didn't mind a political fight and wasn't above employing rhetorical misdirection. In seven years of experience he'd learned a great deal about getting things through a reluctant Congress.

CONGRESS PUSHES BACK

And make no mistake, Congress was very reluctant to go to war. In 1935, it had passed the Neutrality Act, legislation the President signed; related bills were passed later, all of which were signed into law by the President. The impetus for these bills came out of Senate hearings chaired by Gerald Nye which pushed the idea that bankers, arms manufacturers, and other war "profiteers" had manipulated the United States into entering World War I.

On Capitol Hill, the "America Firsters" were an eclectic bunch comprising liberals and conservatives in both parties. In the Senate, Republicans Nye, William Edgar Borah of Idaho, and Arthur H. Vandenberg of Michigan, and Wisconsin's Robert M. La Follette Jr. were key isolationist leaders. They were joined by many Democrats, including Senators Burton K. Wheeler of Montana, David I. Walsh of Massachusetts, and Senator Bob Reynolds of North Carolina. And, of course, California's Hiram Johnson. Isolationism ran strong in the House, too, where the Democrats' leading isolationist was Representative Louis Ludlow of Indiana. On the Republican side, the most prominent proponent of neutrality—*Time* magazine once dubbed him America's "No. 1 isolationist"—was New York Representative Hamilton Fish III.

Roosevelt considered them all misguided, but with one eye on his 1936 reelection campaign, he had signed the 1935 and 1936 Neutrality Acts, and another version again in 1937 for good measure. In 1938, the President roused himself to oppose—but only at the eleventh hour—a constitutional amendment authored by Republican Ludlow that went much further. Ludlow's measure held that "except in the event of an invasion of the United States or its territorial possessions" any declaration of war by Congress would have to be rubber-stamped by the American people in a nationwide referendum. Even with the President's opposition, the amendment only failed by a vote of 209–188.

That was the environment on Capitol Hill, and in the country, as the 1930s came to a close. In still-insular America, the 1938 midterm elections hinged on domestic concerns ranging from FDR's court-packing schemes to the 1937–1938 recession that had undone the nation's progress in digging out of the Great Depression. Campaigning against what they portrayed as Roosevelt's dictatorial impulses, Republicans picked up 72 seats in the House and 7 in the Senate. Meanwhile, while Americans were barely looking, real dictators were on the march abroad.

WORLD CONQUEST

Japan had invaded Manchuria in 1931, and in 1938 occupied Nanking. In 1936, the Italian Army invaded Ethiopia. In March 1938, Hitler annexed Austria. Six months later, with English and French acquiescence, Germany began gobbling up Czechoslovakia, finishing the job in March of 1939. As all this was going on, Americans continued to look inward. Even after Germany rolled into Poland in September 1939, putting Germany at war with France and Great Britain, Americans believed they could, and should, stay out of the fighting.

In October and again in December, a *Fortune* magazine poll asked a scientific cross-section of Americans what the United States should do. In neither poll did as many as 18 percent of respondents choose the answer, "enter the war at some stage." The second choice: "help the Allies, but don't enter the war," garnered 20 percent support in October, but less than half that much in December. The third choice was "impartial neutrality," in which the United States could sell goods to both sides, but only on a cash-and-carry basis. It garnered a huge plurality of support. Even after Czechoslovakia was swallowed up and Poland carved in half, Americans felt safe. The same polls that revealed a desire to stay out of the fight showed that Americans had no illusions about the Axis power's hostility to democracy—or their insatiable desire for conquest, perhaps even in this hemisphere. So why were Americans so unconcerned about their own security?

It is often said today—and was said at that time—that isolationists believed the two vast oceans, the Atlantic and the Pacific, protected the United States. To be sure, prominent isolationists used this imagery. But the truth was more complex. Americans had known since the days of the *Lusitania* that German submarines could patrol the oceans anywhere in the world. The real reason Americans were not overly worried about the threat Germany posed to the United States was because of their faith in the French Army and the English Navy.

The events leading up to Dunkirk upended that equation. Norway was suddenly in Nazi hands, as were the Low Countries. May 1940 had revealed the French Army to be a paper tiger, and the Maginot Line a useless and expensive boondoggle. The British Navy was on the ropes. On May 15, 1940, frantic French Prime Minister Paul Reynaud phoned Churchill. "We are beaten!" he screamed over the phone. "The road to Paris is open!"

Hearing that awful cry, Churchill composed an urgent cable to Franklin Roosevelt. "As you are no doubt aware, the scene has darkened swiftly," Churchill wrote. "The small countries are simply smashed up, one-by-one, like matchwood. . . . We expect to be attacked here ourselves."

Churchill thought the German invasion would come by sea and by air, with paratroopers, "If necessary, we shall continue the war alone, and we are not afraid of that," he told Roosevelt. "But I trust you realize, Mr. President, that the voice and force of the United States may count for nothing if they are withheld too long."

ROOSEVELT AND CHURCHILL

Britain's wartime prime minister asked Roosevelt for a lot, including the "loan" of up to 50 mothballed U.S. Navy destroyers; use of "several hundred" modern fighter planes and bombers; antiaircraft guns; and the deployment of U.S. forces to Ireland and Singapore to keep the Germans and Japanese at bay. He was also asking at a delicate time. But he was asking the right man. In Franklin Delano Roosevelt, the people of the United States— and the people of the world—had chosen the leader with the proper temperament, outlook, experience, and skill set needed to negotiate the swirling political waters ahead. Much later, at a December 1943 news conference, Roosevelt would say that "Dr. New Deal" had become "Dr. Win-the-War." This metamorphosis had actually begun in 1940, notwithstanding the President's protestations to the contrary.

As late as October 30, 1940—a week before the election—FDR had assured voters that no Americans would be sent to fight overseas while he was Commander in Chief. "Your boys are not going to be sent into any foreign wars!" he said in a speech at the Boston Navy Yard. At the same time, Roosevelt doubled the size of the Army and the Navy and announced that the British wanted to purchase an additional 12,000 warplanes—for a total of 26,000. Roosevelt added that he planned to build twice that many for the United States, thereby deftly marrying the idea of economic security of America with the physical security of the Allies.

"Under normal conditions we have no need for a vast army in this country," the President said in Boston. "But you and I know that unprecedented dangers require unprecedented action to guard the peace of America against unprecedented threats."

Roosevelt also noted in his speech how isolationists in Congress had tried to thwart him, except that he didn't call them isolationists—he called them Republicans. "Can such people be trusted with national defense?" he asked the cheering crowd. Here, the President was having it both ways. He assailed the GOP and, by extension, its presidential nominee for not being tough enough—all while simultaneously issuing a Wilson-like declaration that American boys wouldn't be fighting and dying overseas.

In hindsight, Roosevelt's balancing act between what his countrymen wanted to do, and what they needed to do, helped save the world. His foresight and political dexterity in accommodating two competing national desires was on display in the program known as "Lend-Lease." It would take a bit of Roosevelt's disingenuousness as well as a dash of amnesia to sell it to the American people, and passing it signaled Roosevelt's victory over isolationism. The military victories over fascism would follow in due course.

A LEASE ON WAR

When he received Churchill's desperate May 15, 1940 plea, FDR responded the next day. The destroyers were not his to give, he informed the Prime Minister, absent an act of Congress, "and I am not certain that it would be wise for that suggestion to be made to the Congress at this moment." As for the rest of requests, Roosevelt indicated he could finesse them; from that moment on, the two leaders worked in concert.

Despite what he said in Boston, Roosevelt had already laid the ground-work for Lend-Lease—and for war—before his reelection. As he noted, the size of the standing military had been doubled; the factories were already in the midst of their conversion to a wartime economy that would do what the New Deal couldn't—end the Depression. On September 2, 1940, FDR came through with the destroyers, and did so by crafting a "Destroyers for Bases," compromise that gave Britain 50 nearly obsolete warships in exchange for 99-year leases at naval ports in Newfoundland and the Caribbean. Two weeks later, Roosevelt signed another bill he'd shepherded through Congress—a military draft law.

"America stands at the crossroads of its destiny," Roosevelt proclaimed in the official signing statement issued by the White House. "Time and distance have been shortened. A few weeks have seen great nations fall. We cannot remain indifferent to the philosophy of force now rampant in the world. The terrible fate of nations whose weakness invited attack is too well known to us all."

Just a month after being reelected to his third term, Roosevelt learned that Britain could no longer afford the "cash and carry" terms of the aid in armaments it was receiving from the United States. Roosevelt's answer to this was "Lend-Lease"—an inspired bit of legislation fortuitously named House Resolution 1776.

Under the terms of Lend-Lease, the United States could send essential wartime materiel to Britain (and Free France, China, and the Soviet Union) in return for reverse leases of the type Britain used to pay for the 50 destroyers. In truth, little of it was ever going to be paid back, but this was not the primary worry of its critics: their criticism was that it essentially ended American neutrality. So how did Roosevelt sell it?

To rally support for his plan, Roosevelt turned first to one of his strengths: communicating directly with the American people, via his famed radio addresses known as "fireside chats." In one of them, delivered December 29, 1940, Roosevelt told the American people that they, not the federal government, had the ability to alter the course of the war.

"We must be the arsenal of democracy," he added. "We must apply ourselves to our task with the same resolution, the same sense of urgency, the same spirit of patriotism and sacrifice as we would show were we at war." He also reassured the American people: "I believe that the Axis powers are not going to win this war."

RALLYING THE PUBLIC

It was a wartime speech by the leader of a nation not at war, a point noted by infuriated isolationists; it was followed up a week later by a State of the Union address remembered simply as the "Four Freedoms" speech. Those four freedoms, in Roosevelt's telling, were freedom of expression, freedom of worship, freedom from want, and freedom from fear—but it was the phrase used by Roosevelt after he enunciated each freedom—"everywhere in the world"—that gave the speech its soaring rhetorical power, and internationalist implications.

American public opinion shifted significantly in 1940. The year before, fewer than one-in-five Americans foresaw U.S. entry into the war. In late 1940, 62 percent of Americans told the Gallup polling organization that defeating Nazi Germany was more important than staying out of the war. After the military draft was instituted, 89 percent of respondents told Gallup that the Selective Service requirements were "a good thing." Whether this evolution took place because of Roosevelt's and Churchill's rousing rhetoric, or because of the facts on the ground that prompted such speechmaking, is an open question. Either way, Roosevelt shrewdly took advantage of it.

One of the ways that FDR did so was to reframe the question. Previously, the choice Roosevelt posed to the American people had been this: should the United States be involved in the European war? After the 1940, election, Roosevelt recast the question: should America stand by and let England fall—or try help without getting into the fighting ourselves? Even as Roosevelt personally steered the national discourse on this question, he wrapped the legislation in a creative rhetorical package: It wasn't a step in the direction of war, he and his surrogates proclaimed, it was a step *away from war.* FDR was reframing the issue so that isolationist-leaning Democrats who wanted to support their President could do so in good conscience.

ROOSEVELT VERSUS ISOLATIONISTS

Not everyone was buying it, of course. "This is a bill for the destruction of the American Republic," thundered the *Chicago Tribune.*

"Never before has this nation resorted to duplicity in the conduct of its foreign affairs," added Montana Democratic Senator Burton Wheeler. "The lend-lease-give program is the New Deal's triple-A foreign policy; it will plow under every fourth American boy."

Roosevelt's countermove against these criticisms was often to demonize isolationists by name as Nazi sympathizers or worse, and he rarely missed a chance to pounce when one of his adversaries overstepped, as Senator Wheeler did with his "every fourth American boy" remark. Now he pounced: Wheeler's comment was "the rottenest thing that has been said in public life in my generation," the President told the White House press corps. "Quote me on that," he added. And they did.

Lend-Lease still had to pass Congress, however, and White House strategists went to work. After failing to bypass the isolationist-heavy Senate Foreign Relations Committee, Roosevelt launched a multipronged offensive. He reached out to moderate and internationalist Republicans; he sought advice from a wide array of people, including Supreme Court Justice Felix Frankfurter; abandoning his partisan impulses, he recruited former Republican opponent Wendell Willkie to the cause. The defeated Republican nominee in the 1940 presidential election agreed to testify before Congress on behalf of Lend-Lease.

The hearings in the House began on January 15, 1941, and featured the usual suspects on the isolationist side, including Charles Lindbergh and Robert M. Hutchins, President of the University of Chicago. Hutchins espoused a peculiar argument: high U.S. unemployment undermined FDR's high-minded rhetoric about "freedom from want." In Hutchins's bizarre logic,

America lacked the moral authority to tell anyone else—even Hitler—what to do.

The pro-Lend-Lease forces brought more heft to the witness table: The slate of administration witnesses included Secretary of State Cordell Hull, Secretary of the Navy and former Republican vice presidential candidate Frank Knox, and former Republican Secretary of State Henry Stimson. When the committee went into executive session, Hull told them that Germany was planning to invade England in the spring. Another closed-door witness, General George C. Marshall, explained that U.S. military readiness was woefully inadequate should war come to these shores.

Thus educated, the House passed Lend-Lease on February 8, 1941. The vote was 265–165. The Senate outcome was uncertain, however, and hearings were scheduled for February 11. The star witness before the Senate Foreign Relations Committee was Willkie, recently returned from a well-publicized trip to England. Only months earlier, the Republicans on that committee were hoping for Willkie's election as president.

"Do you think that the passage of this bill will take us further away from war or take us closer to war?" Senator Bob Reynolds (D-NC) asked.

"*Much* further away from war," replied Willkie.

Reynolds then asked if the witness foresaw "any possibility of the United States becoming involved in this present war," to which Willkie presciently replied, "You have a couple of madmen loose in the world; and I don't know whom they will strike."

Pressing the point, Reynolds asked, "If the situation continues to exist as it is at this very hour, do you think that we are likely to become involved in this war?"

"Well," Willkie answered, "my judgment is that if Britain collapses tomorrow we would be in a war in a month."

Just as a fever suddenly subsides without any obvious reason, thus did the isolationist fever break. With 54 percent of Americans favoring Lend-Lease, according to a Gallup Poll, the Senate passed Lend-Lease on March 11. Four nights later, at the annual White House Correspondents' Association dinner, "Dr. Win-the-War" made his first public appearance since the hearings.

"We have just now engaged in a great debate," Roosevelt said. "It was not limited to the halls of Congress. It was argued in every newspaper, on every wave-length, over every cracker barrel in all the land; and it was finally settled and decided by the American people themselves."

"Yes, the decisions of our democracy may be slowly arrived at," Roosevelt continued. "But when that decision is made, it is proclaimed not with the voice of any one man but with the voice of one hundred and thirty millions. It is binding on us all. We believe firmly that when our production output is in full swing, the democracies of the world will be able to prove that dictatorships cannot win."

His audience, comprised mostly of seasoned journalists, knew what they were hearing. "There is no turning back," wrote syndicated columnist Raymond Clapper. "Everyone who was in the room when Mr. Roosevelt spoke must have heard the leaf of history turning. Twenty years of isolationism gone."

LESSONS OF HISTORY

For modern political leaders, there are several lessons to be drawn from Roosevelt's strategy in the lead-up to World War II. One lesson involves the juxtaposition between polling and Roosevelt Administration policy. Polling was a recent innovation when FDR went into national politics, and he was keenly interested in it. In 1936, he complained bitterly to his aides about one prominent pollster—as Barack Obama would do 76 years later. (FDR and Obama complained about the same polling organization—Gallup—and for the same reason: they thought Gallup's samples were undercounting their support.) Both men would be proven right, but in Roosevelt's case the dispute produced a significant result: he became more skeptical of polling after that. Good thing, too: the polls in 1939 showed overwhelming opposition to the idea of a third term, just as they did to U.S. involvement in World War II. But FDR had learned from his experience in 1936 that polls are not infallible, and true leadership entails more than just slavishly following public opinion.

Yet Roosevelt also had an uncanny ability to stay abreast of American public opinion—and in sync with it. He understood the dangers of getting too far ahead, or too far behind, the nation's prevailing attitudes.

Then there is the issue of bipartisanship. All presidents invoke this theme, while few are temperamentally suited to actually practice it. This was true of Franklin Roosevelt as well. He would barely acknowledge, let alone cooperate with Herbert Hoover during his 1932–1933 transition—even as U.S. banks were failing by the hundreds. By 1940, however, he'd learned his lesson. Roosevelt didn't only ask Willkie to testify for Lend-Lease. He hosted Willkie in the White House and sent him to London as a personal envoy of sorts.

In that meeting, FDR handed Willkie a note for Winston Churchill. It read: "Wendell Willkie will give you this—He is truly helping to keep politics out over here: I think this verse applies to you people as it does to us:

> 'Sail on, Oh Ship of State!
> Sail on, Oh Union strong and great.
> Humanity with all its fears
> With all the hope of future years
> Is hanging breathless on thy fate.'
>
> As ever yours,
> Franklin D. Roosevelt"

Churchill's famous reply to the Longfellow verse sent to him by Roosevelt has echoed through the decades. "We shall not fail or falter," the Prime Minister said. "We shall not weaken or tire. Neither the sudden shock of battle nor the long-drawn trials of vigilance will wear us down. Give us the tools and we will finish the job."

This inspiring exchange, it is worth stressing, stemmed from Roosevelt's willingness to enlist the man he'd defeated for the presidency, a man from the other political party. Wendell Willkie may have joked with the Senate Judiciary Committee about nearly becoming president himself, but when he was pressed by Senator Nye about whether he'd changed his mind about Roosevelt and war, Willkie spoke from the heart—and said something that goes to the essence of what it means to be an American.

"I struggled as hard as I could to beat Franklin Roosevelt, and I tried to keep from pulling any of my punches," Willkie said. "He was elected president. He is my president now."

♦ ♦ ♦ ♦ ♦

37. A Superpower's Foundation: The National Security Act of 1947

by Katherine A. Scott

The United States emerged victorious from World War II, but the road to victory had been fraught with disaster. The Japanese surprise attack on Pearl Harbor, which drew a reluctant nation into war, had brought the issue of inadequate intelligence into sharp relief. Throughout the war, the nation's military forces had operated largely autonomously to the detriment of coherent, joint operations, leading many to believe that only a fundamental reorganization of the nation's armed services could prevent future tragedies.

"Proof that a divine Providence watches over the United States," wrote then-Senator Harry Truman (D-MO), in 1944, "is furnished by the fact that we have managed to escape disaster even though our scrambled professional military set-up has been an open invitation to catastrophe."[1] President Franklin Roosevelt attempted to address inefficiencies and inadequacies with temporary measures, such as the formation of the Joint Chiefs of Staff and the Office of Strategic Services (OSS), but these entities were set to expire at war's end.

In addition to the experience of World War II, international developments increased the need for the nation to modernize its foreign policy structures. The rise of the Soviet Union and the coming Cold War, as well as the development and use of atomic weapons, presented elected and appointed officials with seismic global challenges. When he became President in 1945, Harry Truman thus made strengthening the nation's national security establishment, including the unification of its armed services, a top legislative priority.

Just months after the war ended in December 1945, Truman outlined his proposal in a message to Congress. His plan would unite air, naval, and ground forces within a single department, under a new Secretary of National Defense. Truman proposed to make permanent the Joint Chiefs of Staff, and to establish a permanent intelligence agency modeled on the OSS. Unifying the military services would, he argued, streamline budget and strategic planning; save money by eliminating duplication in procurement and supplies; encourage coordination among the military and other branches within the government; and unify training of the nation's armed forces. In 1947, a revised version of the President's proposal, known as the National Security Act, became law.

POLITICAL AND INSTITUTIONAL RESISTANCE

Though many recognized that the emerging Cold War posed new national security threats, Truman faced institutional, political, and cultural resistance to his calls to modernize the national security establishment. Congress had deferred to the Executive Branch during the war, and members were eager to reassert legislative prerogatives. There were political considerations as well. In 1947, for the first time in nearly 15 years, Republicans took control of both chambers of Congress. Politics were certain to play a role in the battles over demobilization, budgets, and the removal of wage, price, and rent controls.

On the issue of national security reform, the President counted among his many congressional allies Republicans who had long advocated for such changes. On the other hand, Truman's proposals challenged Americans' deeply held antistatist and antimilitarist beliefs. For all these reasons, the congressional debate over the National Security Act would continue hotly for two years, and the final legislative outcome satisfied few.

Since World War I, members of Congress had considered formal proposals to unify the nation's armed forces by integrating the nation's Departments of War and Navy. During World War II, congressional committees and special investigations revealed that the national security establishment was ill prepared to face modern security threats. Then-Senator Harry Truman had led one of the most thorough and well known of these congressional studies. Responding to a dramatic increase in defense spending, Harry Truman called for a special committee to oversee the awarding of defense contracts. As chairman of the Senate Special Committee to Investigate the National Defense Program, Truman expanded the scope of the committee's investigation to include waste, cost overruns, faulty manufacturing, and labor strikes in the defense sector. The committee's published reports underscored the lack of coordination among the armed services, and called attention to the exorbitant costs associated with it.

Though the final committee report did not call for the unification of the military—a proposal beyond the scope of the inquiry—it went a long way toward informing Congress about the problems that plagued the national security establishment. Democrats and Republicans hailed the committee's work, and Truman later boasted that the inquiry saved the nation billions of dollars.

In the House, Clifton Woodrum (D-VA) chaired the Select Committee on Postwar Military Policy. Known as the Woodrum Committee, its members considered proposals to unify the armed forces within a single department, and coordinate military research and development. Cabinet-level officials from the War and Navy Departments testified, and Secretary of War Henry Stimson assured members of Congress that unifying the War and Navy departments would improve the nation's security.

NAVY PUSHBACK

Representatives from the Department of the Navy, however, generally opposed the proposal. Under Secretary of the Navy James Forrestal (later to serve as Secretary of the Navy and the nation's first Defense Secretary), concluded, "I think [unification] should be studied and examined . . . [however]

I am not prepared to say that the Navy believes that the consolidation into one department is desirable."

Ultimately, the Woodrum Committee proposed individual studies within the Executive Branch to review these issues, but stopped short of making a recommendation for unification, "at this critical period in the war."[2] Supporters of unification in the postwar period would reference the Woodrum Committee's work as dramatic proof of the urgent need to reform the national security establishment.

Truman's wide-ranging modernization bill proposed merging the existing Departments of War and Navy. However, it was his proposal to establish an independent air force service that would be directed by a cabinet-level Secretary of National Defense, which drew the most criticism, especially from the U.S. Navy and its congressional allies. Congressional Navy sponsors worried about how the reforms would affect the future viability of the U.S. Marine Corps and Naval Aviation.

The Navy had powerful congressional allies. House Naval Affairs Appropriations Subcommittee Chairman Carl Vinson (D-GA) and Senator David Walsh (D-MA), chairman of the Senate Naval Affairs Committee, deserved much credit for building the modern U.S. Navy during World War II. These chairmen saw the issue of military unification as personal attacks because, as one historian argues, their "political identities had become inseparable from the institutional interests of [the Navy] over the years."[3]

In 1946, Senator Walsh provided the Navy with a venue for airing its opposition to the President's unification bill. His Naval Affairs Committee held hearings ostensibly to gauge the Navy's position with respect to the unification proposals then being considered by the Senate Military Affairs Committee.[4] Top Navy officials testified against the Military Affairs Committee's recommendation to unify the military services. By opposing a congressional committee's recommendation, they avoided accusations of insubordination; they did not directly challenge the President's position on the matter.

The Navy's carefully articulated opposition to unification confirmed what Vinson and Walsh believed to be true: the Navy had a lot to lose and little to gain from unification. They expressed their unequivocal opposition in a letter to Secretary of the Navy Forrestal, stating in no uncertain terms that Congress would not approve legislative proposals to unify the armed services within one cabinet-level department. With these powerful committee chairman and members of the President's own party in opposition, Truman had arrived at a stalemate. Walsh's opposition to the measure ensured that the

Naval Affairs Committee did not report out the unification bill. Truman, recognizing that he had lost this round, quietly let the proposal die.

INTELLIGENCE REFORM

The military unification proposal proved to be the main point of opposition for critics of the President's national security modernization bill. Other aspects of the draft legislation were less controversial, including the creation of a permanent national intelligence agency. The tragedy at Pearl Harbor had revealed the tragic consequence of inadequate intelligence capacities. The Joint Committee on the Investigation of the Pearl Harbor Attack, which held hearings in 1945–1946, posed the question which had haunted the nation since 1941: "Why with some of the finest intelligence available in our history, why was it possible for a Pearl Harbor to occur?"[5]

The American public's collective desire to prevent another national tragedy helps to explain why a nation which had traditionally opposed the build-up of military power during peacetime did not oppose the creation of a permanent national intelligence agency. For his part, Truman and his advisors, perhaps anticipating such opposition, intentionally crafted a vaguely defined intelligence agency.

After extended conversations with members of Congress and Navy officials, the Truman Administration introduced a revised bill in 1947. The midterm election had granted Republicans control of both chambers of Congress. In addition to these political challenges, the President and his top advisors were engaged in efforts to convince Congress to support sweeping changes to American foreign policy embodied in the Truman Doctrine and the Marshall Plan. Modernizing the national security establishment remained a top legislative priority, but Truman told his advisors that he did not want to expend too much political capital to do it. The new bill reflected the compromises that he was willing to accept in order to gain the support of the bill's most vocal congressional opponents.

DILUTED REFORMS

The new measure made concessions to those who feared the concentration of power within the hands of a new Secretary of National Defense. Naval, ground, and air services would each have their own civilian secretary who would maintain extraordinary powers to oversee their respective branches. Technically, service secretaries would report to the new Secretary of National

Defense. But after consultation with the new Secretary, they were authorized to take their concerns directly to the President. This made the new Defense Secretary little more than a figurehead who could coordinate, but not direct, military strategy and policy for the President. The new secretary would manage the multiservice budget, though he lacked centralized control over the various branches within that structure. Congressional Navy supporters had fought hard for these consequential concessions to ensure that the Navy would maintain authority over its service branch within a newly formed Defense Department.

House and Senate committees immediately began hearings to consider the revised measure. In the House, Chairman Clare Hoffman (R-MI) of the Committee on Expenditures in the Executive Departments handled the legislation; in the Senate, Chan Gurney (R-SD), Chairman of the Armed Services Committee, managed the bill. After months of hearings and markup, Gurney introduced a revised bill on the Senate floor. During the ensuing floor debate, a bipartisan group including Raymond Baldwin (R-CT), Lister Hill (D-AL), Henry Cabot Lodge Jr. (R-MA), Wayne Morse (R-OR), Leverett Saltonstall (R-MA), and Millard Tydings (R-MD), urged their Senate colleagues to support the measure. They argued that the bill would improve national security by enhancing coordination and communication among the Army, Navy, and Air Force. They insisted, furthermore, that a merger would reduce waste and duplication.

Opponents of the measure, led by Republican Edward Robertson of Wyoming, warned that concentrating such extraordinary power in the hands of one man—a Secretary of National Defense—might have dire consequences, bringing the nation closer to a garrison state. Robertson also challenged claims that unification would save money, arguing that evidence suggested just the opposite—it would cost the nation more. Robertson failed to convince his colleagues, however, and the Senate passed the bill with a voice vote.

In the House, debate over the measure boiled down to two outstanding issues: opponents argued that the bill did not do enough to protect Navy interests, especially the Marine Corps and Naval Aviation. Opponents also wanted the new intelligence agency to be led by a civilian with carefully delineated powers. The bill had considerable support from key Republican members of the House Expenditures Committee, including James Wadsworth Jr. (R-NY). The House passed a modified Senate bill by voice vote, and the subsequent conference committee bill retained most of the House changes.

The final bill passed both chambers by voice vote, and included revisions to protect Naval Aviation and the Marine Corps, as well as definitions of some Navy roles and missions. The National Security Act of 1947 established a National Military Establishment (renamed the Defense Department in 1949) comprising air, ground and naval forces, headed by a Secretary of Defense; made permanent the Joint Chiefs of Staff; created a permanent intelligence agency limited to gathering intelligence abroad; and established a National Security Council, a Munitions Board, and a Research and Development Board to better coordinate military preparedness.

President Truman hastily signed the legislation on July 26, 1947, the last day of the legislative session, before leaving for Missouri to visit with his dying mother. The final bill did not contain all of the measures that he thought were vital to protecting the national interests in an increasingly dangerous Cold War environment. In addition, many of the compromise measures, particularly those that empowered the autonomous Secretaries of the Army, Navy, and Air Force, proved unworkable. The first Secretary of Defense, James Forrestal, who had fervently opposed unification, helped draft revisions to the original bill that granted greater powers to the Defense Secretary, and Congress approved these revisions in 1949.

At the end of World War II, many had agreed that the nation needed to modernize its national security establishment. Nevertheless, the long road to the passage of the National Security Act suggests how institutional, political, and cultural considerations shaped and in many instances diluted the final product. Though imperfect, the legislation was notable for laying the national security foundation from which a global superpower would arise over the next half century. Historically after previous wars, the United States had disbanded its armies, sent most of the troops home, and dismantled most wartime structures. With the Marshall Plan to rebuild a devastated Europe and the National Security Act to maintain a globe spanning military, Truman was announcing to the world that the West had a new standard-bearer.

◆ ◆ ◆ ◆ ◆

38. Un-American Investigations: McCarthyism and the Red Scare

by Ellen Schrecker

The term alone brings to mind the near-hysteria whipped up by the anticommunist congressional investigations of the early Cold War. *McCarthyism.* It was named after a disreputable junior Senator from Wisconsin who became famous for leveling scurrilous, and often unfounded, charges of Communism against civil servants and others during the early 1950s. As is so often the case, the actual history is a bit more complicated than the mythology. A more accurate description of the "red scare" phenomenon that gripped America would note that it began more than a decade before Joseph McCarthy arrived on the scene in February 1950, waving a list of 205 (or was it 57? or 81?) supposed communists in the State Department. The anticommunist hysteria that assumed McCarthy's name did not actually abate until a few years after his death in 1957.

Although McCarthy was the most notorious individual associated with what became the longest lasting and most widespread episode of political repression in American history, he was hardly alone in producing that stain. In hindsight, the phenomenon also could have been called *Hooverism,* after J. Edgar Hoover, the tenacious director of the Federal Bureau of Investigation (FBI). Perhaps more than any other individual, Hoover was responsible for advancing the narrative at the center of the "red scare," developing the anticommunist machinery to combat it, and then targeting the men and women he believed were behind it.

Congress was another major player in the drama. If there was any single institutional expression of the anticommunist furor that gripped the nation in the late 1940s and early 1950s, it was the congressional investigating committee. Ostensibly designed to provide lawmakers with the information they needed for carrying out their legislative responsibilities, big-time congressional investigations also gave them an invaluable forum for promoting pet causes. As the Cold War progressed, using such investigations to expose communists became a surefire technique for ambitious politicians to harass political opponents. That was especially true from 1947 to 1949, when a Republican-controlled Congress was looking to make life uncomfortable for the Democrat sitting in the White House.

Although the Communist Party (CP) had been unpopular in the United States virtually since its birth in 1919, it did not become the target of a congressional committee until 1930, which was when Representative Hamilton Fish III (R-NY) decided to explore CP activities. Fish's investigation eventually petered out, but it set a precedent that would be expanded later in the decade as the international scene darkened, and conservatives in both parties turned against Franklin D. Roosevelt's New Deal.

The probes began in earnest early in 1938 when the House voted 191–41 to establish a special U.S. House Committee on Un-American Activities to investigate un-American propaganda. HUAC, as this committee later came to be called, became the most well-known, and ultimately the longest-lived, institutional manifestation of the anticommunist furor. Although it was supposed to look at Nazis as well as Reds, the new body's chair, the right-wing Representative Martin Dies (D-TX), initiated a wide-ranging investigation into the supposed communist infiltration of the labor movement and the New Deal. Dies's hearings embarrassed the Roosevelt Administration, but received such a large amount of public support that Roosevelt could not quash them.

Especially after the signing of the Nazi-Soviet Non-Aggression Pact in August 1939, which plunged Europe into World War II, anticommunism was the order of the day in Washington. Until the United States and the Soviet Union joined forces against Hitler a few years later, Congress busied itself with a flurry of legislation that included the 1940 Smith Act, which essentially made it illegal to belong to the CP. Even after Pearl Harbor pushed the rest of the anticommunist crusade onto the back burner, the Dies Committee continued to accuse the Administration of coddling Reds.

With the end of World War II, the anticommunist movement was resuscitated. In 1945, HUAC transitioned from a temporary body that had to be renewed in every congressional session to a permanent committee. It returned to business by holding hearings on a variety of so-called front groups, organizations that were closely connected to the American CP. The committee thrived on publicity, and it was soon drawn to Hollywood. In October 1947, it initiated a spectacular set of hearings to investigate communist infiltration of the film industry. First, the committee heard a group of so-called friendly witnesses—studio heads and actors, Ronald Reagan among them—who testified that, despite the presence of a few Reds, the industry was fervently opposed to Communism. Then, the committee called up a group of left-wing screenwriters and directors. Known as the "Hollywood Ten," these people—all of whom were or had been in the CP—refused to cooperate. In an often raucous battle with committee members, they claimed that questions about their political activities violated their First Amendment right of free speech and association.

After HUAC's staff members displayed copies of the Hollywood Ten's CP membership cards that the FBI had secretly provided, the committee charged them with contempt of Congress. Though other unfriendly witnesses had also received contempt citations, the Hollywood hearings brought HUAC the publicity its members craved. The case also set the parameters for the future inquisitions by demonstrating that there were scant protections for political dissidents, who risked their jobs by defying an investigating committee.

At first it was not altogether clear whether the unruly proceedings had bolstered or tarnished the committee's reputation. As soon as the Department of Justice indicted the Hollywood Ten, however, the film studio heads met at the Waldorf-Astoria Hotel in New York City to announce that they would bar CP members from the industry, and fire the unfriendly witnesses unless they recanted. Once that precedent was established, the blacklist soon expanded to include similarly uncooperative witnesses in every field, as well as many politically compromised individuals who never even received a HUAC subpoena. Meanwhile, as the Hollywood Ten's contempt case wound its way through the courts, it became increasingly clear that the First Amendment was not going to keep them out of prison. Future witnesses who did not want to cooperate with the committee would have to rely on the Fifth Amendment's protection against self-incrimination if they wanted to avoid a contempt citation.

An even more important set of hearings occurred in the summer of 1948, when the House Un-American Activities Committee began investigating charges that the Democratic administration harbored communists. The main witnesses were the ex-Communists Elizabeth Bentley and Whittaker Chambers, who not only testified about their work in Washington's communist underground, but also named a number of former federal bureaucrats who had been in the CP with them.

When the committee subpoenaed the people that Bentley and Chambers had fingered, most relied on the Fifth Amendment. One, a former State Department official named Alger Hiss, did not. He coolly denied all of Chambers's allegations, including the accusation that the two men had traveled in the same communist circles in the late 1930s. At first, the smooth and well-connected Hiss seemed more credible than the somewhat seedy ex-Communist Chambers. With the FBI secretly feeding him information, however, a tenacious first-term Congressman from California named Richard Nixon was able to force a confrontation between the two men. Eventually Chambers produced evidence that Hiss had actually spied for the Soviet Union. Though the statute of limitations for espionage had run out, Hiss's eventual conviction for perjury early in 1950 launched Nixon's career. The incident also established HUAC's legitimacy, and the charge that the Roosevelt and Truman Administrations had been "soft on Communism" gained political traction.

By the time Joseph McCarthy appeared at a women's Republican Club dinner in Wheeling, West Virginia, on February 9, 1950, waving the first of his ever-changing lists of supposed Communists in the State Department, the anticommunist inquisition was thus already well under way. McCarthy differed from its other practitioners both in the concrete specificity of his charges and in his gift for publicizing them. Although many of those charges were totally without foundation, they greatly embarrassed the Truman Administration. Accordingly, the leaders of the Republican Party urged McCarthy to continue—despite the personal distaste that many of them had for McCarthy's tactics.

Ultimately, McCarthy's charges resulted in an investigation by a special subcommittee of the U.S. Senate Committee on Foreign Relations under Senator Millard Tydings (D-MD). At those hearings, McCarthy amplified his allegations, insisting among other things that a Johns Hopkins University East Asian specialist named Owen Lattimore was a Soviet spy. However, partisanship dogged the Tydings committee from the start. As a result it produced two reports, with the Democratic majority calling McCarthy's charges "a fraud and a hoax," and the Republican minority supporting the charges. The outbreak of the Korean War in June 1950 gave additional salience to the issues involved, in particular to the claim that Soviet agents within the State Department had somehow "lost China" to the Communists.

In the beginning of 1951, the newly formed Senate Internal Security Subcommittee (SISS) of the Senate Judiciary Committee began its own investigation into McCarthy's charges. Perhaps because it seemed more judicious than HUAC or McCarthy, the SISS carried out some of the McCarthy era's most influential investigations (first under the chairmanship of the powerful Pat McCarran (D-NV), and then later under the leadership of William Jenner (R-IN) and James Eastland (D-MS)). The SISS's first and most important hearings focused on the Institute of Pacific Relations (IPR), a highly respected think tank for individuals interested in East Asia. Owen Lattimore had been involved with the organization, as were many eminent diplomats, academics, and a handful of Communists.

The McCarran committee constructed a narrative that the IPR's Communists had manipulated U.S. foreign policy to ensure the victory of Mao Zedong. After hearing the perjured testimony of a professional ex-Communist, the SISS grilled Lattimore for an unprecedented 11 days, and then sought to have him prosecuted for perjury. While Lattimore was ultimately acquitted, the inquisition destroyed his career. More seriously, the IPR hearings twisted the course of American foreign policy, giving credibility to the thoroughly partisan "loss of China" narrative, and leading to a purge of the Foreign Service officers involved. Future administrations were frightened into a rigid posture in East Asia lest they be accused of being insufficiently anticommunist.

In the beginning of 1953, with war hero Dwight Eisenhower in the White House and the Republicans in control of Congress, Joseph McCarthy finally got a committee of his own. As chairman of the Permanent Subcommittee on Investigations of the Senate Committee on Government Operations, McCarthy joined HUAC and the SISS in their continuing investigations of Communism in American society. By this point the committees had adopted ritualized procedures that purported to expose Communists or communist sympathizers, and invariably ensured that uncooperative witnesses would be punished in one way or another.

Despite criticisms that the committees were harassing "innocent liberals," most of the men and women called before HUAC and its counterparts were or had been in the CP. The lawmakers knew that these witnesses had committed no crimes, but Communists had become so demonized by the 1950s that their mere existence was considered a threat to national security. While a massive assault on civil liberties, their public vilification by congressional committees was justified as a necessary cleansing of the body politic.

The committees' standard procedure was to summon prospective witnesses to an executive session to ascertain whether they would answer the so-called $64 question—so named after an early TV quiz show—"Are you now or have you ever been a member of the Communist Party?" The standard follow-up question was whether they would identify their former comrades. Those individuals who refused were subjected to a public hearing. Many of these people were ex-Communists who would have been willing to talk about themselves, but did not want to "name names."

The Supreme Court offered limited protection for witnesses caught in this conundrum. Although the Court allowed the witnesses Fifth Amendment protection against self-incrimination, once they talked about themselves it ruled that they had waived that privilege and could be prosecuted for contempt for refusing to cooperate by naming names. Committee members knew this and thus insisted in the court of public opinion that taking the Fifth was, in Joe McCarthy's words, "the most positive proof obtainable that the witness is a Communist." Though their silence protected them from prosecution, once exposed as "Fifth Amendment Communists," most of the unfriendly witnesses lost their jobs and careers.

Eventually, the anticommunist investigations ran their course and came to an end. By the mid-1950s, the committees had pretty much run out of newsworthy targets. They had questioned most of the top people in the CP and its front groups; looked for atomic spies; exposed Communists in the federal government; investigated the entertainment industry and academic community; and subpoenaed dozens of left-wing labor leaders. In addition, the Supreme Court was finally beginning to place limitations on the committees' activities. For instance, their questions could no longer be used merely to expose Communists, but instead had to be relevant to some legislative purpose. The justices also eventually ruled that taking the Fifth Amendment, in and of itself, could not be used as grounds for dismissing a public servant. The public was also tiring of the inquisition, especially after it became clear that it had not uncovered any major subversion, and the committees were suppressing dissent and damaging innocent people's lives and careers.

Joseph McCarthy's self-destruction was perhaps the most important signal that Congress's anticommunist crusade had lost its momentum. Although President Eisenhower despised the junior Senator from Wisconsin, he refused to, as he put it, "get down in the gutter with that guy." As a result, McCarthy and his staff had rampaged through the federal government for over a year, and in late 1953 they took on the U.S. Army. At that point, Eisenhower, the commander of allied forces in World War II who had spent most of his adult life in the Army, intervened (behind the scenes, of course). A special Senate committee was convened to investigate charges that the Wisconsin Senator had used his influence to get special treatment for one of his committee staffers after he was drafted.

During the course of the televised Army-McCarthy hearings in April 1954, McCarthy accused the Army's chief counsel, an eminent Boston attorney named Joseph Welch, of harboring a former member of a communist front group in his law firm. Welch, who had been prepared for this attack, turned to McCarthy and in an aggrieved manner accused him of trying to ruin a young man's life. "Have you no sense of decency, sir?" he asked. "At long last, have you left no sense of decency?" The applause that greeted Welch's outburst essentially ended McCarthy's career. In December, the Senate voted to censure him, and he died an alcoholic three years later.

Though McCarthy's demise was rapid, the other anticommunist investigators continued their work into the 1960s; but the committees had lost their bite. Once the mainstream media abandoned its enthusiasm for exposing Reds and employers no longer automatically fired or blacklisted supposed subversives, anticommunist investigations became marginal operations. Perhaps the most dramatic indication of the decline of these formerly powerful committees were the 1962 HUAC hearings into a feminist organization called Women Strike for Peace. As each of the group's elegantly dressed leaders walked up to the stand, her supporters cheered and handed her bouquets of flowers. The committee never recovered. Though HUAC and the SISS remained active into the 1970s, the anticommunist fever they had done so much to stoke had finally broken. The damage to the American polity inflicted by their intemperate investigations, however, is still being assessed.

◆ ◆ ◆ ◆ ◆

39. A Blank Check for War: The Gulf of Tonkin Resolution

by Marvin Kalb

A rumor circulating in 1964—though never confirmed—had Lyndon Johnson actually carrying a draft war resolution in his hip pocket, waiting for just the right moment in his presidential campaign to ask Congress for authority to take military action in South Vietnam. There was no doubt that the new president often worried about how the issue affected his image: would he be seen as a country bumpkin, as a few of his critics joked, or as the tough Texan standing tall at the Alamo of America's destiny, as he imagined? A popular, young president had only recently been assassinated, and it was Johnson's job to lead the nation—and the Western world. He was determined that no one was going to push this president around. The Tonkin Gulf resolution, when it passed, had Johnson's imprint all over it—and the clout of a "declaration of war."

For Johnson, the providential moment came at 3:40 A.M. Washington time on August 2, when North Vietnamese patrol boats attacked the USS *Maddox,* an American destroyer on a dangerous spying mission in the Gulf of Tonkin. The warship was nine miles off shore. As it had done in the past, the *Maddox* was checking on enemy troop and supply lines, ignoring repeated warnings from Hanoi to respect its 12-mile territorial claim, or else. Skipper John Herrick, an experienced Navy captain, was concerned that the United States, by continuing these intelligence operations, might be pushing the North Vietnamese too far. Time and again, he had cautioned Washington that these missions carried "unacceptable risk," on one occasion predicting "possible hostile action" if they continued.[1]

However, Washington was absorbed with other things, most especially a presidential campaign. Johnson, having taken office as the result of an assassination, yearned for the glow and glory of his own popular mandate. Not only was Johnson favored to win, but to win big. His opponent was Barry Goldwater, a staunchly conservative, stridently anticommunist Senator from

Arizona, who enjoyed nothing more than tweaking his Democratic rival as weak on national security, a liar to boot, and certainly unworthy of the White House. Johnson, canny and delightfully unprincipled, answered by painting a picture of Goldwater as a reckless extremist, lacking the subtlety and skill to safely steer the United States through the treacherous waters of the Cold War.

From the beginning of the campaign, Johnson realized that a measured use of American military power in Vietnam would arouse waves of patriotism, encouraging voters to rally around their leader. If he was going to take the country into another war—albeit a "limited" one, as he saw it at the time—he wanted the approval and support of his colleagues on Capitol Hill. This was a matter of supreme importance to the former "master of the Senate."

In his autobiography, Johnson wrote with pride that his "first major decision" was to follow President Kennedy's policy on Vietnam; his second was to "seek a congressional resolution in support of our Southeast Asia policy."[2] According to his close confidant, Jack Valenti, the President was "very, very disgruntled and discontented with the fact that we were messing around in Southeast Asia without congressional approval." Johnson often quoted the respected Senator Arthur Vandenberg (R-MI) as saying: "By God, if you want us in on the landing, we sure as hell better be in on the takeoff."[3]

Johnson believed that President Harry Truman had made a terrible mistake by going to war in Korea in 1950 without some sort of congressional authorization. "He could have had it easily," Johnson believed, "and it would have strengthened his hand. I had made up my mind not to repeat that error."[4]

FAST-TRACK CRISIS

And yet, when the August 2nd attack on the USS *Maddox* provided him with the perfect pretext for both retaliation and a congressional resolution of support, Johnson chose to turn the other cheek, at least at that time. He blamed the "crisis" on an "overeager North Vietnamese boat commander," who had clearly "miscalculated." Nonsense, Goldwater thundered, the President was trying to "sweep this [crisis] under the rug." Johnson would not be rattled—he wanted the voters to see him as calm and sober, the leader whose first instinct was the pursuit of peace. Still, as a sign of his toughness and America's resolve, Johnson ordered another destroyer, the USS *Turner Joy,* to join the *Maddox* in the Gulf of Tonkin.

Within 48 hours, Johnson was again challenged and, this time, there was no doubt in his mind that he would have to act. On August 4, a tropical storm was raging in the Gulf, and shipboard radar aboard both the *Mad-dox* and the *Turner Joy* picked up odd signals—"skunks" or "bogies," as they were called. Herrick mistakenly interpreted them as approaching enemy boats or torpedoes. Mindful of his August 2 experience, he assumed he was again under attack. Herrick wired Washington, leaving no doubt that the sit-uation was dire: "under continuous torpedoes attack . . . successfully avoided at least six torpedoes. Four torpedoes in water . . ."[5]

James Stockdale, a Navy pilot from the USS *Ticonderoga,* an aircraft car-rier patrolling protectively a few miles away, was ordered to fly to the scene, just as he had done two days earlier. During the first incident, he had spotted and fired at North Vietnamese patrol boats. Only this time Stockdale saw nothing. "I had the best seat in the house to see that patch of water for two or three miles in radius around these two ships," he told me. "There were no wakes, there were no ricochets, there was nothing but American fire-power . . . I couldn't see anything."[6]

Herrick, like Stockdale, did not see any enemy patrol boats either. He began to question his original judgment that he was again under attack. He decided to run an experiment. He put the *Maddox* into a series of swift turns, kicking up high waves that slapped against the side of the ship, producing strange signals that his sonar specialists interpreted as approaching boats and torpedoes, but that were actually the sounds of the ship's own engine. Noth-ing more. Embarrassed, Herrick wired headquarters in Honolulu and Wash-ington: "Review of action," he wrote, "makes many reported contacts and torpedoes fired appear doubtful. Freak weather effects and overeager sonar man may have accounted for many reports. No actual visual sightings by *Maddox.* Suggest complete evaluation before further action. Nothing more."[7]

CLOUDY INTELLIGENCE

However, senior officials in Washington were confused. Their intelligence was weak, sloppy, and unreliable. Was there an attack or wasn't there? The question was not academic. Everyone understood that the President was leaning toward military retaliation. "We spent about ten hours that day try-ing to figure out what in the hell had happened," Defense Secretary Robert McNamara recalled. Late that afternoon, with his deputy, Cyrus Vance, and the Joint Chiefs of Staff, McNamara tried desperately "to marshal the evi-dence to overcome lack of a clear and convincing showing that an attack on the destroyers had in fact occurred."[8] They concluded that, though the evidence of a North Vietnamese attack was flimsy at best, they would inform Johnson that, in their view, an attack had indeed occurred.

Johnson had his doubts, too, but he knew in his political gut that he had to order a retaliatory strike. Otherwise, Goldwater would accuse him of an election-year cover-up or, worse, moral cowardice. Johnson also knew that he could quickly turn to Congress for a resolution authorizing him to take "whatever action" he considered necessary "to protect the national interest."

The inevitable leaks that accompany any Washington crisis soon followed. The Associated Press and the United Press International learned of the August 4 "attack," and their news bulletins prompted questions from other reporters as well as heartburn at the White House. Johnson immediately instructed McNamara to issue a statement confirming the attack. It used boilerplate language—"two destroyers attacked, no casualties or damage to the destroyers, several of the attacking vessels driven off, more info in the a.m."[9]—but it touched off intense military preparations and political consultations that led to the first American military attacks against North Vietnam. "The world has turned a corner," Stockdale observed. "We are now locked into the Vietnam War—there is no question about it."[10]

Johnson had always assumed that military action would be coupled with congressional approval. Early that evening, at 6:45 P.M., as a key step in the process, he invited nine senators and seven congressmen to the White House for a top-secret briefing from McNamara about the events that day in the Gulf of Tonkin, and what the United States intended to do about them.

After only a few questions, Johnson read the brief statement he intended to deliver on television. Three times he described America's military response to the North Vietnamese "attacks" as "limited," prompting Senator Leverett Saltonstall (R-MA) to suggest substituting the word "determined," and "let the limitation speak for itself." Johnson disagreed. His emphasis on limited retaliation was a crucially important signal to both Hanoi and Beijing. "We are not going to take it [the North Vietnamese 'attacks'] lying down," he stressed, "but we are not going to destroy their cities." Secretary of State Dean Rusk added meaningfully, "We are not doing this as a pretext for a larger war."[11]

Johnson then raised the specific question of a congressional resolution. It should apply, he said, "not just to Vietnam but to our interests in all of Southeast Asia," and it should place no constraints on a president's inherent right to order American forces into action. There were approving nods all around the room. Senator Bourke Hickenlooper (R-IA) spoke for his colleagues when he summed up this exchange. "It is up to the president to prepare the type and kind of resolution he believes would be proper," he said. "It is up to Congress to see whether they will pass it or not. I have no doubt in my mind that concrete action would be taken."[12]

Translation: You write the resolution, Mr. President. We'll support it.

The President then asked each Senator and Representative for his opinion. Yes or no? Should the United States retaliate? Yes was their answer. "I think it will be passed overwhelmingly," said Congressman Charles Halleck (R-IN).[13] Reflecting the rich spirit of bipartisan cooperation on foreign policy that then existed, Speaker John McCormack added, we want to show "a united front to the world."[14]

Johnson was not yet fully satisfied—he wanted Goldwater's approval, too. He got it at 10 P.M. that night, his Republican opponent returning his call from a sailboat off the coast of Southern California.

At 11:36 P.M., well past prime time, Johnson went on television to inform the American people that "renewed hostile actions against United States ships on the high seas in the Gulf of Tonkin have today required me to order the military forces of the United States to take action in reply. That reply is being given as I speak to you tonight." A Harris Poll found that 85 percent of the American people supported the President's decision.

Johnson delivered this somber message to the American people, despite harboring grave doubts about whether there had even been any actual "hostile actions." Earlier in the evening, he had confided to State Department official George Ball: "I just think those dumb sailors were shooting at flying fish. I don't think there was any attack." At the same time, McNamara was telling Congress that he had "unimpeachable evidence" of the North Vietnamese attacks. He also told the National Security Council that the North Vietnamese were "continu[ing] their attacks." (McNamara clearly had trouble telling the truth even to officials with top-secret clearances.) Years later in his 1995 memoirs, the guilt-ridden former defense secretary admitted that "confusion" had reigned that day and "our judgment" was "wrong."[15]

During the American retaliation, the United States lost two planes while damaging or destroying 25 North Vietnamese boats and 90 percent of the oil storage tanks at Vinh.[16]

A BLANK CHECK FOR WAR

Rusk and Ball spent much of the next day drafting the Tonkin Gulf resolution, based essentially on Johnson's earlier consultations with congressional leaders. It supported the President's "right" to "take all necessary measures to repel any armed attack against the forces of the United States and to prevent further aggression." It also stated that the United States was "prepared, as the President determines, to take all necessary steps, including the use of armed force, to assist any member or protocol state of the Southeast

Asia Collective Defense Treaty requesting assistance in defense of their freedom."[17] Johnson jokingly described it as being "like grandma's nightshirt—it
covered everything."[18]

Under White House pressure, the Senate and the House then moved with
uncharacteristic speed. Pro forma hearings were held in the relevant committees. Johnson insisted that roll call votes be taken in the committees and
on the floor of both houses. He wanted the record to be "complete and
indisputable."

In the Senate, the vote was 88 to 2, and in the House, it was unanimous,
416 to 0.

A contented President later explained that he was not going "to commit forces and undertake actions . . . unless and until the American people
through their Congress sign on to go in." He also told reporters that "anybody who has read the resolution" could see that it authorized the President
"to take all, all, all necessary measures," hammering away at "all, all, all" to
eliminate any doubts that he had the authority to go to war, if he deemed
it necessary. McNamara called it a "blank check authorization for further
action."[19]

Johnson had, for a brief time, considered asking Congress for a declaration
of war, as Franklin Roosevelt had done in December 1941, after the Japanese
attack on Pearl Harbor. Johnson changed his mind, however, settling on a
congressional resolution as the better option. His reasoning was fascinating.
A declaration of war conjured up World War II visions of all-out war—of the
entire nation committed to a military victory. For this president, that would
have meant no "great society" program, "my beautiful lady," as he often
referred to his broad program of domestic reforms. He had a limited war in
mind. But he often worried that his limited war had the potential for expanding into a wider war, possibly involving China and/or Russia. "I didn't know
what treaty China might have had with North Vietnam," he told Senator
Wayne Morse (D-OR), one of the two senators who voted against the Tonkin
Gulf resolution, "or Russia might have had with North Vietnam." Johnson felt the need to tread lightly on the communist challenge in Southeast
Asia, because Russia and China always hovered over the near horizon of his
calculations.

Six weeks later, in mid-September, two other American destroyers were
reportedly under attack in the Gulf of Tonkin. This time, Johnson refused to
act, telling McNamara he didn't want "to get sucked in" to a bigger war in
Vietnam on questionable intelligence. Alluding to his Tonkin Gulf experience,
he humorlessly criticized his defense secretary: "You came in . . . and said
that 'Damn, they are launching an attack on us—they are firing on us.' When

we got through with all the firing, we concluded maybe they hadn't fired at all."[20] His earlier doubts about the August 4 attacks had now hardened into a deep skepticism about Pentagon intelligence on Vietnam. He worried that McNamara might have taken him to the cleaners on August 4, and he wanted to avoid a repeat performance, especially before the election.

Months later, in early 1965, after his impressive reelection victory, Johnson faced a policy quandary with the South Vietnamese reeling under ferocious communist attack: should the United States now shift from an advisory to a combat role? Should Johnson order tens of thousands of American troops to South Vietnam and the regular bombing of North Vietnam? And, if he did decide to deepen the American involvement in Vietnam, would Congress begin to raise questions about his authority under the Tonkin Gulf resolution?[21]

On February 22, 1965, McNamara was again summoned to Capitol Hill to defend the Administration's Vietnam policy. He had just been there a few days earlier, and he sensed a growing itchiness among congressmen about the direction of the President's policy. He telephoned Johnson, who seemed ready for the challenge. Tell them, he advised, that "when we went into Korea," Congress had not approved or disapproved of Truman's decision. "For that reason, last summer, . . . we asked the Congress for a resolution . . . And they passed it 504 to 2."

Johnson continued: "I read it last night again . . . and all the statements [we made] at the time . . . Now, anytime anybody asks me . . . I would say, now, the Commander in Chief has certain inherent powers as Commander in Chief, but it so happens in this instance that Congress has expressed theirself very definitely. And here's *what it has said. Period!*"[22] He seemed to be saying that he had a congressional resolution that specifically affirmed his "inherent right" to use military force wherever and whenever he deemed it necessary to protect American interests in Southeast Asia.

A TROUBLING PRECEDENT

Johnson used the Tonkin Gulf resolution as a form of political protection against congressional criticism. It was also his claim to legitimacy as a Commander in Chief who had the power to employ the nation's military might, with or without further congressional approval. If Congress objected to his policy or his actions, Johnson felt that it had its own inherent "right" to disavow the Tonkin Gulf resolution.

Unwittingly, Johnson had set a precedent for presidential war-making powers that would bedevil relations between the Executive and Legislative

Branches of government for decades to come. With faulty intelligence and merely a congressional resolution, however loosely crafted, however hurriedly approved, a president could commit American troops to extended combat on a foreign battlefield. Did a president even need a congressional resolution to go to war? He could argue, as others have, that the President has an inherent power as Commander in Chief to launch offensive military operations, as he deems it necessary to protect the national interests of the country.

This argument over whether presidents have the inherent power to use military force absent a congressional declaration of war has ensnared subsequent chief executives, most recently during the 2013 Syrian crisis. President Barack Obama brought the nation to the brink of military action before changing his mind and going to Congress for authorization that it seemed likely to reject. The White House position at the time was that Obama did not really have to go to Congress; that, as President and as Commander in Chief, he had all the power he needed to take the country to war without any congressional authorization.

At this point in American history, there is still no agreed-upon, broadly accepted blueprint for how the United States legitimately uses lethal military force. Does the Congress "declare war," as the Constitution states, or has it become the President's prerogative as Commander in Chief to wage war, with or without Congress? Has presidential power in the realm of national security become so predominant that only one person ultimately decides matters of war and peace? The answers await the next crisis when a president, sitting alone in the Oval Office, must choose between the costs of acting alone and the risks of Congress deciding not to act at all.

◆ ◆ ◆ ◆ ◆

40. From Draftees to Professionals: The All-Volunteer Force

by James Kitfield

By 1971, President Richard Nixon and the Democrats who controlled Congress agreed on relatively little, but both sides were eager to distance themselves from an unpopular draft. Nixon had run for election calling for an end to conscription, and the White House was anxious to diffuse antiwar protests that had started on college campuses with the burning of draft cards. These protests had spread throughout the country during Nixon's first term in office. Following nearly a decade of an unpopular war that would claim the lives of more than 58,000 Americans, Congress was looking for ways to hasten the return of the remaining U.S. troops in Vietnam.

Needing time to transition to an all-volunteer force, the Nixon Administration requested that Congress extend the draft for just two additional years. Opponents of the war were led by Senator Mike Gravel (D-AK), an Army veteran who tried to filibuster the draft renewal legislation as a way to scuttle the draft and hasten an end to the war. After a lengthy debate, the Administration's supporters prevailed, overcoming the filibuster and ensuring that a Cold War draft that began with World War II and lasted 33 years would end in 1973.

While a number of conservative lawmakers, including Senator Sam Nunn (D-GA), opposed ending the draft, antiwar sentiment was running high on Capitol Hill in the early 1970s. In acceding to the end of the draft and establishment of an all-volunteer force, however, Congress was surrendering important leverage and a key restraint on a president's war-fighting powers. The tradition before World War II, for instance, was for Commanders in Chief to go to Congress and request conscription authority. Franklin Roosevelt did that in 1940 with war clouds gathering on the horizon in Europe and Asia, and the Selective Training and Service Act Congress passed that year created the first peacetime draft in U.S. history. At the time, there was significant isolationist sentiment around the country and on Capitol Hill; the following year when Roosevelt asked for an extension of the draftees' terms of duty beyond 12 months, the House of Representatives approved it by only a single vote.

In the early 1970s, the United States was undergoing another dizzying period of change and societal transformation. The Equal Rights Amendment had just passed in 1972, signaling a redefinition of the role of women in society. Race riots and the assassination of Martin Luther King Jr. were still fresh memories, and African Americans continued to resist the institutional racism prevalent in so much of society. Additionally, drug use was becoming a shared experience for much of a new generation. Meanwhile, a scandal was already brewing in Washington over a break-in at the Watergate complex that would topple a U.S. president, and with him the fading vestiges of respect for authority in America.

MILITARY STRONGLY OPPOSED

With the U.S. military staggered by its first defeat in war, and flailing in the eddy of social currents that brought racial tensions and rampant drug abuse into the ranks, the senior officer corps was strongly opposed to the concept of an all-volunteer force. The draft had been a fixture of military planning for decades, during which military ranks were swelled by both plumbers and Princeton PhDs, sons of sharecroppers and scions of great wealth and position. Even during the Vietnam War, new entrees through the draft had averaged 950,000 men annually. The idea of abruptly closing that spigot at a moment of defeat and vulnerability for the U.S. military was seen as purely political maneuvering on the part of the Nixon Administration.

More fundamentally, the issue of a draft versus an all-volunteer army struck at the very heart of the relationship between those in uniform and the society they served. The idea that national service was a moral responsibility and the bedrock of patriotism was deeply embedded in American culture at the time, as was the belief that the country's armed forces should have a breadth that spanned all strata of American society—regional, racial, and socioeconomic. Almost no one denied that the gross inequities in the draft revealed during the Vietnam era needed reforming, beginning with deferments that made colleges and the reserves sanctuaries for those trying to evade service. There were profound fears among senior military officers, however, that a volunteer force would become disproportionately skewed toward minority or lower-income recruits who had limited choices, or else attract too many "trigger-happy psychos." Military leaders worried that the services could become such a haven for society's rejects that public support for the military would continue to decline, isolating the U.S. military further.

Accustomed to a captive audience of draftees, military leaders also resented being thrown into the open market for recruits in the bitter aftermath of the Vietnam War, vying for the services of one of the most antiauthoritarian and rebellious generations in modern American history. Already many of their most promising young career officers were resigning their commissions.

Few in uniform took comfort from what was seen as the rubber-stamping of the all-volunteer idea by the Gates Commission (named for its chair, former Secretary of Defense Thomas Gates Jr.), which was tasked by President Nixon to study the issue. Nor were many military leaders comforted by Defense Secretary Melvin Laird's assurances that "long range . . . we do not foresee any significant difference between the racial composition of the all-volunteer force and the racial composition of the nation." Fears that it would be dominated by low-income or disadvantaged youth were, in Laird's words, likewise "false and unfounded."

A ROCKY START

Despite the Pentagon's efforts to entice a new generation of Americans into military service, by the end of the decade the earlier predictions about the all-volunteer force had proven to be correct. With the end of the draft, the proportion of African American recruits in the ground forces ballooned, from 12 percent in the early 1970s, or roughly in line with the eligible population of American youngsters, to a peak of 37 percent in 1979. While the number of African American officers increased nearly twofold during the same period, it still lagged far behind those numbers. U.S. military leaders discovered that units with such a high percentage of minorities and an overwhelming white officer cadre typically suffered severe racial tensions and a lack of cohesion.

The number of women joining the armed services also grew dramatically, as recruiters relied on them to make up for shortfalls in recruiting men (women recruits were also far more likely than their male counterparts to have high school diplomas, thus helping the Pentagon counter a growing "quality" problem). Military support systems for women and families predictably lagged. In the decade after the draft ended in 1973, the proportion of enlisted men in the Army who were married also nearly doubled from one-fourth to one-third of the total force, spelling an end to an army centered on barracks life. Once again, U.S. military personnel experts struggled to adapt.

Warnings that an all-volunteer force would mean digging deeper into the recruitment barrel were also coming true. Nearly half of all new recruits in 1979 were rated as CAT IV, the lowest mental category the military accepted. That same year, only 62 percent of Army recruits were high school graduates, the lowest since the all-volunteer force began. For the first time that year, the Army experienced a manpower shortage of 15,400 troops because of its inability to recruit even marginally qualified soldiers. The U.S. Navy was likewise short 20,000 petty officers, its most skilled enlisted crew members. Chronic drug and alcohol problems also persisted, with surveys indicating that as many as half of service members were regular drug users.

Put simply, in its first decade, the all-volunteer military hemorrhaged talent that the Pentagon was increasingly unable to replace. The fears expressed by opponents of the all-volunteer force had largely come true. Rather than reflecting a broad cross section of American society, the all-volunteer force was becoming increasingly racially skewed and economically disadvantaged, raising the specter of a permanent military underclass.

Armed with those grim personnel numbers, Army Chief of Staff General Edward "Shy" Meyer briefed President Jimmy Carter at Camp David in November 1979, shortly after Iranian militants had overrun the U.S. Embassy in Tehran, taking the embassy staff hostage, and just before the Soviet Union would invade Afghanistan. On the sorry state of the Army at a moment of national crisis, General Meyer was unequivocal. "Mr. President," he said, "basically what we have is a hollow Army."

THE REAGAN TURNAROUND

The U.S. military has always cast an imperfect mirror on American society, reflecting its weaknesses but also magnifying its strengths. By 1980, the manifest weaknesses of the all-volunteer force were evident for all to see. The dual crises in Iran and Afghanistan served as shock therapy to awaken the country from a decade of post-Vietnam malaise. The election of President Ronald Reagan in 1980, followed by largest peacetime defense buildup in the nation's history, signaled another inflection point. The nation was ready to change course once again.

How else to explain the dizzying turnaround in the fortunes of the all-volunteer force? Compared to the last three years of the 1970s, for instance, the proportion of new recruits with at least a high school diploma jumped from 62 percent to an unprecedented 85 percent by 1983, higher than the national average and more than 10 percentage points higher than the Army's average level even during the draft. The CAT IVs, or those who scored below average on the Armed Forces Qualification Test, had registered a corresponding drop from 44 to 20 percent, while those who scored above average had risen from 18 to 31 percent.

A collateral benefit of the rapid rise in the quality of recruits quickly became evident: soldiers with high school diplomas and higher aptitudes were more likely not only to successfully complete their initial tours, but also to reenlist once they were completed. That cut down on training demands and led to a force whose experience level steadily rose. Those retention levels pointed to a virtuous cycle, with the U.S. military able to become more selective about whom it recruited into a personnel pool that gained in maturity and experience throughout the 1980s. By the end of the decade, the all-volunteer force had largely become what its creators had originally envisioned: a truly professional army.

The question of what factors produced that tipping point and virtuous cycle is a matter of debate. Some experts credit the rapid rise in military pay and defense spending; others point to President Reagan for helping bring overt patriotism out of the closet where it remained hidden for much of the post-Vietnam 1970s.

Another possible factor was the increase in educational benefits, with the Montgomery G.I. Bill rewarding enlistees for their initial three-year tour of duty with $10,800 toward a college education. Still others credit the U.S.

military's adoption of improved recruitment techniques and strategies, reflected in the Army's widely acclaimed "Be All You Can Be" commercials.

The sheer speed of the reversal of fortune for the all-volunteer force, however, suggests that more elemental forces were at work. The post-Vietnam decade was in many ways an anomaly, following one of the longest and most unpopular wars in the nation's history, and the fortunes of the U.S. military during that period predictably suffered. After staring into the abyss of the hostage crisis and witnessing the humiliation of the United States at the hands of Iranian mullahs and extremists, however, the American public decided to change course. Once again the U.S. military held a mirror up to society, and it reflected a nation determined to confront a hostile world with renewed confidence and embrace core ideals such as patriotism and service. The U.S. military and all-volunteer force magnified that sense of renewed strength and optimism, captured in Ronald Reagan's 2004 reelection campaign slogan, "It's morning again in America."

PROFESSIONAL BUT SEPARATE

Today it has become commonplace for senior U.S. military leaders to insist that the all-volunteer force is the best the nation has ever fielded, and in one sense they are right. It is quantifiably the most professional force, comprising more careerists and staffed by volunteers who joined in order to learn the military craft. That is particularly important at a time when rapid advances in technology are revolutionizing the art of war, requiring increased levels of technological sophistication and advanced training and education. Senior military leaders would not return to a draft army of relative amateurs even if given the choice, and politicians fearing a popular backlash against reinstatement of the draft are not about to give them one.

However, the creation of an all-volunteer force severed an important bond that once tied the fate of the U.S. military more closely to Congress, the nation's political class, and to society at large through shared sacrifice and service. As originally envisioned in the depths of the Cold War, for instance, the all-volunteer military was intended to be a core cadre of professionals around which the nation would mobilize via the draft in the event of a major or extended conflict with the Soviet Union.

To prepare for the possibility that the Commander in Chief would have to mobilize the entire country behind a war effort, then–Army Chief of Staff Creighton Abrams in 1973 engineered a wholesale transfer of many critical support missions from the active-duty force into the National Guard and reserves. That insured that a future president would have to make the politically charged decision to activate and call up Guardsmen and reservists from virtually every congressional district in America even in the early stages of a conflict (a move Lyndon Johnson avoided throughout Vietnam, much to the consternation of Abrams and other senior military leaders).

After the 9/11 terrorist attacks led to wars in Afghanistan and Iraq, President George W. Bush was indeed required to activate the reserves and the Pentagon initially leaned heavily on the reserve component to deploy forces. Unhappy with that dependency, however, former Secretary of Defense Donald Rumsfeld moved to loosen close ties with reserves by shifting critical support missions back into the active-duty forces.

Such public passivity highlights another disturbing characteristic of the all-volunteer force. Today's military rank-and-file are the working-class sons and daughters of America's middle class, the offspring of schoolteachers, firemen, and police, and especially of military families whose service goes back multiple generations. Yet there are very few of the sons and daughters of America's privileged class to be found there, a change driven home by the fact that military experience is disappearing from congressional resumes. According to the Congressional Research Service, the percentage of legislators with military experience has dropped from 73 percent in 1971 to 20 percent in 2013.

Following more than a decade of war, there's reason to worry that a "political decoupling" has taken place, degrading the quality of congressional oversight of the military and the Commander in Chief's wartime decision making. Without energized constituents with a direct stake in the conflict, and no military experience on which to draw in judging its execution, Congress too often acquiesces to the Executive Branch and shows undue deference to leaders in uniform.

Former U.S. Ambassador to Afghanistan and Lieutenant General Karl Eikenberry witnessed that dynamic firsthand. In one 18-month period, he notes that 46 coalition soldiers were murdered by their Afghan allies in so-called green on blue incidents, and yet Congress held only one brief, 95-minute hearing on the issue. "In seeking a balance between displays of deferential respect for the volunteer military, and exercise of sober, demanding oversight, members [of Congress] have often found political expediency in prioritizing the former."

There's also reason to question the decision by the Bush Administration and Congress to actually reduce taxes during a decade of war, further insulating the American public from any sacrifices associated with the conflict. That left the burdens of more than a decade of war in Afghanistan and Iraq on the narrow shoulders of a small all-volunteer force and its families, while no sacrifice was asked of other American citizens. Little wonder that service members who served multiple combat tours in Iraq and Afghanistan frequently complain of feeling a profound sense of alienation on returning home to a nation that doesn't seem to be at war.

Another question looming over the all-volunteer force after its first extended wars is how its tenuous ties to the larger society impacts decision making on when to use military force. The *Washington Quarterly* recently noted that the number of military deployments has increased by a factor of five in the all-volunteer force era (versus the post–World War II draft era 1945–1973). Would the United States have invaded Iraq in 2003, or have 100,000 troops in Afghanistan more than a decade after the start of that conflict, if the country had a draft military? Writing for the publication, Lieutenant General Eikenberry doesn't think so.

One lawmaker who also doesn't think so is Representative Charles Rangel (D-NY), a staunch liberal who has repeatedly proposed legislation to reinstate the draft. The Universal National Service Act he proposed would have committed all Americans aged 18–26 to two years of national service, either in the active-duty or reserve military or in a civilian position that supports the national defense. In October 2004, the House defeated what became known as the "Reinstate the Draft Bill" by a lopsided vote of 402–2.

"Why is a kid who is going to Harvard or Yale or has alternatives not included in the sacrifice for our country? Why will you recruit people who have less options?" Rangel, a decorated Korean War veteran and a lawyer to the draft board during the Vietnam War, told Fox News in 2006. A draft would help discourage lawmakers, he insisted, from reckless wars. "Every time someone says more troops, or the military option is on the table in Iran, and the military option is on the table in North Korea, they're saying that somebody's kids are going to be placed in harm's way, but not mine."

In his book *Breach of Trust: How Americans Failed Their Soldiers and Their Country*, national security scholar, West Point graduate and Vietnam veteran Andrew J. Bacevich likewise takes direct aim at this civil-military relationship "founded on the principle that a few fight while the rest watch." His own son, 1st Lieutenant Andrew John Bacevich, was one of those few who fought in Iraq, and paid the ultimate sacrifice.

"Rather than offering an antidote to problems, the military system centered on the all-volunteer force bred and exacerbated them. It underwrote recklessness in the formulation of policy and thereby resulted in needless, costly, and ill-managed wars," Bacevich writes. "From pulpit and podium, at concerts and sporting events, expressions of warmth and affection shower down on the troops. Yet when . . . the state heedlessly and callously exploits those same troops, the people avert their gaze. Maintaining a pretense of caring about soldiers, state and society actually collaborate in betraying them."

Out of a long-ago desire to diffuse protests against the Vietnam War and the draft, Congress and the Nixon Administration embarked on a grand experiment that has fundamentally changed the balance of power between the Legislative and Executive Branches, and the compact between citizen and society. For all its admirable strengths and noble attributes, the all-volunteer force has in essence evolved into an American Foreign Legion, one with few ties to Washington decision-makers who left it to fight unpopular wars in Iraq and Afghanistan for more than a decade without so much as imposing a war tax on the other 99 percent of the citizenry. One does not need to be an alarmist to wonder whether the nature of the deal is in the long-term interest of either the soldiers or the society they serve.

◆   ◆   ◆   ◆   ◆

41. Congress Takes a Stand: The 1973 War Powers Resolution

by Dan Mahaffee

One of the U.S. Constitution's greatest "invitations to struggle" between the Executive and Legislative Branches, as constitutional scholar Edward Corwin described them, concerns the gravest decision its elected leaders can make—the decision to go to war. While the Founding Fathers placed a significant amount of authority in the hands of the Congress regarding wars, modern trends have strengthened the hand of the President in his role as Commander in Chief.

However, during the zenith of U.S. involvement in Vietnam in the 1960s, and the greatly unpopular expansion of that war into Cambodia and Laos, Congress sought to reassert its authority through the War Powers Resolution. Thoroughly bipartisan—a testament to the fatigue with the Vietnam War and a congressional desire to check executive power—this resolution sought to provide clear restrictions on how U.S. military forces could be deployed overseas.

The story of the War Powers Resolution serves as a useful window into the Constitutional and legal issues surrounding the use of U.S. military force. It also provides a notable example of how traditional partisan rivalries can give way to efforts to address great national challenges. The tensions between the

Executive and Legislative Branches that are at the core of the story are as real today as when the Resolution originally passed in 1973, with two-thirds of Congress voting to override a presidential veto.

WAR POWERS AND THE CONSTITUTION

In Article I, Section 8 of the Constitution, Congress is given clearly enumerated powers regarding matters concerning national security. It is given the power to "raise and support Armies" and "provide and maintain a Navy." Additionally, Congress is given power to set the rules governing the military; call forth and organize the state militias in federal service; and handle issues regarding piracy and other "Offences against the Law of Nations." Most importantly, it is Congress that has the sole power "to declare War."

On the other hand, all that Article II, Section 2 says about presidential power is that the President "shall be the Commander in Chief of the Army and Navy" and command state militia in federal service. Scholars who have analyzed the proceedings of the Constitutional Convention have found that only one proposal was made to vest any kind of power to declare war in executive hands, and it was promptly tabled and never revisited. It was assumed that the President—as well as naval commanders or army outposts leaders far afield—would act immediately in self-defense, but significant offensive action, exemplified by a declaration of war, would be the responsibility of the Congress.[1] Indeed, in *Federalist No. 74*—regarding "The Command of the Military and Naval Forces, and the Pardoning Power of the Executive"—the discussion of the powers of the Commander in Chief is limited to a brief explanation of why a unified command would be needed in wartime.

The Constitution's division of responsibilities over the conduct of war quickly raised another question: What was the role of Congress and the Commander in Chief in situations that did not rise to the level of declared war? With the turmoil of the French Revolution and conflict between key trading partner Great Britain and crucial ally France, the United States found its neutrality repeatedly violated on the high seas. With its limited resources a young America could not hope to challenge European powers, and yet it could not afford to continue fighting a purely defensive battle against French commerce raiding. Thus on July 9, 1798, Congress passed "An Act Further to Protect the Commerce of the United States," allowing U.S. vessels to attack, and seize, French ships.[2] Thus a precedent was set wherein Congress would authorize the use of military force but not go so far as to commit the nation to a declared war.

Although Congress did declare war during the War of 1812, the Mexican-American War, the Spanish-American War, World War I, and World War II, notably, war was never declared during the Civil War, so as to avoid acknowledgement of any Confederate sovereignty. However, during that conflict Congress formed the Joint Committee on the Conduct of the War, which left a significant imprint on the war. Filled largely with radical Republicans, the committee pushed for more aggressive military strategies and pro-emancipation policies, and its stances often aggravated members of the Lincoln Administration and Union military commanders, and likely hindered the war effort.[3] Congress also had significant impact on the conduct of the war in other ways, notably through passing laws allowing for conscription, as well as a law prohibiting the purchase of officers' commissions—remedying the issue of wealthy or well-connected, yet incompetent, commanders that plagued the war effort at the beginning of the conflict.

THE POST–WORLD WAR II ERA

Following World War II, the United States found itself in a geopolitical position unlike any in its previous experience. As the de facto political, economic, and military leader of the "free world," America suddenly had to shoulder global responsibilities far beyond its previous global involvement.

The National Security Act of 1947 and other pieces of legislation thus created a permanent national security bureaucracy within the Executive Branch, institutionalizing many of the executive powers assumed by the President during World War II. (See "A Superpower's Foundation: The National Security Act of 1947," Chapter 37.) With the creation of the Central Intelligence Agency, the National Security Agency, and the broader intelligence community, presidents in the future would increasingly have tools for covert action ready at hand. Additionally, through the Charter of the United Nations (UN) and the North Atlantic Treaty, the United States was, for the first time, diplomatically and legally bound to provide military force in times of conflict, at least under some circumstances.

When Communist North Korean forces invaded South Korea on June 25, 1950, instead of going to Congress, the Truman Administration went to the United Nations Security Council (UNSC). With the Soviet Union boycotting the UNSC and thus unable to veto the resolution, on June 27, 1950, UNSC Resolution 83 deemed the North Korean attack a "breach of the peace" and called on UN member nations to "furnish such assistance . . . as may be necessary to repel the armed attack and to restore international peace and security in the area."[4]

When he met with congressional leaders on June 27, President Truman's goal was not to seek approval, but merely to "inform them of important decisions that he had made in the past 24 hours." Additionally, the congressional leaders in attendance felt that U.S. assistance to South Korea was vital to show commitment to both the United Nations and strength in the face of Communist aggression.[5] With few exceptions, Truman found bipartisan support for the deployment of U.S. combat forces pursuant to UN resolutions. As the war went on, however, the growing stalemate and the firing of General Douglas MacArthur resulted in increased congressional opprobrium.[6] Often described as a "police action," the Korean conflict set the precedent of near unilateral executive power to not only enter a war, but also to prosecute it.

As the United States began to support South Vietnam in the late 1950s and early 1960s, it was largely through military assistance and covert action. However, as U.S. involvement in the region expanded, American forces were increasingly drawn into the conflict between North and South Vietnam. For President Kennedy, U.S. military assistance to Vietnam was pursuant to treaty obligations and commitments under the 1954 Geneva Conference and the SEATO Pact (South East Asia Treaty Organization), a collective defense organization that included the United States.

While Congress was informed of U.S. military assistance programs, it was often within the context of these treaty obligations, as well as the overall policy of the Kennedy Administration to actively confront what was perceived as Communist expansion.[7]

By the time of the Gulf of Tonkin incident in August 1964, U.S. advisors and covert forces were heavily involved with South Vietnamese military forces. However, with the reported attack on the USS *Maddox*, President Johnson felt the need to gain congressional approval for an escalation of U.S. involvement in Vietnam. Seeking to avoid the criticism that Truman faced during the Korean conflict, the Johnson Administration worked closely with congressional leadership to develop a resolution that would give the President as much leeway as possible in Southeast Asia. With no opposition in the House of Representatives and only two nay votes in the Senate, the Gulf of Tonkin Resolution gave President Johnson near total power to expand the war in Vietnam. (See "A Blank Check for War: The Gulf of Tonkin Resolution," Chapter 39.)

THE VIETNAM QUAGMIRE

Despite broad congressional authorization and the deployment of half a million American troops to South Vietnam, the North Vietnamese Army and Viet Cong insurgents proved to be a tenacious adversary. During the 1968 presidential election, Richard Nixon vowed "to bring an honorable end to the war in Vietnam," and reached out to an American public tired of combat—both in Southeast Asia and during antiwar demonstrations on the streets and campuses of the United States.[8]

The Communist losses in men and materiel during the Tet Offensive allowed Nixon to pursue a strategy of "Vietnamization" where U.S. forces were gradually withdrawn from combat operations in favor of U.S.-supported South Vietnamese forces. To the chagrin of antiwar advocates, however, Nixon made no sound commitment to a total withdrawal of U.S. forces or an end date for U.S. combat operations.[9] In addition, Communist sanctuaries in Cambodia and Laos continued to thwart the U.S. goal of ensuring that South Vietnamese forces could stand on their own.

Despite the open-ended authorization for the Vietnam War, the Nixon Administration realized that the expansion of the war into Laos and Cambodia would be met with both congressional and public anger. In 1969, shortly after Nixon's inauguration, the U.S. Air Force launched Operation MENU, airstrikes against North Vietnamese and Viet Cong camps in Cambodia. Operation MENU was considered one of the tightest held secrets in the Nixon White House, and only six Members of Congress—chosen due to their leadership positions and perceived hawkishness—were briefed on the airstrikes: Senators Richard Russell (D-GA), John C. Stennis (D-MS), and Everett Dirksen (R-IL), and Representatives Lucius M. Rivers (D-SC), Gerald Ford (R-MI), and Leslie Arends (R-IL).[10]

In 1970, as Communist Khmer Rouge rebels overthrew the Cambodian king, President Nixon publicly announced a U.S.-South Vietnamese incursion into Cambodia to attack Communist bases. In 1971, U.S. forces also supported South Vietnamese incursions into ostensibly neutral Laos, fueling the narrative that the Nixon Administration was deaf to the war-weariness of the American public and their political leaders.

In response to the escalation of the war, Congress began to move to limit U.S. involvement in Cambodia. The 1970 Cooper-Church Amendment, originally attached to the Foreign Military Sales Act, was passed in 1971, limiting offensive operations in Cambodia. Other legislative measures sought to defund the Vietnam War (though many legislators were wary of casting a vote perceived as pulling funding for American troops in combat).[11] New revelations about Vietnam policy, notably the 1971 publication of the "Pentagon Papers," furthered the perception that the White House was not keeping the American people and the Congress fully informed about the war. All of those factors raised a broader question for congressional leaders—what role is left for Congress in deciding to send American troops into combat? Ultimately, the debate over this question, combined with the snowballing scandals of the Nixon Administration, drove congressional leaders to try and define Congress's modern war powers.

WAR POWERS DEBATE

At the same time Congress was debating the merits of the Cooper-Church Amendment, several Members of Congress began to push for some form of resolution requiring the President to notify or consult Congress when U.S. forces were deployed overseas. A major force behind these proposals—and the eventual 1973 War Powers Resolution—was Representative Clement J. Zablocki (D-WI). A staunch anticommunist from the heavily Polish south side of Milwaukee and a supporter of the Vietnam War, Zablocki was the chairman of the U.S. House Committee on Foreign Affairs. While Zablocki continued to support the objectives of the war, he was alarmed that the Foreign Affairs Committee was losing influence, as the majority of legislation regarding the Vietnam War was instead coming through the Appropriations Committees via defunding measures.[12] He thus charted a careful course over the next several years, avoiding direct criticism of the war, while vigorously defending the role of Congress and the jurisdiction of his committee.

During initial hearings on war powers legislation in June through August 1970, witnesses ranging from then-Assistant Attorney General William Rehnquist to former National Security Advisor McGeorge Bundy (who advised both Presidents Kennedy and Johnson) opposed formalizing Congress's role in the decision to go to war. When asked if Congress had a role before the nation was committed to war, State Department legal advisor, John Stevenson, stated, "There is a role. We simply feel codifying it would be counterproductive."[13] Expressing the sentiments of many of his colleagues, Zablocki asked Stevenson, "How else can we get our feet in the door?"[14]

The White House tried to run out the clock by prolonging the discussion, and thus the status quo. But in September 1970, the House considered H.J. Res. 1355, which called for the President to consult Congress before a military deployment, or to notify Congress promptly after a deployment about the scope and objectives of the deployment, as well as the reasons Congress was not consulted in advance. The resolution passed by a 288–39 margin. However, the Senate failed to act on the House resolution and focused largely on the Cooper-Church Amendment.

In early 1972, the Senate began to take up the issue of war powers in earnest—an effort that was driven by the unlikely coalition of Senators John C. Stennis (D-MS) and Jacob K. Javits (R-NY). Stennis, the Chairman of the U.S. Senate Armed Services Committee and one of the six aforementioned Congressmen briefed on Operation MENU, was considered one of the leading Democratic hawks. Javits, on the other hand, was a liberal Republican who found himself more often at odds with his own party.

For Stennis, the push for war powers legislation came from a deeply held belief—reaffirmed by the Vietnam War—that clear congressional approval or a declaration of war was necessary to mobilize the nation behind a war effort. Stennis, like Zablocki in the House, carefully couched discussions about war powers in a way that separated the issue from the ongoing war in Vietnam.[15] As a respected legislator—especially in military matters—Stennis carefully addressed concerns that the President's hands would be tied during a Cold War crisis, or that passage of such legislation would lead NATO allies to question American treaty commitments.[16]

The arguments of Stennis and Javits—framed in terms of Congress's Constitutional prerogatives and issues of national mobilization—helped their proposal gain bipartisan support in the Senate. Senator Robert Taft Jr. (R-OH), who would join the bill's cosponsors, announced his support by saying "War is not only too important to be left to the generals, the American people abhor war to such an extent that it is too important to be left to the President alone."[17]

The Stennis-Javits measure passed the Senate 68–16 in April 1972, and the House passed the Senate bill with minimal modification, 344–13. However, concerns about the bill—namely its impact on the Vietnam War and perceptions about American Cold War power—as well as disagreements about the timeframe in which the President would be required to report military deployments to Congress, resulted in a deadlocked conference committee. At the time, Zablocki was still unwilling to provide specific timeframes for congressional approval or disapproval of a deployment. Zablocki's relatively vague legislation was the best chance the White House had to satisfy congressional demands, while ensuring maximum flexibility for military operations.

Despite this setback, Zablocki, Stennis, and Javits redoubled their efforts in 1973, and this time, they benefitted from the scandals which soon engulfed the Nixon Administration.

At the time the United States continued to support South Vietnamese incursions into Cambodia and Laos, and conduct airstrikes against North Vietnamese and Khmer Rouge forces. The Linebacker II bombing raids during the 1972 holiday season, combined with the breakdown in peace negotiations, furthered congressional perceptions of a Nixon Administration unwilling to end the war.

Among the political elite, there was increasing disquiet about the issue of war powers. In the *New York Times*, Arthur Schlesinger Jr. asked, "Why, after nearly two years of independence, should there now seem to be no visible checks on the personal power of an American President to send troops into combat?"[18]

Despite the success of Paris peace negotiations following the Linebacker II raids, Congress was still concerned about the issue of seemingly unchecked presidential war powers. As U.S. forces were withdrawn from Vietnam, many in Congress wanted to ensure that American forces were never again deployed to such a murky conflict.

Additionally, after Nixon's successful reelection, many lawmakers began to resent the hubris of the White House. A story, perhaps exaggerated, exemplified this attitude. On March 27, 1973, when William H. Sullivan, Deputy Assistant Secretary of State for East Asia, was asked about the legal basis for the continued airstrikes in Cambodia, it was reported that his reply was "For now, I'd just say the justification is the re-election of President Nixon."[19] This hubris, combined with growing revelations about the illegal behavior of the Nixon Administration, further affected congressional attitudes about executive power—and not just regarding war powers.

In May 1973, the Senate and House thus began to move in the same direction, quickly reintroducing the legislation that had died in conference in 1972.[20] By July, both bills came before the floor for debate. As both bills moved through Congress, three key points of contention emerged: the Senate bill required congressional approval for a deployment within 30 days, compared to 120 days in the House version; the Senate bill would call for a military withdrawal via Joint Resolution, which is subject to a presidential veto, while the House version called for a Concurrent Resolution; and the Senate version exempted current conflicts from the law, while the House version did not.[21] The House version was passed, 244–170, on July 18, 1973; the Senate version passed 72–18 two days later.

By early October, the conference committee tasked with reconciling the versions reached compromises on the differences between the bills. Without congressional approval, military operations would be terminated within 60 days. The President would be able to extend this deadline 30 days if he was able to certify that continued deployment was required to secure the withdrawal of forces. The legislation would not apply to ongoing conflicts, and a concurrent resolution would be used to end military action. Three exceptions were provided to the law: a declaration of war, specific statutory authority to use force, or an attack upon the United States.

With the compromises, the legislation came under attack from the far right and the far left. On the right, concerns were raised about whether the Congress would destroy the necessary unity of command in wartime. On the left, some argued that by acknowledging this 60-day timeframe, the President was granted an unconstitutional amount of leeway to make war, albeit briefly.[22]

Outside events gave ammunition to both sides. Further revelations about the Watergate scandal fed the narrative of an administration run amok, and, in August, hearings before the Senate Armed Services Committee revealed the scope of Operation MENU. Members of Congress were taken aback by the Administration's belief that briefing six members was a sufficient consultation with Congress.

At the same time, President Nixon's repeated veto threats raised the specter of a showdown with the White House, with Congress needing a two-thirds majority in both houses to override a veto. In October, the outbreak of the Yom Kippur War between Israel and its Arab neighbors, and the need for rapid resupply of Israeli forces by the U.S. military, raised concerns about whether the law would hamstring the President during international crises.

With this backdrop, on October 10, the Senate passed the conferenced bill 75–20—well beyond the two-thirds needed to override a veto—while the House passed the bill 238–123—3 short of two-thirds—though 74 members were absent.

President Nixon exercised his threatened veto on October 24, stating that the legislation would place undue burdens on the Commander in Chief. His veto statement used a well-worn Washington tactic, as he suggested forming a commission to examine the issue of presidential and congressional war powers. Nixon also used his statement to provide a thorough defense of presidential powers, "[The bill] would purport to take away, by a mere legislative act, authorities which the President has properly exercised under the Constitution for almost 200 years."[23] Using recent examples as evidence for his stand, he also declared,

> We may well have been unable to respond in the way we did during the Berlin crisis of 1961, the Cuban Missile Crisis of 1962, the Congo rescue operation in 1964, and the Jordanian crisis of 1970—to mention just a few examples. In addition, our recent actions to bring about a peaceful settlement of the hostilities in the Middle East would have been seriously impaired if this resolution had been in force.[24]

Despite the presidential warnings and the veto, Cold War tensions, and opposition from the far right and left, on November 7, the House and Senate overrode the veto, 284–135 and 75–18, respectively.

AN UNCERTAIN LEGACY

Initial analyses focused on the fact that, for the first time, a Nixon veto had been overridden by the Congress.

However, this was more than a mere political setback; this was a bipartisan statement by the Congress pushing back against presidential overreach. Certainly the scandals surrounding Nixon provided cover for Republicans to vote against the White House. Still, during the first three decades of the Cold War, trends in domestic politics, foreign policy, and military organization placed increasing power in the hands of the Executive, and in 1973, the Legislative Branch finally pushed back.

In his remarks before the Senate as it debated overriding Nixon's veto, Senator Javits hinted at the uncertain legal future that awaited the War Powers Resolution,

> I doubt very much that any court would have decided [the constitutionality of the Resolution] before or would decide it now. It is almost a classic example of what the courts have considered a "political question." That was the reason we had to settle it through legislation, including a veto override.[25]

Indeed, no court has taken up a legal challenge based on the War Powers Resolution, and only one President—Gerald Ford during the evacuation of U.S. nationals from South Vietnam and the retaking of the SS *Mayaguez*— has specifically cited the War Powers Resolution when reporting military operations to Congress.[26] Each presidential administration has continued to take the stance that the War Powers Resolution is unconstitutional. Reflecting the legal disagreements at a semantic level, reports from the President to Congress state that they are "consistent" with the War Powers Resolution— not "pursuant to."

Despite this legal disagreement, the War Powers Resolution has provided Congress with a vehicle to discuss and challenge the President, and it has often been raised in discussions ranging from the Iran Hostage Crisis to the deployment of Marines to Lebanon to the more recent U.S. support for NATO operations in Libya in 2011.

In major military interventions—the Gulf War, the War in Afghanistan, and the Invasion of Iraq—the President has continued to seek statutory authorization from Congress for military operations. Still, the continued ability of Congress to shape national security policy is uncertain given the evolving nature of warfare. A modern president seeking to take military action can draw on an array of tactics that his predecessors did not have: Special Forces, drones, or cyber-attacks. Indeed, during the intervention in Libya, the Obama Administration argued that U.S. participation in the conflict was not covered by the War Powers Resolution, as standoff operations using unmanned aerial vehicles and cruise missiles did not represent "imminent hostilities" for U.S. troops.[27]

The debate about when and how Congress will be consulted on these military actions involve the careful balancing of security, secrecy, and Constitutional values. While it is unclear what shape this debate might take in the future, it is likely that Congress will continue to defend its institutional role in this process.

♦ ♦ ♦ ♦ ♦

42. Shining a Light on Spycraft: The Church and Pike Committees

by Loch K. Johnson

In 1974 the American public was transfixed by the Watergate scandal, which revealed criminality in the White House and led to the first resignation of a U.S. President when Richard Nixon stepped down in August of that year. Close on the heels of Watergate, *The New York Times* published a series of articles in the fall and winter of 1974 that revealed serious abuses of power in the U.S. intelligence apparatus, raising an outpouring of public concern that there was rot at the core of the U.S. government.

Reported by investigative journalist Seymour M. Hersh, the *Times* articles disclosed details of covert actions overseas, including those against the democratically elected regime of Salvador Allende in Chile. Intelligence sources quoted in the *Times* further claimed that "the Agency," as the Central Intelligence Agency (CIA) is known by insiders, had collected dossiers on over 10,000 American citizens. Additionally, the CIA had conducted "massive" spying program against anti–Vietnam War activists, despite the fact that the

National Security Act of 1947 expressly barred the CIA from engaging in espionage inside the United States. Arriving so soon after Watergate, this news of intelligence skullduggery brought intense pressure on government officials to launch an official inquiry into the allegations

On January 27, 1975, the U.S. Senate voted 82–4 in favor of establishing a special committee to conduct an inquiry into America's intelligence agencies. The Senate Majority Leader Mike Mansfield (D-MT) chose a fellow Westerner and senior member of the Foreign Relations Committee, Frank Church (D-ID) to lead the investigation. The House of Representatives established a counterpart panel, and after initially experiencing internal strife, it finally settled in July on a permanent leader, Otis Pike (D-NY). Senator Church and Representative Pike met in midsummer to discuss how they could avoid unnecessary overlap between their two investigations. Church's panel would concentrate on alleged abuses of power, and Pike agreed to focus mainly on how well the agencies performed their core mission of intelligence collection and analysis. Meanwhile, President Gerald R. Ford initiated a separate probe: the Rockefeller Commission, chaired by Vice President Nelson A. Rockefeller.

The life spans of the Rockefeller Commission and the Pike Committee proved shorter than the Church Committee. The Rockefeller Commission narrowed its focus to alleged wrongdoings related to CIA domestic spying and issued its report by the summer of 1975. The Pike Committee labored on during the fall, but continued to suffer from internal dissention and combative relations with the intelligence agencies. In contrast, the Church Committee subjected the CIA and its companion agencies to a 16-month investigation. As a result of its broader probe, the Committee ultimately had greater influence on intelligence reform.

CONGRESSIONAL LEADERS STEP FORWARD

The Church Committee consisted of six Democrats and five Republicans, and its staff numbered more than 150 investigators and researchers. Senator Church led the Democrats and Senator John G. Tower (R-TX) led the Republicans.

As the Church Committee investigation unfolded, different senators assumed leadership roles according to their personal interests and opportunities. Church's foremost concern was foreign policy and he spent most of his efforts looking into CIA covert actions. In 1973, he was the chair of a Foreign Relations Subcommittee on Multinational Corporations. During that time, he had already explored the role of International Telephone and Telegraph (ITT) and the CIA in secret anti-Allende activities in Chile. Church also had a strong interest in the subject of foreign assassination plots, an issue that came to the attention of the Committee as it investigated past covert actions.

Senator Tower also took a lively interest in the assassination plots. He and Church, though far apart ideologically, worked together closely to unravel these Cold War operations aimed at eliminating the likes of Fidel Castro of Cuba and Patrice Lumumba of Congo (among other targets, none of whom died at the hands of the Agency as all the plots failed). Senator Walter F. Mondale (D-MN) emerged as the Committee's leader on domestic intelligence matters. Having served earlier in his career as state attorney general, Mondale had an interest in the Federal Bureau of Investigation (FBI) and law enforcement. He ended up spending more hours than any other member working with the staff in preparation for hearings on the Bureau's counter-intelligence program (COINTELPRO), which involved spying on antiwar dissenters, civil rights advocates, and members of the Ku Klux Klan.

Additional committee members stepped forward to provide leadership in different areas. Gary W. Hart (D-CO) became fascinated by the assassination plots against Castro and their possible relationship to President John F. Kennedy's own death at the hands of an assassin. He joined forces with Senator Richard S. Schweiker (R-PA) to form an ad hoc working group. They examined the available evidence in CIA files, and concluded that the Cuban leader may have decided to retaliate against President Kennedy. Other committee members, though, steered clear of this controversial and unproven sidebar.

Although ill with terminal cancer, Senator Philip A. Hart (D-MI) assumed leadership during the Committee's hearing on the FBI's COINTELPRO program. In a Senate Caucus Room of the Russell Building that was packed with media, government officials, and tourists, Hart spoke in a weakened voice that was nonetheless deeply moving to those in earshot. "I've been told for years by, among others, members of my own family that this is what the Bureau has been doing all this time," Hart said, summarizing the findings presented by the Committee's top staff attorneys. "As a result of my superior wisdom in high office, I assured them that they were on pot—it just wasn't true. They [the FBI] just wouldn't do it." Hart paused and cleared his throat as the Caucus Room fell silent. "What you have described is a series of illegal actions intended to deny certain citizens their First Amendment rights—just like my children said." Even hardened staff members felt choked with emotion as they listened to Hart's heartfelt response. This popular Senator would never appear again at a Committee hearing or work session, but he had provided the most dramatic moment in the investigation.

Beneath its formal hierarchy, the Church Committee—like all congressional inquiries—wrestled with disagreements over how to proceed: what topics to investigate, what hearings to hold in public, which witnesses to call, what to say in the final report. The liberals, led by Church and Mondale, wished to see strong new regulations that would make the intelligence agencies more accountable to Congress. The conservatives, led by Senators Tower, Howard H. Baker Jr. (R-TN), and Barry Goldwater (R-AZ), sided with the Republican White House most of the time in opposing more stringent oversight. The moderates on the Committee—Walter "Dee" Huddleston (D-KY), Robert B. Morgan (D-NC), and Charles Mathias (R-MD)—played an important role in arbitrating disagreements between the liberals and conservatives.

These ideological conflicts were complicated by personal ambitions, as individuals on the Committee jockeyed for position and tried to advance their party's interests in upcoming presidential elections. For instance, Church became a presidential candidate in the spring of 1976, as the work of the Committee wound down. At the staff level, disagreements between social scientists and attorneys about how such a broad investigation should be run produced further tensions. The social scientists emphasized the importance of interviewing key intelligence personnel, for example, while the attorneys focused on the acquisition of documentary evidence.

A TUG-OF-WAR BETWEEN BRANCHES

Institutional rules about handling classified information became significant for both the Church and the Pike Committees. The Church Committee decided to negotiate with the Executive Branch for access to documents and witnesses, and worked with the intelligence agencies to declassify selected documents. By Committee vote, some of the findings were released publicly, including those surrounding the National Security Agency's (NSA) domestic surveillance programs. However, Senator Church eventually bowed to the insistence of Republicans that Senate Rule 36 required full Senate approval for release of the panel's final report, and the report on CIA assassination plots. After extensive debate, the Senate voted that both documents be released to the public.

On the House side the atmosphere between the branches was far more acrimonious. The Pike Committee demanded immediate access to documents and witnesses, and Chairman Pike insisted that his panel had the right to declassify documents on its own accord if it received full House approval. In a disastrous finale, the "top secret" Pike Committee report leaked to *The Village Voice* in February 1976. Relations in the House grew so poisonous over the Pike Committee inquiry that a majority of lawmakers refused to even consider creating a permanent intelligence oversight committee in the House until emotions had cooled down in 1977.

The Ford Administration found the Pike Committee so belligerent that the White House eventually refused to cooperate with its requests for documents and witnesses. Even with the Church Committee, the Administration periodically resorted to stonewalling and slow rolling, refusing initially to provide key documents and witnesses and, when relenting, doing so in a manner that dragged the investigations out seemingly forever. The White House always had an eye on the calendar, knowing that time would eventually run out on both congressional investigations. The Church Committee's more honey-laden approach to the Executive Branch often worked better, but not always. For example, after repeated requests for more documents on the assassination plots, covert action, and NSA activities went unanswered, the staff escalated the Committee's demands, which were followed when necessary by formal letters of complaint signed by Church and Tower. The Committee staff also took some disputes to the U.S. District Court for the District of Columbia for arbitration, and waved subpoenas in the faces of witnesses who balked at requests to appear in hearings. The modus operandi of the Executive Branch was to seek more delays, and then—on most topics—finally to comply.

On one occasion, the Department of Defense responded to a document request by backing up a huge truck filled with documents to the Church Committee's offices in the Dirksen Building. The staff was initially elated, only to discover that the papers were about as relevant to the panel's proceedings as copies of the *Congressional Record* from the 1980s. After the Committee's leaders rebuked the Secretary of Defense, documents more germane to the investigation arrived a few weeks later.

Another ploy used by the Executive Branch was preemption. While the investigations were still ongoing, the White House created the Intelligence Oversight Board (IOB) as a symbolic gesture toward reform, and it issued an executive order banning assassination plots. The creation of the Rockefeller Commission was itself an effort at preemption, although it failed to halt the gathering momentum toward reform created by the Church and Pike inquiries.

THE INTELLIGENCE WARS

Throughout what became known on Capitol Hill as the "Year of Intelligence" (or "The Intelligence Wars," as CIA officers often referred to it), a running battle raged inside the Executive Branch itself. On one side was CIA Director William E. Colby who decided it would be prudent to cooperate with the Church Committee (although not the obstreperous Pike Committee), rather than risk the potential abolition of the Agency. On the other side was the Ford White House, which proposed hunkering down until the congressional storm blew over. President Ford finally fired Colby in December 1975, near the end of the investigations. Colby was right, however, in believing that if the CIA had refused to cooperate with the Church Committee, lawmakers in the Senate would likely have gone after his organization with a vengeance, much as the Pike Committee had done.

The Church Committee's three most conservative Republicans—Tower, Goldwater, and Baker—ended up voting against the release of the Committee's final report. Nonetheless, during the course of the investigation, even they acquiesced to most of the substantive and procedural decisions reached by the Democratic majority. In the Senate, shock among lawmakers over CIA covert actions, assassination programs, and NSA and FBI domestic spying eventually trumped partisanship. When the full Senate finally voted on the key reform of creating an intelligence oversight committee—the Senate Select Committee on Intelligence (SSCI)—the final tally of 72 to 22 was a lopsided bipartisan victory for the Church Committee. Members of the House were also unhappy about shortcomings in intelligence collection-and-analysis, but the disorganized and shrill, anti-CIA tilt of the Pike Committee managed to alienate the entire House of Representatives. In January 1976, lawmakers voted 146–124 against the release of the Committee's official report (the document that later leaked to *The Village Voice*). It would take another year before memory of the Pike Committee's squabbling was sufficiently behind them before lawmakers agreed to establish a House Permanent Select Committee on Intelligence (HPSCI).

GROUNDBREAKING REFORM, CONSTANT VIGILANCE

Despite some bickering along party lines—with Democrats seeking greater intelligence transparency, and Republicans attempting to preserve the status quo—the Church Committee investigation ranks as one of the most significant congressional inquiries ever conducted. It provided the first serious examination into America's intelligence agencies, and set in motion forces that would revolutionize U.S. espionage activities, including the tightening of accountability through oversight by the Senate and House intelligence committees.

Later Congress also enacted legislation initially drafted by the Church Committee, including: the 1978 Foreign Intelligence Surveillance Act (FISA), which required court warrants for national security wiretaps; and the 1980 Intelligence Oversight Act, which importantly required advance notice of all significant intelligence operations before they were actually carried out. Above all, the Church Committee set a new tone when it came to espionage activities. Henceforth, the CIA and its companion agencies were expected to operate under the rule of law, with proper supervision by members of Congress.

Even with the Church Committee reforms, however, accountability has fallen short from time to time. The Iran-Contra scandal in the 1980s demonstrated that serious intelligence abuses could occur even in an era of stepped-up congressional oversight of the nation's spy agencies. Additionally, after the 9/11 terrorist attacks, the George W. Bush Administration bypassed the FISA warrant requirements, and allowed the CIA to engage in a number of over-zealous counterterrorism operations that included the use of secret prisons abroad. This included the torture of suspected terrorists through "enhanced interrogation techniques" such as waterboarding, and extraordinary renditions (kidnapping terrorist suspects for imprisonment and interrogation by third-party nations). Further questionable intelligence activities in the post-9/11 era included the expansive "metadata" collection programs that the NSA ran inside the United States. In response, the Obama Administration outlawed the secret prisons, renditions, and torture, but permitted the NSA operations to continue. Members of the Senate and House intelligence oversight committees have investigated the NSA's "dragnet" procedures, and in October 2013, they vowed to establish new rules to better align this agency with accepted counterterrorism norms and practices.

The Church Committee ushered in an era of greater intelligence oversight and accountability represented most notably by the establishment of the intelligence oversight committees in Congress. To function properly and live up to the spirit of the Church Committee reforms, however, those committees require constant vigilance on the part of members.

◆ ◆ ◆ ◆ ◆

43. Against All Odds: The Goldwater-Nichols Defense Reorganization

by James Kitfield

By the mid-1980s, the United States was well into the largest peacetime defense buildup in the nation's history. President Ronald Reagan's signature foreign policy initiative had been to abandon détente and adopt a more confrontational approach with the Soviet Union. In the President's mind, that required restoring the strength and vitality of a U.S. military that Army Chief of Staff General Edward "Shy" Meyer had publicly disparaged as "hollow" the year Reagan took office in 1980. So between 1980 and 1984, the defense budget more than doubled, and all of the armed services went on a buying spree for new weapons systems. When Reagan won a landslide reelection in 1984, Defense Secretary Caspar Weinberger saw it as a clear mandate to continue the defense buildup.

There were already signs that a backlash was building, however, especially among Democrats who believed Reagan was throwing too much money at the Pentagon, too fast. Each week, there was a steady stream of "spare parts horror stories" that publicized $700 hammers and $400 toilet seats purchased by the Defense Department, as well as reports of defense contractors who kenneled their pets and entertained at posh retreats at government expense. The result was a steady drumbeat of negative headlines and "waste, fraud and abuse" stories involving profligate Pentagon spending.

Beyond the daily headlines, there was also a sense among military reformers in Washington that something was fundamentally askew with the U.S. military. Evidence included the humiliating failure to rescue 52 American hostages in Iran in 1980, an operation that ended in a calamity in the Iranian desert when rescue aircraft collided, killing eight U.S. service members. That operation EAGLE CLAW was followed in rapid succession by the terrorist bombing of the U.S. Marine barracks in Beirut, Lebanon, in 1983 that killed 241 Marines; and the Operation Urgent Fury to rescue U.S. medical students caught up in a Marxist coup on the tiny Caribbean island of Grenada that same year, which very nearly ended with U.S. forces mistakenly bombing the facility where the students were held. The investigative commissions that examined those operations cited a familiar litany of shortcomings, including: a muddled chain-of-command structure; an inability of the armed services to work together and cooperate on joint operations; poor appreciation for the proper uses of Special Operations Forces; and frequently faulty intelligence. Shortly before their retirement, Air Force General David Jones, Chairman of the Joint Chiefs of Staff, and Army Chief General Meyer, both echoed those criticisms in calling for fundamental reform of the Joint Staff system.

Despite the tenor of the times and unfavorable publicity surrounding the Pentagon, the forces arrayed against substantive military reforms seemed insurmountable in the mid-1980s. The wall of resistance to reform included an extremely popular Republican President; a Secretary of Defense and service secretaries in the Pentagon who, along with the current Joint Chiefs of Staff, were all adamantly opposed; and a powerful committee chairman of the Armed Services Committee in the Republican-controlled Senate. Against that wall of resistance was arrayed a few members of Congress and their staffs who were trying to reform the largest bureaucracy in the free world, one that had successfully resisted similar efforts for nearly four decades.

That a determined band of reformers ultimately succeeded against all odds, pushing through the most sweeping reorganization of the Defense Department since the 1947 National Security Act, is a testament to how powerful personalities and behind-the-scenes experts with intricate knowledge of the often arcane ways of Congress and the Pentagon can team together to drive transformational change. The passage of the Goldwater-Nichols Department of Defense Reorganization Act of 1986 also serves as a reminder of what can be achieved in Washington, D.C. when a worthy cause finds an unlikely champion.

INSTITUTIONAL RESISTANCE

A conservative Democrat from rural Alabama, Representative Bill Nichols made for an unlikely military reformer. He had first come to Congress in 1966, a George Wallace Democrat from the kind of Southern district that tended to stick loyally with its politicians. In two decades on the House Armed Services Committee, Nichols had risen to become chairman of the Investigations Subcommittee, where he held exhaustive hearings on the bombing of the Marine barracks in Beirut, as well as spare-parts procurement scandals. An Army veteran who had lost a leg in World War II to a land mine, Nichols personally traveled to Beirut, where he saw and heard enough to believe that the Pentagon's command structure had let the Marines down in Lebanon. At these hearings, witnesses continually pointed to the problems that occurred when a joint military response was needed—Vietnam, *Mayaguez, Pueblo,* EAGLE CLAW, Beirut. As details continued to emerge on Operation Urgent Fury in Grenada, even that "victory" had written on it many of the problems that had doomed other operations to failure.

Nichols instructed Archie Barrett, his chief staffer on the investigations subcommittee, to write up a relatively modest reform rider and attach it to the 1985 Defense Authorization Bill. A recently retired Air Force lieutenant colonel with an undergraduate degree from West Point and a doctorate from Harvard, Barrett had spent his last two years in uniform studying the subject of defense reorganization on the staff of former Secretary of Defense Harold Brown. Before retiring from the military, Barrett spent a year at the National Defense University compiling his files on reorganization for a forthcoming book. Having literally written the book on defense reorganization, Barrett was well placed to try and help effect real change from his largely unseen perch as a subcommittee aide.

That a relatively faceless staff member such as Barrett was at the center of the defense reform debate would have surprised observers unaccustomed to the workings of Capitol Hill. The whole concept of unelected professional staff was a relatively recent development begun in earnest only after the Legislative Reorganization Act of 1946. In 1900, for instance, congressional employees numbered fewer than 300. To combat the ever-expanding staffs of various agencies in the Executive Branch, and to keep pace with the volume and overwhelming complexity of modern legislation, Congress had steadily increased the number of its professional staff members since World War II. By the early 1980s, they numbered more than 19,000. Though chartered to act primarily as clerks, translating the policies of the elected members of Congress into reports and legislation, in truth staff members accounted for much of the expertise in Congress. There were simply too many arcane subjects for each member of Congress to master, even within the realm of his or her chosen committees.

The problem for Representative Bill Nichols and Archie Barrett was that an even more astute power player stood between them and meaningful reform. Senator John Tower (R-TX), chairman of the Senate Armed Services Committee (SASC), was a consummate politician who commanded respect, if not loyalty. A brainy, partisan politician with an acerbic bent, he kept a tight grip on his committee. Tower had been a key hawk on increases in defense spending in support of Reagan's buildup, and he harbored a deep ambition to succeed Caspar Weinberger as Secretary of Defense. By 1984, when Nichols attached his reform rider to the Defense Authorization Bill, Tower had plans to retire from the Senate soon, and he was not about to leave having alienated his key constituencies in the Pentagon and the White House by forcing unwanted reform on them.

Given the strong ties between many members of the SASC and the military, Tower also rightly concluded that they had no appetite for an acrimonious battle with the Pentagon that any major reform effort was sure to provoke (Senator John Warner (R-VA) was a former Navy Secretary with major naval bases in his district; Senator Jeremiah Denton (R-AL) was a retired Navy admiral; Senator Strom Thurmond (R-SC) retired from the Army reserves as a general; both Senator John East (R-NC) and Senator John Glenn (D-OH) were former Marines; Senator Barry Goldwater (R-AZ) had been a general in the Air Force reserves).

As Chairman of the House/Senate Conference tasked with reconciling the House and Senate Defense Authorization Bills, Tower controlled the agenda on the hundreds of amendments that are part of any major authorization bill. So each time Bill Nichols's reform measure came up for a discussion, Tower simply placed it at the bottom of the stack with assurances that they would get to it later, and then he ran out the clock. Nichols and Barrett, who watched a year's worth of hearings and legislative preparation disappear down the unexpected trap, were furious. The House/Senate Conference became so tense that some members later recalled fearing that actual physical blows might be struck.

When he had studied legislative affairs for his doctorate at Harvard, Barrett had learned about House/Senate Conferences held at the end of each legislative session to work out compromises between competing legislation. He knew the chairmanship of those conferences rotated each year between the two bodies of Congress. No one had ever mentioned, however, the pivotal power the chairman wielded in controlling the agenda. It was an oversight and lesson in hardball politics delivered by Senator John Tower, and neither Representative Bill Nichols nor Arch Barrett would ever forget it.

REFORM'S DON QUIXOTE

When 75-year-old Barry Goldwater (R-AZ) assumed the chairmanship of the SASC a few months later, the appointment caused little alarm at the Pentagon. Goldwater was the granddaddy of the conservative movement, a noted hawk on defense who was also close to his predecessor John Tower. Both men shared in common a painful electoral loss to Lyndon Johnson. Goldwater's 1964 campaign as the Republican nominee for president against Johnson forever solidified his national image when he memorably proclaimed, "Extremism in the defense of liberty is no vice."

The reality of the man was far more complex and nuanced than the outsized image. Goldwater had made a career out of saying exactly what he thought, frequently on the Senate floor. In a deliberative body where speechwriters could haggle for hours over the political ramifications of an adverb, that candor and bluntness won Goldwater grudging respect and a large measure of tolerance for the "old man" of Arizona politics. Goldwater's fundamental belief in less government and strong defense harkened back to the Taft Republicans of the 1940s. He was neither a close confidant of Ronald Reagan, nor a darling of the New Right, nor of the supply-siders, and most certainly not of the Moral Majority. Goldwater went his own way in a town where a premium was still put on consensus, and thus his ascension to the chairmanship of SASC added an unknown quantity to the already volatile military-reform campaign.

Goldwater had personally witnessed the Tower and Nichols reform show-down a few months earlier, and it intrigued him. One of his first meetings as the incoming SASC chairman was thus with retired General Andrew Goodpaster, the former Supreme Allied Commander, Europe. Along with an impressive cast of defense experts, Goodpaster had been studying military reorganization for the Center for Strategic and International Studies (CSIS) a prestigious Washington think tank cofounded by David M. Abshire (Vice Chairman of the Center for the Study of the Presidency & Congress), and famed Navy strategist Admiral Arleigh Burke. Other participants in the CSIS study included Senator Sam Nunn (D-GA), the ranking minority member on SASC, and a man Goldwater considered to be one of the most capable in Congress; Representative Les Aspin (D-WI), the brainy Democratic chair-man of the House Armed Services Committee who would go on to serve as Secretary of Defense under President Bill Clinton; General "Shy" Meyer, who after leaving the Pentagon had renewed his calls for reforming the Joint Chiefs of Staff (JCS); and General David Jones, who had continued agitating for major reform of the Joint Chiefs after relinquishing the chairmanship.

The episode reveals the critically important role that think tanks play in advancing the policy agenda in Washington, particularly in providing military expertise for members of Congress to utilize. As Goodpaster briefed him on the upcoming CSIS report that would advocate a major reorganization of the Pentagon's command structure, for instance, Goldwater kept harking back to his own experiences as a general in the Air Force reserve who had served during World War II. Every time Goodpaster laid out a problem, Goldwater would nod his head and add an anecdote from his own long experience in the military.

After the CSIS briefing, Goldwater huddled with his SASC aide Jim Locher, a West Point graduate with an MBA from Harvard. The 38-year-old Locher had spent nearly a decade inside the Pentagon working in the Office for Program Analysis and Evaluation, the spawning ground for former Sec-retary of Defense Robert McNamara's systems-analysis whiz kids. Locher had witnessed firsthand the dismay of defense secretaries who felt the advice they received from the Joint Chiefs was frequently factored down to the "lowest common denominator," and the frustration of JCS chairmen who tried to get the service chiefs or the Joint Staff to operate independently of the individual armed services. While his own report arguing for fundamental JCS reform had been quashed by John Tower, the new SASC chairman Barry Goldwater had other ideas.

Goldwater and Locher developed a year-long campaign for military reform. When Congress reconvened in January 1985, Goldwater established a bipartisan task force for reform, and made Sam Nunn an equal cochairman. They could never collect the necessary votes on an issue so emotionally charged, Goldwater reasoned, if an eventual vote broke down along party lines. The Senator from Arizona knew better than anyone that the odds were heavily stacked against them, and that a conservative Republican with major military bases in his backyard would have to be crazy to provoke a public battle with the Pentagon. He just didn't give a damn.

What many people failed to understand about Barry Goldwater was that he had first put on a uniform as a 14-year-old boy in a Virginia military academy, and as far as Goldwater was concerned, he had never taken it off. When he died, Goldwater wanted to be cremated in his Air Force uniform and have his ashes scattered over the Grand Canyon. Tilting at the windmills of military reform, Goldwater would be fighting one last grand battle in a long career that had known its share of hopeless causes. The military reform effort had found its Don Quixote.

MANIPULATING LEVERS OF POWER

It was Goldwater's idea to send early copies of the defense reorganization report to Robert McFarlane, the President's National Security Adviser and a former SASC professional staff member. McFarlane had seen right away that the Administration was on a collision course with Congress. There was no love lost between McFarlane and Secretary of Defense Caspar Weinberger, however, and McFarlane saw a way to give the Administration cover on the reform effort and neutralize Weinberger's opposition in a single stroke. He convinced President Reagan to appoint his own Blue Ribbon Commission on Defense Reform in the summer, headed by David Packard, a respected former Defense Department official and the successful businessman of Hewlett-Packard fame. Initially Weinberger had strongly opposed the idea and, when it looked as if Reagan was going through with it anyway, had argued that the commission should focus on defense acquisition, and not reform of the Joint Chiefs of Staff and the Pentagon command structure. David Packard and his fellow commission members such as retired Air Force General Brent Scowcroft regularly visited Barry Goldwater to learn what the SASC was doing, however, and to coordinate their efforts.

Outside the Beltway and even among many members of Congress, the assumption was that the reorganization and reform effort was thus mostly about $700 hammers and procurement "waste, fraud and abuse." That was the story that kept the effort alive, and ultimately the vote on the complex reform package would hinge on the vague sense that something was wrong at the Pentagon that needed "reforming." Those who worked closely on the effort wondered, however, if the press and the country at large would wake up one day to discover that they had been engineering the most fundamental reorganization of the military command structure in 40 years.

The SASC deliberations on the reform bill began in February 1986, and Barry Goldwater quickly recognized that the opposition's end-game strategy for defeating it was to be death by amendment, with Senator John Warner serving as the designated executioner. Frequently during deliberations, Warner would excuse himself from the room and Goldwater had no doubt his friend had an open line going to the Navy Department and Secretary John Lehman's office. A few minutes later Warner would come back into the room and propose a dozen amendments. Goldwater suspected that much of the Navy staff at the Pentagon were standing by to write those amendments designed to gut his reform bill.

After an entire day was wasted debating Warner's amendments, Goldwater had Jim Locher prepare a list of measures that would put pressure on opponents on the committee and at the Pentagon to stop the amendment shenanigans. The list of potential pressure points included halting all Pentagon requests for budget reprogramming; stopping all planned budget hearings; freezing promotions as well as nominations for civilian appointments at the Pentagon; and halting the "strategic home-porting plan," a pet project of John Lehman's that called for dispersing the Navy fleet to numerous ports around the country to guard against a surprise nuclear strike by the Soviet Union (not coincidentally, "home-porting" had the additional benefit of spreading Navy largess into the districts of far more members of Congress, thus exponentially expanding the service's political base during budget battles). Goldwater told Locher to implement every one of the measures designed to pressure the Pentagon and Lehman to abandon the strategy of "death by a thousand amendments."

With cries for relief beginning to sound from the Pentagon after two weeks of deliberations, the reform camp began picking up votes as each measure of the reform bill was debated and voted on. When the reformers on the committee reached 15 votes, the opposition collapsed, and the committee overwhelmingly sent the reform bill to the floor of the Senate. On May 7, 1986, the Senate voted 95–0 to support Goldwater's defense reorganization bill. During the August recess, Arch Barrett, Jim Locher, and their aides worked 16-hour days, seven days a week, hammering out the final compromises that produced the Goldwater-Nichols Defense Reorganization Act of 1986. The House/Senate Conference that formalized approval of the bill, chaired by Barry Goldwater, was a study in contrast to the tension-filled meeting chaired by Senator Tower less than two years earlier, with Goldwater having already coordinated his reform measures with those of Representative Bill Nichols.

A HIGH-WATER MARK

Goldwater-Nichols was complex beyond the understanding of all but Congress's most devoted defense experts, but the unmistakable thrust was in the direction of what the military called "jointness." The Chairman of the Joint Chiefs, the only JCS member not dual-hatted as chief of a military service, became the principal uniformed adviser to the civilian Secretary of Defense and the President. Commands to, and requests from, the geographical commanders in chief in the field, the essential warfighters, were to be channeled through the chairman, de facto putting him directly in the operational chain-of-command. The Joint Staff of over a thousand officers was put under the exclusive direction of the chairman, representing a fundamental shift in power within the Pentagon from the massive service staffs to the chairman's Joint Staff. Service in a joint assignment, either on the Joint Staff or elsewhere, became necessary for promotion to flag or general rank, and thus a required stepping stone for the services' best officers. A joint curriculum was established at each service war college, and officers were required to complete a joint-duty assignment following graduation.

The Pentagon's true warlords, the commanders in chief (CINCs)—later renamed Combatant Commanders (COCOMs) in 2002—of the unified commands, meanwhile, gained broader authority over their subordinate commands and joint task forces. A four-star vice chairman was added as a sixth member of the JCS, both to assist the chairman and to represent the voices of the CINCS in internal discussions on budget matters and resource allocation.

Congress's triumph with Goldwater-Nichols was also critical in breaking down the services' ironclad resistance to the establishment of two new unified, joint commands. In 1987, U.S. Special Operations Command was established to coordinate the training and equipping of the services' special operations forces. A new position of Assistant Secretary of Defense for Special Operations and Low Intensity Conflict was also established. U.S. Transportation Command was also created that same year on a direct recommendation of the Packard Commission report, finally integrating global air, land, and sea assets under a single commander. As expected, the Packard Commission endorsed the Goldwater-Nichols reforms, and suggested changes that put the services' vast acquisition bureaucracies under more direct oversight of the Office of the Secretary of Defense, and a newly created undersecretary for acquisition.

In many ways, Congress's passage of Goldwater-Nichols and Reagan's endorsement of the Packard Commission were the high-water mark of an activist era of both unprecedented defense spending, and pioneering defense reforms. It resulted from a rare consensus between Congress and ultimately the White House that the U.S. military needed radical revitalization into a more well-resourced and joint force, with a unified and more coherent command structure. Goldwater-Nichols was also the product of a bygone era when many members of Congress had served in the military, and thus were not unduly cowed by opponents in uniform, and relevant committee staffs were stocked with experts to rival the most powerful think tanks in Washington. The superb performance of the U.S. military in the 1991 Persian Gulf War, and in the numerous successful military operations that followed, are a testament to the wisdom of the underlying vision.

And yet the entire reform might well have foundered but for the efforts of a single lawmaker that many contemporaries mistakenly thought was well past his prime. Barry Goldwater retired shortly after passage of the legislation bearing his name. Recalling the day his colleagues on the floor of the Senate rose in unison to applaud and pay tribute to that accomplishment with a 95–0 vote, Barry Goldwater insisted that Goldwater-Nichols was the best damn thing he did in 35 years in the U.S. Senate. The reforms thus anchored the legacy of one of the great lions of the modern Congress.

◆ ◆ ◆ ◆ ◆

44. The Triumph of Process over Politics: The Base Closure Commissions

by David Berteau

The history of base closures is relatively simple and straightforward. Article II of the Constitution establishes the President as the Commander in Chief. From the time the new federal government built the first military base in the 1790s, up until the 1970s, every president used that authority to establish, or dismantle, military installations as necessary for the country's defense. Bases were built, abandoned, torn down, and closed for many reasons. That was especially true after World War II, when nearly half of the bases in America were closed. Many towns across America have an airport originally built as an Army Air Corps base.

Base closures became more complicated and political in the 1960s, when victorious presidents sometimes closed bases in districts that had voted for their opponent in a recent election. Congress complained but had little authority to stop the practice. Congress could, and did, create bases, authorizing the funds and establishing the base through appropriations. The President could exercise with relative impunity his Article II constitutional authority to terminate operations at a military base, however, declaring the property to be excess and disposing of it.

CONGRESS CONSTRAINS BASE CLOSURES

However, in 1970, Congress passed—and President Nixon signed—the National Environmental Policy Act (NEPA) to provide for environmental assessments and public scrutiny of such property disposal decisions. Subsequently, Congress tried to apply NEPA processes to base closures, but Presidents Nixon and Ford vetoed the legislation. Finally, in 1977 Congress passed a third such bill, and President Carter signed it—voluntarily yielding his constitutional authority to open or close bases and giving Congress a larger role.

NEPA did not prevent base closures. In fact, Section 2687 of Title 10 of the U.S. Code permits the U.S. Department of Defense (DoD) to close bases under NEPA. However, if DoD attempts to close a base, Congress can add a provision to an appropriations act with wording like "of the funds appropriated in this act, none shall be expended on environmental impact studies for closing base X." That would effectively shut down compliance with the NEPA process. Just the threat of such legislation meant that no major base closed for a decade.

By the early 1980s, however, the military services were complaining about spending money to maintain excess capacity and unneeded facilities. Secretary of Defense Caspar Weinberger repeatedly sought expanded authority to close bases, but Congress resisted. Many bases are the biggest economic drivers in their communities, sustaining jobs and votes.

DoD argued that communities would be better off in the long run, if they replaced an underused military base with other economic engines of development. From the time of Secretary McNamara, DoD's Office of Economic Adjustment has helped cities and towns recover economically from base closures. In the long run, most communities actually were better off after base closures, with more diverse economies that were less vulnerable to fluctuations in the Pentagon's budget.[1]

Members of Congress, however, don't run for reelection in the long run. Representative Arthur B. Ravenel Jr. (R-SC) from Charleston typified their reaction. Responding to a DoD witness explaining the potential for recovery, he said, "What you say may very well be true, but let me tell you, if you close my base, a thousand angels sent down from heaven ain't going to help Arthur B. Ravenel, Jr., get reelected." Members don't care about economic recovery 5 or 10 years after the base is closed; they worry about getting reelected.

BASE CLOSURE COMMISSIONS

After Congress rebuffed Secretary of Defense Weinberger on base closures, he took another approach. The Grace Commission, created by President Ronald Reagan in 1982 to seek federal government efficiencies, proposed an independent commission for closing bases. DoD agreed with the recommendation, but it failed to appear in any legislation. However, when Frank Carlucci replaced Weinberger in November 1987, he created a commission process to close bases under executive authority, following internally developed criteria for comparing bases by function and utility.

Carlucci also proposed legislative language to support the process he was already undertaking. At the last minute, with the transition to President George H.W. Bush already underway, Congress authorized a one-time Base Closure Commission. This occurred a few days before the 1988 commission created by Carlucci announced its list of some 26 to 86 base closures. Congress recognized the political reality that the defense budget was declining and the number of bases had to come down. It played no role other than approving the process as a one-time deal.

Within a year of Carlucci's commission, however, the Berlin Wall fell, the Warsaw Pact collapsed, the Cold War ended, and the defense budget was thus rapidly reduced by Congress. At an internal Pentagon budget meeting, President Bush's new defense secretary Dick Cheney said, in effect, "This budget is going to keep falling until it directly impacts the members. The only way I know to do that is to start closing bases." Using Title 10 authorities, Cheney initiated environmental impact statements to close bases across the country. Throughout 1990, DoD officials testified before Congress defending this approach. In every hearing, nearly every lawmaker present had a direct stake in the ongoing studies, either a base being considered for closure or a base set to expand after receiving missions and functions from closing bases.

Due to the large number of affected installations, Congress found it difficult to simply prohibit funds for studies as a way to derail the process.

Secretary Cheney was clearly going to close bases, if necessary without input from or participation by Congress. Eventually, legislators began to see value in a different process, one that didn't leave the decision of closures entirely to the Pentagon. Working together quietly, the Pentagon and Congress drafted legislation to create a new, congressionally mandated Base Closure Commission process. The commission language was not voted on as part of the defense authorization bills that passed either the House or the Senate. Instead, it was added in conference, meaning that the first time Congress voted on it was as part of a package deal, up or down, all or nothing. That foreshadowed what became a fundamental principle behind the Base Closure Commission process—reliance on up-or-down votes on an overall package.

DOD'S SELECTION PROCESS

As the first step in that process, the military departments nominated bases they proposed to close, following criteria set forth in law. Using a standardized method of analysis permitted comparisons of the value of many different kinds of bases, such as a submarine base, an Army brigade post, a repair depot, or a helicopter station. The primary criterion was military value, and each military service established its own measures for making evaluations. Bases were then ranked within categories such as operating bases, support bases, training bases, and so on. Such rankings mattered most when there was excess capacity within one of the categories, because the lower ranked bases were the most likely to be closed.

To establish capacity requirements within each category, the base closure law required DoD to project forces 20 years into the future. That force structure included the number of Army brigades, Air Force air wings, Navy carrier groups, Marine Corps regiments, and so on. Those operating units also needed support bases, training and testing ranges, engineering centers, and all the other facilities and installations required to sustain military operations. The requirements and rankings enabled the services to start identifying candidate bases for closure or realignment and consolidation.

Beyond the force structure projections and the criterion of military value, the base closure law listed additional criteria that affected which bases to close. Chief among those additional criteria were the costs to close a base and the time it took to recoup those costs through savings. Closure costs increased when there was a requirement to move an ongoing mission or existing unit to another base, for instance, putting a premium on closing bases when and where forces were being eliminated or reduced, rather than simply relocated.

WINNERS AND LOSERS

The need to relocate some ongoing missions created winners as well as losers from base closures. Bases which received ongoing missions became "gaining bases," and the congressional delegation for those gaining bases became supporters of the closure list.

"Gaining bases" also created internal support for base closures from the military services themselves. Base closure costs were paid from a separate DoD account and were not debited from the services' own budgets; essentially, both the cost of closure and the costs of building new facilities at receiving bases were free gifts to the services, and in turn they got to reapply the savings. Those benefits helped persuade the military departments to support closing bases that otherwise would have been painful for them to jettison.

The internal process that DoD settled on for closing bases thus ranked bases by their military value, selected bases that represented excess capacity based on the projected force structure, and found the best combination of costs and savings to identify base closures. The services submitted their separate lists to the Secretary of Defense, who further refined them before submitting the lists to the Base Closure Commission, together with an assessment by the Chairman of the Joint Chiefs of Staff of the military impact of the proposed closures.

COMMISSIONS WEIGH IN

Under the law, the Base Closure Commission's role was to review the recommendations from DoD. The commission could change, modify, or reject a proposal from DoD, but it could make those changes only on the basis of a finding that DoD "substantially deviated" from the established criteria in making its recommendations. The statute did not define what constitutes substantial deviation; the Base Closure Commission defined it when it voted on such a finding. Before the commission voted, though, its members held hearings, visited bases proposed for closure, assessed DoD's analysis and recommendations, and evaluated closure alternatives.

At those hearings, affected members of Congress appeared and testified, often delivering impassioned speeches, populated with data about the civil service and military employees of the threatened base. The commission members might have driven to the hearing along a highway lined with schoolchildren with signs reading, "Please don't fire my Daddy."

That process created the potential for every politician to have their day in court, as it were, in front of their home crowd. Then members of Congress got a second chance to be seen, at the Commission's final votes. Those votes were held in public over several days, leading to decisions to approve, reject, or change DoD's recommended closures. Members were not allowed to speak at those votes, but they could show up at the right time and be seen on national television in support of their base. Eventually, Commission votes overturned or modified roughly 20 percent of DoD's recommended closures and realignments.

THE ROLE OF POLITICS

Politicians not only had input at public hearings and during commission visits, but they also had private meetings with commissioners and staff. They made emotional pleas, frequently noting long-standing community support for their base, the potential loss of jobs and income, and the sacrifices of the past. But to sway the commission, politicians needed to make the case for a Finding of Substantial Deviation. To do that, they hired consultants, refined data, and pointed out flaws in DoD's analysis, trying to persuade the commission that DoD made mistakes in applying the criteria and determining its recommendations. While commissioners may have been moved by the emotional appeals, in the end, they could only change a DoD proposal with a Finding of Substantial Deviation.

Undoubtedly, in cases where the vote could have gone either way, politics may have tilted the vote of one or more commissioner in favor of closing or keeping open a base. Without staff evidence to support Substantial Deviation, though, there was relatively little room for politics to change the outcome or the process. The clear predisposition of the Base Closure Commission was to accept the DoD's recommendations unless there was the right combination of policy, analysis, and politics to warrant a change.

In 1991, in the first round of three base closures that followed the end of the Cold War, Secretary Cheney rejected only one of the base closures recommended by the services. In that case, the Army proposed using the base closure process to reorganize the Corps of Engineers. Cheney demurred, saying that he was not ready to take on public works committees at the same time as the defense committees.

When one of the services offered Cheney their assessment of the impact of the base closures on Congress, he rejected it, saying the decisions should be independent of politics. Other than the Corps of Engineers proposal, Cheney recommended the same closure packages the services proposed to him. As the Base Closure Commission evaluated and decided on Cheney's recommendations, he stood behind each of the service recommendations, and the commission approved roughly 85 percent of them.

Politics played a somewhat larger role in the recommendations made by Secretary Les Aspin in round two in 1993. Aspin's main problem was that neither he nor the White House supported all the closures recommended by the military services. With one exception, however, Aspin had no logical basis to reject the service proposals.

With instructions that he receive daily updates on the process, Aspin was arguably the Secretary of Defense most involved in base closures. Perhaps that was in part because of his prior support for a base closure process as chairman of the U.S. House Committee on Armed Services. In the end, like his predecessor, Aspin saw 85 percent of his recommendations approved by the commission.

THE WHITE HOUSE ROLE

The White House has three key policy and political functions in the base closure process. The first and most important is providing political support to the Secretary of Defense in undertaking base closures in the first place. The twin goals of reducing excess infrastructure (and therefore saving money over the long run) and supporting community economic redevelopment postclosure are potentially offset by the near-term impact on some of the administration's allies in Congress. White House backing is also essential for the military services to propose closures or realignments; otherwise, they risk irritating Congress without the reward of savings.

The second key White House role is to assemble and nominate the commissioners, including the chairman. The most recent law provided that congressional leadership would be consulted on six of the nine commissioners (two each from the Senate Majority Leader and the Speaker of the House, and one each from the Minority Leaders), with the administration picking the remaining three. Each of these picks have historically represented a balance among the constituencies represented, with the strongest engagement from the House and Senate Armed Services Committees, but the White House creates the final mix of backgrounds, experiences, and viewpoints. Most commissions, for example, have had at least one former member of Congress and one or more retired military officers. The resulting balance of party representation on the commission guarantees minority views in every final vote. With many commission decisions approved unanimously, no political faction can point to obvious political bias in the commission votes.

The third role for the White House comes once the commission has made its final votes and submitted its complete package of base closure recommendations to the President. At that point, the Commander in Chief has three options: the President can approve the list in its entirety and send it to Congress; return it to the commission with recommendations for adjustments; or reject it outright, terminating the entire base closure process. In five previous base closure rounds of the modern era, the President has always approved the list and sent it to Congress.

However, there was one close call during this final stage. In 1995, the commission voted to close two huge bases that DoD had not recommended: the Sacramento Air Logistics Center (employing 12,000 people) and the San Antonio Air Logistics Center (employing 14,000 people, including the largest Hispanic workforce in America at the time). These were politically sensitive decisions on the eve of Bill Clinton's reelection campaign. Reportedly, White House Chief of Staff Leon Panetta called former Senator Al Dixon (D-IL)—Clinton's selection as commission chairman—and asked what the commission might do if the President asked them to reconsider its recommendations and to take those bases off of the list. Dixon reportedly replied that the commission would vote unanimously to send it right back unchanged. President Clinton approved the full list and sent it to Congress, adding a proviso that the logistics centers would be "privatized in place," in an effort to save the local jobs.

That was the final round of three base closures under the 1990 law. Starting in 1998, DoD requested another round of base closures, but Congress refused for three years because of claims of White House political interference. Only when a Republican recaptured the presidency did Congress approve a fifth base closure round in December 2001, set for 2005. Following the 9/11 terrorist attacks, however, members pushed to postpone the 2005 base closures, with threats of presidential veto needed to preserve the law. In 2005, Secretary Rumsfeld proposed dozens of closures and realignments, and a new commission reviewed them, accepted roughly 80 percent of DoD's recommendations, and forwarded them through the President to Congress.

THE UP-OR-DOWN CONGRESSIONAL VOTE

Congress has never liked base closures. Applying NEPA to base closures was a way to stop them, but eventually the need for savings from base closures outweighed the aversion. However, the commission process allows members of Congress to challenge publicly base closures, while not altogether derailing the process. Those fights start before DoD makes its recommendations and continue throughout the commission's hearings and reviews.

In the end, Congress receives the recommendations of the commission, along with a powerful impediment to tinkering. This is the well-known, all-or-nothing, up-or-down vote that has come to symbolize the Base Closure Commission process. Unless there is a resolution of disapproval passed by both houses within 45 days of submission, the closures become law. In each base closure round of the modern era (1988, 1991, 1993, 1995, and 2005), a resolution of disapproval was introduced and failed to pass one house, effectively advancing the entire package of closures.

The politics of that final up-or-down vote are simple. Members whose base is on that list tend to vote in disapproval. Members with no base on the list, or with a base that is scheduled to expand because of the closures elsewhere, tend to vote to approve.

LESSONS OF BASE CLOSURE COMMISSIONS

The base closure commission process ensures that politicians can defend their base and in the end argue that the system won.[2] This raises an important question: could that same process work for other issues?

The lessons from 20 plus years of base closures suggest that the all-or-nothing, up-or-down vote is not necessarily the key to success. Rather, it's the process leading up to that vote that would need to be replicated if it were applied to other seemingly intractable problems, from tax reform to cancelling unneeded programs. Key elements of that process include establishing uniformed, predetermined criteria for judging options (such as which bases to close), laid out in advance to avoid favoritism; standardized analysis for ranking those options and comparing costs and benefits; a review group such as the Base Closure Commission, with staff and resources to conduct its own independent analysis; establishing clear grounds for challenging or changing those options, such as the "Finding of Substantial Deviation" criteria; public and political input into the process through open hearings, field visits, and opportunities for political figures at all levels to weigh in; and the full backing of the President and the Executive Branch in choosing commission members, endorsing its recommendations, and supporting the process from the very beginning.

Without all of these elements, the final all-or-nothing vote will not prove to be credible. In the end, the commission process reflects the fundamental constitutional tension between the Executive and Legislative Branches, and closing a military base brings it into high relief. At different times, one side or the other may gain the upper hand, but the struggle and tension will endure as long as we remain a Republic.

◆ ◆ ◆ ◆ ◆

45. A Powers Tug-of-War: The Iraq War Resolutions

by James Kitfield

They stand almost as mirror images separated by more than a decade of time, George H. W. Bush in 1991 and George W. Bush in 2002, the father and son each asking Congress for the authority to wage offensive war against Iraq, both opposed by the same tyrant in Saddam Hussein. Though they led in very different times and adopted different tactics, both Commanders in Chief won the approval they sought from Congress. In the process, they demonstrated the White House's growing predominance over Capitol Hill in the modern struggle over war powers.

There is a truism that no vote will prove more sobering or profound for a member of Congress than the decision to send U.S. troops into harm's way. That is as true today as ever. What is really remarkable about the modern era, however, is how infrequently lawmakers render that weighty judgment in a period when the U.S. military has been sent into hostilities repeatedly and often.

Since Vietnam, U.S. presidents have submitted 136 reports to Congress notifying them that U.S. military forces were being introduced into situations where hostilities were imminent or possible. In only a few instances did Congress explicitly authorize the President to use military force: the 1991 Iraq War Resolution; the 2001 Authorization for the Use of Military Force in response to the September 11, 2001 terrorist attacks, used to justify the Afghan war and global war against Al Qaeda; and the 2002 Iraq War Resolution. In 1999, President Bill Clinton asked for a resolution authorizing airstrikes against Yugoslavia and was rebuffed when the House failed to pass the measure. The Clinton Administration bombed anyway, and the federal courts dismissed a suit by some members of Congress that Clinton had violated the War Powers Act.[1] Thus is the period between the Iraq War Resolutions of 1991 and 2002 an important window into the modern struggle over war powers in America.

SEPARATION OF POWERS

The United States bracketed by the Iraq War Resolutions of 1991 and 2002 would be all but unrecognizable to the Founding Fathers. Mindful of the unchecked powers of European kings and queens to wage bloody wars on a personal whim, the Constitution separated war powers between a Commander in Chief charged with defending the nation from attack and leading the armed forces, and a Congress given the sole authority to declare war and "raise and support Armies . . . and to provide and maintain a Navy." The Constitution also allows Congress to appropriate money for those armies for only two years at a time, revealing the Founding Fathers' deep suspicion of large, standing armies.[2]

That balance in war powers shifted decisively at the end of World War II, and with the beginning of the Cold War in the late 1940s. Out of necessity, the United States assumed the role of standard bearer for the Western democracies from a Great Britain devastated by the war. Rather than demobilizing military forces after the war in keeping with tradition, Washington maintained a globe-spanning U.S. military in order to contain the Soviet Union. The superpower that emerged in what was to become the "American Century" was not one the Founding Fathers envisioned. The country's security also was tied to a collective defense system in NATO that resembled the "entangling alliances" that Thomas Jefferson said should be avoided. Feeding that outsized role in global affairs was the massive "military industrial complex" that former President and World War II hero General Dwight Eisenhower famously cautioned about. The Commander in Chief who sits at the top of that global architecture casts such a large shadow on world affairs that some observers have talked about the era of the "imperial presidency," and it has been marked by an inexorable shifting in the balance of war powers from Congress to the White House.[3]

After the United States became embroiled in protracted yet undeclared wars in Korea in the 1950s and Vietnam in the 1960s, however, congressional leaders became alarmed at the erosion of their authority in deciding if and when the nation goes to war. Many lawmakers also had "buyer's remorse" over Congress's 1964 Gulf of Tonkin Resolution, which was based on questionable intelligence and amounted to a blank check for the use of military force in Vietnam that Presidents Lyndon Johnson and Richard Nixon used to justify nearly a decade of conflict, at a cost of more than 58,000 U.S. troops killed. (See "A Blank Check for War: The Gulf of Tonkin Resolution," Chapter 39.)

Congress answered by passing the 1973 War Powers Resolution, which stipulated that the President could only introduce U.S. military forces into hostilities with a formal declaration of war or specific authorization by Congress, or in response to an attack on the United States or its forces. Under the law, the President also has to notify Congress whenever troops are introduced into potentially hostile situations, at which point Congress has 60 to 90 days to authorize their deployment or else the troops must be withdrawn. After Richard Nixon vetoed the War Powers Resolution and was overridden by Congress, every president has insisted that the law is an unconstitutional infringement on his role as Commander in Chief. Famously uninterested in getting in the middle of a separation of powers battle between the Executive Branch and Congress, the courts have been silent on the issue.[4] (See "Congress Takes a Stand: The 1973 War Powers Resolution," Chapter 41.)

OPERATION DESERT STORM

When Iraqi dictator Saddam Hussein invaded and occupied neighboring Kuwait in early August, 1990, putting his elite Republican Guards on the border with Saudi Arabia and astride the world's energy jugular, he revealed a penchant for poor timing. The Soviet empire was in the process of disintegrating and the Cold War was ending, leaving America as that rarest of historical anomalies—the lone superpower in a unipolar world, with a global military and suddenly no peer competitor to tie it down or constrain its actions. President George H.W. Bush and his seasoned foreign affairs and national security team recognized an opportunity to use U.S. military superiority to create a "new world order," one in which the great scourge of the 20th century—state-on-state aggression—was abolished. Almost immediately Bush signaled his intension to reverse Iraq's invasion: "This naked aggression will not stand," Bush stated publicly.

After taking the issue to the United Nations Security Council, Bush won backing for a series of tough economic sanctions designed to compel Saddam Hussein to reverse course and withdraw his forces from Kuwait. Bush also built a broad coalition, eventually deploying a massive force of 500,000 U.S. and allied troops to Saudi Arabia by the end of 1990. The Senate Armed Services Committee convened a pivotal series of hearings in the fall of 1990 that some observers compared to the hearings convened by Senator J. William Fulbright (D-AR), in 1966 that brought initial opposition to the Vietnam War out into the open. During the 1990 hearings, a long parade of respected statesmen and former military leaders urged restraint and caution, and advised that the economic sanctions on Iraq be given time to work.[5]

With so much at stake, some of Bush's senior advisers, including National Security Adviser Brent Scowcroft, advised against asking Congress to formally approve a military operation to liberate Kuwait. Though the administration continued to argue that congressional authorization was not required, Bush decided to risk a vote, but only after waiting until the very eve of hostilities before requesting that Congress pass the Authorization for Use of Military Force against Iraq Resolution. It authorized the President to "use United States armed forces pursuant to United Nations Security Council Resolution 678," which permitted member states to use "all necessary means" to compel Iraqi forces to withdraw from Kuwait.

The shadow hanging over three days of solemn congressional debate was the Vietnam War. For the first time since what many considered the disastrous 1964 Gulf of Tonkin Resolution, Congress was being asked to approve offensive military operations against another nation. The mostly Democratic lawmakers who opposed the operation wanted to give sanctions more time to work. U.S. Senate Majority Leader George Mitchell (D-ME) spoke for many in the Democratic majority when he asked, "How many people will die? How many young Americans will die? And for the families of those young Americans who die, for every one of us, the truly haunting question will be, did they die unnecessarily?" Senator Sam Nunn (D-GA), the influential chairman of the U.S. Senate Committee on Armed Services, sounded a similar theme in opposition: "We are playing a winning hand. I see no compelling reason to rush to military action."

By shrewdly front-loading the deployment of hundreds of thousands of troops into a foreign theater before ever putting the issue before Congress, Bush put tremendous pressure on lawmakers not to do anything to undermine the troops or the Commander in Chief on the eve of war. "Let's not pull the rug out from under the President when the pressure is building on Saddam Hussein by the minute," Senate Minority Leader Robert Dole (R-KS) said during debate on the Iraq Resolution. "Let's don't give him any relief." House Minority Leader Robert H. Michel (R-IL) stressed the same argument. "President Bush has openly and forthrightly asked for our help. How can we turn our backs on him?"

In the end, the vote to authorize military action against Iraq was a cliff-hanger, passing in the Senate by a tally of just 52–47 (with 10 Democrats, mostly from the conservative South, joining 42 Republicans in voting "aye"). The House vote passed by a wider margin (250–183, with 86 Democrats joining 164 Republicans). Just four days after the vote, on January 17, 1991, U.S. forces commenced Operation DESERT STORM.

In the first vote of its kind in a generation, Congress's authorization for war against Iraq was notable on several fronts. Though the debate rose above purely partisan politics, the vote showed that members of the President's party were clearly more inclined to support the Commander in Chief, with Republicans overwhelmingly supporting Bush and the majority of Democrats voting to oppose the war.

After Operation DESERT STORM culminated in one of the most lopsided military victories in U.S. history, the vote on authorization also factored into the political calculus of several presidential aspirants, seeming to bolster supporters—such as Senator Al Gore (D-TN), who went on to share the successful ticket with Bill Clinton in 1992—and work against opponents—the vote was seen as a blow to the aspirations of Senator Sam Nunn, who decided against a run in 1992 that he had been contemplating. By waiting until 500,000 troops were poised at the very precipice of war before asking Congress for its authorization, President Bush also revealed the immense leverage that Commanders in Chief wield in terms of setting the conditions and timing for votes authorizing war.

Many members of Congress concluded that the vote on the Iraq war resolution was the most important of their careers. Their views were summarized eloquently by Representative Charles E. Bennett (D-FL), a Silver Star awardee from World War II who had voted for the Gulf of Tonkin Resolution authorizing military force in Vietnam, and had lived to regret it. "Out of the 17,000 votes I have cast, the only one I really regret was the one I cast for the Bay of Tonkin Resolution," Bennett said during the debate, as quoted in *The New York Times*.[6] Though he voted against the Iraq war resolution, Bennett insisted that "a vote ought to be cast on the basis of what you think is best for our country, not best for the Republican or the Democratic Party, not best for the President, not best for you. But what's best for our country and what's best for the world."

OPERATION IRAQI FREEDOM

The shadow hanging over the 2002 Iraq War Resolution was not the distant memory of Vietnam or even the first Iraq war, but the still fresh memory of the September 11, 2001 terrorist attacks that killed more than 3,000 civilians on American soil. In its aggressive response, the Bush Administration had declared a "global war on terrorism," and identified the enemy broadly as a nexus of terrorists, weapons of mass destruction, and rogue states—the famous "Axis of Evil" that Bush called out in his 2002 State of the Union address, naming Iraq, Iran, and North Korea. By the fall of 2002, Iraq was clearly in the Bush Administration's crosshairs, and the war drums were beating.

In September 2002, the administration unveiled its new National Security Strategy, the seminal blueprint for the post-9/11 reordering of world affairs. The Bush strategy, which received wide play in the domestic and international media, essentially downgraded the defensive doctrines of containment and deterrence that had triumphed in the Cold War, arguing that they were inadequate to new threats posed by terrorists and rogue states armed with weapons of mass destruction (WMD). The new Bush strategy thus anticipated preemptive U.S. military action against terrorists and rogue states.[7]

That aggressive and forward-leaning strategy diminished Congress's role in carefully deliberating and authorizing the use of military force, a fact revealed in October 2002, when the administration pushed for an Iraq War Resolution— formally the Authorization for the Use of Military Force against Iraq Resolution. By that time, the administration already had put the issue of Iraq's suspected stockpiles of WMD squarely before the United Nations Security Council, implying that if UN weapons inspectors failed to deal decisively with Saddam Hussein's defiance of earlier UN resolutions, the United States was prepared to act without UN backing, which it eventually did.

Whereas Bush's father had frontloaded the deployment of U.S. military forces to the Iraqi theater before putting the matter before Congress, Bush "43" took the opposite tack: he asked Congress to authorize war with Iraq far in advance—nearly a half year—of actual hostilities. At that early stage, it was still an open question whether the UN inspectors would successfully disarm Iraq, or indeed, whether there were actually any WMD stockpiles to discover and destroy—as it turned out after the U.S. invasion, there were not. The administration also improved its chances of winning authorization by pushing for a vote only a month before midterm elections. With the one-year anniversary of the 9/11 attacks and the quick routing of Al Qaeda and the Taliban in Afghanistan still fresh memories, few politicians were eager to buck a popular wartime Commander in Chief.

Congress did not disappoint. The Iraq War Resolution of 2002 was introduced on a bipartisan basis in both chambers, by Senators Tom Daschle (D-SD) and Trent Lott (R-MS), and Representatives Dennis Hastert (R-IL) and Richard Gephardt (D-MO). Compared to the 1991 resolution, the 2002 measure sailed through comfortably, with the vote authorizing war passing by 296–133 in the House, and by 77–23 in the Senate.

As with its 1991 predecessor, the 2002 Iraq Resolution revealed that politics and ideology play a role in the decision to authorize military force, just as they do in other weighty matters that come before Congress. Though a majority of House Democrats, 61 percent, supported the resolution, House Republicans were overwhelming in their support, 94 percent, for a Republican Commander in Chief. That partisan split was reflected in the Senate vote as well, with a majority of Democrats, 58 percent, voting "aye," and only a single Republican Senator, Lincoln Chafee (R-RI), opposed.[8]

By pushing for an Iraq War Resolution just before midterm elections and well in advance of any actual hostilities, the Bush Administration all but insured that the issue would be caught up in preelection politics. In his speech before voting to support the resolution, Senator Chuck Hagel, (R-NE), a Vietnam War veteran, brought up the issue of its timing:

"The decision to possibly commit a nation to war cannot and should not ever be considered in the context of either party loyalty or campaign politics. I regret that this vote will take place under the cloud and pressure of elections next month. Some are already using the Iraq issue to gain advantage in political campaigns. It might have been better for our vote to have been delayed until after the elections, as it was in 1990. Authorizing the use of force against Iraq or any country for any purpose should always be weighed on its own merits, not with an eye on the politics of the vote or campaign TV spots. War is too serious, the human price is too high, and the implications unforeseen."[9]

In contrast to the 1991 Iraq War Resolution, Democrats with presidential aspirations were later left to explain why they supported a war that went decidedly bad and became increasingly unpopular throughout the decade. When she ran for president in 2008, for instance, Senator Hillary Clinton (D-NY) insisted that she wasn't voting for war, but rather a reinsertion of UN inspectors into Iraq: "What I was told directly by the White House in response to my question, 'If you are given this authority, will you put the inspectors in and permit them to finish their job,' I was told that's exactly what we intended to do."

TUG-OF-WAR POWERS

As milestones in the ongoing struggle between Congress and the White House, the Iraq War Resolutions reflect how the constitutional balance of powers has shifted decisively toward the Executive Branch in matters of war and the use of military force. Even when Congress decides to weigh in, as it did on the Iraq Wars of 1991 and 2002, the ability of presidents to manipulate the timing and political context of votes gives them the upper hand. For their part, lawmakers hamstrung by incomplete intelligence information are often reluctant to take a firm "yes" or "no" position on difficult and complex matters of life-and-death, with uncertain political fallout.

Since the 2002 vote, Congress's role in decisions about the use of the military has continued to diminish. When the Bush Administration negotiated a strategic framework agreement that would have left thousands of U.S. troops in harm's way in Iraq after 2011, Congress neither debated nor voted on the agreement. Likewise, as the Obama Administration has negotiated a similar long-term agreement that could yet leave thousands of U.S. forces in harm's way in Afghanistan after 2014, no congressional leaders from either party have requested a debate or scheduled a vote.[10]

Or the Commander in Chief can simply ignore Congress while ordering U.S. forces to use deadly force. When U.S. air forces joined NATO's months-long war against Libyan dictator Muammar el-Qaddafi in 2011, President Obama did not ask for Congress's authorization, nor did Congress formally debate a conflict that unseated the Libyan strongman and left behind a chaotic country with no functional government.

"President Obama has arguably established the authority of the president to intervene militarily virtually anywhere without the consent or the approval of Congress, at his own discretion and for as long as he wishes," former Senator Jim Webb (D-VA), a Vietnam veteran and former Secretary of the Navy, wrote in the *National Interest*. "Few leaders in the Legislative Branch even asked for a formal debate over this exercise of unilateral presidential power, and in the Senate any legislation pertaining to the issue was prevented from reaching the floor. One can only wonder at what point these leaders or their successors might believe it is their constitutional duty to counter unchecked executive power exercised on behalf of overseas military action."

More recently, President Obama decided to ask Congress to authorize military strikes against Syria in response to the Bashar al-Assad regime using chemical weapons against civilians. When it appeared that Congress would reject the request, the administration backed off. And yet the plausible threat of U.S. military force was decisive in pressuring the Assad regime to relinquish its chemical weapons to international inspectors. That suggests that the debate will continue over how to reconcile the obligations of America's superpower status with the system of checks and balances established by the Founding Fathers.

◆ ◆ ◆ ◆ ◆

46. An Imperfect Compromise: "Don't Ask, Don't Tell"

by James Kitfield

In every country, the military holds up a mirror to the society it serves, reflecting its strengths and sometimes magnifying its weaknesses. By 1992, the

U.S. military was emerging victorious after more than four decades of Cold War, and fresh off its lopsided defeat of the Iraqi army in the 1991 Persian Gulf War. With the recent, rapid dissolution of the Soviet Union, the nation reflected in the U.S. military's image was ascendant, a lone-superpower in a suddenly unipolar world. America was riding high.

After 12 years of a Republican occupying the White House, Democrat Bill Clinton was elected president in 1992, representing a passing of the torch from the World War II generation of Ronald Reagan and George H. W. Bush. Clinton was the first baby-boomer Commander in Chief. For his generation, the seminal experiences were not the unifying crises of the Great Depression or World War II, but rather antiwar protests over Vietnam and the polarizing cultural wars of the 1960s and 1970s. Like all of the candidates for the Democratic presidential nomination in 1992, Clinton had run on a platform that supported lifting the U.S. military's ban on gays and lesbians, an increasingly influential constituency. Most Republicans and many conservative Southern Democrats were opposed to the idea. In retrospect, perhaps it was inevitable that some of the nation's unresolved cultural issues would follow Clinton to Washington, D.C., and the U.S. military would quickly find itself at the center of those disputes.

Since the earliest days of the Republic, the government has specified who would serve in the military in ways that reflected society's evolving norms, and often its prejudices against minorities in particular. Black Americans were barred from service in the Continental Army, for instance, and treated as second-class citizens in uniform even after President Harry Truman's historic 1948 order that "there shall be equality of treatment and opportunity for all persons in the armed forces without regard to race, color, religion, or national origin." Debilitating racial tensions in the uniformed ranks persisted during and after the Vietnam War. The reliance on a disproportionate number of black Americans to fill the ranks of the all-volunteer force in the 1970s and 1980s finally led to a number of policies that facilitated a smoother and deeper racial integration of the U.S. military. Largely as a result, General Colin Powell, the nation's first black chairman of the Joint Chiefs of Staff, had in 1991 helped orchestrate one of the most lopsided victories in U.S. military history.

As recently as Vietnam, the small numbers of women in uniform had served mostly in the nursing ranks. The Pentagon leaned heavily on women recruits, however, to fill its depleted ranks after the draft ended and the all-volunteer force was established in the 1970s. The Defense Department was slow to come to grips with the contradiction of denying women jobs in combat units in an organization where promotions were tied to such service. After 41,000 female troops served in Operation DESERT STORM in 1991, representing the largest deployment of women to a war zone in American history, advocates also began pressing for a lifting of the "combat exclusion" ban on women. The result was a 1994 policy opening all military jobs to women, to include flying combat aircraft, with the exception of direct ground combat units at the battalion-level or below.

A policy of banning sodomy among the uniformed ranks had been in place since the Revolutionary War. In 1982, the Defense Department reaffirmed a ban on gays and lesbians, stating that "homosexuality is incompatible with military service" based on the need to maintain "discipline, good order and morale." Many gays and lesbians had served in the Persian Gulf War, however, and with the gay rights movement having gained increased political influence in the 1980s, advocates believed their time for equality in the uniformed ranks had also come. In 1991, Senator Brock Adams (D-WA), and Representative Barbara Boxer (D-CA) thus introduced the Military Freedom Act, legislation to end the gay ban completely. A number of major newspapers endorsed the legislation, including *USA Today*, the *Los Angeles Times*, and the *Detroit Free Press*.

In this context in early 1993, a brash, young Democrat moved into the White House prepared to quickly make good on his promise to end the ban on gays and lesbians in the uniformed ranks. Clinton had never served in the military, however, and his avoidance of military service during the Vietnam War had become an issue during his campaign against George H.W. Bush, a former World War II naval aviator. In fact, the shift from a draft to a professional army back in the 1970s had insured that the day would come when relatively few of the country's civilian leaders would list military service on their resumes. One of the downsides of that cultural divide between an all-volunteer military and a political class with little military experience was about to become evident. Clinton could not have guessed it at the time, but he was about to step into what some experts considered the worst crisis in civil-military relations since President Harry Truman relieved General Douglas MacArthur in 1951 for gross insubordination.

STAUNCH MILITARY OPPOSITION

Bill Clinton had badly misjudged the degree of opposition in the military to his proposal to allow homosexuals to serve openly in uniform. All of the four-star flag officers on the Joint Chiefs of Staff opposed lifting the ban, as did the Veterans of Foreign Wars, the American Legion, and the Retired Officers Association. According to a *USA Today*—Gallup poll at the time—a 50 to 43 percent plurality of the American public were also opposed to lifting the ban.

For senior U.S. military leaders at the time, the issue of gays in the military felt like too much social engineering, coming too soon on the heels of groundbreaking changes underway governing women in combat. The issue also fell on a fault line that separated how individual freedoms and group responsibility were viewed. In the civilian world, the rights of the individual are rightfully given precedence unless they infringe on others. In the military, those rights were—and are still—routinely subjugated to the good of the group in ways both petty and profound. Service members adhere to an autocratic society where rank governs, everyone wears the same uniform and cuts their hair according to strict guidelines, privacy is routinely invaded, and entrance and acceptance is denied for reasons as arbitrary as age, weight, height, eyesight, and political memberships (communists and Ku Klux Klansmen need not apply). For the top military leadership and many of the rank-and-file who signed on to that group ethic, the idea of quickly adjusting themselves to an openly homosexual lifestyle was undeniably jarring.

General Carl Mundy Jr., the Marine Corps Commandant, led the uniformed opposition to relaxing the ban. In a letter to all of his senior officers, Mundy trumpeted a position paper authored by a Marine Corps chaplain that said that "in the unique, intensely close environment of the military, homosexual conduct can threaten the lives, including the physical (e.g., AIDS) and psychological well-being of others." Commander Craig Quigley, a senior Navy spokesman at the time, expressed the feeling of many senior uniformed leaders when he charged that "homosexuals are notoriously promiscuous" and would make other service members uncomfortable in "shared shower situations."

Privately, Mundy and other senior military leaders reached out to conservative politicians on Capitol Hill who were also either opposed outright, or uneasy with lifting the ban. They included many Republicans as well as pro-defense, Blue Dog Democrats, many of them from the more conservative South. Most importantly, military opponents of lifting the ban found a champion in Senator Sam Nunn (D-GA), a Southern conservative and the powerful chairman of the Senate Armed Services Committee, who favored maintaining the absolute ban on gays in uniform.

In his first months in the Oval Office, Bill Clinton thus experienced pushback against a signature policy from two unexpected directions: from a powerful committee chairman and fellow Southerner in his own Democratic Party, and from uniformed military leaders who were expected to show deference to civilian authority in all matters. The experience offered an abject lesson in Washington power politics, and the difficulty even a newly minted president bursting with political capital faced in trying to overcome the unified opposition of two pillars of the military-industrial complex.

CIVIL-MILITARY CRISIS

Clinton's apparent misreading of the depth of the military's unease with open homosexuality in the ranks highlighted concerns about the first Vietnam War–generation president and Commander in Chief. The press predictably picked up on the rising tensions between the White House and senior U.S. military leaders. In one story that made front-page headlines, Lieutenant General Barry McCaffrey, a Vietnam and Persian Gulf War hero and the most-decorated general in uniform, was reportedly insulted at the White House by a Clinton aide who met his greeting with a curt, "I don't talk to the military." The incident was recounted in *U.S. News and World Report* and *The Baltimore Sun*, and was used by Clinton's political opponents as evidence that the White House was virulently antimilitary.

Other media stories hammered on the same theme of antipathy between the White House and U.S. military. False stories circulated that Chelsea Clinton reportedly refused to ride to school with a military driver, and that Hillary Rodham Clinton supposedly banned uniforms from the White House. Many such anecdotes were apparently fed to the media by disgruntled officers in the Pentagon, some of whom displayed an antipathy to the Commander in Chief that spilled over into outright insubordination. That rancor surfaced openly at an Air Force banquet in the Netherlands, for instance, when Major General Harold Campbell publicly chastised the Commander in Chief's "womanizing," "draft dodging," and "pot smoking." Campbell was relieved of duty, but the deterioration in civil-military relations was apparent for all to see.

General Colin Powell, the hugely popular Chairman of the Joint Chiefs, eventually recognized the danger of the U.S. military seeming to be at odds with a popular new president. Coming so early in Clinton's term, the controversy over gays in the military was threatening to cut short the President's political honeymoon. It also thrust the U.S. military into the middle of the kind of partisan political battle from which it rarely emerged unscathed. More to the point, a professional military whose leadership openly opposes a president's policies, and in some cases denigrates the civilian atop the chain of command, is a threat to the democracy it is pledged to protect. Powell delayed his planned retirement until a compromise could be reached on the issue of gays and lesbians in the military, and ended talk of a schism between the White House and the military. His chief military assistant and the target of the snub by a White House aide, Lieutenant General Barry McCaffrey, was later photographed jogging with President Clinton, and eventually became the President's "drug czar."

AN IMPERFECT COMPROMISE

The Defense Authorization Act passed in 1993 and signed by President Clinton essentially upheld the ban on gays in the military. As part of a compromise reached with Senator Nunn, Clinton issued a directive that same year that military recruits and applicants were not to be asked about their sexual orientation. Limitations were placed on launching investigations into a service member's sexual orientation. The directive also made clear, however, that a public statement of homosexuality was enough to instigate a discharge. The name given to the policy was "Don't Ask, Don't Tell, Don't Pursue." After a number of cases emerged in which service members were attacked and even killed because of their sexual orientation, a "Don't Harass" provision was added to ensure the military targeted harassment or violence against any service member.

As a political compromise to defuse a crisis in civil-military relations, and remove a serious distraction from a new president's crowded agenda, "Don't Ask, Don't Tell" was arguably a qualified success. The policy bought time for the U.S. military, and for society writ large, to evolve on the issue of the rights of gays and lesbians.

However, as a policy, "Don't Ask, Don't Tell" left much to be desired. The Pentagon's accompanying directive upheld the legal position that homosexuality was incompatible with military service, and declared that persons who engaged in homosexual acts or openly stated that they were homosexual or bisexual faced discharge. More than 13,000 service members would ultimately be discharged over the life of the policy. A Pentagon review of the policy in 2000 also found that antigay sentiments were still widely expressed and tolerated in the military.

Predictably there were also costs to the U.S. military, and a price paid in civil-military relations. At a time when the U.S. military faced difficulty filling the ranks to fight the post-9/11 wars in Iraq and Afghanistan, for instance, some universities refused to allow military recruiters to visit their campuses because of their perceived discrimination against gays and lesbians. Many national security experts remain disturbed by the spectacle of senior U.S. military leaders knowingly pushing back against the policies of their civilian master. The collusion of powerful politicians on military oversight committees on Capitol Hill, and senior military leaders in the Pentagon, recalled warnings of an unholy alliances at the heart of the military industrial complex that former President Dwight Eisenhower spoke about in 1961.

Perhaps the most important takeaway from the "Don't Ask, Don't Tell" drama was the importance of timing in setting the stage for social change. If militaries truly present a mirror on society, then the images, norms and values reflected there must be recognizable and accepted by both sides. As was the case with black Americans after Vietnam and women following the Persian Gulf War, the wars in Iraq and Afghanistan were watersheds in changing perceptions about gays and lesbians serving in uniform. Citing evidence that as many as 65,000 gay men and women were serving in the armed forces in 2007, many of them risking life and limb in combat zones to protect America, 28 retired generals and admirals wrote a letter that year urging Congress to repeal "Don't Ask, Don't Tell." In 2008, *60 Minutes* ran a segment on an Army medic who served in Iraq after coming out to his unit. A 2010 survey by the Pew Research Center found that 58 percent of the public favored allowing gays and lesbians to serve openly in the military. Citing changes in public attitudes, both Colin Powell and Sam Nunn eventually argued for revisiting "Don't Ask, Don't Tell" with an eye toward repeal. In 2010, a U.S. Circuit Court ruled that the policy was an unconstitutional violation of the First and Fifth Amendments to the constitution.

In December 2010, President Barack Obama signed the "Don't Ask, Don't Tell Repeal Act." The following year, Obama, Secretary of Defense Leon Panetta, and Joint Chiefs Chairman Admiral Mike Mullen certified that the ending of the policy was consistent with the standards of "military readiness, military effectiveness, unit cohesion, and recruiting and retention of the Armed Forces." In 2012, a photograph of Marine Sergeant Brandon Morgan kissing his partner at a homecoming celebration on a Marine Corps Base went viral. Asked about the photo, a Marine Corps spokesperson commented, "It's your typical homecoming photo." Nudged by a new generation of "millennials" for whom tolerance of gays and lesbians is an article of faith, America has moved on.

♦ ♦ ♦ ♦ ♦

47. License to Spy: The USA PATRIOT Act

by James Kitfield

Everyone remembers how blue the sky was that morning. Later, we would recall the indelible silhouette of the New York City skyline with its gleaming towers reflecting sky, water, and the vibrancy of Manhattan; the broad-shouldered brawn of the Pentagon and the feelings of strength it evoked;

the confident swagger of Washington, D.C., the capital city on a hill whose superpower beacon was supposed to shine into virtually every corner of the globe. On the morning of September 11, 2001, Americans tasted firsthand the venom of those who rejected that light and all that it represented. And just like that the sky turned threatening, New York's once-proud skyline was gap-toothed and broken, and smoke hovered over the deserted and eerily quiet streets of Washington, D.C. Even the sense of what it meant to be an American seemed somehow altered that day. Everything had changed, not least of all the fundamental balance between civil liberties and security that is central to any democracy.

For the generation of Americans that came of age in the 9/11 era, the Al Qaeda terrorist attacks were a defining moment, not unlike Pearl Harbor and Victory Day for the World War II generation, or the assassination of President John F. Kennedy and the Vietnam War for the baby boomers. The worst attack on U.S. soil since Pearl Harbor created a national *zeitgeist* that was a mixture of fear, shock, and righteous anger.

Part of Osama Bin Laden's sinister brilliance was to turn on its head the U.S. counterterrorism strategy before 9/11. U.S. policy had treated terrorism as a criminal matter, with terrorists brought to justice in federal courts. What use was the threat of tough sentences or even the death penalty against a seemingly endless stream of martyrs willing to take their own lives in exchange for mass murder? Al Qaeda cells had also become adept at operating in the shadowy gaps between the United States' vast intelligence, defense, and domestic law enforcement bureaucracies, exploiting legal boundaries and distinct cultures that kept those agencies from effectively cooperating with one another. The Central Intelligence Agency (CIA) was barred from spying on individuals inside the United States, for instance, while the Federal Bureau of Investigation (FBI) lacked the overseas presence and domestic intelligence-gathering expertise to pick up the trail of terrorists headed for U.S. borders, and to preemptively thwart their plots at home.

Those legal firewalls were erected by an earlier act of Congress after it was revealed that the FBI and CIA had spied on antiwar activists and civil-rights advocates in the 1960s and 1970s. (See "Shining a Light on Spycraft: The Church and Pike Committees," Chapter 42.) In response to those abuses, Congress passed the Foreign Intelligence Surveillance Act (FISA), requiring the government to seek warrants from a special FISA court to monitor citizens' private communications. It seemed a simple line of defense against government overreach at the time, but one that Congress was willing to erase in the dark days following the 9/11 terrorist attacks.

A TERRORIZED CAPITOL

When a seemingly innocuous letter arrived in the office of Senate Major-ity Leader Thomas Daschle (D-SD), on October 15, 2001, with a cryptic note and a small amount of white powder, it seemed as if Al Qaeda had struck again, and the prospect dealt a severe psychological blow to a Con-gress already badly on edge. Immediately the letter tested positive for the deadly biological agent anthrax, leading to the closure of the Senate and House office buildings and throwing Capitol Hill into a near panic. In the initial sweep, 33 congressional staffers tested positive to exposure to anthrax.

Not surprisingly, suspicions immediately focused on Al Qaeda and intel-ligence reports that Osama Bin Laden had proclaimed that acquiring chemi-cal and biological weapons was a "religious duty" for his jihadists. There were also reports that Mohammed Atta, the tactical ringleader of the 9/11 hijackers, had made inquiries about crop dusting airplanes, possibly as a delivery mechanism to dispense chemical or biological weapons. Though much later it would be revealed that the anthrax came from a U.S. Army biological weapons lab, in October 2001 Congress was forced to confront the specter of nihilistic terrorists armed with weapons of mass destruction, a growing threat that many reports and blue ribbon commissions had warned against.

By that time, President Bush had already decided that the 9/11 attacks were the opening salvo in a global war on terrorism, declaring: "This is a different type of battle, a different type of battlefield, and a different type of war . . . this is really the first war of the 21st century." Congress had already responded by giving the Bush Administration wartime authorities to prosecute the military campaign against Al Qaeda with the September 14, 2001 Authorization for Use of Military Force. The Justice Department was also pressing Congress to put the nation's intelligence and law enforce-ment agencies on a wartime footing by passing a hastily assembled package of counterterrorism measures that would essentially knock down the walls separating them. The proposed legislation would greatly expand the ability of the law enforcement and intelligence apparatus to intercept electronic communications of all types, target money-laundering operations, and pros-ecute terrorists and those who harbored or abetted them.

Congress's eager response was the sweeping USA PATRIOT (Uniting and Strengthening America by Providing Appropriate Tools Required to Inter-cept and Obstruct Terrorism) Act of 2001. The broad scope of the legislation was evident in the fact that it was crafted with the input of no less than seven congressional committees. Representative Frank James "Jim" Sensenbrenner Jr. (R-WI), a conservative Republican, best known for playing a leading role in the House's impeachment of former President Bill Clinton in 1998 (see "Political Warfare on the Potomac: The Lewinsky Scandal and Clinton Impeachment," Chapter 52), shepherded the legislation through the House and was recognized as a key architect and supporter.

Even the name "USA PATRIOT Act" suggested the groundswell of congressional and popular support for the legislation in the weeks after 9/11. Many of its provisions were shrouded in the arcane language of law and technology, and relatively few lawmakers seemed overly concerned with the details. Notably, the USA PATRIOT Act expanded the ability of the government to conduct electronic surveillance for an expanded list of terrorist offenses; allowed judges to approve "roving wiretaps" on all the communications of individuals targeted in terrorist investigations; permitted law enforcement to delay notification that a search warrant has been executed on a suspect; allowed the government to issue "national security letters" that demand business records from third-party entities (including libraries and banks), that might aid a terrorist investigation; and removed the major legal barriers that previously prevented law enforcement, intelligence, and national security agencies from cooperating on investigations.

The USA PATRIOT Act passed the House and Senate with overwhelming bipartisan majorities (357–66 in the House, 98–1 in the Senate), and was signed into law by President Bush on October 26, 2001. Many lawmakers noted that in some particulars it simply extended to terrorist investigations authorities that law enforcement already had in pursuing the heads of drug cartels or organized crime families. "The FBI could get a wiretap to investigate the mafia, but they could not get one to investigate terrorists," Senator Joe Biden (D-DE) noted during floor debate. "To put it bluntly, that was crazy! What's good for the mob should be good for terrorists."

The lone Senate opponent to the USA PATRIOT Act was liberal Russell "Russ" Feingold (D-WI) best known for cosponsoring the McCain-Feingold campaign reform legislation with Senator John McCain (R-AZ). Feingold felt that in its rush to provide the Bush Administration with the tools to fight Al Qaeda, the Senate was needlessly compromising cherished civil liberties protections. His early warnings would ultimately prove prescient.

CIVIL LIBERTY CONCERNS

With many of the provisions of the legislation set to expire at the end of 2005, civil libertarians began publicly questioning the extent to which the USA PATRIOT Act enabled the government to spy almost without restraint, including monitoring the communications of American citizens who were not suspected of any crime. This government power seemed to violate constitutional protections against unreasonable search and seizure.

Earlier that year, for instance, *The New York Times* revealed that President Bush had authorized the National Security Agency (NSA) to intercept, without warrants, the private communications of millions of Americans. Bush was unapologetic: "We know that a two-minute phone conversation between somebody linked to Al Qaeda here and an operative overseas could lead directly to the loss of thousands of lives."

Once again, Senator Feingold led the opposition to a blanket renewal of the USA PATRIOT Act, but this time he had more company—including Senators Lisa Murkowski (R-AK), Ken Salazar (D-CO), Larry Craig (R-ID), Dick Durbin (D-IL), and John Sununu (R-NH). After Feingold led a filibuster of the renewal, some mild civil liberties protections were added, and the renewal bill passed in 2006 on a bipartisan 89–10 vote. Notably, Feingold voted against the renewal anyway, complaining that it did not go far enough in protecting civil liberties.

In 2009 the USA PATRIOT Act was again up for renewal, only this time with Democrat Barack Obama in the White House. As a Senator, Obama (D-IL) had opposed a FISA Amendment Act that codified the government's power to tap Americans' international communications and even gave retroactive immunity to telecommunications companies that assisted in the earlier warrantless taps of the Bush Administration. But as the Commander in Chief, Obama reversed course and supported the FISA Amendment Act, and his administration fought a lawsuit by the American Civil Liberties Union that challenged the FISA changes.

In October 2009, Feingold once again sounded a warning about the U.S. government's ever-expanding surveillance powers during a Senate Judiciary Committee hearing, one that foreshadowed a massive intelligence scandal a few years later. He singled out for criticism Section 215 of the USA PATRIOT Act, which allows the FISA court to compel businesses to turn over unspecified information. "Mr. Chairman, I am also a member of the Intelligence Committee. I recall during the debate in 2005 that proponents of Section 215 argued that these authorities had never been misused," said Feingold. "They cannot make that statement now. They have been misused. I cannot elaborate here. But I recommend that my colleagues seek more information in a classified setting."

THE SNOWDEN SCANDAL

When a young NSA contractor and computer specialist named Edward Snowden walked out of an NSA facility in Hawaii in May 2013, carrying millions of classified documents detailing the agency's operations, he precipitated perhaps the greatest breach in the history of U.S. intelligence. Through a series of periodic disclosures coordinated with a small group of journalists, Snowden revealed a globe-spanning communications intercept and intelligence-gathering operation of breathtaking breadth and scope. The guiding principle behind NSA operations was clearly that if intelligence can be gathered, it will be. Whether or not the private communications of civilians ranging from the Chancellor of Germany to millions of unsuspecting American citizens actually should be intercepted seems not to have been a factor in internal NSA deliberations. And largely because of rapid advances in communication technology, coupled with the enabling authorities of the USA PATRIOT Act, the amount of intelligence that the NSA could gather was staggering.

Among the Snowden revelations, leaked in a series of water-torture revelations that have bedeviled the Obama Administration: the NSA routinely collects the communications records of millions of U.S. citizens by using secret FISA court orders to access bulk records of telephone companies such as Verizon; the agency has infiltrated and compromised the servers of the biggest U.S. technology companies, including Apple, Google, and Microsoft; the NSA routinely spies on diplomats and foreign leaders even of allied nations; the NSA has the ability to tap into emails, contacts folders, and text messages to determine the physical location of all the major smartphones on the market; the NSA has tapped into the large, fiber-optic cables that span the Atlantic and Pacific Oceans and carry much of the world's internet and telephone traffic; the NSA stores "metadata" of millions of people on massive computer databases; and the NSA broke U.S. laws and violated its own internal regulations nearly 3,000 times in the space of just one year (April 2011–March 2012).

Responding to the public outrage and diplomatic blowback prompted by the Snowden revelations, President Obama issued new guidelines in January 2014 that will somewhat limit NSA access to bulk telephone data, establish some privacy safeguards for foreign nationals, and assign a public advocate to argue civil liberty concerns before the FISA court. Notably, he suggested that a third party or the telecommunications companies themselves could store the "metadata" on electronic communications, though the companies themselves oppose the idea. Nor did the administration require that the FISA court first approve the issuance by the FBI and other law enforcement agencies of so-called national security letters requesting business records, a reform that civil liberties groups had strongly advocated.

Though a welcome corrective, those reforms will not fully restore the fundamental balance between civil liberties and security that was skewed on September 11, 2001. As the 9/11 attacks mercifully recede into memory, it has become increasingly clear that the hybrid nature of the terrorist threat (part criminal, part military), and the endless horizon of a "war on terrorism," makes this period in American history almost uniquely dangerous. The lack of any definable end to the threat forestalls the self-correcting cycle that followed past wars and crises, when civil-liberties abuses—the internment of Japanese Americans during World War II, for instance—were reexamined and reversed. In an endless conflict, the exigencies of war get embedded not only in statutory and legal structures, but also in the consciousness of the American people. As Founding Father Benjamin Franklin warned, "They who would give up essential liberty, to purchase a little temporary safety, deserve neither liberty nor safety."

♦ ♦ ♦ ♦ ♦

48. Reforming National Intelligence: The 9/11 Commission

by Michael Allen

On September 11, 2001, in a daring surprise attack, 19 Al Qaeda terrorists penetrated the nation's security and hijacked four airplanes, flying three of them into the World Trade Center Towers in New York and the Pentagon in Washington, D.C., causing the deaths of nearly 3,000 individuals. In the aftermath of this strategic intelligence failure, Congress created a commission to study the 9/11 attacks and propose changes to the national security infrastructure created after World War II.

A half century earlier, the National Security Act of 1947 had sought to guarantee there would be no more strategic surprises like Japan's attack on Pearl Harbor, and "to ensure through [the creation of the Central Intelligence Agency] that never again would the U.S. government be disadvantaged because it failed to consider as a whole all the information available to its parts."[1] (See "A Superpower's Foundation: The National Security Act of

1947," Chapter 37.) In a similar way, the 9/11 Commission set out to make substantial improvements to the intelligence structure to enable higher performance for a generational struggle against new threats, especially stateless international terrorists.

To succeed, the Commission had to navigate through substantial obstacles. A reallocation of authority, control, and money between national security and intelligence agencies, for instance, inspired fierce bureaucratic opposition. Compounding the challenge of shifting authority between long-established institutions was the complexity of the political environment. The attacks of 9/11 profoundly affected the political landscape, creating a charged electoral environment and raising the central question of whether President Bush had made the country safer.

REFORMING NATIONAL INTELLIGENCE

The formal creation of the CIA in the National Security Act of 1947 laid the foundation for the "permanent national intelligence structure."[2] While the National Security Act had given the Director of Central Intelligence (DCI) the job of "coordinating the intelligence activities of the several government departments and agencies," it had "provided no language compelling these various agencies to cooperate. The director of central intelligence, who also headed the CIA, had no levers—no general budget authority, no overall intelligence personnel authority, no exclusive access to the President—to force inter-agency collaboration."[3] Although the covert action mission flourished, the coordinating of responsibilities, the inspiration for the "Central" in CIA, was hollow. In that sense, the CIA was "centralized in name only."[4]

Of course, the DCI's impotence in coordinating intelligence functions was fine with many of the more established Cabinet departments. This was especially the case for the military services, which routinely opposed centralizing more power in the DCI because it threatened their own direct control over intelligence programs.[5]

The Commission's review of the government's performance before September 11, 2001, convinced commissioners that the lack of an effective centralizing authority had contributed to an intelligence community that was poorly postured to meet an emerging terrorism threat. For instance, in 1998, the DCI had issued a "declaration of war" against Al Qaeda. To the Commission, the declaration was a call to arms for all the intelligence agencies to devote more time, money, and effort to the fight against this terrorist network. Instead, the agencies largely ignored the pronouncement, leading investigators to conclude that the DCI was little more than a figurehead who could not back up his orders with any redirection of funds or people. A new structure was needed that would enable the head of the intelligence community to make good on future "declarations of war," and to ensure greater responsiveness to new priorities.

Despite the enormity of the 9/11 attack, the adoption of such a sweeping remedy was hardly a foregone conclusion. Any attempt to establish more central authority over the intelligence community would inspire fierce bureaucratic opposition, especially during an election year when centrifugal forces loomed. The Commission needed to marshal convincing arguments, and be seen as impartial and qualified to carry the day on wholesale change. But in some cases its hearings and actions contributed to wariness of the Commission. President Bush's Chief of Staff, Andrew Card, remembered, "The 9/11 Commission was perceived by a lot of people to be a place where you had license to slap the president around."[6]

With the election just months away, a former member of President Bush's national-security staff, counterterrorism czar Richard Clarke, launched a provocative series of attacks on President Bush's national-security record. Clarke's assertions—on *60 Minutes,* in a book, and before the 9/11 Commission—cut to the heart of Bush's presidency. He laid blame for the greatest attack on U.S. soil directly at Bush's feet. Clarke's attacks on Bush's national-security record predictably proved political dynamite. On *60 Minutes,* Clarke painted an image of President Bush "sitting by a warm fireplace in the White House drawing X's through al-Qaida leaders and thinking that he's got most of them and therefore he's taken care of the problem, and while George Bush thinks he's crossing them out one by one there are all these new al-Qaida people who are being recruited who hate the United States in large measure because of what Bush has done."

Clarke's use of a 9/11 Commission hearing as a platform to attack the President seemed to validate the White House's fears about the Commission becoming a partisan instrument. Expressing his skepticism about the Commission, Senator Mitch McConnell (R-KY) said: "Sadly, the Commission's public hearings have allowed those with political axes to grind, like Richard Clarke, to play shamelessly to the partisan gallery of liberal special interests seeking to bring down the president."[7]

The Clarke attacks forced the commissioners to take sides. In the hearings, the Democratic commissioners seemed to pursue a strategy sympathetic to Clarke, while the Republicans impeached his credibility. Clarke's appearance before the Commission also provoked the Bush White House to counterattack. "I was furious, I was furious,"[8] former National Security Adviser Condoleezza Rice recalled. At the time she told the press that, "Dick Clarke just does not know what he's talking about."[9] Rice labeled some of his comments as "arrogance in the extreme."[10] Seen as a turncoat, Clarke was in for a counterassault that further painted him as a bitter, disingenuous opportunist selling a book in an election year, and hoping for a job in a future Kerry Administration. Rice's rejoinder before the Commission—that 9/11 was caused by structural and legal impediments decades in the making—brought into stark relief the two competing narratives on whether President Bush deserved reelection.

STAYING ABOVE POLITICS

Throughout 2003–2004, Commission Chairman and Republican Tom Kean, and Vice Chairman and Democrat Lee Hamilton, worried that the Commission would fall victim to the rising election year politics. Although the Clarke and Rice appearances had given the 9/11 Commission a national stage, there was risk that the factionalism it inspired could seep into the Commission's report due later in 2004. If the report were seen as a partisan political document, a product of election year politics, the Commission's plans to fundamentally restructure the intelligence community would be at risk. Kean recalled that, "We worried that the Clarke episode might break us apart because of the partisanship that resulted." Hamilton would later say the Clarke book gave a "political edge"[11] to the 9/11 Commission's hearings.

Kean and Hamilton strove to keep the Commission from breaking into warring camps. Remembering that previous commissions' recommendations had been ignored, Kean believed an absolute prerequisite was unanimity. "I worried about the recommendations; that's where I thought we would come apart."[12] Kean remembers one instance when two commissioners brought him their disagreement about a Commission recommendation on increased centralized management of the intelligence community. Undeterred, Kean asked a third commissioner to take them to lunch and broker a compromise. Steadfast mediation by the Chairman and Vice Chairman ensured that the Commission remained united, avoiding a pitfall that might have allowed opponents to exploit divisions.

When the Commission unveiled its report in July 2004, its findings were widely heralded as fact-based and shorn of partisan aspersions. The commissioners, which only months earlier had teetered on the brink of partisan division, were now praised as statesmen who had transcended politics for the good of the country. To be sure, the Commission also benefited from deep frustration with the intelligence community for its failures on 9/11, and, as it came into full view that summer, misjudgments about nonexistent weapons of mass destruction stockpiles in Iraq. But their unanimity cast the Commission in a flattering light and catapulted their recommendations onto the national policy agenda.

The Commission recommended a new leader, a Director of National Intelligence (DNI), with the tools—enhanced budget and personnel authority—to be a "quarterback" providing centralized management of the intelligence community. The Commission's DNI would force unity of effort by breaking down "stovepipes" that prevented the effective sharing of information that may, if properly correlated, have revealed Al Qaeda's 9/11 plot. The Commission imagined a DNI as a "spymaster" with sweeping authority to manage the vast intelligence bureaucracies whose budgets rose to nearly $80 billion at their peak.

The Commission added a second major recommendation to centralize greater authority in the intelligence community, namely a National Counterterrorism Center (NCTC) that would build upon President Bush's efforts to fuse intelligence data collected domestically and internationally. By bringing counterterrorism analysts and databases from all the major intelligence, law enforcement and military agencies together, the Commission intended for the NCTC to be an innovative advancement in interagency cooperation.

The Commission's recommendations were celebrated. Senator Lieberman (D-CT) thought they had a "shining white horse" quality to them.[13] The 9/11 Commission thus commanded the national policy agenda in the fall of 2004. Instead of going unnoticed in a presidential election, the Commission's recommendations were quickly endorsed by the Democratic presidential nominee, Senator John Kerry (D-MA), as well as by President Bush. By the end of October 2004, the Senate and the House of Representatives had taken up and passed legislation to enact its recommendations (although the final text would not come until December 2004). The 9/11 Commission— aided by the families of those killed on 9/11, evidence of the intelligence failures, and election-year politics—had produced the most comprehensive reorganization of intelligence since the National Security Act of 1947.

The Commission's avoidance of partisanship allowed it to capitalize on the looming presidential election and gain bipartisan support for enacting its recommendations into law. The Commission was able to set the congressional and executive agenda in the fall of 2004, and the commissioners wielded considerable influence during the development and passage of the Intelligence Reform and Terrorism Prevention Act of 2004 (IRTPA) (which created the DNI and an NCTC largely as the Commission recommended). The mere fact that the IRTPA even passed was a tremendous accomplishment.

Numerous commissions since 1947 had made similar recommendations that had gone nowhere, stymied by determined opposition.

To be sure, the friction generated by the creation of a DNI has limited progress on some of the issues that have long hampered the ability of intelligence agencies to act as a coherent enterprise. Ironically, the quick pace of the legislation's passage—just four-and-half months—contributed to a lack of a full agreement on the DNI's precise roles, missions, and authority.

Nonetheless, the IRTPA fundamentally changed the structure of the intelligence community by creating a central authority in the DNI and stripping the community management functions from CIA. This allows the DNI to lead and manage a system that more efficiently collects and analyzes the hardest to obtain information for the benefit of our national security policy makers. It also empowers the DNI to make budgetary judgments and to reorient intelligence collection to meet new threats. The 9/11 Commission, through its recommendations embodied in the IRTPA, created new institutions that, while still being refined, will have a tremendous impact on U.S. national security. That record of achievement easily ranks the 9/11 Commission as one of the most successful commissions in U.S. history.

Author's Note: This essay is derived in part from my book, *Blinking Red, Crisis and Compromise in American Intelligence after 9/11* (Potomac Books, October 2013).

♦ ♦ ♦ ♦ ♦

49. Changing Course in a Time of War: Congress and the 2006 Iraq Study Group

by Jordan Tama

The story of the 2006 Iraq Study Group demonstrates the power—and the limits—of blue-ribbon commissions to challenge indirectly the President's dominance of national security policy.

By 2006, Iraq was unraveling and spiraling toward all-out civil war, raising the specter of ignoble defeat for U.S. forces charged with stabilizing the country. Total U.S. and Iraqi deaths from the war rose from several hundred per month in early 2005 to roughly 2,000 per month by the summer of 2006.[1]

As the violence in Iraq escalated, the war also became increasingly unpopular in the United States. Starting in 2005, opinion polls consistently found that more than half of Americans thought it was a mistake for the United States to have gone to war in Iraq.[2] At the same time, there was strong evidence that the war was taking a serious toll on public attitudes toward the Republican Party. By late 2005, President George W. Bush's approval rating tumbled below 40 percent for the first time, and Americans generally expressed a strong preference for the Democratic Party in opinion polls—partly because of their dissatisfaction with the war.[3] These trends in public opinion became even more pronounced as sectarian violence in Iraq surged to new heights following the February 2006 bombing in the city of Samarra of the holiest Shiite mosque.

With a congressional election approaching in November 2006, the Iraq crisis greatly concerned many Republican lawmakers. But Republicans on Capitol Hill were generally not inclined to criticize Bush's handling of the war, or to challenge the President directly by introducing legislation that would force a change in course in how the war was conducted. Instead, a few congressional Republicans sought to indirectly generate pressure for a strategy change by supporting the creation of a blue-ribbon commission called the Iraq Study Group (or Baker-Hamilton Commission, after its cochairmen, former Secretary of State James Baker and former Congressman Lee Hamilton).

When this commission issued a sharp critique of the war effort in December 2006, it did indeed add to the pressure facing Bush, and its proposals for gradually winding down the war were embraced by centrist lawmakers on Capitol Hill. But neither Bush nor the Democratic congressional leadership backed the study group's plan, ultimately leaving it to Barack Obama to implement the study group's ideas when he became president two years later.

CREATING THE IRAQ STUDY GROUP

The idea of an independent Iraq commission originated with Representative Frank Wolf (R-VA), who represented a politically moderate district in northern Virginia. Wolf said he wanted to create the study group because "at the time, there were no real solutions being offered on Iraq."[4] Wolf surely also realized that the deteriorating situation in Iraq threatened to become an albatross around Republicans' necks in future elections.

Wanting to gain Bush's blessing for the idea of a commission, Wolf first proposed the idea privately at a November 2005 meeting with senior Bush Administration officials. After Vice President Dick Cheney resisted the idea,

Wolf worked with a few allies outside government—David M. Abshire, President of the Center for the Study of the Presidency; John Hamre, President of the Center for Strategic and International Studies; and Richard Solomon, President of the United States Institute of Peace—to gain Bush's support by circumventing Cheney. On November 29, Abshire, Hamre, and Solomon met with Secretary of State Condoleezza Rice and pitched the commission idea to her. Rice liked the idea because she too was dissatisfied with the administration's existing Iraq strategy. The next day, Rice gained Bush's backing for creating the study group—before Cheney could lobby the President against the idea.[5]

Wolf then used his position within Congress to establish the commission. Rather than trying to achieve congressional approval of a statute that provided a charter for the commission—the typical legislative approach for creating commissions—Wolf inserted into an emergency appropriation bill a $1 million earmark to the U.S. Institute of Peace for the purpose of coordinating the work of an Iraq study group.[6] Wolf was well positioned to follow this approach because he served as chairman of the House appropriations subcommittee with jurisdiction over the U.S. Institute of Peace. Wolf's principal Senate partner in this effort was Armed Services Committee Chairman John Warner (R-VA), another moderate Republican from Virginia who shared Wolf's hope that a commission would place pressure on the Bush administration to change course.

In early 2006 the backers of the Iraq Study Group (Solomon principally, in consultation with Abshire, Hamre, Warner, and Wolf) selected James Baker, a Republican, and Lee Hamilton, a Democrat, to cochair the commission. Baker and Hamilton then chose the study group's eight other members:

- Former Director of Central Intelligence Robert Gates (who was replaced by former Secretary of State Lawrence Eagleburger when Gates was named Secretary of Defense after the 2006 election);
- Former New York Mayor Rudolph Giuliani (who was replaced by former Attorney General Ed Meese after Giuliani failed to attend the study group's initial meetings);
- Democratic power broker Vernon Jordan;
- Former U.S. Supreme Court Justice Sandra Day O'Connor;
- Former White House Chief of Staff Leon Panetta;
- Former Secretary of Defense William Perry;
- Former Democratic Senator Charles Robb; and
- Former Republican Senator Alan Simpson.

SHIFTING THE DEBATE

The group of five Republicans and five Democrats began their work in March 2006. After a joint trip to Iraq and many hours of deliberations, they reached consensus on key findings and 79 recommendations. Their 142-page report, issued on December 6, 2006, offered a highly critical assessment of conditions in Iraq, captured by its stark opening sentence: "The situation in Iraq is grave and deteriorating."[7] The report went on to highlight three principal proposals: (1) launching a diplomatic offensive in the Middle East, including direct engagement with Iran and Syria and pursuit of Arab-Israeli peace; (2) changing the primary mission of U.S. forces in Iraq from combat to training and counterterrorism; and (3) conditioning aid to Iraq on the Iraqi government's progress toward the achievement of milestones in the areas of national reconciliation, security, and governance.

The report also endorsed a gradual troop withdrawal from Iraq, stating, "By the first quarter of 2008, subject to unexpected developments in the security situation on the ground, all combat brigades not necessary for force protection could be out of Iraq."[8] At the same time, the study group stated that it could "support a short-term redeployment or surge of American combat forces to stabilize Baghdad, or to speed up the training and equipping mission, if the U.S. commander in Iraq determines that such steps would be effective."[9]

The study group's report attracted tremendous public interest and attention. All of the major television networks provided live coverage of the press conference held by the study group when it issued the report, and more than 2 million copies of the report were downloaded in the first two weeks after its release. Public opinion surveys also found that the study group's proposals were viewed favorably by the American people. The recommendations to negotiate with Iran and Syria, pursue Israeli-Palestinian peace talks, shift the military mission from combat to training, and reduce aid if the Iraqis failed to meet milestones were each backed by at least 60 percent of the public.[10]

One month before the study group reported, Republican electoral fears had been validated, as the Democrats decisively won the midterm election, gaining control of Congress for the first time in 12 years. In the wake of that defeat, and as public support for the Iraq war continued to fall, many moderate Republicans, including Senators Judd Gregg (R-NH), Gordon Smith (R-OR), and John Sununu (R-NH), endorsed the commission's ideas and called on Bush to change course. A *Wall Street Journal* reporter noted that the study group was giving "moderate Republicans political cover to condemn the handling of the war."[11]

However, the Iraq Study Group report was not embraced by the audience of one that mattered most: George W. Bush. On January 10, 2007—five weeks after the study group reported—Bush announced a decision to send five new combat brigades to Iraq to carry out a new counterinsurgency strategy aimed at protecting the Iraqi people. Bush's announcement of this surge was the outcome of a series of internal administration reviews of Iraq strategy during the second half of 2006.[12] Bush's choice to double down on the U.S. military commitment to Iraq reflected a desire on his part to salvage a war effort central to his legacy—a common calculus for presidents who begin wars that do not produce clear victories.[13] Although the study group indicated that it could support a short-term troop surge, Bush's new policy departed from the main thrust of the study group's key proposals, as it did not change the primary U.S. military mission to training and counterterrorism. Nor did Bush endorse the study group's proposals concerning diplomacy and milestones.

The study group report also received a cool reception from Democratic congressional leaders. Representative Nancy Pelosi (D-CA) and Senator Harry Reid (D-NV) were disappointed that the study group did not recommend setting a deadline for the rapid withdrawal of U.S. troops from Iraq. Given the strong political advantage held by the Democrats on the Iraq issue at the time, Pelosi and Reid also had little political incentive to endorse an approach that would not only allow troops to remain in Iraq longer than they preferred, but would also give Congress partial ownership of the course of the unpopular war.

Nevertheless, as conditions in Iraq remained bleak and U.S. public opinion remained strongly opposed to the war during the first half of 2007, the study group's proposals were at the center of the Capitol Hill debate on Iraq policy. During this time, the proposals served as the lodestar for centrist Republicans and Democrats in Congress who sought to advance an alternative to the Bush Administration's policy. Two weeks after Bush announced the troop surge, a bipartisan group of nine senators led by John Warner cosponsored a "sense of the Senate" resolution that followed the study group's recommendations in calling for changing the military mission to counterterrorism and training, and for greater diplomacy with Iraq's neighbors.[14] In subsequent months, a bipartisan group of lawmakers drafted binding legislation that mandated the adoption of most of the study group's proposals. In the Senate, this group was led by Senators Ken Salazar (D-CO) and Lamar Alexander (R-TN); in the House, it was led by Frank Wolf and Representatives Chris Shays (R-CT) and Mark Udall (D-CO). On June 5, the legislation was introduced in both chambers, with 15 Senate and 62 House cosponsors.[15]

This legislation did not advance in either chamber, however, partly because Reid and Pelosi opposed bringing it up for a vote. In July, Salazar sought to force a vote on the legislation by reintroducing it as an amendment to the defense appropriation bill, but Reid pulled the appropriations measure from the floor without allowing a vote on the amendment.[16] In the House, meanwhile, the Rules Committee turned down requests from the legislation's supporters to allow a floor vote on the bill.[17]

SHIFTING TIDES OF WAR AND POLITICS

Meanwhile, during the summer of 2007, conditions on the ground in Iraq started to improve, and by the fall, it became clear that violence in Iraq was declining. This improvement quickly took the wind out of the sails of efforts to legislate the adoption of the study group's proposals, and led to the fracturing of the bipartisan coalition that had coalesced around that effort.

The study group's ideas remained alive, however, thanks to the presidential campaign of then-Senator Barack Obama, whose Iraq platform was heavily influenced by the study group report. Seven weeks after the study group reported, Obama introduced his own Iraq legislation, which was based largely on the study group's proposals. The bill mandated a gradual withdrawal of U.S. troops to "achieve the goal of the complete redeployment of all United States combat brigades from Iraq by March 31, 2008, consistent with the expectation of the Iraq Study Group." The bill also authorized retaining troops in Iraq after that date for training and counterterrorism, conditioning aid to Iraq on Iraqi progress in meeting benchmarks, and mandating regional and international diplomatic initiatives.[18] On all of these issues, the bill was intentionally patterned on the study group's proposals.[19]

The plan laid out in Obama's legislation remained his Iraq platform during the presidential campaign, and was the foundation for the policy he adopted when he became President two years later. The only significant differences in the policy he adopted as President were that he moved forward the date for ending the combat mission to August 31, 2010, and he did not make economic aid to Iraq conditional on its progress toward benchmarks. As President, Obama did follow the study group's recommendations to reach out to Iran and Syria, shift the military mission from counterinsurgency to counterterrorism and training, and gradually reduce the number of American troops in Iraq.

The story of the Iraq Study Group suggests broader conclusions about Congress and the effectiveness of independent commissions. During times of crisis or war, it can be politically risky and unappealing for lawmakers to criticize the President directly—particularly if they share the same political party—or to put their own necks on the line by proposing a specific alternative to the President's policy. By establishing a commission, lawmakers can indirectly introduce potentially influential new ideas into the public debate on an important national security issue, without necessarily committing themselves to those ideas. In this way, commissions can be seen both as a tool for lawmakers to avoid blame, and as a creative and flexible vehicle for policy making.[20] The effectiveness of such commissions can be increased when, as was the case with the Iraq Study Group, the commission's unanimous recommendations help create a bipartisan coalition among lawmakers that had not previously existed.[21]

However, commissions are far from a panacea for partisanship and polarization. While the Iraq Study Group had a significant impact on the U.S. debate over Iraq policy and on the Iraq policy of the Obama Administration, it could not force the Bush Administration and congressional leaders to compromise on a highly charged and polarizing issue. Sometimes partisan divides are simply too great for commissions and centrist lawmakers to overcome.

In the end, Frank Wolf's hope that the U.S. President would follow the study group's ideas became reality—it was just not the President he had in mind.

Author's Note: Much of this chapter is adapted from Jordan Tama, "The Power and Limitations of Commissions: The Iraq Study Group, Bush, Obama, and Congress," *Presidential Studies Quarterly* 41, no. 1 (March 2011): 135–55.

◆ ◆ ◆ ◆ ◆

Congress and Presidential Scandal

50. A President Resigns: The Watergate Scandal

by Keith Olson

Officially, Congress's investigation of the Watergate affair ran from 1973 to 1974. Yet, the constitutional crisis that led to the first resignation of a U.S. President in history was the culmination of a decade of upheaval and instability. Assassins killed three of the nation's most charismatic leaders: John and Robert Kennedy and Martin Luther King Jr. Black leader Malcolm X and several civil rights leaders also died from assassins. Champions for and opponents of equal civil rights for all Americans clashed violently. Opposition to the Vietnam War swept from college campuses to the nation's capital. And all the while, groups that had not previously played a significant role in politics—women, minorities, the young, the poor—were asserting their right to be heard.

Watergate became a major news story on June 17, 1972, when Washington, D.C., police arrested five burglars in the Democratic National Committee headquarters in the Watergate complex along the Potomac River. On August 9, 1974, Watergate reached its climax when President Richard M. Nixon resigned.

Watergate was unique in that all three branches of the federal government were involved. Both Houses of Congress played indispensable roles in forging the political consensus that forced Nixon to resign or face impeachment and conviction. The extensive media coverage also resulted in an unusual public awareness. By the summer of 1974, one national poll reported that 66 percent of Americans favored impeachment or resignation, a rare example of public unanimity on a political issue of such grave importance.

SHADOW OVER NIXON'S INAUGURATION

The situation looked very much different in November 1972 when Richard Nixon won reelection despite several months of media coverage about the break-in. In fact, in January 1973 he matched his greatest popularity when polls recorded that 68 percent of Americans approved of his performance.

Ten days before Nixon's inauguration, however, the trial of the Watergate burglars opened in U.S. District Court in Washington with Judge John J. Sirica presiding. Four of the burglars and one of the planners of the operation, E. Howard Hunt, pleaded guilty. Hunt had a White House office, and one of the burglars was on the Central Intelligence Agency (CIA) payroll. On

January 30, 1973, a jury returned a guilty verdict on the two men who were arrested but plead not guilty. Sirica, known as a "law and order judge," concluded the trial was a cover-up and delayed sentencing until March 23, 1973.

Senator Sam J. Ervin (D-NC) had been waiting for the trial's conclusion. For himself and the Democratic Majority Leader, Mike Mansfield (D-MT), Ervin introduced a resolution to establish a Select Committee on Presidential Campaign Activities. Two days after its introduction, the Senate voted 77–0 to adopt Resolution 60 establishing a Select Committee of seven members, four Democrats and three Republicans. Resolution 60 identified three areas of investigation: the 1972 campaign of alleged dirty tricks and espionage; the break-in and cover-up; and possible illegal campaign financing. The resolution gave the Committee authority to subpoena, a budget of $500,000, and a deadline of February 28, 1974, to submit a final report.

Ervin, who was widely viewed as honest and nonpartisan, was selected to chair the Select Committee. Although an honors graduate of Harvard Law School and a constitutional scholar, the folksy Ervin quoted the Bible and maintained the image of a common sense country lawyer. At age 76, he was also too old to have any presidential ambitions.

The other Democrats named to the Committee were Joseph M. Montoya (D-NM), Herman E. Talmadge (D-GA), and Daniel K. Inouye (D-HI). None of the three came from the Northeast, and none had a strong liberal image; all were unlikely presidential hopefuls. The Senate Republican leadership essentially made similar low-profile appointments: Lowell P. Weicker Jr. (R-CT), Edward J. Gurney (R-FL), and Howard H. Baker (R-TN), who was chosen to be the ranking minority member of the Committee.

For chief counsel of the Committee, Ervin selected Samuel Dash, a distinguished Georgetown University law professor who had previously worked in the Philadelphia District Attorney's office, the Justice Department, and in private practice, and had served as president of the National Association of Criminal Defense Lawyers. For minority counsel, Baker named Fred D. Thompson, a lawyer who had managed Baker's 1972 reelection campaign. Ervin and Baker wanted their staffs to cooperate yet maintain separate identities. Resolution 60 had even called for separate budgets. At its peak, the Committee employed more than 100 staff plus more than 20 people who managed an early computer system for record-keeping.

WHITE HOUSE STORY UNRAVELS

Before the Committee even met, three disclosures outside of the Committee's work began undermining the White House's story that it was not involved in any wrongdoing. On February 28, 1973, the Senate Judiciary Committee considered the confirmation of L. Patrick Gray as director of the Federal Bureau of Investigation (FBI). One document he submitted recorded a payment made by Nixon's appointment secretary to Donald H. Segretti for his operation of the dirty tricks campaign. On March 23, Judge Sirica read a letter from one of the burglars, James McCord, who described pressure on all of them to remain silent and to plead guilty. McCord also claimed that during the trial some defendants had committed perjury. Early in April, during the trial of Pentagon Papers defendant Daniel Ellsberg, it was revealed that Hunt and G. Gordon Liddy had burglarized the office of Ellsberg's psychiatrist. At the time, Hunt and Liddy were on the While House payroll.

On April 30, the President addressed the nation to discuss Watergate. He announced the resignation of John Erhlichman and H. R. Haldeman and Attorney General Richard Kleindienst, and the dismissal of John Dean, the White House Counsel. Nixon's speech and the latest disclosures prompted Republican Senator Charles H. Percy of Illinois to introduce a "sense of the Senate" resolution requesting the President to appoint a special prosecutor to investigate. Ten other Republicans joined Percy as cosponsors as did seven Democrats. The Senate adopted Percy's resolution by voice vote.

Meanwhile, other disclosures continued to draw the White House deeper into the scandal. Former Attorney General John Mitchell admitted that in 1972 Liddy had given him a proposal for burglary and telephone taping to obtain "political intelligence." A Senate subcommittee released a document indicating that in the summer of 1972 the director of the CIA had ended cooperation with the White House because the White House had gone "too far" regarding Watergate.

The weight of these revelations caused Nixon's January 68 percent approval rating to fall to 44 percent by the middle of May of 1973. Mid-May polls also reported that 96 percent of Americans had heard or read about Watergate and that 56 percent of Americans believed that the President had participated in the cover-up. At 10 A.M. on May 17, 1973, Senator Ervin called the Committee to order in the Caucus Room of the Old Senate Office Building. The opening of the hearings attracted extensive media coverage. For the first two weeks all three networks—ABC, CBS, and NBC—broadcasted the hearings. After that, the networks rotated coverage with one channel covering the hearings and the other two channels returning to their regular programs.

In his opening statement, Ervin said that the hearings began "in an atmosphere of the utmost gravity" but emphasized that the hearings were neither prosecutorial nor judicial. The objective was "investigative and informative." Baker then remarked that "This is not in any way a partisan undertaking, but, rather it is a bipartisan search for the unvarnished truth." In turn, the other members of the Committee presented short opening statements echoing similar sentiments.

For weeks prior to the May 17 hearing, Dash and his staff had interviewed those who had taken part in the break-in and cover-up. The order of appearance was intended to build a foundation of information and establish a timeline of events. On the second day of hearings, Nixon's nominee for Attorney General, Secretary of Defense Elliot Richardson, promised to immediately appoint Harvard law professor Archibald Cox as Special Prosecutor upon confirmation. Six days later, the Senate confirmed the nomination of Elliot Richardson for Attorney General by a vote of 82–3.

During the hearings, Liddy's secretary, Sally J. Harmony, told of creating stationery with George McGovern's letterhead and typing transcripts of documents and telephone tapes from the Democratic National Committee. Herbert L. Porter, the director of scheduling for the reelection campaign, confessed to having committed perjury before the grand jury and at the trial of the burglars. On June 14, 1973, Jeb Stuart Magruder, who initially had headed up the reelection efforts, confirmed that Mitchell had approved Liddy's espionage plan. Magruder also told of the participation of Dean, Mitchell, and Haldeman in the cover-up and of his perjury before the grand jury and at the trial of the burglars.

The witness who might implicate the President in the cover-up was John Dean, the President's lawyer. Known only to Ervin and Dash, Dean had held a series of meetings during a six-week period. On June 25, Dean took the witness oath and admitted obstructing justice and assisting someone to commit perjury, adding "that when the facts come out I hope the President is forgiven." In an unemotional steady voice, Dean then read for five hours his prepared statement of 245 pages. He opened: "the Watergate matter was an inevitable outgrowth of . . . an insatiable appetite for political intelligence . . . regardless of the law." Dean described at length the involvement in the cover-up of Mitchell, Haldeman, and Ehrlichman. Dean also discussed the 15 meetings he had had with Nixon in late February to late March, 1973. After the March 23 meeting, Dean testified that he realized Nixon knew of, and planned to continue, the cover-up and obstruction of justice.

After his long prepared statement with charges against the President, Dean spent the next four days answering questions from committee members and majority and minority counsel. Although he had leveled charges against the President, Dean had no documentary proof. Baker framed the situation succinctly, "What did the President know and when did he know it?"

On July 10, 1973, John N. Mitchell testified before the Committee. He had managed Nixon's 1968 campaign and served as Attorney General. Often Mitchell's answers were contemptuous and disagreed with the testimonies of earlier witnesses. At one point he justified his June 1972 attitude: "I still believe that the most important thing to this country was the reelection of Richard Nixon. And I was not to countenance anything that would stand in the way of that re-election."

THE SECRET TAPES

The testimony of the next witness, Alexander P. Butterfield, fundamentally altered the entire Watergate investigation. From January 21, 1969 to March 14, 1973, Butterfield had served as a deputy assistant to the President. Butterfield revealed the existence of voice-activated recording systems in the Oval Office, in the President's office in the Executive Office building, and in the Cabinet Room. Taping devices also operated on the telephones in the Oval Office, the President's office in the old Executive Office building, the Lincoln sitting room in the family residence, and the President's desk at Camp David. Butterfield had the responsibility for storage of the tapes. Only Nixon, Haldeman, and Haldeman's assistant Larry Higby, and the Secret Service knew of the system.

Knowledge of the tapes aroused immediate attention. They could answer questions about contradictory testimonies. Most importantly, the tapes could answer Baker's question: "What did the President know, and when did he know it?" The next day Ervin wrote: "Dear Mr. President: Today the Select Committee on Presidential Campaign Activities met and unanimously voted that I request you provide the Committee with all relevant documents and tapes. . . ." Nixon replied six days later and denied the request. After Ervin read Nixon's letter, the Committee voted unanimously to issue two subpoenas to obtain the tapes and documents.

The testimonies of Haldeman and Ehrlichman were anticlimactic. Existence of the taping system and the struggle to obtain the tapes replaced the Committee hearings as the focus of the Watergate investigation. The Special Prosecutor and Judge Sirica also requested Nixon to release the tapes.

Events in the fall of 1973 increased public anxiety. On October 10, Vice President Spiro T. Agnew resigned as part of a plea bargain for federal income tax evasion. Ten days later, Nixon offered a compromise. Rather than transfer tapes to Judge Sirica, he would summarize the subpoenaed tapes and have Senator John Stennis (D-MS) listen to the tapes and authenticate the accuracy. Special Prosecutor Cox rejected Nixon's plan, which precipitated the incident that would become known as the Saturday Night Massacre. The President then ordered Attorney General Richardson to fire Cox. Richardson refused, resigned, and reminded Nixon that he had given the Special Prosecutor absolute authority in all decisions. Deputy Attorney General William Ruckelshaus also refused to fire Cox and resigned. Solicitor General Robert Bork carried out Nixon's order and dismissed Cox. The FBI sealed the office of the Special Prosecutor.

The public outcry forced Nixon to have the acting Attorney General appoint a new Special Prosecutor. House Democratic leaders started to consider impeachment charges based on abuse of power. Meanwhile, on October 30, former Attorney General Kleindienst confessed he committed perjury at his confirmation hearings. Five days later, Senator Edward W. Brooke (R-MA) called for the President to resign. *Time* magazine, which had endorsed Nixon in his three presidential campaigns, published its first-ever editorial urging the President to resign.

NIXON RESIGNS

In mid-November 1973, the White House counselor informed Sirica that the subpoenaed tape of June 20, 1972, had an eighteen-and-a-half-minute buzz tone but no conversation. Other tapes had short blank gaps. In his January 1974 State of the Union Address, the President promised to cooperate with the U.S. House Committee on the Judiciary. On February 6, the House voted 410–4 to authorize the Judiciary Committee to subpoena any person, any document, and any tape it needed in its investigation. Committee Chairman Peter Rodino (D-NJ) directed the staff to gather information from other congressional committees, grand jury proceedings, and available White House records. After a month, the President's lawyer, James D. St. Clair informed the Judiciary Committee that Nixon would refuse further requests. Soon thereafter James L. Buckley, the Conservative Party Senator from New York, declared that "Richard Nixon must resign as President."

On April 11, 1974, by a vote of 33–3, the Judiciary Committee subpoenaed 42 tapes it earlier had requested. This was the first time any House Committee ever had subpoenaed a president. Nixon explained his response to the subpoena on a national television and radio address on April 30. Rather than send the tapes, the President would send the Judiciary Committee transcripts of the tapes. On camera, he pointed to a pile of notebooks on a table. "Everything that is relevant is included," he proclaimed. Nixon's strategy proved disastrous. The transcripts revealed the President's foul language, contained vital gaps of knowledge, and revealed his involvement in obstruction of justice. The Special Prosecutor and his staff found the manuscripts unreliable after comparing them with eight tapes in their possession. After that, Nixon responded that he would reject any further subpoenas.

On July 2, 1974, Rodino opened public hearings that included testimony from Butterfield, Dean, and Mitchell. Three weeks later, on July 24, approximately 40 million Americans watched television at 7:45 P.M., when the Judiciary Committee began formal debate on impeachment. Three days later, the Committee adopted impeachment Article 1 (obstruction of justice) by a vote of 27–11 with six Republicans voting with the majority. Article 2 (abuse of power) was adopted by a 28–10 margin, and Article 3 (contempt of Congress) was adopted by a 21–17 margin. Two proposed Articles dealing with the secret bombing of Cambodia and tax violations were rejected. If accepted by the full House, the Articles mandated impeachment and Senate trial and possible removal from office.

Earlier in the day that Rodino opened formal impeachment debate, the Supreme Court announced its unanimous decision that Nixon must turn over 64 subpoenaed tapes. The President complied on August 5 with the "smoking gun tape" from June 23, 1972, that recorded Nixon obstructing justice and abusing power. Within 24 hours, every Republican member of the Judiciary Committee announced publicly that he favored impeachment. On August 9, Nixon became the only president to resign. Thirteen days later, the full House accepted the impeachment report by a vote of 412–3.

A month after Nixon left office, President Gerald Ford pardoned his predecessor for all crimes he "committed or may have committed" as president. Ford's decision was highly controversial, generating additional congressional hearings but effectively bringing an end to two years of investigations. Nevertheless, 40 years later, the legacy of Watergate continues to affect how the three branches of government relate to one another, how the press covers politics, and how the public perceives its leaders.

◆ ◆ ◆ ◆ ◆

51. In Watergate's Shadow: The Iran-Contra Scandal

by Ross Cheit

On November 3, 1986, the day before the U.S. midterm elections, a Lebanese magazine reported that the United States was secretly selling weapons to Iran in exchange for the release of hostages. At the time, President Ronald Reagan was nearing the final two years of his Presidency and, although the Democrats took control of the Senate for the first time in six years (and already controlled the House), Reagan remained an extremely popular president. But what became known as the Iran-Contra scandal challenged Reagan's presidency like never before, strained his relationship with Congress, and resulted in dramatic Watergate-like hearings.

The allegations of arms sales to Iran were shocking because Iran had been designated a terrorist state in 1984. Selling arms to Iran was not against the law, but it was contrary to a stated U.S. policy against negotiating with hostage takers. The President instructed Attorney General Edwin Meese to investigate the matter. At a news conference in November 1986, Meese informed the public that he had uncovered a "diversion" scheme whereby the profits from secret arms sales to Iran were used to support the Contras, rebels against the Soviet-leaning Sandinista government in Nicaragua. President Reagan then announced that his National Security Adviser, Adm. John Poindexter, and a member of his staff, Lt. Col. Oliver North, USMC, had "left their posts."[1] The revelations about clandestine support for the Contras did not have as strong an impact on the public because of widespread hatred of Iran in the aftermath of the 1979 U.S. Embassy hostage crisis. By contrast, Nicaragua was not well known to the public, and many in Congress supported the cause of the Contras. Nevertheless, the "diversion" of funds to help the Contras was designed to circumvent Congress, which had placed specific restrictions on aid to the Contras shortly after a cover story in *Newsweek* revealed "America's Secret War" in Nicaragua.[2] The "diversion" was in clear violation of the spirit, and likely the letter, of the Boland Amendment, named for its sponsor, Representative Edward Boland (D-MA).

These covert operations—both the arms-for-hostages effort in Iran and the subsequent diversion of funds to the Contras in Nicaragua—were not conducted by the CIA. Rather, they were run by a relatively low-ranking White House staffer, Lieutenant Colonel North, who worked in the National Security Council (NSC). The NSC had no statutory authority to conduct such operations, and it had never before acted as an operational organization. Lacking the infrastructure to carry out such actions, virtually all of the operations were conducted by private parties—some of whom were later referred to as privateers. Foreign governments also made secret "donations" to help fund these operations. The existence of what appeared to be a secret foreign policy that bypassed Congress and the State Department created what many considered a constitutional crisis.

Following the revelations about the "diversion," President Reagan appointed John Tower, a former Republican Senator from Texas, to investigate these matters in more detail. After initially denying reports that the United States had sold arms to Iran or negotiated for hostages, President Reagan eventually confirmed the arms-for-hostages deal in an address to the nation in March 1987. His popularity dropped significantly in the wake of these revelations, but it rebounded before his term ended.

CONGRESS INVESTIGATES

There was considerable interest in Congress in investigating both aspects of the scandal. Numerous committees could claim jurisdiction over at least some aspect of the matter. The top leaders in the Senate, Robert Byrd (D-WV) and Robert Dole (R-KS), announced a month before the 100th Congress convened in January 1987 that they intended to appoint a select committee to investigate the Iran-Contra matter. Byrd named six senators to the committee; Dole named five. Byrd also selected Daniel Inouye (D-HI) to chair the committee. Inouye, a decorated war veteran with a no-nonsense demeanor, was widely respected in the Senate.

Inouye then made the remarkable decision to appoint Warren Rudman (R-NH) as vice chair. Senate committees do not generally have a vice chair, and the ranking minority member generally does not have a leadership role in Senate committees. Rudman, a Korean War veteran, had a reputation for independence and candor. Inouye's decision signaled to the Republicans on the committee that "they would be full partners."[3] To others, it signaled that the committee would be bipartisan—or at least not highly partisan. One structural feature that helped promote this ethic was a "unitary" staff for the entire committee. Inouye's experience on the Watergate committee told him that having a staff divided by party lines fostered polarization.

The House committee had 15 members: 9 Democrats and 6 Republicans. The committee was chaired by Representative Lee Hamilton (D-IN). Hamilton, elected to the House in 1965, had made his reputation as an expert on foreign policy, and he had a measured approach that was straightforward and courteous. Many observers thought Hamilton conveyed the same sense of fairness and seriousness as Inouye. Representative Dante Fascell (D-FL) was the vice chair, although that meant very little on the House committee. The ranking minority member was Representative Richard "Dick" Cheney (R-WY). Elected to the House in 1978, Cheney also had considerable experience with foreign policy, and he would eventually take the lead in presenting the minority view on Iran-Contra. Cheney would leave the House in 1989 when he was appointed Secretary of Defense.

There was no joint agreement about exactly what the two committees would investigate. The differing names of the committees formed in each chamber suggested one difference. The Senate created the Select Committee on Secret Military Assistance to Iran and the Nicaraguan Opposition. The House created the Select Committee to Investigate Covert Arms Transactions with Iran. There was apparently some ambivalence about the extent to which this inquiry was about supporting the Contras in Nicaragua. One later criticism of the congressional investigation of Iran-Contra was that the committee scarcely reflected the strongest opposition to Reagan's policy toward the Contras. Seven of the 11 Senate members, for instance, had voted to continue armed support for the Contras. The House committee included one outspoken critic of the Reagan Administration: Edward Boland, the Massachusetts Democrat who sponsored the original restriction on aid to the Contras.

The committees quickly agreed on a timetable that was intended to prevent the hearings from overshadowing the fall elections. They agreed to finish their hearings by August 1987 and issue a report by the end of October. Critics would later argue that this decision unduly limited the quality and scope of the inquiry, but the decision could also be seen as bipartisan since it was apparently aimed at preventing the hearings from becoming embroiled in the 1988 elections.

The Senate select committee played the dominant role between the chambers. The leadership of the Senate select committee reportedly agreed "from the outset," according to later reports, that "specific evidence of a Presidential 'act of commission' would be necessary before Reagan himself would become a target."[4] In other words, they adopted the "smoking gun" frame that came to characterize Watergate. If there were no smoking gun, the committee would not go after the President. Watergate had resulted in the departure of a president only 13 years earlier. That fact was later cited as one of the primary reasons why impeachment proceedings were never seriously considered in connection with the Iran-Contra scandal. Many thought that the country did not have the appetite for another impeachment drama. But the scandal did precipitate significant Watergate-like hearings.

TELEVISED HEARINGS

On March 18, 1987, the Senate and House select committees announced an agreement to hold televised joint hearings. Senators Cohen and Mitchell would later describe the decision as "virtually unprecedented."[5] This decision was also informed by Watergate, where separate House and Senate hearings added six to eight months to the process. Special rules were crafted in an attempt to prevent each witness from being subjected to questioning by as many as 26 members of Congress, plus lawyers for both committees. Arthur Liman, the lead counsel for the Senate select committee, and John Nields, his counterpart on the House select committee, became major players in the hearings.

The hearings involved a combination of high drama and mind-numbing details about the intricacies of financing covert operations. In many ways, Oliver North, who was on loan to the NSC from the Marines, came to define the hearings. He testified in uniform and presented an earnest but unapologetic image that many Americans found compelling. In the court of public opinion, the members of the committee did not fare as well. The hearings ended on August 6, and the *Report of the Congressional Committees Investigating the Iran-Contra Affair*[6] was submitted to Congress on November 18. In 10 months, the congressional committees had examined more than 1 million pages of documents and interviewed or taken depositions from more than 500 witnesses.

If bipartisanship marked at least some aspects of the hearings, it was much less apparent in the final report. The joint committee issued a 430-page report, along with a 150-page Minority Report that was signed by all of the House Republicans. Only three Republicans signed the report of the full joint committee, making it modestly bipartisan. The report concluded that the "common ingredients of the Iran and Contra policies were secrecy, deception, and disdain for law." The committee also concluded that the scandal did not result from "deficiencies in existing law or in our system."[7] They noted that the record concerning the involvement of President Reagan on these matters was "incomplete," but the President was nevertheless "ultimately responsible" for the events. The Minority Report rejected the notion that there had been a constitutional crisis or even a systematic disrespect for the law. It criticized "the *'j'accuse'* atmosphere with which witnesses were confronted" and the use of "witnesses as objects for lecturing the cameras."[8]

THE INDEPENDENT COUNSEL

A week after disclosing the existence of the "diversion," Attorney General Meese requested the appointment of an independent prosecutor under the provisions of the Ethics in Government Act, a post-Watergate statute intended to address the inherent conflict with Executive Branch prosecutors investigating allegations of high-level wrongdoing in the Executive Branch. A three-judge panel selected Lawrence Walsh, a former judge and deputy attorney general in the Eisenhower Administration, later that month to be the independent counsel.

Walsh clashed almost immediately with the joint congressional committee over conferring "use" immunity on witnesses. Use immunity provides the legal assurance that the testimony before Congress would not be used against the witness in a subsequent criminal proceeding. Without such immunity, Congress could not compel testimony from witnesses who might be subject to criminal charges. Walsh did not want anyone immunized, particularly North and his immediate superior at the NSC, John Poindexter. Nevertheless, the joint committee eventually offered to use immunity to 21 witnesses, including Poindexter and North. North was later convicted in a criminal trial, but the conviction was overturned on appeal for precisely the reason that worried Walsh in the first place: the appellate court decided that witnesses in the case against North might have been influenced by his "immunized" testimony before Congress.[9] That result highlighted the trade-off between holding high-profile congressional hearings in the wake of a political scandal when criminal changes were still being pursued.

Walsh's investigation lasted six years and cost $46 million. He charged 14 people with criminal offenses, "11 of whom were convicted after trial or plea agreements."[10] But the criminal cases against North and Poindexter were undone by the appellate decision. President George H.W. Bush also issued a preemptive pardon to Caspar Weinberger, the former Secretary of Defense, who was about to go to trial along with five others. Some were cheered by the pardons, others credited Walsh for having "secured sufficient evidence to convict principal offenders."[11] The independent counsel provisions in the Ethics in Government Act would eventually expire with bipartisan support after many Democrats came to see Kenneth Starr in the Monica Lewinsky investigation in much the same light that many Republicans viewed Lawrence Walsh in the Iran-Contra affair.

CONGRESS AND FOREIGN POLICY

The Iran-Contra scandal was part of a larger conflict between the Executive and Legislative Branches over foreign policy in general, and covert activities in particular. That conflict was expressed in the War Powers Resolution of 1973 (see "Congress Takes a Stand: The 1973 War Powers Resolution," Chapter 41), enacted over President Nixon's veto and intended to prevent future Vietnams. But the act does not speak to covert wars, and presidents, including Nixon, have claimed it is unconstitutional and, therefore, not binding. That expansive view of executive power in foreign affairs was expressed by many witnesses in the Iran-Contra hearings. Louis Fisher described the Iran-Contra hearings as a "constitutional drama" that helped to demonstrate why foreign policy "must be carried out with funds appropriated by Congress."[12] An alternative view is that the hearings demonstrated how certain circles within the Reagan Administration viewed Congress with disregard and even disdain.

The congressional inquiry and the Walsh investigation focused on possible wrongdoing by Executive Branch officials, but the "fact-intensive, personality-oriented nature of the hearings" left larger institutional issues unexamined.[13] One criticism of the hearings was that they did not engage questions about the extent to which Congress itself was complicit, by "barely [paying] attention to their responsibility for 'oversight.'"[14] The Minority Report emphasized the problem of inconsistent congressional policy toward the Contras and the problem of congressional leaks, which was North's famous justification for lying to Congress: it was lies versus lives.

There was a shared sentiment on all sides of the Iran-Contra hearings that Congress and the President needed to figure out how to work together better. Yet, the select committee did not offer any specific recommendations to make that happen. A quarter of a century later, Congress is still struggling to play a meaningful role in overseeing foreign policy, particularly covert actions. Some commentators have concluded that "only a structural solution aimed at revitalizing both Congress and the court" can fully redress the "constitutional imbalance in national security decision-making that the Iran-Contra affair has exposed."[15]

◆ ◆ ◆ ◆ ◆

52. Political Warfare on the Potomac: The Lewinsky Scandal and Clinton Impeachment

by Kirk Victor

On December 19, 1998, Senate Majority Leader Trent Lott (R-MS) watched as the House of Representatives voted, almost entirely along party lines, to impeach President Bill Clinton for perjury and obstruction of justice stemming from an affair he had with a White House intern. At that moment, Lott understood that his every action would suddenly be the focus of intense scrutiny and second-guessing. Nothing less than the reputation of the Senate as an institution was at stake as it proceeded to conduct a trial of the President.

Lott, a Mississippi Republican who was far more pragmatic as a leader than the media portrayed, quickly sized up the situation and began to work on a game plan. It was not the way he wanted to spend his Christmas holidays, but he had no choice. Lott knew the stakes were profound for the governing institutions involved, and for the nation at large. The trial had to be conducted with solemnity and could not come off as just the latest chapter in Washington's endless partisan warfare.

"As we approached Clinton's trial, I believed that the honor of Congress was at stake: the power of the presidency was threatened, and the reputation of the Senate could be won or lost during this last act of the impeachment melodrama," Lott wrote in his autobiography, *Herding Cats*. "I also quickly accepted the fact that as Senate majority leader, I was the man who needed to prove that the system still worked."[1]

The bespectacled 57-year-old leader with never a hair out of place wrote that he "had hoped against hope that the House would find a way to stop this runaway train." But House Republicans, driven by partisan fury and righteous indignation, were determined to pursue the political equivalent of the nuclear bomb—impeachment—rather than seek a censure resolution, which would have signaled tough condemnation of Clinton's conduct, and probably would have received bipartisan support.[2]

So, for only the second time in history, senators would sit as the jury in an impeachment trial of a president. In the earlier case, shortly after the Civil War, Andrew Johnson was impeached in a battle with Congress over presidential powers involving personnel decisions. He was acquitted in 1868 when the Senate fell a single vote short of the two-thirds margin required to convict him and remove him from office.

Lott knew that the odds of getting two-thirds of the Senate to vote to convict Clinton—and throw him out of office—were very long. Clinton's defenders were adamant that the President's wrongdoing did not come close to the standard set by the Constitution for impeachment and removal from office: "treason, bribery or other high crimes and misdemeanors."

The Majority Leader figured there simply was no way to get 67 votes when 45 of the 100 senators were Democrats, who, along with a handful of Republican moderates, were not likely to endorse what they saw as this draconian step for Clinton's personal moral failings. "The Republican senators simply didn't have the two-thirds majority necessary to convict Clinton and remove him from office," Lott wrote. "And we would never have them."[3]

FIERCE POLITICAL WARFARE

So how had the country reached this point at which the President had been impeached and the Senate would have to develop rules to conduct a trial?

Impeachment really was the culmination of fierce political warfare that had erupted repeatedly in Washington in the 1990s. The battle lines between the White House and House Republicans were drawn early on in the Clinton presidency. When Republicans grabbed control of the House in 1994 for the first time in 40 years, their animus toward the President was a key—but not the sole—driver of their actions. Their moves also stemmed from a pent-up desire of GOP lawmakers to flex their muscles after having been consigned to the political wilderness of the minority for four decades. Since Republicans also won control of the Senate in 1994, they were well positioned to drive the agenda.

Having nationalized the 1994 midterm elections by running on the Contract with America—a campaign blueprint that called for sweeping policy changes from welfare reform and tax cuts to tort reform and term limits—the House Republicans chose the hard-charging, take-no-prisoners Newt Gingrich (R-GA) as Speaker of the House. Gingrich was determined to make Congress the center of gravity in the federal government.

From the time they took the committee gavels, the House Republicans put Clinton on the defensive. Congressional investigations were the order of the day, as the relationship between the two branches deteriorated. Republicans sought independent counsels to look into various allegations against four cabinet members—Secretary of Housing and Urban Development Henry Cisneros, Interior Secretary Bruce Babbitt, Labor Secretary Alexis Herman, and Commerce Secretary Ron Brown—as well as AmeriCorps director Eli Segal.[4]

Indeed, the locus of power seemed to shift to Capitol Hill. Just a few months after the GOP had taken control, in a prime-time news conference in April 1995, Clinton was reduced to pleading the continuing relevance of the presidency. "The Constitution gives me relevance. The power of our ideas gives me relevance," he said. "The record we have built up over the last two years and the things we're trying to do to implement it give it relevance. The President is relevant here, especially an activist President."

That Clinton had to declare to the nation that he was still an important player underscored how far the Executive Branch had slipped in a short period, and how much Congress was driving policy debates. Of course, such shifts in power are not uncommon, and in a few short years, in the aftermath of the 9/11 attacks, complaints about a dominant Executive Branch would resound through the Capitol.

During that news conference in 1995, Clinton also held out an olive branch to his GOP critics. "I am willing to work with the Republicans," he said. "The question is, are they willing to work with me?"

But Republicans were determined to pursue allegations of wrongdoing in the Executive Branch, especially by Clinton. Given their newly gained power, they were also well positioned to conduct investigations. And Clinton, by his reckless, indefensible behavior with White House intern Monica Lewinsky, gave Republicans plenty of ammunition.

Not even the President's staunchest allies were willing to defend Clinton's conduct and the lies he told his wife, his closest colleagues, his cabinet members, and the American public. On January 26, 1998, a week after the allegations of impropriety had surfaced, Clinton faced reporters and cameras and vehemently denied a relationship in a clip that would be replayed repeatedly for the rest of the year. "I did not have sexual relations with that woman, Miss Lewinsky. I never told anybody to lie, not a single time. Never. These allegations are false, and I need to go back to work for the American people."

AGGRESSIVE INDEPENDENT COUNSEL

Even as Clinton stonewalled, a determined Independent Counsel, Kenneth W. Starr, was aggressively investigating various allegations about the President. He had begun by scouring records and looking into alleged wrongdoing in a failed land deal in which the Clintons had invested before he was elected president in 1992. That investigation into what was known as Whitewater later was broadened when Starr received an expanded mandate to examine other aspects of Clinton's past, including allegations of sexual misconduct. Ultimately, the tenacious Starr and his zealous staff uncovered lurid details of Clinton's affair with Lewinsky and, given Clinton's denial under oath that he had had a sexual relationship with her, they believed they had a case for impeachment that they took to the House.

Clinton—faced with the knowledge that Starr had incontrovertible evidence that he had had the affair—reversed course after months of denying such a sexual relationship. In August 1998, he admitted publicly that he had "a relationship with Miss Lewinsky that was not appropriate. In fact, it was wrong. It constituted a critical lapse in judgment and a personal failure on my part for which I am solely and completely responsible." Clinton acknowledged that "my public comments and my silence about this matter gave a false impression. I misled people, including even my wife. I deeply regret that."

At the same time, Clinton could barely conceal his contempt for the investigation in general, and specifically for Kenneth Starr. "I had real and serious concerns about an independent counsel investigation that began with private business dealings 20 years ago, dealings I might add about which an independent federal agency found no evidence of any wrongdoing by me or my wife over two years ago," he said in August 1998. "The independent counsel investigation moved on to my staff and friends, then into my private life. . . . This has gone on too long, cost too much and hurt too many innocent people."

"Even presidents have private lives," he continued. "It is time to stop the pursuit of personal destruction and the prying into private lives and get on with our national life."

On September 9, 1998, shortly after that speech, Starr issued his report— a 453-page document replete with graphic, lurid details of the President's sexual relationship with Lewinsky in the White House. Starr alleged 11 impeachable offenses—from lying under oath in a deposition in a case in which a former Arkansas state employee (Paula Corbin Jones) charged him with sexual harassment, to lying under oath to a grand jury about his sexual relationship with Lewinsky, to obstructing justice and witness tampering.

In a stunning move, the House voted overwhelmingly to release the report to the public even before Clinton or his lawyers or the lawmakers themselves had read the document. Millions of citizens read it on the Internet. If those in the House who favored impeachment saw it as a way to poison feelings toward Clinton and force the Senate to vote to convict him, they badly miscalculated. In fact, polls showed that increasing numbers of citizens saw Starr, his report and Republican lawmakers as pursuing a partisan agenda. The report was seen by critics as more of a political document than a reasoned legal treatise that set out the basis for impeachment.

Starr defended the report as providing details that countered Clinton's denial of "sexual relations" as the President parsed words over the definition of that phrase, even as he admitted an inappropriate relationship. And Starr wrote that the charges—perjury and obstruction of justice—"are profoundly serious matters," and that when those acts "are committed by the President of the United States, we believe those acts 'may constitute grounds for impeachment.'"

When Democrats on the House Judiciary Committee, during the impeachment hearing, lashed out at Starr for, among other things, performing as "a federally paid sex policeman," Starr responded that "perjury is an extraordinarily serious business—it is insidious."

Democrats were quick to contrast the "tawdry, salacious" report issued by Starr with the balanced, even dry impeachment referral of Leon Jaworski, the special prosecutor in the Watergate scandal that eventually led to President Richard Nixon's resignation in 1974. Clinton, whose contempt for Starr was palpable, picked up on that theme and argued in his autobiography, *My Life,* that the special prosecutor had stepped beyond his authority and had usurped the power of Congress in his determination to press the case for impeachment.

"The independent counsel was supposed to report his findings to Congress if he found 'substantial and credible' evidence to support an impeachment; Congress was supposed to decide whether there were grounds for impeachment," wrote Clinton, who noted that Jaworski's report was never made public. "In Starr's report, the word 'sex' appeared more than 500 times; Whitewater was mentioned twice. He and his allies thought they could wash away all their sins over the last four years in my dirty laundry."

The report's salacious details of Clinton's sexual behavior with Lewinsky made plenty of folks, on both sides of the aisle, uncomfortable. "I think Starr could have toned down his report substantially and still made his points," then-Senator Arlen Specter (R-PA) wrote in his book, *Passion for Truth.* "More important I think the report should not have been released publicly the way it was."

MOUNTING A DEFENSE

Meanwhile, the President's legal team wasted no time in portraying the Starr Report as falling far short of the standard for impeachment as set out in the Constitution. "The referral is so loaded with irrelevant and unnecessary graphic and salacious allegations that only one conclusion is possible: Its principal purpose is to damage the president," the lawyers wrote. The details really constitute "part of a hit and run smear campaign, and their inclusion says volumes about [Starr's] tactics and objectives."

The majority of the public, wearying of this battle, sided with Clinton's defenders. Gingrich had tried to exploit the allegations against Clinton to help Republicans win big at the ballot box, but his tactic failed. Republicans actually lost five seats in 1998—the first time the President's party gained seats in a midterm election since 1934. And in the Senate, Republicans failed to pick up any seats, as the status quo prevailed. In the wake of those disappointing election returns, Gingrich stunned everybody by stepping down as Speaker.

Still, the drive toward impeachment continued. Emotions were high as House leaders began the debate even before a new Congress was seated. In two days of debate, the anger on both sides exploded into the open. The refusal to consider a vote on censure was something that could be expected of "Hitler's parliament . . . or Stalin's parliament," Representative Tom Lantos (D-CA) exclaimed. Representative Jerrod Nadler (D-NY) scorned the process as a Republican "coup d'état."

The acrimonious debate culminated in the nearly party-line House votes to impeach Clinton on perjury to a grand jury and obstruction of justice. However, Lott and Senate Democratic Leader Tom Daschle (D-SD) succeeded in their efforts to conduct a more restrained proceeding. The House managers' move to summon Lewinsky to testify on the Senate floor was rebuffed in a 70–30 vote that included nearly half of the Republican senators. Lott writes in his book that he persuaded some of his GOP colleagues to drop the idea of votes on "findings of fact" resolutions that would detail Clinton's wrongdoing, but would not change the ultimate outcome of the trial.

After two days of questioning and speeches by almost every senator, the Upper Chamber voted to acquit Clinton of the perjury article by a 55–45 margin, with all 45 Democrats joined by 10 Republicans. The other article, obstruction of justice, failed on a 50–50 vote, with five Republicans joining every Democrat. The votes were far short of the 67 needed to convict the President.

Clinton's presidency ended two years later, and at a time of relative peace and prosperity, the public gave his performance very high grades—66 percent approval, according to Gallup in January 2001. In fact, throughout the impeachment trial, the public's approval of Clinton did not waver. The President's highest ratings during his eight years in office, according to Gallup, came the very day the House voted to impeach him. Seventy-three percent of the public approved of his performance even as he became the second president in history to be impeached.

Those numbers showed how seriously out of step with the public the House Republicans were in pursuing impeachment, rather than seeking a punishment like censure or reprimand that could have garnered bipartisan support. In the end, it is difficult to determine any real winners of this bloody political battle. The unavoidable conclusion is that Clinton's impeachment damaged the stature of both Congress and the Presidency—a downhill slide from which neither branch has yet fully recovered.

♦ ♦ ♦ ♦ ♦

Notes

CHAPTER 2

1. *National Review*, February 27, 1987, p. 24.

2. Keith Krehbiel, *Information and Legislative Organization* (Ann Arbor: University of Michigan Press, 1991).

3. Christopher J. Deering and Steven S. Smith, *Committees in Congress, 3rd ed.* (Washington, DC: CQ Press, 1997).

4. Richard L. Hall and Kris C. Miler, "Interest Group Subsidies to Legislative Overseers," *Journal of Politics* 70, no. 4 (October 2008): 990–1005.

5. Gary M. Cox and Mathew McCubbins, *Legislative Leviathan* (Berkeley: University of California Press, 1994).

6. R. Douglas Arnold, *The Logic of Congressional Action* (New Haven, CT: Yale University Press, 1992).

7. Steven S. Smith, *Call to Order* (Washington, DC: Brookings Institution, 1989).

8. Bryan W. Marshall, *Rules for War: Procedural Choice in the U.S. House of Representatives* (Burlington, VT: Ashgate, 2005).

9. Ibid.

10. Stanley Bach and Steven S. Smith, *Managing Uncertainty in the U.S. House of Representatives* (Washington, DC: Brookings Institution, 1988).

11. The Senate Committee on Rules and Administration does not set the floor agenda, and instead focuses on campaign finance issues, Senate rule changes, and the internal administrative operations of the chamber.

12. Gregory Koger, *Filibustering: A Political History of Obstruction in the House and Senate* (Chicago: University of Chicago Press, 2010).

13. Barbara Sinclair, *Party Wars* (Norman: University of Oklahoma Press, 2006).

14. Charles Babington, "Hastert Launches a Partisan Policy," *The Washington Post,* November 27, 2004.

15. Barbara Sinclair, *Unorthodox Lawmaking, 4th ed.* (Washington, DC: CQ Press, 2011).

16. Ibid.

CHAPTER 3

1. Hugh Heclo, "Campaigning and Governing: A Conspectus," in *The Permanent Campaign and Its Future,* ed. Norman Ornstein and Thomas Mann (Washington, DC: AEI/Brookings, 2000).

2. Thomas E. Mann and Norman J. Ornstein, *It's Even Worse than It Looks: How the American Political System Collided with the New Politics of Extremism* (New York: Basic Books, 2012).

CHAPTER 4

1. Richard L. Hall and Alan V. Deardorff, "Lobbying as Legislative Subsidy," *American Political Science Review* 100, no. 1 (2006): 69.

2. Lee Drutman and Daniel J. Hopkins, "The Inside View: Using the Enron E-Mail Archive to Understand Corporate Political Attention," *Legislative Studies Quarterly* 38, no. 1 (February 17, 2013): 24. doi:10.1111/lsq.12001. http://doi.wiley.com/10.1111/lsq.12001.

3. Nicholas W. Allard, "Lobbying Is an Honorable Profession: The Right to Petition and the Competition to Be Right," *Stanford Law and Policy Review* 19, no. 1 (2008): 43.

4. Lee Drutman and Bruce E. Cain, "Congressional Staff and the Revolving Door: The Impact of Regulatory Change," *Election Law Journal* 13, no. 1 (March 2014): 27–44.

5. Kenneth M. Goldstein, *Interest Groups, Lobbying, and Participation in America* (New York: Cambridge University Press, 1999). http://books.google.com/books?id=raPgCM53hUsC.

6. Private Interview with the author.

7. Stephen Ansolabehere, John M. de DeFigueiredo, and James M. Snyder, "Why Is There So Little Money in U.S. Politics?" *The Journal of Economic Perspectives* 17, no. 1 (2003): 114. http://www.jstor.org/stable/3216842.

8. President's Advisory Panel on Federal Tax Reform. "Simple, Fair, and Pro-Growth: Proposals to Fix America's Tax System," 2005, p. xi.

9. Interview with the author.

10. Lorelei Kelly, *Congress' Wicked Problem: Seeking Knowledge inside the Information Tsunami* (Washington, DC: New America Foundation, 2012), p. 1.

CHAPTER 5

1. D. B. Hardeman and Donald Bacon, *Rayburn: A Biography* (Austin: Texas Monthly Press, 1987), pp. 375–76.

2. Alen Rich, "Quiet Ceremony Commemorates Anniversary of the Passing of Sam Rayburn," ntxe-news.com, December 17, 2007.

3. Nicol C. Rae, *Southern Democrats* (New York: Oxford University Press, 1994), p. 66.

4. Anthony Champagne, Douglas B. Harris, James W. Riddlesperger Jr., and Garrison Nelson, *The Austin-Boston Connection* (College Station: Texas A&M University Press, 2009), p. 124.

5. Alfred Steinberg, *Sam Rayburn: A Biography* (New York: Hawthorn Books, 1975), pp. 220–22.

6. Anthony Champagne, *Congressman Sam Rayburn* (New Brunswick: Rutgers University Press, 1984), p. 174.

7. Ibid., p. 154.

8. Ibid.

9. "Rayburn Is Dead; Served 17 Years as House Speaker," *New York Times,* November 17, 1961.

CHAPTER 6

1. Ford had been the second-string center of the University of Michigan's 1932 and 1933 national championship football teams. In 1934, he made the first string and was named team captain, but Michigan lost seven of its eight games that year.

CHAPTER 7

1. *Congressional Record,* March 8, 1994.

2. *Washington Post,* November 6, 1980. David Stockman, *The Triumph of Politics,* 1986; John A. Farrell, *Tip O'Neill and the Democratic Century,* 2001.

3. *Newsweek,* November 24, 1980.

4. Wright interview with author, quoted in *Tip O'Neill and the Democratic Century,* p. 547.

5. Stockman, *The Triumph of Politics.*

6. O'Donnell interview with author, quoted in *Tip O'Neill and the Democratic Century,* p. 571.

7. O'Neill press conference transcript, May 13, 1981, O'Neill papers, Boston College, quoted in *Tip O'Neill and the Democratic Century,* p. 572.

8. O'Neill quoted in *Tip O'Neill and the Democratic Century,* p. 573–75.

9. Gingrich interview with author, quoted in *Tip O'Neill and the Democratic Century,* p. 580.

10. Baker interview with author, quoted in *Tip O'Neill and the Democratic Century,* p. 597.

11. *Washington Post,* November 7, 1982.

12. Fred Barnes, "TV News: The Shock Horror Welfare Cut Show," *Policy Review,* Spring 1983.

13. O'Donnell interview with author, quoted in *Tip O'Neill and the Democratic Century,* p. 605

14. Richard Darman, *Who's in Control?,* 1996.

CHAPTER 8

1. Richard E. Cohen, *Rostenkowski: The Pursuit of Power and the End of the Old Politics* (Chicago: Ivan R. Dee Publisher, 1999), p. 136.

2. Ralph Whitehead, "Rusty Counts the House," Chicago, April 1978, p. 114.

3. Cohen, p. 190.

CHAPTER 13

1. Zell Miller, "Richard Russell, Georgia's Senator" in *Dedication and Unveiling of the Statue of Richard Brevard Russell, Jr.* (Washington, DC: United States Government Printing Office, 1997), p. 17.

2. Robert C. Byrd, "Behind the Scenes Leadership: Richard B. Russell, Jr." in *A Guide to the Richard B. Russell, Jr. Collection* (Athens, GA: Richard B. Russell Library for Political Research and Studies, 1997), p. 11.

3. Sally Russell, *Richard B. Russell, A Life of Consequence* (Macon, GA: Mercer University Press, 2011), p. 140.

4. Miller, "Richard Russell, Georgia's Senator," p. 18.

5. Byrd, "Behind the Scenes Leadership," p. 11.

6. Charles E. Campbell, *Senator Richard B. Russell and My Career as a Trial Lawyer* (Macon, GA: Mercer University Press, 2013), pp. 26–27.

7. Ted Stevens, "Richard Russell, A Senator's Senator" in *Dedication and Unveiling of the Statue of Richard Brevard Russell, Jr.* (Washington, DC: United States Government Printing Office, 1997), pp. 14–15.

8. Richard B. Russell Jr., "Talk to Freshmen Members in House of Representatives (Congress)," Washington, DC., March 26, 1953, Speech, Speech/Media Series, Richard B. Russell, Jr. Papers, Richard B. Russell Library for Political Research and Studies, University of Georgia.

9. Campbell, *Senator Richard B. Russell,* p. 27.

10. Hiram L. Fong, interview by Hugh Cates, April 28, 1971, transcript, Richard B. Russell Oral History Collection, Russell Library, pp. 1, 3–4.

11. Carl T. Curtis, interview by Hugh Cates, April 21, 1971, transcript, Russell Oral History Collection, Russell Library, p. 6.

12. Samuel J. Ervin Jr., interview by Hugh Cates, April 28, 1971, transcript, Russell Oral History Collection, Russell Library, p. 1.

13. Clifford P. Hansen, interview by Hugh Cates, April 19, 1971, transcript, Russell Oral History Collection, Russell Library, p. 5.

14. John C. Stennis, interview by Hugh Cates, April 21, 1971, transcript, Russell Oral History Collection, Russell Library, p. 15.

15. Campbell, *Senator Richard B. Russell,* pp. 29–30.

16. Ibid., p. 30.

17. Richard B. Russell Jr., "Coosa Valley Area Planning and Development Commission," Rome, Georgia, July 15, 1964, Speech, Speech/Media Series, Russell Jr. Papers, Russell Library.

18. Russell, *A Life of Consequence,* p. 240.

CHAPTER 16

1. Ernest B. Furgurson, *Hard Right: The Rise of Jesse Helms* (New York: W.W. Norton, 1986), p. 97.

2. Ibid., p. 104; Senator Jesse Helms, *Here's Where I Stand: A Memoir* (New York: Random House, 2005), p. 177.

3. Helms, *Here's Where I Stand,* pp. 67, 94; Furgurson, *Hard Right,* p. 109.

4. Laura Kalman, *Right Star Rising: A New Politics, 1974–1980* (New York: W.W. Norton, 2010), pp. 119–20.

5. Christopher J. Deering, "Principle or Party? Foreign and National Security Policymaking in the Senate," in *The Contentious Senate: Partisanship, Ideology, and the Myth of Cool Judgment,* ed. Colton C. Campbell and Nicol C. Rae (Lanham, MD.: Rowman & Littlefield, 2001), pp. 54–55.

6. Helms, *Here's Where I Stand,* pp. 59, 64.

7. William A. Link, *Righteous Warrior: Jesse Helms and the Rise of Modern Conservatism* (New York: St. Martin's, 2008), p. 388.

8. Ibid., pp. 312–16.

9. Furgurson, *Hard Right*, p. 281.

10. Link, *Righteous Warrior*, pp. 348–63.

11. Ibid., pp. 413–15.

12. James M. McCormick, "Decision Making in the Foreign Affairs and Foreign Relations Committees," in Randall B. Ripley and James M. Lindsay, eds., *Congress Resurgent: Foreign and Defense Policy on Capitol Hill* (Ann Arbor: University of Michigan Press, 1993), pp. 142–43, 129; Link, *Righteous Warrior*, pp. 400–403.

13. Ibid., pp. 433–35.

14. Helms, *Here's Where I Stand*, p. 220.

15. Ibid., p. 210; Link, *Righteous Warrior*, p. 426.

CHAPTER 17

1. Susan Milligan, "A Towering Record, Painstakingly Built," *The Boston Globe*, February 20, 2009.

2. Edward M. Kennedy, Speech to the Democratic National Convention, Denver, Colorado, August 25, 2008.

3. Steven Pearlstein, "Kennedy Saw Health-Care Reform Fail in the '70s," *The Washington Post*, August 28, 2009.

4. Edward M. Kennedy, interview with the author, December 5, 2004.

5. Raymond Hernandez and Patrick D, Healy, "The Evolution of Hillary Clinton, *The New York Times*, July 13, 2005.

6. "HIPAA Background," The University of Chicago HIPAA Program Office, updated February, 2010, http://hipaa.bsd.uchicago.edu/back ground.html.

7. Robert Pear, "Hatch Joins Kennedy to Back a Health Program," *The New York Times*, March 14, 1997.

8. Orrin Hatch, eulogy for Edward M. Kennedy, John F. Kennedy Library and Museum, Boston, Massachusetts, August 28, 2009.

9. Milligan, "A Towering Record, Painstakingly Built."

10. The Team at The Boston Globe, *Last Lion: The Fall and Rise of Ted Kennedy*, ed. Peter S. Canellos (Simon & Schuster, 2009), pp. 145–73.

11. Ronald J. Ostrow, "Police Report Details Kennedy Incident," *Los Angeles Times*, April 13, 1991.

12. Robin Toner, "For Kennedy, No Escaping a Dark Cloud," *The New York Times*, April 17, 1991.

13. Esther Scott, *Keeping a Campaign Promise: George W. Bush and Medicare Prescription Drug Coverage* (John F. Kennedy School of Government, 2007) pp. 1–21.

14. George W. Bush, *Decision Points* (Crown, 2010), p. 304.

15. Susan Milligan, "Fulfilling a Nation's Promise," *The Boston Globe,* August 26, 2009.

16. Stephen J. Glain and Susan Milligan, "Kennedy Vows Fight over GOP Drug Bill," *The Boston Globe,* November 17, 2003.

17. Susan Milligan, "Stunning Return and a Vital Vote," *The Boston Globe,* July 10, 2008.

18. Philip Rucker and Eli Saslow, "Patrick Kennedy Leaves Note for Ted on Gravesite: 'Dad, the Unfinished Business Is Done,'" *The Washington Post,* March 23, 2010.

CHAPTER 18

1. John Tower, *Congressional Record,* June 20, 1984, 7725.

2. Sam Nunn, *Congressional Record,* June 20, 1984, 7745.

CHAPTER 21

1. U.S. Constitution, Article I, Section 8, Clause 3.

2. See *Wickard v. Filburn,* 317 U.S. 111 (1942); *Heart of Atlanta Motel v. U.S.,* 379 U.S. 241, (1964); *Pacific Co. v. Arizona,* 325 U.S. 761 (1945); *Gonzales v. Raich,* 545 U.S. 1 (2005).

3. Michael Downing, *Spring Forward: The Annual Madness of Daylight Saving Time* (Berkeley: Counterpoint Press, 2005).

4. Alexander Abad-Santos, "Daylight Saving Time is America's Greatest Shame," www.theatlanticwire.com/entertainment/2013/11/daylight-saving-time-americas-greatest-shame/71172/.

5. P.L. 65–106, 40 Stat. 450.

6. William P. Borland, Memorial Addresses Delivered in the House of Representatives of the United States, 65th Congress, 3rd Session, March 2, 1919.

7. http://www.indystar.com/article/99999999/NEWS06/101108002/.

8. http://www.greenwichmeantime.com/daylight-saving-time/usa/index-htm.

9. William Willett, *The Waste of Daylight,* http://www.webexhibits.org/daylightsaving/willett/html.

10. For an excellent discussion of "Willett Time," see David Prerau, *Seize the Daylight: The Curious and Contentious Story of Daylight Saving Time* (New York: Thunder's Mouth Press, 2006).

11. Lyric Wallwork Winik, "Daylight-Saving Time," *Parade Magazine*, March 27, 2005.

12. Testimony before the House Committee on Interstate and Foreign Commerce, U.S. House of Representatives, June 2, 1919.

13. Robert Garland, *Ten Years of Daylight Saving from the Pittsburgh Standpoint*, Carnegie Library of Pittsburgh, p. 12, http://www.clpgh.org/exhibit/dst.html.

14. For a humorous, carefully researched account of some of DST's supporters' hyperbolic claims, see Michael Downing, *Spring Forward: The Annual Madness of Daylight Saving Time* (New York: Counterpoint Press, 2005).

15. Garland, *Ten Years of Daylight Saving*, p. 19.

16. Timeline of Farming in the U.S., http://www.pbs.org/wgbh/amex/trouble/timeline/.

17. Donna Vestal, "Daylight Saving Time: The Ultimate Rural Legend?" Harvest Public Media: Cultivating Stories from the Ground Up, http://harvestpublicmedia.org/blog/daylight-saving-time-ultimate-rural-legend#.UpoV4cRDuSp.

18. Indian Country Today Media Network, November 2, 2013, http://indiancountrytodaymedianetwork.com/2013/11/02/clocks-go-back-hour-though-you-still-cant-turn-back-time-152051.

19. Correspondence of J. Henkel Henry of Winchester, VA, to Chairman John J. Esch, Committee on Interstate and Foreign Commerce, June 2, 1919.

20. Pub. L. 66–40, 41 Stat. 280, August 20, 1919.

21. U.S. Senate, Statistics and Lists, https://www.senate.gov/reference/Legislation/Vetoes/vetoCounts.htm.

22. Statement of Mr. Elliot H. Goodwin, Hearing before the Committee on Interstate and Foreign Commerce, June 2, 1919.

23. *Massachusetts State Grange v. Benton*, 272 U.S, 525 (1926).

24. P. L. 89–387, 80 Stat. 107, April 13, 1966.

25. http://www.webexhibits.org/daylightsaving/k.html.

26. Douglas E. Kneeland, "Protests on Daylight Time Persist despite New Federal Law on Uniformity," http:// academics.smcvt.edu/geography/daylight%20savings.htm.

27. Ibid.

28. Marc-Antoine Baudoux, "Golf, BBQ Lobbyists Responsible for Daylight Savings (sic) Time," *Agence France Presse*, March 28, 2013.

29. News Release, October 26, 2001, "Enzi Proposes Halloween Safety for Children," http://enzi.senate.gov; Congressional Record, S 1803, October 30, 2003.

30. National Journal, Congress Daily Report, July 21, 2005.

31. Brian Snyder, "U.S. Lost Almost Half a Billion Dollars Due to Daylight Saving Time," Reuters, http://rt.com/usa/us-lost-almost-half-billion-dollars-due-to-daylight-saving-time-153/.

32. http://www.nist.gov/pml/div688/dst.cfm.

33. http://www.webexhibits.org/daylightsaving/k.html.

34. http://www.dot.gov/regulations/time-act.

CHAPTER 22

1. Ted Morgan, *FDR: A Biography* (New York: Simon & Schuster, 1985), p. 379; Robert A. Caro, *The Years of Lyndon Johnson: Master of the Senate* (New York: Alfred A. Knopf, 2002), p. 55.

2. Frances Perkins, *The Roosevelt I Knew* (New York: Penguin Books), 239.

3. Clapper and Commager quoted in Charles A. Beard, "In Defense of Congress," *Atlantic Monthly* 172 (July 1943): 91–92.

4. Clinton Rossiter, *The American Presidency* (New York: Harcourt Brace, 1960), p. 261.

5. R. W. Apple to Patrick J. Maney, May 27, 1993.

6. Arthur M. Schlesinger Jr., *The Coming of the New Deal* (Boston: Houghton Mifflin Company, 1958), pp. 554–55; William E. Leuchtenburg, *Franklin D. Roosevelt and the New Deal, 1933–1940* (New York: Harper and Row, 1963), footnote 3, p. 327.

CHAPTER 24

1. See GovTrack Statistics and Historical Comparison: Bills by Final Status, https://www.govtrack.us/congress/bills/statistics.

2. See David Garrow, *Protest at Selma: Martin Luther King, Jr., and the Voting Rights Act of 1965* (New Haven, CT: Yale University Press, 1978).

3. Ibid.

4. Ibid.

5. John Lewis and Michael D'Orso, *Walking with the Wind: A Memoir of the Movement* (New York: Simon & Schuster, 1998).

6. Taylor Branch, *Parting the Waters: America in the King Years 1954–63* (New York: Simon & Schuster, 1988).

7. Ibid.

8. Richard E. Neustadt, *Presidential Power and the Modern Presidents: The Politics of Leadership from Roosevelt to Reagan* (New York: Free Press, 1990)

9. See, President Lyndon B. Johnson's Special Message to the Congress: The American Promise March 15, 1965, http://www.lbjlib.utexas.edu/johnson/archives.hom/speeches.hom/650315.asp.

10. Ibid.

11. See 42 U.S.C. § 1973 et seq.

12. Ibid.

13. See Chandler Davidson and Bernard Grofman (eds.), *Quiet Revolution in the South* (Princeton, NJ: Princeton University Press, 1994).

14. Thomas Byrne Edsall and Mary D. Edsall, *Chain Reaction: The Impact of Race, Rights, and Taxes on American Politics* (New York: W.W. Norton & Company, 1992).

15. See Merle Black and Earl Black, *The Rise of the Southern Republicans* (Cambridge, MA: Harvard University Press, 2002).

CHAPTER 25

1. Herman M. Somers and Anne R. Somers, *Medicare and the Hospitals: Issues and Prospects* (Washington, DC: Brookings Institution), 1967.

2. Frank D. Campion, *The AMA and U.S. Health Policy since 1940* (Chicago: Chicago Review Press), 1984; Robert J. Myers, *Medicare. McCahan Foundation Book Series* (Homewood, IL: Richard D. Irwin), 1970.

3. Karen Davis and Cathy Schoen, *Health and the War on Poverty: A Ten-Year Appraisal* (Washington, DC: Brookings Institution Press), 1978; Ronald Andersen, Joanna Lion, and Odin W. Anderson, *Two Decades of Health Services: Social Survey Trends in Use and Expenditure* (Cambridge, MA: Ballinger Publishing Co.), 1976.

4. Theodore R. Marmor, *The Politics of Medicare* (Chicago: Aldine Publishing Co.), 1970.

5. Jonathan Oberlander, *The Political Life of Medicare* (Chicago: University of Chicago Press), 2003.

6. Marilyn Moon, *Medicare: A Policy Primer* (Washington, DC: Urban Institute Press), 2006.

7. Myers, *Medicare.*

8. Michael Gluck and Virginia Reno, *Reflections on Implementing Medicare* (Washington, DC: National Academy of Social Insurance), 2001.

9. Davis and Schoen, *Health and the War on Poverty.*

10. Ronald Andersen, Joanna Kravits, Odin W. Anderson, and Joan Daley, *Expenditures for Personal Health Services: National Trends and Variations, 1953–1970* (Washington, DC: U.S. Department of Health, Education and Welfare), 1973.

CHAPTER 26

1. Full text of the bill, with amendments, can be obtained online: http://www.house.gov/legcoun/Comps/BUDGET.pdf. Some notable amendments include the Balanced Budget and Emergency Deficit Control Act of 1985, the Budget Enforcement Act of 1990, and the Balanced Budget Act of 1997.

2. http://thomas.loc.gov/cgi-bin/query/z?c112:S.365.

3. http://thomas.loc.gov/cgi-bin/bdquery/z?d112:h.r.8.

4. Congressional Budget Office (CBO), *The Budget and Economic Outlook* (various years).

5. Congressional Budget Office (CBO), *The Budget and Economic Outlook* (various years).

6. Author's calculations based on various data from the Congressional Budget Office and the Office of Management and Budget.

7. Peter G. Peterson Foundation, Chart Pack (2014), http://pgpf.org/sites/default/files/sitecore/media%20library/PGPF/Chart-Archive/PGPF-Chart-Pack.pdf.

CHAPTER 28

1. Jonathan Masters, "The Renewing America Interview: Bill Bradley on Leadership and U.S. Tax Reform," Council on Foreign Relations, September 12, 2013.

2. For a detailed chronology of enactment of the Tax Reform Act of 1986, see Jeffrey H. Birnbaum and Alan S. Murray, *Showdown at Gucci Gulch* (New York: Vintage Publishing, 1987).

3. Richard E. Cohen *Rostenkowski: The Pursuit of Power and the End of the Old Politics* (Chicago: Ivan R. Dee, 1999), p. 139.

4. Albert R. Hunt, introduction to *Showdown at Gucci Gulch*, p. xvi.

5. Henry J. Aaron, "Lessons for Tax Reform," in *Do Taxes Matter?*, ed. Joel Slemrod (Cambridge, MA: The MIT Press, 1990), p. 322.

6. Michael J. Graetz, "Tax Reform Unraveling," *Journal of Economic Perspectives*, 21, Winter 2007, p. 69.

CHAPTER 29

1. Senator Alan Simpson, "Let 'Er Rip," Reflections of a Rocky Mountain Senator, Conversations with History, Institute of International Studies, University of California Berkeley, September 17, 1997, http://globetrotter .berkeley.edu/conversations/Simpson/simpson3.html (accessed November 15, 2013).

2. Select Commission on Immigration and Refugee Policy, *U.S. Immigration Policy and the National Interest*, 97th Cong., 2d Sess., Final Report (Comm. Print 1981).

3. Aristide R. Zolberg, *A Nation by Design: Immigration Policy in the Fashioning of America* (Cambridge: Harvard University Press, 2008).

4. Select Commission on Immigration and Refugee Policy, *U.S. Immigration Policy and the National Interest*, 97th Cong., 2d Sess., Final Report (Washington: Comm. Print, 1981).

5. Ira Shapiro, *The Last Great Senate: Courage and Statesmanship in Times of Crisis* (Public Affairs Press, 2012).

6. On Thurmond generally, see Nadine Cahodas, *Strom Thurmond and the Politics of Southern Change* (Macon: Mercer University Press, 1995). On IRCA specifically, see Lawrence H. Fuchs, "The Corpse That Would Not Die: The Immigration Reform and Control Act of 1986," in *Revue europeenne de migrations internationales* 6, no. 1 (L'immigration auz Etats-Unis, 1990): 118; and Harris N. Miller, "The Right Thing to Do: A History of Simpson-Mazzoli," in *Clamor at the Gates: The New American Immigration*, ed. Nathan Glazer (San Francisco: Institute for Contemporary Studies Press, 1985): p. 62.

7. Harris N. Miller, "The Right Thing to Do: A History of Simpson-Mazzoli," in *Clamor at the Gates: The New American Immigration*, ed. Nathan Glazer (San Francisco: Institute for Contemporary Studies Press, 1985): p. 67 and explanatory endnote 10.

8. Lawrence H. Fuchs, "The Corpse That Would Not Die: The Immigration Reform and Control Act of 1986," in *Revue europeenne de migrations internationales* 6, no. 1 (L'immigration auz Etats-Unis, 1990): 115.

9. Among other reasons for the bill's death speculated on by congressional participants and other observers: (1) a decided lack of enthusiasm for the bill by Speaker O'Neill and other Democratic partisans, who feared among other things that passage of the bill might depress Hispanic voter turnout in the 1984 elections, or conversely that a rumored Reagan veto of the bill might divert Latino voters away from the Mondale-Ferraro ticket into the Reagan camp; (2) the likely failure of the bill to include a guest worker

program robust enough to satisfy agricultural interests close to the Reagan White House, or conversely the strong opposition of Judiciary Chairman Peter Rodino (D-NJ) to any temporary worker program at all; and (3) Senator Simpson and others argued that the practice of holding the conference committee in open session, where lobbyists and lawmakers opposed to core provisions of the bill had full access to the proceedings, encouraged time-wasting posturing and other dilatory tactics. See, for example, Ellis Cose, *A Nation of Strangers: Prejudice, Politics, and the Populating of America* (New York: William Morrow and Company, 1992): pp. 175–77.

10. Lawrence H. Fuchs, "The Corpse That Would Not Die: The Immigration Reform and Control Act of 1986," in *Revue europeenne de migrations internationales* 6, no. 1 (L'immigration auz Etats-Unis, 1990): 123.

11. Interviews with lobbyists and congressional staffers involved in the negotiations, who requested anonymity; records on file with junior author.

12. See Rosanna Perotti, "Resolving Policy Conflict: Congress and Immigration Reform," (Doctoral diss., University of Pennsylvania, 1989); and Ellis Cose, *A Nation of Strangers: Prejudice, Politics, and the Populating of America* (New York: William Morrow and Company, 1992), for details of the provisions promoted by Torres, largely at the behest of Latino advocacy groups, which are also documented in the junior author's interview with Albert Jacquez, former Chief of Staff to Representative Esteban Torres, November 14, 2012.

13. Robert Pear, "Washington Talk: Congress; Immigration Bill: How 'Corpse' Came Back to Life," *New York Times,* October 13, 1986, http://www.nytimes.com/1986/10/13/us/washington-talk-congress-immigration-bill-how-corpse-came-back-to-life.html (accessed December 2, 2013). See Fuchs for a brief blow-by-blow account of the developments in the 99th Congress. For more detailed discussions of the bill's passage, see Rosanna Perotti, *Resolving Policy Conflict: Congress and Immigration Reform* (Doctoral diss., University of Pennsylvania, 1989); and Michael C. LeMay, *Anatomy of a Public Policy: The Reform of Contemporary Immigration Law* (Westport, CT: Praeger Press, 1994).

14. See Michael C. LeMay, *Anatomy of a Public Policy: The Reform of Contemporary Immigration Law* (Westport, CT: Praeger Press, 1994) for a more detailed analysis of voting patterns on the Immigration Reform and Control Act of 1986.

15. John W. Kingdon, *Agendas, Alternatives, and Public Policies, 2nd ed.* (New York: Addison Wesley Longman, 1995).

16. See *Mexico-US Migration: A Shared Responsibility*, Carnegie Endowment for International Peace, 2001, and Doris Meissner, Deborah W. Myers,

Demetrious G. Papademetriou, and Michael Fix, *Immigration and America's Future: A New Chapter* (Washington, DC: Migration Policy Institute, 2006).

17. Rachel L. Swarns, "Senate, in Bipartisan Act, Passes an Immigration Bill," *New York Times,* May 26, 2006, http://www.nytimes.com/2006/05/26/washington/26immig.html (accessed December 2, 2013).

18. For a detailed but relatively brief summary of these developments as well as the "State of Play" from 2001 through 2011, see Marc R. Rosenblum, *US Immigration Policy since 9/11: Understanding the Stalemate over Comprehensive Immigration Reform* (Woodrow Wilson International Center for Scholars and Migration Policy Institute, August 2011).

19. "The Grand Collapse," *New York Times,* editorial, June 30, 2007, http://www.nytimes.com/2007/06/30/opinion/30sat1.html (accessed December 2, 2013).

20. Marc R. Rosenblum, "US Immigration Policy since 9/11: Understanding the Stalemate over Comprehensive Immigration Reform," Woodrow Wilson International Center for Scholars and Migration Policy Institute, August 2011. Senators McCain, Sam Brownback (R-KS), Chuck Hagel (R-NE), Lindsey Graham (R-SC), and Mel Martinez (R-FL) are among those whose support for the bill waned.

21. Robert Pear and Jim Rutenberg, "Senators in Bipartisan Deal on Immigration Bill," *New York Times,* May 18, 2007, http://www.nytimes.com/2007/05/18/washington/18immig.html (accessed December 2, 2013). The article quoted then-Senator Barack Obama (D-IL) as "troubled" by the bill's temporary worker provisions, and then-Senator Hilary Clinton (D-NY) as withholding judgment.

22. Advocates for immigrants' rights and business have indicated that they had 58 of 60 votes needed to invoke cloture, but lacking the decisive margin a number of the bill's supporters changed their votes. For insider accounts of the 2006 and 2007 Senate debates, see the *The Senate Speaks* and *Last Best Chance*," documentary films by Shari Robertson and Michael Camerini, in their *How Democracy Works Now* series (Epidoko Pictures, 2010–2013), http://www.howdemocracyworksnow.com (accessed December 2, 2013).

23. Steven Kelman, *Making Public Policy: A Hopeful View of American Government* (New York: Basic Books, 1987): pp. 3–5.

24. For an insider account of O'Neill's actions during this period, see Chris Mathews, *Tip and the Gipper: When Politics Worked* (New York: Simon and Schuster, 2013). For a discussion of the Social Security compromise, see Mathew Dallek, "Bipartisan Reagan-O'Neill Social Security Deal in 1983 Showed It Can Be Done," U.S. News and World Report, April 2009,

http://www.usnews.com/opinion/articles/2009/04/02/bipartisan-rea
gan-oneill-social-security-deal-in-1983-showed-it-can-be-done   (accessed
November 9, 2013). For a detailed account of the 1986 tax reform legisla-
tion, see Jeffrey H. Birnbaum and Alan S. Murray, *Showdown at Gucci Gulch:
Lawmakers, Lobbyists, and the Unlikely Triumph of Tax Reform* (New York:
Vintage Books, 1988).

25. For example, several Latino advocates, including the League of United
Latin American Citizens and the National Council of La Raza, moderated
their opposition and encouraged Representative Torres's efforts to improve
the bill from their perspective. NCLR President Raul Yzaguirre called the
final product, "probably the best immigration legislation possible under current political conditions." Restrictionists, already prepared to swallow hard
to accept a legalization program to obtain employer sanctions, were deeply
opposed to the SAW program. The leading restrictionist group, the Federation for American Immigration Reform, said, "We wanted a Cadillac, we were
promised a Chevy, and we got a wreck," but it too declined to derail the bill.
See Lawrence H. Fuchs, "The Corpse That Would Not Die: The Immigration Reform and Control Act of 1986," in *Revue europeenne de migrations
internationales* 6, no. 1 (L'immigration auz Etats-Unis, 1990): 124–26. See
also Rosanna Perotti, "Resolving Policy Conflict: Congress and Immigration
Reform" (Doctoral diss., University of Pennsylvania, 1989), and the junior
author's interview with Roger Connor, Former Executive Director of the
Federation for American Immigration Reform, February 11, 2013.

26. Ezra Klein, "The 13 Reasons Washington Is Failing," *Washington
Post Wonkblog*, October 7, 2013, http://www.washingtonpost.com/blogs/
wonkblog/wp/2013/10/07/the-13-reasons-washington-is-failing/
(accessed November 14, 2013). As Klein notes: It used to be that politicians
could try and work out deals in private and sell them in public. Now the deals
essentially get worked out in public—which means it's far easier for a delicate
discussion to be crushed as fuzzy reports leak and enraged interest groups
blitz the proceedings.

27. These "macro" factors are discussed in Thomas E. Mann and Norman J.
Ornstein, *It's Even Worse than It Looks: How the American Constitutional System
Collided with the New Politics of Extremism* (New York: Basic Books, 2013).

28. The filibuster threat occurred in 1984, when retiring Senator John
Tower (R-TX) was said to have made a commitment to a Latino lobbyist to
filibuster the conference report if the conference committee had been able to
come to an agreement. See Ellis Cose, *A Nation of Strangers: Prejudice, Politics, and the Populating of America* (New York: William Morrow and Company, 1992): p. 175.

29. In 1984, House Democrats split 138 to 125 against the Immigration Reform and Control Act, while Republicans supported it by a 91–73 margin. In 1986, however, facing a slightly different bill, Republicans opposed the bill 105 to 62, while Democrats supported it by a 168–61 margin. See Lawrence H. Fuchs, "The Corpse That Would not Die: The Immigration Reform and Control Act of 1986," in: *Revue europeenne de migrations internationales* 6, no. 1 (L'immigration auz Etats-Unis, 1990): 124. By contrast, 203 of 230 (92 percent) Republicans supported and 164 of 200 (82 percent) Democrats opposed the 2005 Sensenbrenner bill, per the official House roll call at: http://clerk.house.gov/evs/2005/roll661.xml (accessed November 11, 2013); while 208 of 246 (85 percent) Democrats supported the DREAM Act in 2010, 160 of 168 (95 percent) Republicans opposed the bill. See Scott Wong, "House Sends DREAM Act to Senate," *Politico,* December 8, 2010.

CHAPTER 30

1. Bork labeled as "unprincipled" or otherwise wrong landmark decisions that recognized the right of married couples to purchase contraceptives, prohibited sterilization of criminals, prohibited racially restrictive covenants, and protected the concept of "one man, one vote," just to name a few decisions.

2. According to Harvard constitutional law professor Larry Tribe in his testimony before the Committee, Bork would have been the "first to read 'liberty' (in the Constitution) as though it was exhausted by the rights that the majority expressly conceded to individuals in the Bill of Rights." (p. 257 Matters of Principle)

3. Several national polls indicated that public opinion swung against him during his five days of testimony. (p. 55 Matters of Principle)

4. The Jay Treaty ratified in 1794 was negotiated by the Washington administration to settle outstanding trade issues with Great Britain from the revolutionary period. It was a highly partisan issue between the Federalists and the Jeffersonians.

5. In the summer of 1987, polls by *The New York Times* and the *Los Angeles Times* found that over 60 percent of Americans believed that a nominee's views should be considered by the Senate.

CHAPTER 31

1. The freshmen also attracted many bright, deeply committed conservative staffers to serve in the 104th Congress, most notably future Congressman and vice presidential candidate Paul Ryan (R-WI), who worked for then-Representative Sam Brownback (R-KS).

CHAPTER 32

1. For an overview of the Republican bill and the many political fights that took place over the course of the two-year debate, see Ron Haskins, *Work over Welfare: The Inside Story of the 1996 Welfare Reform Law* (Washington DC: Brookings, 2006).

2. Bureau of Labor Statistics, "Women in the Labor Force: A Databook," *BLS Reports*, Report 1040, February 2013, Washington, DC: U.S. Department of Labor,

3. By contrast, Obama assumed the Presidency at the beginning of the worst recession since the Great Depression. Unemployment was 5.8 percent in 2008, but increased rapidly to 9.3 percent in 2009, the year he assumed office, and remained above 8 percent through 2012. Obama also had to struggle with a federal deficit, which exceeded a record-setting $1 trillion during each of his first four years in office, although the rising deficit was due in part to spending during his administration. Between the stagnant economy and the unprecedented deficit, the environment for bipartisan policy making was not favorable. But neither was the environment for bipartisanship favorable during the more successful Clinton presidency.

4. Gertrude Himmelfarb, *The Idea of Poverty: England in the Early Industrial Age* (New York: Vintage, 1985).

5. Sheldon Danziger, Robert Haveman, and Robert Plotnick, "How Income Transfer Programs Affect Work, Savings, and the Income Distribution: A Critical Review," *Journal of Economic Literature*19 (1981): 975–1028.

6. Charles Murray, *Losing Ground: American Social Policy, 1950–1980* (New York: Basic Books, 1984).

7. Walter I. Trattner, *From Poor Law to Welfare State: A History of Social Welfare in America, 6th ed.* (New York: Free Press, 1989).

8. For 1968 spending, see Vee Burke, *Cash and Noncash Benefits for Persons with Limited Income: Eligibility Rules, Recipient and Expenditure Data, F2000–FY2002*, Order Code RL32233, Washington, DC: Congressional Research Service, November 25, 2003; for 2011 spending, see Congressional Research Service, "Spending for Federal Benefits and Services for People with Low Income, FY2008–FY2011: An Update of Table B-1 from CRS Report R41625, Modified to Remove Programs for Veterans," A Memo to the Senate Budget Committee, October 16, 2012.

9. Jon F. Hale, "The Making of the New Democrats," *Political Science Quarterly* 110, no. 2 (1995): 207–32.

10. Robert Cherry, *Welfare Transformed: Universalizing Family Policies That Work* (New York: Oxford, 2007); Stanley B. Greenberg, *Dispatches from*

the War Room: In the Trenches with Five Extraordinary Leaders (New York: Thomas Dunn, 2009).

11. Jeffrey B. Gayner, "The Contract with America: Implementing New Ideas in the U.S.," Washington, DC: Heritage Foundation, October 12, 1995. The 10 items in the Contract addressed budget balance, crime, welfare reform, family restoration, a child tax credit, national security, income limits on Social Security recipients, job creation and wage enhancement, legal reforms, and term limits.

CHAPTER 33

1. U.S. Government Printing Office, "Public Papers of the Presidents of the United States: William J. Clinton (1997, Book II), Remarks on Signing the Balanced Budget Act of 1997 and the Taxpayer Relief Act of 1997." Last modified August 5, 1997. http://www.gpo.gov/fdsys/pkg/PPP-1997-book2/html/PPP-1997-book2-doc-pg1051.htm (accessed December 3, 2013).

2. John F. Harris and Eric Pianin, "Bipartisanship Reigns at Budget Signing," *Washington Post*. Last modified August 6, 1997. http://www.washingtonpost.com/wp-srv/politics/special/budget/stories/080697.htm (accessed December 3, 2013).

3. Kwame Holman, "Background: The Re-Election of Speaker Gingrich," *PBS News Hour*. Last modified January 7, 1997. http://www.pbs.org/newshour/bb/politics/jan-june97/gingrich_01–07a.html (accessed December 3, 2013).

4. "Gingrich as Speaker: Remembering When," *ABC News*. Last modified September 28, 2007. http://abcnews.go.com/blogs/politics/2007/09/gingrich-as-spe/ (accessed December 3, 2013).

5. June E. O'Neill, "The Economic and Budget Outlook: Fiscal Years 1997–2006," Congressional Budget Office. Last modified May 1996. http://www.cbo.gov/sites/default/files/cbofiles/ftpdocs/47xx/doc4755/entirereport.pdf (accessed December 3, 2013).

6. June E. O'Neill, "The Economic and Budget Outlook: Fiscal Years 1998–2007," Congressional Budget Office. Last modified January 1997. http://www.cbo.gov/sites/default/files/cbofiles/attachments/Eb01–97.pdf (accessed December 3, 2013).

7. June E. O'Neill, "The Economic and Budget Outlook: An Update," Congressional Budget Office. Last modified September 1997. https://www.cbo.gov/sites/default/files/cbofiles/attachments/Eb09–97.pdf (accessed December 3, 2013).

8. Ibid.

9. O'Neill, "The Economic and Budget Outlook: An Update." Congressional Budget Office. Last modified 1997. https://www.cbo.gov/sites/default/files/cbofiles/attachments/Eb09–97.pdf (accessed December 3, 2013).

10. "Historical Budget Data—February 2013," Congressional Budget Office. Last modified February 5, 2013. http://www.cbo.gov/publication/43904 (accessed December 3, 2013).

11. Jerry Gray, "Gingrich Offers an Agenda, but the Christian Coalition Attacks Sharply," *The New York Times*. Last modified March 7, 1997. http://www.nytimes.com/1997/03/07/us/gingrich-offers-an-agenda-but-the-christian-coalition-attacks-sharply.html?src=pm (accessed December 3, 2013).

12. U.S. Senate Budget Committee, "INFORMED BUDGETEER, Special Edition: Year-End Summary & Final Omnibus Scoring." Last modified November 16, 1998. http://www.budget.senate.gov/republican/public/index.cfm/files/serve?File_id=4ac46152–723a-4fd9–8bf1-e11e865db7ea (accessed December 3, 2013).

13. Stephen Slivinski, "How Speaker Newt Gingrich Betrayed the Republican Revolution," United Liberty. Last modified December 14, 2011. http://www.unitedliberty.org/articles/9188-how-speaker-newt-gingrich-betrayed-the-republican-revolution (accessed December 3, 2013).

14. Katherine Q. Seele, "The Speaker Steps Down: The Overview; Facing a Revolt, Gingrich Won't Run for Speaker and Will Quit Congress," *The New York Times*. Last modified November 7, 1998. http://www.nytimes.com/1998/11/07/us/speaker-steps-down-overview-facing-revolt-gingrich-won-t-run-for-speaker-will.html?pagewanted=all&src=pm (accessed December 3, 2013).

15. Richard F. Fenno Jr., "Learning to Govern: An Institutional View of the 104th Congress," The Brookings Institution. Last modified 1997. http://books.google.com/books?id=2R6jBjM3uhsC&pg=PA31&lpg=PA31&dq=speaker+abolished+some+committees+and+subcommittees,+appointed&source=bl&ots=4O5JqoFKuC&sig=e-jWFSvZuLHCGBtEeJZvCdMHdUY&hl=en&sa=X&ei=j6JqUsnOH_av4APG5YCYCQ&ved=0CCkQ6AEwAA#v=onepage&q=speaker%20abolished%20some%20committees%20and%20subcommittees%2C%20appointed&f=false (accessed December 3, 2013).

CHAPTER 34

1. Alison Mitchell, "Daschle Takes Part in Shot as Congress Breaks," *The New York Times*, October 19, 2002.

2. Robert E. Dewhirst and John David Rausch, *Encyclopedia of the United States Congress* (New York: Infobase Publishing, 2009), p. 288.

3. Katharine Q. Seelye, "A Nation Challenged: Capitol Hill; In Congress, 2 Chambers, Incongruent," *The New York Times,* October 19, 2001.

4. Federal Election Commission, "The Federal Election Campaign Laws: A Short History," http://www.fec.gov/info/appfour.htm (accessed December 13, 2013).

5. Marty Meehan, interview with the author, Fall 2010; Susan Trausch, "The Few, the Brave, the Pac-less: Rare Is House Freshman Who Keeps Pledge," *The Boston Globe,* September 13, 1993.

6. Center for Responsive Politics, "Soft Money Backgrounder," http://www.opensecrets.org/parties/softsource.php (accessed December 13, 2013).

7. Robert L. Jackson, "Trial of Former Gore Fund-Raiser Hsia Opens," *Los Angeles Times,* February 8, 2000.

8. Edwin Chen, "Free Speech Will Pay Heavy Price under Campaign Finance Reform, Key Foe Says," *Los Angeles Times,* March 15, 1997.

9. Walter Oleszek, *Congressional Procedures and the Policy Process* (Washington, DC: Sage, 2013), p. 297.

10. House of Representatives Committee on Rules, "About the Committee on Rules—History and Processes," http://rules.house.gov/about (accessed December 13, 2013).

11. Mark Strand, "Discharging Their Duties," Congressional Institute, March 7, 2008.

12. Mitch McConnell, *Congressional Record—Senate,* March 29, 2001.

13. George W. Bush, "Statement on Signing the Bipartisan Campaign Reform Act of 2002," March 27, 2002.

14. *McConnell v. Federal Election Commission,* 540 U.S. 93 (2003).

15. Jeffrey Toobin, "Money Unlimited: How Chief Justice John Roberts Orchestrated the Citizens United Decision," *The New Yorker,* May 21, 2012.

16. *Citizens United v. Federal Election Commission,* 558 U.S. 310 (2010).

17. John McCain, interview with the author, Washington, DC, October, 2013.

18. Center for Responsive Politics, "2012 Presidential Race," http://www.opensecrets.org/pres12/ (accessed December 13, 2013).

19. McCain, interview with the author.

20. Barack Obama, State of the Union Address, Washington, DC, January 27, 2010.

21. Robert Barnes, "Alito's State of the Union Moment," *The Washington Post,* January 28, 2010.

CHAPTER 35

1. As cited in Jack Jennings, "Republicans and Democrats Warily Move toward Agreement on ESEA," *Center on Education Policy Newsletter* 10, no. 3 (Spring 2001).

2. "George Walker Bush Inaugural Address," January 20, 2001. http://odur.let.rug.nl/'usa/P/gwb43/speeches/gwbush1.htm (accessed March 19, 2002).

3. "Reform School: Bush Seeks Compromise on Education Proposals." ABCNews.com (accessed January 23, 2001).

4. As cited in Siobhan Gorman, "The Education of House Republicans," *National Journal* 33 (March 31, 2001): 955.

5. Ibid.

6. John Boehner, "Making the Grade," *National Review Online,* April 6, 2001.

7. Interview with the author, March 11, 2003.

8. See for example, "Blacks v. Teachers; Blacks and Vouchers," *The Economist,* March 10, 2001, p. 1.

9. David Nather, "As Education Bills Head for Floor Votes, Big Ideological Tests Loom in House," *CQ Weekly,* May 19, 2001, p. 1157.

10. For more on business' support of education reform, see Milton Goldberg and Susan Traiman, "Why Business Backs Education Standards," in *Brookings Papers on Education Policy,* ed. Diane Ravitch (Washington, DC: Brookings Institution Press, 2001).

11. A February 10, 2001 poll found that 73 percent of respondents approved of Bush's reform proposals while only 22 percent opposed them, and a poll taken in March found an 80 percent/15 percent split. Newsweek poll conducted between February 8 and 9, 2001, accession number 0378681, question number 5. Harris poll conducted between February 22 and March 3, 2001, accession number 0379989, question number 3. Support for Bush's handling of education had declined somewhat by the summer, but polls continued to show that respondents were supportive by more than a 2–1 margin. Fox News poll conducted between June 6 and 7, 2001, accession number 0383115, question number 9. ABC News poll conducted between September 6 and 9, 2001, accession number 0386555, question number 5. All polls accessed from Roper Center, Public Opinion Online.

12. For a detailed analysis of the provisions of NCLB see: *No Child Left Behind: A Desktop Reference* (Washington DC: U.S. Department of Education, 2002). Available online at www.ed.gov/pubs/edpubs.html. See also

Erik Robelen, "An ESEA Primer," *Education Week*, January 9, 2002; "Major Changes to ESEA in the NCLB Act," Learning First Alliance, www.learningfirst.org; and "A New Federal Role in Education" Center on Education Policy, January 2002, www.ctredpol.org.

13. For detailed analyses of the NCLB from the viewpoint of state implementers, see "State Requirements Under NCLB," Education Commission of the States, January 2003, www.ecs.org; and "NGA Summary of the Timeline Requirements of NCLB," National Governors Association, www.nga.org.

CHAPTER 37

1. *Congressional Record*, March 14, 1947 (Washington, DC: Government Printing Office, 1947), pp. 2064–65.

2. U.S. Congress, First Report of the House Select Committee on Post-War Military Policy Pursuant to H. Res. 465, a Resolution Creation a Select Committee on Post-War Military Policy, *A Single Department of Armed Services* (Washington, DC: US Government Printing Office, 1944), pp. 2–3.

3. Douglas Stuart, Creating the National Security State: A History of the Law That Transformed America (Princeton: Princeton University Press, 2008), p. 94.

4. The Military Affairs and Naval Affairs Committees would combine to become the Senate Armed Services Committee in 1947.

5. U.S. Congress, Report of the Joint Committee on the Investigation of the Pearl Harbor Attack (Washington, DC: Government Printing Office, 1946), 79th Cong., 2d sess., 251–53.

CHAPTER 39

1. Marvin Kalb, *The Road to War: Presidential Commitments Honored and Betrayed* (Washington, DC: Brookings, 2013), p. 83.

2. Lyndon Baines Johnson, *The Vantage Point: Perspective of the Presidency 1963–1969* (New York: Holt, Rinehart and Winston, 1971), p. 116.

3. Kalb, ibid. pp. 81–82

4. Johnson, ibid. p. 115.

5. Author interviewed Stockdale, Herrick, and others for an NBC News documentary he anchored called "Vietnam—Lessons of a Lost War," broadcast on April 27, 1995.

6. NBC News Documentary, ibid.

7. Kalb, ibid. p. 84.

8. Michael R. Beschloss, *Taking Charge: The Johnson White House Tapes, 1963–1964* (New York: Simon & Schuster, 1997), p. 500.

9. Beschloss, ibid. p. 500.

10. NBC News Documentary, ibid.

11. Johnson, ibid. p. 117.

12. Johnson, ibid. p. 116.

13. Johnson, ibid. p. 117.

14. Johnson, ibid. p. 117.

15. Robert McNamara, *In Retrospect: The Tragedy and Lessons of Vietnam* (New York: Times Books, 1995) (this admission is made repeatedly throughout the book).

16. Johnson, ibid, p. 117.

17. Johnson, ibid, p. 118.

18. Robert Dallek, *Lyndon B. Johnson* (Oxford University Press, 2003), p. 179.

19. Beschloss, ibid, p. 507.

20. Michael Beschloss, *Reaching for Glory: Lyndon Johnson's Secret White House Tapes, 1964–1965* (New York: Simon and Schuster, 2001), p. 191.

21. Foreign Relations of the US, 1964–1968, vol. II, Vietnam, January–June 1965, Doc 42.

22. Beschloss, *Reaching for Glory*, ibid. p. 191.

CHAPTER 41

1. Louis Fisher, "Statement by Louis Fisher before the Subcommittee on International Organizations, Human Rights, and Oversight of the U.S. House Committee on Foreign Affairs—'War Powers for the 21st Century: A Constitutional Perspective'" (Law Library of the U.S. Library of Congress, April 10, 2008), http://loc.gov/law/help/usconlaw/pdf/war-fa-2008.pdf.

2. "5th Congress, Sess. 2, Ch. 68, 1 Stat. 578-'An Act Further to Protect the Commerce of the United States,'" in *Statutes at Large* (U.S. Library of Congress, 1798), pp. 578–80, http://memory.loc.gov/cgi-bin/ampage?collId=llsl&fileName=001/llsl001.db&recNum=701.

3. Bruce Tap, *Over Lincoln's Shoulder: The Committee on the Conduct of the War* (Lawrence: University Press of Kansas, 1998).

4. United Nations Security Council, "#83 Resolution of 27 June 1950 'Complaint of Aggression upon the Republic of Korea'" (The United Nations, June 27, 1950), http://www.un.org/en/sc/documents/resolutions/1950.shtml.

5. "Notes Regarding Meeting with Congressional Leaders, June 27, 1950" (The Truman Library, June 27, 1950), http://www.trumanlibrary.org/whistlestop/study_collections/korea/large/documents/pdfs/ki-2-40.pdf.

6. "Congress at War," *Foreign Affairs,* May 3, 2008, http://www.foreignaffairs.com/articles/64297/louis-fisher-ryan-hendrickson-and-stephen-r-weissman/congress-at-war.

7. Denise Bostdorff and Steven Goldzwig, "Idealism and Pragmatism in American Foreign Policy Rhetoric: The Case of John F. Kennedy and Vietnam," *Presidential Studies Quarterly* 24, no. 3 (Summer 1994).

8. Richard Nixon, "Accepting the Republican Nomination, 1968," *PBS American Experience—Nixon,* August 8, 1968, http://www.pbs.org/wgbh/americanexperience/features/primary-resources/nixon-accept68/.

9. Amy Belasco et al., *Congressional Restrictions on U.S. Military Operations in Vietnam, Cambodia, Laos, Somalia, and Kosovo: Funding and Non-Funding Approaches,* CRS Report for Congress (Congressional Research Service, January 16, 2007), http://www.fas.org/sgp/crs/natsec/RL33803.pdf.

10. U.S. Department of Defense, "Report on Selected Air and Ground Operations in Cambodia and Laos," September 10, 1973.

11. Belasco et al., *Congressional Restrictions on U.S. Military Operations in Vietnam, Cambodia, Laos, Somalia, and Kosovo: Funding and Non-Funding Approaches.*

12. A. D. Horne, "House Gets War Powers Fight," *The Washington Post,* July 4, 1970.

13. Ibid.

14. Quoted in ibid.

15. Joseph A. Fry, *Debating Vietnam: Fulbright, Stennis, and Their Senate Hearings* (Rowman & Littlefield Publishers, 2006), 161–63.

16. Spencer Rich, "Stennis Tells Hill War Powers Bill Won't Hurt Safety," *The Washington Post,* March 31, 1972.

17. Quoted in ibid.

18. Arthur Schlesinger Jr., "Presidential War: 'See If You Can Fix Any Limit to His Power,'" *The New York Times Magazine,* January 7, 1973.

19. Quoted in I. F. Stone, "Can Congress Stop the President?," *The New York Review of Books,* April 19, 1973, http://www.nybooks.com/articles/archives/1973/apr/19/can-congress-stop-the-president/.

20. John W. Finney, "Senate Unit Votes War Powers Curb," *The New York Times,* May 18, 1973.

21. Spencer Rich, "Debate Set on War Powers," *The Washington Post,* July 17, 1973.

22. Richard L. Madden, "House Passes Restrictions on President's War-Making Powers," *The New York Times,* October 13, 1973.

23. Quoted in Richard L. Madden, "Nixon Vetoes a Bill to Cut War Power of the Presidency," *The New York Times,* October 25, 1973.

24. Quoted in ibid.

25. Quoted in William B. Spong Jr., "The War Powers Resolution Revisited: Historic Accomplishment or Surrender," *William and Mary Law Review* 16, no. 4 (1975), http://scholarship.law.wm.edu/cgi/viewcontent.cgi?article=2543&context=wmlr.

26. Richard Grimmett, *The War Powers Resolution: After Thirty-Eight Years,* CRS Report for Congress (Congressional Research Service, September 24, 2012), http://www.fas.org/sgp/crs/natsec/R42699.pdf.

27. Charlie Savage and Mark Landler, "War Powers Act Doesn't Apply for Libya, Obama Says," *The New York Times,* June 15, 2011, sec. U.S. / Politics, http://www.nytimes.com/2011/06/16/us/politics/16powers.html.

CHAPTER 44

1. Mark A. Hooker and Michael M. Knetter. "Measuring the Economic Effects of Military Base Closures," *Economic Inquiry* 39, no. 4 (October 2001): 583–98.

2. Only one member of Congress claims he lost his seat due to base closures, and there were extenuating circumstances that could easily have led to his defeat even if his base had remained open.

CHAPTER 45

1. Juliet Eilperin, "What the 2002 Use of Force Resolution against Iraq Can Tell Us about Syria Vote," *The Washington Post,* September 1, 2013, http://www.washingtonpost.com/blogs/the-fix/wp/2013/09/01/what-the-2002-use-of-force-resolution-against-iraq-can-tell-us-about-syria-vote/.

2. Jim Webb, "Congressional Abdication," *National Interest,* March, 1, 2013, http://nationalinterest.org/article/congressional-abdication-8138.

3. Ibid.

4. Richard F. Grimmett, "War Powers Resolution: Presidential Compliance," *Congressional Research Service,* September 25, 2012.

5. James Kitfield, *Prodigal Soldiers: How the Generation of Officers Born of Vietnam Revolutionized the American Style of War* (Lincoln, NE: Potomac Books Inc., 1997).

6. Adam Clymer, "Confrontation in the Gulf: Congress Acts to Authorize War in Gulf," *The New York Times,* January 13, 1991, http://www.nytimes.com/1991/01/13/world/confrontation-gulf-congress-acts-authorize-war-gulf-margins-are-5-votes-senate.html.

7. James Kitfield, *Prodigal Soldiers: How the Generation of Officers Born of Vietnam Revolutionized the American Style of War* (Lincoln, NE: Potomac Books Inc., 1997).

8. Juliet Eilperin, "What the 2002 Use of Force Resolution against Iraq Can Tell Us about Syria Vote," *The Washington Post,* September 1, 2013, http://www.washingtonpost.com/blogs/the-fix/wp/2013/09/01/what-the-2002-use-of-force-resolution-against-iraq-can-tell-us-about-syria-vote/

9. Charles Pierce, "Chuck Hagel on the Iraq War," *Esquire,* January 8, 2013, http://www.esquire.com/blogs/politics/chuck-hagel-iraq-2002-010813.

10. Jim Webb, "Congressional Abdication," *National Interest,* March 1, 2013, http://nationalinterest.org/article/congressional-abdication-8138.

CHAPTER 48

1. James Taylor et al., *American Intelligence: A Framework for the Future.* (Washington: internal classified CIA report approved for release February 2002). http://www.gwu.edu/-nsarchiv/NSAEBB/NSAEBB144/document%2010.pdf, 1975), 1.

2. Ibid.

3. Amy Zegart, *Flawed by Design* (Redwood City: Stanford University Press). 188.

4. Ibid.

5. James Schlesinger, *A Review of the Intelligence Community*, report for President Nixon, March 10, 1971.

6. Interview with Andrew Card, June 19, 2012, McLean, VA.

7. David Sanger, "August '01 Brief Is Said to Warn of Attack Plans," *New York Times,* April 10, 2004.

8. Interview with Condoleezza Rice, May 10, 2010, Palo Alto, CA.

9. Romesh Ratnesar, "Richard Clarke, at War with Himself," *Time*, March 25, 2004. http://www.time.com/time/nation/article/0,8599,604598,00.html.

10. Condoleezza Rice, Interview by network correspondents, March 24, 2004, 4:53 P.M.

11. Thomas Kean and Lee Hamilton, *News Conference*, March 30, 2004.

12. Interview with Tom Kean, July 20, 2010, Washington, DC.

13. Interview with Senator Lieberman, November 30, 2010, Washington, DC.

CHAPTER 49

1. Iraq War casualties data are available at http://www.icasualties.org/Iraq/IraqiDeaths.aspx (accessed on September 13, 2013).

2. Ole R. Holsti, *American Public Opinion on the Iraq War* (Ann Arbor: University of Michigan Press, 2011), p. 60.

3. The opinion poll data are available at http://www.gallup.com/poll/116500/presidentialapprovalratingsgeorge-bush.aspx and http://www.realclearpolitics.com/epolls/other/2006_generic_Congressional_vote-2174.htm (both accessed on September 13, 2013).

4. Interview by the author of Frank Wolf, October 2, 2007. (All subsequent interviews cited in this chapter were also conducted by the author.)

5. Interview of David M. Abshire, April 11, 2007.

6. This appropriation was enacted by Public Law 109–234.

7. Iraq Study Group, *The Iraq Study Group Report* (New York: Vintage Books, 2006), p. xiii.

8. Iraq Study Group, *The Iraq Study Group Report,* p. xvi.

9. Iraq Study Group, *The Iraq Study Group Report,* p. 73.

10. Peter Baker and Jon Cohen, "Americans Say U.S. Is Losing War," *Washington Post,* December 10, 2006; Susan Page, "USA More Pessimistic on Iraq War," *USA Today,* December 12, 2006.

11. Yochi J. Dreazen, "Republican War Critics Find Cover," *Wall Street Journal,* December 13, 2006.

12. Stephen Benedict Dyson, "George W. Bush, the Surge, and Presidential Leadership," *Political Science Quarterly* 125, no. 4 (Winter 2010–2011): 557–85; Peter Feaver, "The Right to Be Right: Civil-Military Relations and the Iraq Surge Decision," *International Security* 35, no. 4 (Spring 2011): 87–125; Andrew J. Polsky, *Elusive Victories: The American Presidency at War* (New York: Oxford University Press, 2012), pp. 312–17.

13. Michael Abramowitz and Peter Baker, "Embattled, Bush Held to Plan to Salvage Iraq," *Washington Post,* January 21, 2007; Andrew J. Polsky, "Staying the Course: Presidential Leadership, Military Stalemate, and Strategic Inertia," *Perspectives on Politics* 8, no. 1 (March 2010): 127–39.

14. The resolution was S. Con. Res. 4, introduced on January 24, 2007.

15. The legislation was the Iraq Study Group Recommendations Implementation Act of 2007.

16. Shailagh Murray and Paul Kane, "Democrats Won't Force War Vote," *Washington Post*, July 19, 2007. Reid did not bring the appropriations bill back to the floor until October.

17. Interview of Frank Wolf, October 2, 2007; interview of congressional aide, October 2007.

18. This bill was S. 433, the Iraq War De-Escalation Act of 2007.

19. Interview of Ben Rhodes, July 7, 2010.

20. Colton C. Campbell, *Discharging Congress: Government by Commission* (Westport, CT: Praeger, 2002); R. Kent Weaver, "The Politics of Blame Avoidance," *Journal of Public Policy* 6, no. 4 (October–December 1986): 371–98.

21. Jordan Tama, *Terrorism and National Security Reform: How Commissions Can Drive Change during Crises* (New York: Cambridge University Press, 2011).

CHAPTER 51

1. Benard Weintraub, "Iran Payment Found Diverted to Contras; Reagan Security Adviser and Aide Are Out," *New York Times*, November 26, 1986.

2. "America's Secret War: Nicaragua," *Newsweek*, November 8, 1982.

3. William Cohen and George Mitchell, *Men of Zeal: A Candid Inside Story of the Iran-Contra Hearings* (Viking, 1988), p. 22.

4. Seymour M. Hersh, "The Iran-Contra Committees: Did They Protect Reagan?" *New York Times*, April 29, 1990.

5. Cohen and Mitchell, *Men of Zeal*, p. 25

6. *Report of the Congressional Committees Investigating the Iran-Contra Affair.* https://archive.org/details/reportofcongress87unit.

7. *Report of the Congressional Committees Investigating the Iran-Contra Affair*, p. 423.

8. *Report of the Congressional Committees*, p. 438.

9. *U.S. v. North*, 910 F.2d 843, Washington, DC, 1990.

10. Katy J. Harriger, *The Special Prosecutor in American Politics* (University Press of Kansas, 2000), p. 6.

11. Samuel Dash, "Saturday Night Massacre II," *Foreign Policy* No. 96 (Autumn 1994), 173.

12. Louis Fisher, "Foreign Policy Powers of the President and Congress," *AAPSS*, September 1988, p. 157.

13. Harold Hongju Koh, "Why the President (Almost) Always Wins in Foreign Policy Affair: Lessons of the Iran-Contra Affair," *Yale Law Journal* (June 1988): 1279.

14. Theodore Draper, *A Very Thin Line* (Touchstone, 1991), p. 596.
15. Koh, "Why the President (Almost) Always Wins," p. 1258.

CHAPTER 52

1. Trent Lott, *Herding Cats: A Life in Politics* (New York: ReganBooks, HarperCollins, 2005), p. 176.
2. Thomas E. Mann and Norman Ornstein, *The Broken Branch* (Oxford University Press, 2006), p. 120.
3. *Herding Cats,* p. 177.
4. *The Broken Branch,* p. 117.

Selected Bibliography

Aaron, Henry J. "Lessons for Tax Reform." In *Do Taxes Matter?: The Impact of the Tax Reform Act of 1986*, edited by Joel Slemrod. Cambridge, MA: The MIT Press, 1990.

Abad-Santos, Alexander. "Daylight Saving Time Is America's Greatest Shame." *The Wire*, November 1, 2013. www.theatlanticwire.com/entertainment/2013/11/daylight-saving-time-americas-greatest-shame/71172/.

Abramowitz, Michael, and Peter Baker. "Embattled, Bush Held to Plan to Salvage Iraq." *The Washington Post*, January 21, 2007.

"America's Secret War: Nicaragua." *Newsweek*, November 8, 1982.

Arnold, R. Douglas. *The Logic of Action*. New Haven, CT: Yale University Press, 1992.

Babington, Charles. "Hastert Launches a Partisan Policy." *The Washington Post*, November 27, 2004.

Bach, Stanley, and Steven S. Smith. *Managing Uncertainty in the U.S. House of Representatives*. Washington, DC: Brookings, 1988.

Baker, Peter, and Jon Cohen. "Americans Say U.S. Is Losing War." *The Washington Post*, December 10, 2006.

Barnes, Fred. "TV News: The Shock Horror Welfare Cut Show." *Policy Review*, Spring 1983, 57–73.

Barnes, Robert. "Alito's State of the Union Moment." *The Washington Post*, January 28, 2010.

Baudoux, Marc-Antoine. "Golf, BBQ Lobbyists Responsible for Daylight Savings (sic) Time." *Agence France Presse*, 2013. Quoted in *Huffington Post*, March 28, 2013. http://www.huffingtonpost.com/2013/03/28/daylight-savings-time-lobbyists-golf-bbq_n_2972702.html.

Beard, Charles A. "In Defense of Congress." *Atlantic Monthly,* 172, July 1943.

Beschloss, Michael R. *Reaching for Glory: Lyndon Johnson's Secret White House Tapes, 1964–1965.* New York: Simon & Schuster, 2001.

Beschloss, Michael R. *Taking Charge: The Johnson White House Tapes, 1963–1964.* New York: Simon & Schuster, 1997.

Birnbaum, Jeffrey H., and Alan S. Murray. *Showdown at Gucci Gulch.* New York: Vintage, 1987.

Black, Earl, and Merle Black. *The Rise of the Southern Republicans.* Cambridge, MA: Harvard University Press, 2002.

"Blacks v. Teachers; Blacks and Vouchers." *The Economist,* March 10, 2001.

Boehner, John. "Making the Grade." *National Review Online,* April 6, 2001.

Bostdorff, Denise, and Steven Goldzwig. "Idealism and Pragmatism in American Foreign Policy Rhetoric: The Case of John F. Kennedy and Vietnam." *Presidential Studies Quarterly* 24, no. 3 (Summer 1994): 515–30.

Branch, Taylor. *Parting the Waters: America in the King Years 1954–63.* New York: Simon & Schuster, 1988.

Bureau of Labor Statistics. "Women in the Labor Force: A Databook." *BLS Reports,* Report 1040. Washington, DC: U.S. Department of Labor, February 2013.

Bush, George W. *Decision Points.* New York: Crown Publishers, 2010.

Bush, George W. "Statement on Signing the Bipartisan Campaign Reform Act of 2002." Speech at the White House, March 27, 2002.

Byrd, Robert C. "Behind the Scenes Leadership: Richard B. Russell, Jr." In *A Guide to the Richard B. Russell, Jr. Collection.* Athens, GA: Richard B. Russell Library for Political Research and Studies, 1997.

Cahodas, Nadine. *Strom Thurmond and the Politics of Southern Change.* Macon, GA: Mercer University Press, 1995.

Campbell, Charles E. *Senator Richard B. Russell and My Career as a Trial Lawyer.* Macon, GA: Mercer University Press, 2013.

Campbell, Colton C. *Discharging Congress: Government by Commission.* Westport, CT: Praeger, 2002.

Canellos, Peter S., ed. The Boston Globe. *Last Lion: The Fall and Rise of Ted Kennedy.* New York: Simon & Schuster, 2009.

Caro, Robert A. *The Years of Lyndon Johnson: Master of the Senate.* New York: Alfred A. Knopf, 2002.

Center for Responsive Politics. "2012 Presidential Race." http://www.opensecrets.org/pres12/ (accessed December 13, 2013).

Center for Responsive Politics. "Soft Money Backgrounder." http://www.opensecrets.org/parties/softsource.php (accessed December 13, 2013).

Champagne, Anthony. *Congressman Sam Rayburn.* New Brunswick, NJ: Rutgers University Press, 1984.

Champagne, Anthony, Douglas B. Harris, James W. Riddlesperger Jr., and Garrison Nelson. *The Austin-Boston Connection*. College Station: Texas A&M University Press, 2009.

Chen, Edwin. "Free Speech Will Pay Heavy Price Under Campaign Finance Reform, Key Foe Says." *Los Angeles Times*, March 15, 1997.

Cherry, Robert. *Welfare Transformed: Universalizing Family Policies That Work*. New York: Oxford, 2007.

Clymer, Adam. "Confrontation in the Gulf: Congress Acts to Authorize War in Gulf." *The New York Times*, January 13, 1991. http://www.nytimes.com/1991/01/13/world/confrontation-gulf-congress-acts-autho rize-war-gulf-margins-are-5-votes-senate.html.

Cohen, Richard E. *Rostenkowski: The Pursuit of Power and the End of the Old Politics*. Chicago: Ivan R. Dee, 1999.

Cohen, William, and George Mitchell. *Men of Zeal: A Candid Inside Story of the Iran-Contra Hearings*. New York: Viking Adult, 1988.

Cose, Ellis. *A Nation of Strangers: Prejudice, Politics, and the Populating of America*. New York: William Morrow and Company, 1992.

Cox, Gary M., and Mathew McCubbins. *Legislative Leviathan*. Berkeley: University of California Press, 1994.

Curtis, Carl T. Interview by Hugh Cates, April 21, 1971, transcript, Richard B. Russell Library for Political Research and Studies.

Dallek, Mathew. "Bipartisan Reagan-O'Neill Social Security Deal in 1983 Showed It Can Be Done." U.S. News and World Report, April 2009. http://www.usnews.com/opinion/articles/2009/04/02/biparti san-reagan-oneill-social-security-deal-in-1983-showed-it-can-be-done (accessed November 9, 2013).

Dallek, Robert. *Lyndon B. Johnson*. New York: Oxford University Press, 2003.

Danziger, Sheldon, Robert Haveman, and Robert Plotnick. "How Income Transfer Programs Affect Work, Savings, and the Income Distribution: A Critical Review." *Journal of Economic Literature* 19 (1981): 975–1028.

Dash, Samuel. "Saturday Night Massacre II." *Foreign Policy* No. 96 (Autumn 1994): 173.

Davidson, Chandler, and Bernard Grofman, eds. *Quiet Revolution in the South*. Princeton, NJ: Princeton University Press, 1994.

Deering, Christopher J. "Principle or Party? Foreign and National Security Policymaking in the Senate." In *The Contentious Senate: Partisanship, Ideology, and the Myth of Cool Judgment*, edited by Colton C. Campbell and Nicol C. Rae, 43–64. Lanham, MD: Rowman & Littlefield, 2001.

Deering, Christopher J., and Steven S. Smith. *Committees in Congress, 3rd ed*. Washington, DC: CQ Press, 1997.

Dewhirst, Robert E., and John David Rausch. *Encyclopedia of the United States Congress*. New York: Infobase Publishing, 2009.

Downing, Michael. *Spring Forward: The Annual Madness of Daylight Saving Time.* Berkeley, CA: Counterpoint Press, 2005.

Draper, Theodore. *A Very Thin Line.* New York: Touchstone, 1991.

Dreazen, Yochi J. "Republican War Critics Find Cover." *Wall Street Journal,* December 13, 2006.

Dyson, Stephen Benedict. "George W. Bush, the Surge, and Presidential Leadership." *Political Science Quarterly* 125, no. 4 (Winter 2010–2011): 557–85.

Edsall, Thomas Byrne. *Chain Reaction: The Impact of Race, Rights, and Taxes on American Politics.* New York: W.W. Norton & Company, 1992.

Eilperin, Juliet. "What the 2002 Use of Force Resolution against Iraq Can Tell Us about Syria Vote." *The Washington Post,* September 1, 2013. http://www.washingtonpost.com/blogs/the-fix/wp/2013/09/01/what-the-2002-use-of-force-resolution-against-iraq-can-tell-us-about-syria-vote/.

Enzi, Mike. "Enzi Proposes Halloween Safety for Children." *Enzi.senate .gov,* October 26, 2001. http://www.enzi.senate.gov/public/index .cfm/news-releases?ContentRecord_id=5048b126–802a-23ad-4cba-fc7facdc6015.

Ervin, Samuel J., Jr. Interview by Hugh Cates, April 28, 1971, transcript, Richard B. Russell Library for Political Research and Studies.

Farrell, John A. *Tip O'Neill and the Democratic Century: A Biography.* New York: Little, Brown and Company, 2001.

Feaver, Peter. "The Right to Be Right: Civil-Military Relations and the Iraq Surge Decision." *International Security* 35, no. 4 (Spring 2011), 87–125.

Federal Election Commission. "The Federal Election Campaign Laws: A Short History." http://www.fec.gov/info/appfour.htm (accessed December 13, 2013).

Fenno, Richard F., Jr. "Learning to Govern: An Institutional View of the 104th Congress." Washington, DC: The Brookings Institution. Last modified 1997. http://books.google.com/books?id=2R6jBjM3uhsC&pg=PA31&lpg=PA31&dq=speaker+abolished+some+committees+and+subcommittees,+appointed&source=bl&ots=4O5JqoFKuC&sig=e-jWFSvZuLHCGBtEeJZvCdMHdUY&hl=en&sa=X&ei=j6JqUsnOH_av4APG5YCYCQ&ved=0CCkQ6AEwAA#v=onepage&q=speaker%20abolished%20some%20committees%20and%20subcommittees%2C%20appointed&f=false (accessed December 3, 2013).

Finney, John W. "Senate Unit Votes War Powers Curb." *The New York Times,* May 18, 1973.

Fisher, Louis. "Foreign Policy Powers of the President and Congress." *ANNALS, AAPSS* 499 (September 1988): 148–59.

Fisher, Louis. "Statement by Louis Fisher before the Subcommittee on International Organizations, Human Rights, and Oversight of the U.S. House Committee on Foreign Affairs—'War Powers for the 21st Century: A Constitutional Perspective.'" *Law Library of the U.S. Library of Congress,* April 10, 2008. http://loc.gov/law/help/usconlaw/pdf/war-fa-2008.pdf.

Fisher, Louis, Ryan Hendrickson, and Stephen R. Weissman. "Congress at War." *Council on Foreign Affairs: Foreign Affairs,* May 3, 2008. http://www.foreignaffairs.com/articles/64297/louis-fisher-ryan-hendrickson-and-stephen-r-weissman/congress-at-war.

Fong, Hiram L. Interview by Hugh Cates, April 28, 1971, transcript, Richard B. Russell Library for Political Research and Studies.

Fry, Joseph A. *Debating Vietnam: Fulbright, Stennis, and Their Senate Hearings.* Lanham, MD: Rowman & Littlefield Publishers, 2006.

Fuchs, Lawrence H. "The Corpse That Would not Die: The Immigration Reform and Control Act of 1986." *Revue europeenne de migrations internationals* 6, no. 1, L'immigration auz Etats-Unis (1990): 111–27. http://www.persee.fr/web/revues/home/prescript/article/remi_0765-0752_1990_num_6_1_1230.

Furgurson, Ernest B. *Hard Right: The Rise of Jesse Helms.* New York: W.W. Norton, 1986.

Garland, Robert. *Ten Years of Daylight Saving: From the Pittsburgh Standpoint.* Pittsburgh: Carnegie Library of Pittsburgh, 1927. www.clpgh.org/exhibit/dst.html.

Garrow, David J. *Protest at Selma: Martin Luther King, Jr., and the Voting Rights Act of 1965.* New Haven: Yale University Press, 1980.

Gayner, Jeffrey B. "The Contract with America: Implementing New Ideas in the U.S." *The Heritage Foundation.* Washington, DC: Heritage Foundation, October 12, 1995.

"George Walker Bush Inaugural Address." January 20, 2001. http://odur.let.rug.nl/'usa/P/gwb43/speeches/gwbush1.htm (accessed on March 19, 2002).

"Gingrich as Speaker: Remembering When." *ABCNews.go.com* (blog). 28 September 2007 (10:02 A.M.). http://abcnews.go.com/blogs/politics/2007/09/gingrich-as-spe/.

Glain, Stephen J., and Susan Milligan. "Kennedy Vows Fight over GOP Drug Bill." *The Boston Globe,* November 17, 2003.

Goldberg, Milton, and Susan Traiman. "Why Business Backs Education Standards." In *Brookings Papers on Education Policy,* edited by Diane Ravitch. Washington, DC: Brookings Institution Press, 2001.

Gorman, Siobhan. "The Education of House Republicans." *National Journal* 33, March 31, 2001.

Graetz, Michael J. "Tax Reform Unraveling." *Journal of Economic Perspectives* 21, no. 1 (Winter 2007): 69–90.

"The Grand Collapse." *The New York Times*. Editorial. 30 June, 2007. http://www.nytimes.com/2007/06/30/opinion/30sat1.html.

Gray, Jerry. "Gingrich Offers an Agenda, but the Christian Coalition Attacks Sharply." *The New York Times*. Last modified March 7, 1997. http://www.nytimes.com/1997/03/07/us/gingrich-offers-an-agenda-but-the-christian-coalition-attacks-sharply.html?src=pm (accessed December 3, 2013).

Greenberg, Stanley B. *Dispatches from the War Room: In the Trenches with Five Extraordinary Leaders*. New York: Thomas Dunn, 2009.

Hale, Jon F. "The Making of the New Democrats." *Political Science Quarterly* 110, no. 2 (Summer 1995): 207–32.

Hall, Richard L., and Kris C. Miler. "What Happens After the Alarm? Interest Group Subsidies to Legislative Overseers." *Journal of Politics* 70, no. 4 (October 2008), 990–1005.

Hansen, Clifford P. Interview by Hugh Cates, April 19, 1971, transcript, Richard B. Russell Library for Political Research and Studies.

Hardeman, D. B., and Donald Bacon. *Rayburn: A Biography*. Austin: Texas Monthly Press, 1987.

Harriger, Katy J. *The Special Prosecutor in American Politics*. Lawrence: University Press of Kansas, 2000.

Harris, John F., and Eric Pianin. "Bipartisanship Reigns at Budget Signing." *The Washington Post*. Last modified August 6, 1997 http://www.washingtonpost.com/wp-srv/politics/special/budget/stories/080697.htm (accessed December 3, 2013).

Haskins, Ron. *Work over Welfare: The Inside Story of the 1996 Welfare Reform Law*. Washington, DC: Brookings Institution Press, 2006.

Hatch, Orrin. Eulogy for Edward M. Kennedy, John F. Kennedy Library and Museum, Boston, MA, August 28, 2009.

Heclo, Hugh. "Campaigning and Governing: A Conspectus." In *The Permanent Campaign and Its Future*, edited by Norman J. Ornstein and Thomas E. Mann. Washington, DC: AEI/Brookings, 2000.

Helms, Jesse. *Here's Where I Stand: A Memoir*. New York: Random House, 2005.

Hernandez, Raymond, and Patrick D. Healy. "The Evolution of Hillary Clinton." *The New York Times*, July 13, 2005.

Hersh, Seymour M. "The Iran-Contra Committees: Did They Protect Reagan?" *The New York Times*, April 29, 1990.

Himmelfarb, Gertrude. *The Idea of Poverty: England in the Early Industrial Age*. New York: Vintage, 1985.

"HIPAA Background." *The University of Chicago HIPAA Program Office*. http://hipaa.bsd.uchicago.edu/background.html (updated February, 2010).

Holman, Kwame. "Background: The Re-Election of Speaker Gingrich." *PBS News Hour*. Last modified January 7, 1997. http://www.pbs.org/news

hour/bb/politics/jan-june97/gingrich_01–07a.html (accessed December 3, 2013).

Holsti, Ole R. *American Public Opinion on the Iraq War.* Ann Arbor: University of Michigan Press, 2011.

Hooker, Mark A., and Michael M. Knetter. "Measuring the Economic Effects of Military Base Closures." *Economic Inquiry* 39, no. 4 (October 2001): 583–98.

Horne, A. D. "House Gets War Powers Fight." *The Washington Post,* July 4, 1970.

House of Representatives Committee on Rules. "About the Committee on Rules—History and Processes." http://rules.house.gov/about (accessed December 13, 2013).

Iraq Study Group. *The Iraq Study Group Report.* New York: Vintage Books, 2006.

Jackson, Robert L. "Trial of Former Gore Fund-Raiser Hsia Opens." *Los Angeles Times,* February 8, 2000.

Jennings, Jack. "Republicans and Democrats Warily Move toward Agreement on ESEA." *Center on Education Policy Newsletter* 10, no. 3 (Spring 2001).

Johnson, Lyndon B. "President Lyndon B. Johnson's Special Message to the Congress: The American Promise." Speech presented at a joint session, March 15, 1965 (9:02 P.M.) http://www.lbjlib.utexas.edu/johnson/archives.hom/speeches.hom/650315.asp.

Johnson, Lyndon Baines. *The Vantage Point: Perspective of the Presidency 1963–1969.* New York: Holt, Rinehart and Winston, 1971.

Kalb, Marvin. *The Road to War: Presidential Commitments Honored and Betrayed.* Washington, DC: Brookings, 2013.

Kalman, Laura. *Right Star Rising: A New Politics, 1974–1980.* New York: W.W. Norton, 2010.

Kean, Thomas, and Lee Hamilton. *News Conference,* March 30, 2004.

Kelman, Steven. *Making Public Policy: A Hopeful View of American Government.* New York: Basic Books, 1987.

Kennedy, Edward M. Speech to the Democratic National Convention, Denver, Colorado, August 25, 2008.

Kingdon, John W. *Agendas, Alternatives, and Public Policies, 2nd ed.* London: Longman Publishing Group, 1995.

Kitfield, James. *Prodigal Soldiers: How the Generation of Officers Born of Vietnam Revolutionized the American Style of War.* Dulles, VA: Potomac Books Inc., 1997.

Klein, Ezra. "The 13 Reasons Washington Is Failing." *The Washington Post, Wonkblog,* October 7, 2013. http://www.washingtonpost.com/blogs/wonkblog/wp/2013/10/07/the-13-reasons-washington-is-failing/ (accessed November 14, 2013).

Kneeland, Douglas E. "Protests on Daylight Time Persist Despite New Federal Law on Uniformity." *The New York Times*, February 27, 1967. http://select.nytimes.com/gst/abstract.html?res=F50F14FF355F137A93C5AB1789D85F438685F9.

Koger, Gregory. *Filibustering: A Political History of Obstruction in the House and Senate*. Chicago: University of Chicago Press, 2010.

Koh, Harold Hongju. "Why the President (Almost) Always Wins in Foreign Policy Affair: Lessons of the Iran-Contra Affair." *Yale Law Journal* vol. 97, no. 7 (June 1988): 1255–342.

Krehbiel, Keith. *Information and Legislative Organization*. Ann Arbor: University of Michigan Press, 1991.

LeMay, Michael C. *Anatomy of a Public Policy: The Reform of Contemporary Immigration Law*. Westport, CT: Praeger Press, 1994.

Leuchtenburg, William E. *Franklin D. Roosevelt and the New Deal, 1932–1940*, edited by Henry S. Commager, and Richard B. Morris. New York: Harper & Row, 1963.

Lewis, John. *Walking with the Wind: A Memoir of the Movement*. New York: Simon & Schuster, 1998.

Link, William A. *Righteous Warrior: Jesse Helms and the Rise of Modern Conservatism*. New York: St. Martin's, 2008.

Lott, Trent. *Herding Cats: A Life in Politics*. New York: HarperCollins Publishers, 2005.

Madden, Richard L. "House Passes Restrictions on President's War-Making Powers." *The New York Times*, October 13, 1973.

Madden, Richard L. "Nixon Vetoes a Bill to Cut War Power of the Presidency." *The New York Times*, October 25, 1973.

"Major Changes to ESEA in the NCLB Act." *Learning First Alliance*. www.learningfirst.org.

Mann, Thomas E., and Norman Ornstein. *The Broken Branch*. New York: Oxford University Press, 2006.

Mann, Thomas E., and Norman J. Ornstein. *It's Even Worse Than It Looks: How the American Political System Collided with the New Politics of Extremism*. New York: Basic Books, 2012.

Marshall, Bryan W. *Rules for War: Procedural Choice in the U.S. House of Representatives*. Burlington, VT: Ashgate, 2005.

Masters, Jonathan. *The Renewing America Interview: Bill Bradley on Leadership and U.S. Tax Reform*. Council on Foreign Relations, September 12, 2013. http://blogs.cfr.org/renewing-america/2013/09/12/the-renewing-america-interview-bill-bradley-on-leadership-and-u-s-tax-reform/.

Mathews, Chris. *Tip and the Gipper: When Politics Worked*. New York: Simon & Schuster, 2013.

McCormick, James M. "Decision Making in the Foreign Affairs and Foreign Relations Committees." In *Congress Resurgent: Foreign and Defense*

Policy on Capitol Hill, edited by Randall B. Ripley and James M. Lindsay. Ann Arbor: University of Michigan Press, 1993.

McNamara, Robert. *In Retrospect: The Tragedy and Lessons of Vietnam.* New York: Times Books, 1995.

Meissner, Doris, Deborah W. Myers, Demetrious G. Papademetriou, and Michael Fix. *Immigration and America's Future: A New Chapter.* Washington, DC: Migration Policy Institute, 2006.

Miller, Harris N. "The Right Thing to Do: A History of Simpson-Mazzoli." In *Clamor at the Gates: The New American Immigration,* edited by Nathan Glazer. San Francisco: Institute for Contemporary Studies Press, 1985.

Miller, Zell. "Richard Russell, Georgia's Senator." In *Dedication and Unveiling of the Statue of Richard Brevard Russell, Jr.* Washington, DC: United States Government Printing Office, 1997.

Milligan, Susan. "Fulfilling a Nation's Promise." *The Boston Globe,* August 26, 2009.

Milligan, Susan. "Stunning Return and a Vital Vote." *The Boston Globe,* July 10, 2008.

Milligan, Susan. "A Towering Record, Painstakingly Built." *The Boston Globe,* February 20, 2009.

Mitchell, Alison. "Daschle Takes Parting Shot as Congress Breaks." *The New York Times,* October 19, 2002.

Morgan, Ted. *FDR: A Biography.* New York: Simon & Schuster, 1985.

Murray, Charles. *Losing Ground: American Social Policy, 1950–1980.* New York: Basic Books, 1984.

Murray, Shailagh, and Paul Kane. "Democrats Won't Force War Vote." *The Washington Post,* July 19, 2007.

Nather, David. "As Education Bills Head for Floor Votes, Big Ideological Tests Loom in House." *CQ Weekly,* May 19, 2001.

Neustadt, Richard E. *Presidential Power and the Modern Presidents: The Politics of Leadership from Roosevelt to Reagan.* New York: Free Press, 1991.

"A New Federal Role in Education." *Center on Education Policy,* January 2002. www.ctredpol.org.

Nixon, Richard. "Accepting the Republican Nomination, 1968." *PBS American Experience—Nixon,* August 8, 1968. http://www.pbs.org/wgbh/americanexperience/features/primary-resources/nixon-accept68/.

No Child Left Behind: A Desktop Reference. Washington, DC: U.S. Department of Education, Office of the Under Secretary and Office of Elementary and Secondary Education 2002. www.ed.gov/pubs/edpubs.html.

Obama, Barack. "State of the Union Address." Speech at Washington, DC, January 27, 2010.

Oleszek, Walter. *Congressional Procedures and the Policy Process.* Los Angeles: Sage Publications, 2013.

"Operation Iraqi Freedom." *Icasualties.org: Iraq Coalition Casualty Count*, 2011. http://www.icasualties.org/Iraq/IraqiDeaths.aspx.

Ostrow, Ronald J. "Police Report Details Kennedy Incident." *Los Angeles Times*, April 13, 1991.

Page, Susan. "USA More Pessimistic on Iraq War." *USA Today*, December 12, 2006.

Pear, Robert. "Hatch Joins Kennedy to Back a Health Program." *The New York Times*, March 14, 1997.

Pear, Robert. "Washington Talk: Congress; Immigration Bill: How 'Corpse' Came Back to Life." *The New York Times*, October 13, 1986. http://www.nytimes.com/1986/10/13/us/washington-talk-congress-immi gration-bill-how-corpse-came-back-to-life.html (accessed December 2, 2013).

Pear, Robert, and Jim Rutenberg. "Senators in Bipartisan Deal on Immigration Bill." *The New York Times*, 18 May 2007. http://www.nytimes .com/2007/05/18/washington/18immig.html.

Pearlstein, Steven. "Kennedy Saw Health-Care Reform Fail in the '70s." *The Washington Post*, August 28, 2009.

Pierce, Charles. "Chuck Hagel on the Iraq War." *Esquire*, January 8, 2013. http://www.esquire.com/blogs/politics/chuck-hagel-iraq-2002–010813.

Polsky, Andrew J. *Elusive Victories: The American Presidency at War*. New York: Oxford University Press, 2012.

Polsky, Andrew J. "Staying the Course: Presidential Leadership, Military Stalemate, and Strategic Inertia." *Perspectives on Politics* 8, no. 1 (March 2010).

Prerau, David. *Seize the Daylight: The Curious and Contentious Story of Day-light Saving Time*. New York: Thunder's Mouth Press, 2006.

Rae, Nicol C. *Southern Democrats*. New York: Oxford University Press, 1994.

Ratnesar, Romesh. "Richard Clarke, at War with Himself." *Time*, March 25, 2004. http://www.time.com/time/nation/article/0,8599,604598,00 .html.

"Reform School: Bush Seeks Compromise on Education Proposals." *ABC News.com*, January 23, 2001.

Rich, Allen. "Quiet Ceremony Commemorates Anniversary of the Passing of Sam Rayburn." *ntxe-news.com*, December 17, 2007.

Rich, Spencer. "Debate Set on War Powers." *The Washington Post*, July 17, 1973.

Rich, Spencer. "Stennis Tells Hill War Powers Bill Won't Hurt Safety." *The Washington Post*, March 31, 1972.

Rizzo, Jane, Mark Suozzo, Rachel Salmon, and Jeni Morrison. *The Senate Speaks* and *Last Best Chance*. DVD. Directed by Shari Robertson and Michael Camerini. *How Democracy Works Now* series. New York:

Epidoko Pictures, 2010–2013, http://www.howdemocracyworksnow. com (accessed December 2, 2013).

Robelen, Erik. "An ESEA Primer." *Education Week,* January 9, 2002.

Rosenblum, Marc R. "US Immigration Policy since 9/11: Understanding the Stalemate over Comprehensive Immigration Reform." *The Regional Migration Study Group.* Washington, DC: Woodrow Wilson International Center for Scholars and Migration Policy Institute, August 2011. http://www.wilsoncenter.org/sites/default/files/us_immigration_pol icy_since_9_11.pdf.

Rossiter, Clinton. *The American Presidency.* Baltimore: Johns Hopkins University Press, 1960.

Rucker, Philip, and Eli Saslow, "Patrick Kennedy leaves note for Ted on gravesite: 'Dad, the Unfinished Business Is Done,'" *The Washington Post,* March 23, 2010.

Russell, Richard B., Jr. "Coosa Valley Area Planning and Development Commission." In *Richard B. Russell Library for Political Research and Studies.* Richard B. Russell, Jr. Collection, Subgroup C, Series III: Speech/Media, July 15, 1964.

Russell, Richard B., Jr. "Talk to Freshmen Members in House of Representatives (Congress)." In *Richard B. Russell Library for Political Research and Studies.* Richard B. Russell, Jr. Collection, Subgroup C, Series III: Speech/Media, March 26, 1953.

Russell, Sally. *Richard B. Russell, A Life of Consequence.* Macon, GA: Mercer University Press, 2011.

Sanger, David. "August '01 Brief Is Said to Warn of Attack Plans." *New York Times,* April 10, 2004.

Savage, Charlie, and Mark Landler. "War Powers Act Doesn't Apply for Libya, Obama Says." *The New York Times,* June 15, 2011, sec. U.S./Politics. http://www.nytimes.com/2011/06/16/us/politics/16powers.html.

Schlesinger, Arthur M., Jr. *The Coming of the New Deal.* Boston: Houghton Mifflin Company, 1958.

Schlesinger, Arthur M., Jr. "Presidential War: 'See If You Can Fix Any Limit to His Power.'" *The New York Times,* January 7, 1973.

Schwar, Harriet D., and David S. Patterson, eds. "Foreign Relations of the US, 1964–1968." Vol. II. *Vietnam: January–June 1965.* http://history .state.gov/historicaldocuments/frus1964-68v02

Scott, Esther. *Keeping a Campaign Promise: George W. Bush and Medicare Prescription Drug Coverage.* John F. Kennedy School of Government, 2007.

Seelye, Katharine Q. "A Nation Challenged: Capitol Hill; In Congress, 2 Chambers, Incongruent." *The New York Times,* October 19, 2001.

Seelye, Katharine Q. "The Speaker Steps Down: The Overview; Facing a Revolt, Gingrich Won't Run for Speaker and Will Quit Congress."

The New York Times, Last modified November 7, 1998. http://www
.nytimes.com/1998/11/07/us/speaker-steps-down-overview-fac
ing-revolt-gingrich-won-t-run-for-speaker-will.html?pagewanted=all&
src=pm (accessed December 3, 2013).

Shapiro, Ira. *The Last Great Senate: Courage and Statesmanship in Times of
Crisis*. New York: Public Affairs Press, 2012.

Simpson, Alan K. "Conversation with Alan Simpson." Interview by Harry
Kreisler. *UC Berkeley*, September 17, 1997: 3. http://globetrotter.berke
ley.edu/conversations/Simpson/simpson3.html.

Simpson, Alan K. "Let 'Er Rip: Reflections of a Rocky Mountain Senator."
Conversations with History, Institute of International Studies, University of California Berkeley, September 17, 1997. http://conversations
.berkeley.edu/content/alan-k-simpson (accessed November 15, 2013).

Sinclair, Barbara. *Party Wars*. Norman: University of Oklahoma Press, 2006.

Sinclair, Barbara. *Unorthodox Lawmaking, 4th ed*. Washington, DC: CQ
Press, 2011.

Slivinski, Stephen. "How Speaker Newt Gingrich Betrayed the Republican Revolution." *United Liberty*. Last modified December 14, 2011.
http://www.unitedliberty.org/articles/9188-how-speaker-newt-gin
grich-betrayed-the-republican-revolution (accessed December 3, 2013).

Smith, Steven S. *Call to Order*. Washington, DC: Brookings Institution,
1989.

Snyder, Brian. "U.S. Lost Almost Half a Billion Dollars due to Daylight
Saving Time." *RT*, March 12, 2013. rt.com/usa/us-lost-almost-half-
billion-dollars-due-to-daylight-saving-time-153/.

Spong, William B., Jr. "The War Powers Resolution Revisited: Historic
Accomplishment or Surrender." *William and Mary Law Review* 16, no. 4
(1975). http://scholarship.law.wm.edu/cgi/viewcontent.cgi?article=
2543&context=wmlr.

Steinberg, Alfred. *Sam Rayburn: A Biography*. New York: Hawthorn Books,
1975.

Stennis, John C. Interview by Hugh Cates, April 21, 1971, transcript,
Richard B. Russell Library for Political Research and Studies.

Stockman, David. *The Triumph of Politics*. New York: Harper & Row, 1986.

Stone, I. F. "Can Congress Stop the President?" *The New York Review of Books*,
April 19, 1973. http://www.nybooks.com/articles/archives/1973/
apr/19/can-congress-stop-the-president/.

Strand, Mark. "Discharging Their Duties." *The Congressional Institute*,
March 7, 2008.

Stuart, Douglas. *Creating the National Security State: A History of the Law
that Transformed America*. Princeton, NJ: Princeton University Press,
2008.

Swarns, Rachel L. "Senate, in Bipartisan Act, Passes an Immigration Bill." *The New York Times,* May 26, 2006. http://www.nytimes.com/2006/05/26/washington/26immig.html (accessed December 2, 2013).

Tama, Jordan. *Terrorism and National Security Reform: How Commissions Can Drive Change during Crises.* New York: Cambridge University Press, 2011.

Tap, Bruce. *Over Lincoln's Shoulder: The Committee on the Conduct of the War.* Lawrence: University Press of Kansas, 1998.

Taylor, James et al. *American Intelligence: A Framework for the Future.* Washington, DC: CIA, 1975.

Toner, Robin. "For Kennedy, No Escaping a Dark Cloud." *The New York Times,* April 17, 1991.

Toobin, Jeffrey. "Money Unlimited: How Chief Justice John Roberts Orchestrated the Citizens United Decision." *The New Yorker,* May 21, 2012.

Trattner, Walter I. *From Poor Law to Welfare State: A History of Social Welfare in America, 6th ed.* New York: Free Press, 1989.

Trausch, Susan. "The Few, The Brave, The Pac-less: Rare Is House Freshman Who Keeps Pledge." *The Boston Globe,* September 13, 1993.

United Nations Security Council. "#83 Resolution of 27 June 1950 'Complaint of Aggression upon the Republic of Korea.'" The United Nations, June 27, 1950. http://www.un.org/en/sc/documents/resolutions/1950.shtml.

United Press International. "Rayburn Is Dead; Served 17 Years as House Speaker." *New York Times,* November 17, 1961.

The U.S.-Mexico Migration Panel. "Mexico-US Migration: A Shared Responsibility." *Carnegie Endowment for International Peace* and *Instituto Tecnológico Autónomo de México,* 2001. http://carnegieendowment.org/pdf/files/M%20exicoReport2001.pdf.

U.S. Government Printing Office. "Public Papers of the Presidents of the United States: William J. Clinton (1997, Book II), Remarks on Signing the Balanced Budget Act of 1997 and the Taxpayer Relief Act of 1997." Last modified August 5, 1997. http://www.gpo.gov/fdsys/pkg/PPP-1997-book2/html/PPP-1997-book2-doc-pg1051.htm (accessed December 3, 2013).

U.S. Senate Budget Committee. "Informed Budgetteer, Special Edition: Year-End Summary & Final Omnibus Scoring." Last modified November 16, 1998. http://www.budget.senate.gov/republican/public/index.cfm/files/serve?File_id=4ac46152–723a-4fd9–8bf1-e11e865db7ea (accessed December 3, 2013).

Vestal, Donna. "Daylight Saving Time: The Ultimate Rural Legend?" *Harvest Public Media: Cultivating Stories from the Ground Up,* November 5,

2010. harvestpublicmedia.org/blog/daylight-saving-time-ultimate-rural-legend#.UpoV4cRDuSp.

Weaver, R. Kent. "The Politics of Blame Avoidance." *Journal of Public Policy* 6, no. 4 (October–December, 1986): 371–98.

Webb, Jim. "Congressional Abdication." *National Interest,* March 1, 2013. http://nationalinterest.org/article/congressional-abdication-8138.

Weintraub, Benard. "Iran Payment Found Diverted to Contras; Reagan Security Adviser and Aide Are Out." *The New York Times,* November 26, 1986.

Willett, William. "The Waste of Daylight." In *William Willett's Pamphlet.* London: Sloan Square, 1907. www.webexhibits.org/daylightsaving/willett/html.

Winik, Lyric Wallwork. "Daylight-Saving Time." *Parade Magazine,* March 27, 2005.

Wong, Scott. "House Sends DREAM Act to Senate." *Politico,* December 8, 2010. http://www.politico.com/news/stories/1210/46175.html.

Zegart, Amy. *Flawed by Design: The Evolution of the CIA, JCS, and NSC.* Stanford: Stanford University Press, 1999.

Zolberg, Aristide R. *A Nation by Design: Immigration Policy in the Fashioning of America.* Cambridge, MA: Harvard University Press, 2008.

Contributors

David M. Abshire—Vice Chairman and Counselor, Center for the Study of the Presidency & Congress; Founder and Vice Chairman of the Center for Strategic and International Studies; Former U.S. Ambassador to NATO; Author, *Saving the Reagan Presidency: Trust is the Coin of the Realm* and *A Call to Greatness: Challenging Our Next President.*

Michael Allen—Founder and Managing Director, Beacon Global Strategies; Former Majority Staff Director of the House Permanent Select Committee on Intelligence; Former Special Assistant to the President and Senior Director for Legislative Affairs, President George W. Bush; Author, *Blinking Red: Crises and Compromise in American Intelligence after 9/11.*

Ross K. Baker—Professor, Department of Political Science, Rutgers University; Author, *Friend and Foe in the U.S. Senate, House and Senate,* and *American Government.*

David Berteau—Senior Vice President and Director of National Security Program on Industry and Resources, Center for Strategic and International Studies; Adjunct Professor, Georgetown University.

Joseph A. Califano Jr.—was President Lyndon B. Johnson's chief assistant for domestic affairs and served as Secretary of Health, Education, and Welfare from 1977 to 1979. His book, *The Triumph and Tragedy of Lyndon Johnson,* originally published in 1991, is being republished by Simon and Schuster in February 2015.

Carl Cannon—Washington Bureau Chief of Real Clear Politics; Past Recipient of the Gerald R. Ford Journalism Prize for Distinguished Reporting and the Aldo Beckman Award.

Anthony Champagne—Professor, University of Texas—Dallas; Author, *Congressman Sam Rayburn,* and *Sam Rayburn: A Bio-Bibliography.*

Ross Cheit—Professor of Political Science and Public Policy, Brown University; Supervisor, Understanding the Iran-Contra Affairs Project, Brown University, Taubman Center for Public Policy.

Muzaffar Chishti—Director, Migration Policy Institute, Office at New York University School of Law.

Richard Cohen—Veteran Washington correspondent who has covered Congress for *National Journal, Politico,* and *Congressional Quarterly;* Author, *Rostenkowski: The Pursuit of Power and the End of the Old Politics.*

Kareem U. Crayton—Associate Professor of Law, University of North Carolina School of Law.

Michael Dorning—White House Correspondent, Bloomberg News.

Lee Drutman—Senior Fellow, The Sunlight Foundation; Adjunct Professor of Political Science, Johns Hopkins University and the University of California.

C. Lawrence Evans—Newtown Family Professor of Government, the College of William & Mary; Author, *Congress under Fire: Reform Politics and the Republican Majority,* and *Leadership in Committee: A Comparative Analysis of Leadership Behavior in the U.S. Senate.*

John A. Farrell—Contributing Editor and Correspondent, *The Atlantic and National Journal;* Writer, *The Denver Post, The Boston Globe;* Author, *Tip O'Neill and the Democratic Century.*

Jason J. Fichtner—Senior Research Fellow, Mercatus Center, George Mason University; Former Senior Economist, Joint Economic Committee, U.S. Congress.

David B. Frisk—Resident Fellow, Alexander Hamilton Institute for the Study of Western Civilization; Author, *If Not Us, Who?–William Rusher, National Review, and the Conservative Movement.*

Mark Gitenstein—Special Counsel, Mayer Brown, LLP; Former U.S. Ambassador to Romania; Former Chief Counsel, U.S. Senate Judiciary Committee.

Ron Haskins—Senior Fellow, The Brookings Institution; Former Senior Advisor to the President for Welfare Policy, President George W. Bush; Author, *Work Over Welfare: The Inside Story of the 1996 Welfare Reform Law.*

Loch K. Johnson—Regents Professor, School of Public and International Affairs; Author, *The Threat on the Horizon: An Inside Account of America's Search for Security after the Cold War.*

Marvin Kalb—Edward R. Murrow Professor of Practice, and Senior Fellow of the Joan Shorenstein Center on the Press, Politics, and Public Policy, Harvard University, John F. Kennedy School of Government; Author, *Haunting Legacy: Vietnam and the American Presidency from Ford to Obama.*

Charles Kamasaki—Fellow, Migration Policy Institute; Executive Vice President of the National Council of La Raza (NCLR).

Linda Killian—Washington Journalist; Political Analyst; Author, *The Swing Vote: The Untapped Power of Independents, The Freshmen: What Happened to the Republican Revolution?*

James Kitfield—Senior Fellow, The Center for the Study of the Presidency & Congress; Senior Correspondent, *National Journal*; Three-time recipient of the Gerald R. Ford Award for Distinguished Reporting on National Defense; Author, *War & Destiny: How the Bush Revolution in Foreign and Military Affairs Redefined American Power*, and *Prodigal Soldiers: How the Generation of Officers Born of Vietnam Revolutionized the American Style of War.*

Susan Sullivan Lagon—Senior Fellow, Government Affairs Institute, Georgetown University; Former Professor of American Politics and Constitutional Law, Government Department, Georgetown University.

Joe Lieberman—Senior Counsel, Kasowitz, Benson, Torres & Friedman; Former U.S. Senator from Connecticut.

Scott Lilly—Senior Fellow, Center for American Progress; Former Staff Director, U.S. House Committee on Appropriations.

Dan Mahaffee—Director of Policy and Board Relations, Center for the Study of the Presidency & Congress.

Patrick Maney—Professor, Boston College; Author, *The Forgotten New Deal Congress, 1933–1945,* and *The Roosevelt Presence: The Life and Legacy of FDR.*

Patrick McGuinn—Associate Profess, Drew University; Author, *No Child Left Behind and the Transformation of Federal Education Policy.*

Susan Milligan—Political and Foreign Affairs Contributor, *U.S. News & World Report*; Contributor, *Last Lion: The Fall and Rise of Ted Kennedy.*

Marilyn Moon—Institute Fellow, American Institutes for Research; Former Public Trustee, Social Security and Medicare trust funds; Writer, "The Patient's Advocate" (column on health reform), *The Washington Post.*

Keith Olson—Professor, Department of History, University of Maryland; Author, *Watergate: The Presidential Scandal That Shook America.*

Norman Ornstein—Senior Fellow, The Center for the Study of the Presidency & Congress; Senior Fellow, American Enterprise Institute; Author, *The Permanent Campaign and Its Future, The Broken Branch: How Congress Is Failing America and How to Get It Back on Track,* and *It's Even Worse than It Looks: How the American Constitutional System Collided with the Politics of Extremism.*

James Patterson—Ford Foundation Professor of History Emeritus, Brown University; Author, *Mr. Republican: A Biography of Robert A. Taft.*

Rudolph G. Penner—Institute Fellow, and Arjay and Frances Miller Chair in Public Policy, Urban Institute; Former Director, Congressional Budget Office; Author, *The Moving Pieces of Social Security Reform.*

Elaine S. Povich—Adjunct Professor, University of Maryland; Journalist; Author, *Nancy Pelosi: A Biography.*

Richard Reeves—Journalist; Writer; Senior Lecturer, Annenberg School for Communication and Journalism, University of Southern California; Author,

Portrait of Camelot: A Thousand Days in the Kennedy White House, and *A Ford, Not a Lincoln.*

Jan Reid—Former Senior Editor, *Texas Monthly;* Contributor, *Esquire, GQ, Slate,* and *The New York Times.*

Katherine A. Scott—Assistant Historian, U.S. Senate Historical Office; Adjunct Professor, Cornell University.

John T. Shaw—Congressional Correspondent, Market News International; Author, *Richard G. Lugar, Statesmen of the Senate.*

Ellen Schrecker—Professor of History Emerita, Yeshiva University; Author, *The Age of McCarthyism: A Brief History with Documents.*

Jordan Tama—Assistant Professor, School of International Service, American University; Author, *Terrorism and National Security Reform: How Commissions Can Drive Change during Crises.*

Kirk Victor—Contributing editor of *National Journal* and coauthor of former Senator Ernest F. "Fritz" Hollings memoir, *Making Government Work.*

Sheryl B. Vogt—Director, Richard B. Russell Library for Political Research and Studies, University of Georgia.

Acknowledgments

On behalf of the Center for the Study of the Presidency & Congress, I would like to thank the following for their contributions to the *Triumphs and Tragedies of the Modern Congress:*

Dr. David M. Abshire, Vice Chairman & President *Emeritus* of the Center, whose lifelong commitments to learning from the lessons of history and to building consensus in Washington are driving principles behind the work of this Center.

Our trustees whose generous support was essential to the book: Andrew Barth, Dr. Malik Hasan, Dr. Ray Irani, Daniel Lubin, B. Francis Saul III, Pamela Scholl, Ambassador Robert Tuttle, and Stanley Zax.

Daniel Lubin deserves special thanks for first encouraging us to produce this congressional anthology and thus grow the *Triumphs and Tragedies* series. Additionally, I am deeply grateful for funding from the Dr. Scholl Foundation that enabled us to convert the vision into a reality.

Our staff and interns, including Kathleen Aldrich, Marili Alvarado, Phyllis d'Hoop, Summer Fields, Natalia Jaramillo, Jonathan Murphy, Collin Odell, Ann Marie Packo, Elizabeth Perch, Hurst Renner, Jeff Shaffer, Sara Spancake, Ben Stutts, Madeline Vale, Alexandra White, and Melanie Zook.

Dan Mahaffee and Nick Platt have been invaluable as the coordinators of this project, spending countless hours to ensure that this book was completed on time—not an easy feat with an edited volume.

Praeger Publishing and its exceptional team, especially Steve Catalano. I also thank Chris Howard for his efforts to help launch this project.

The outstanding authors whose contributions of time, experience, and historical knowledge are evident in the final product.

Finally, I would like to thank my very distinguished coeditors, James Kitfield, Chris Lu, and Norm Ornstein, for their leadership of this project. Their complementary experiences and talents make this volume both highly informative and very entertaining.

Maxmillian Angerholzer III
President & CEO
Center for the Study of the Presidency & Congress

Index

National Military Establishment
(renamed Defense Department), 231
National Security Act of 1947, xx,
225–31, 264, 271, 307; background,
225–26; diluted reforms, 229–31;
intelligence reform, 229; Navy
pushback, 227–29; political and
institutional resistance to, 226–27;
Woodrum Committee and, 227–28.
See also Truman, Harry
National Security Agency (NSA), 266,
269, 304–5
National Security Council (NSC), 328
Native Americans: Daylight Saving Time
(DST) and, 122; Jack Abramoff and,
115–16
Naval Affairs Committee, 228–29
Nazi Germany, xx, 216, 221. *See also*
Roosevelt, Franklin D. vs. congressional isolationists leading to WWII
Nazi-Soviet Non-Aggression Pact, 233
Neutrality Acts of 1935 and 1936, 217
New Deal Congress, 125–30, 232–33;
major pieces of legislation during
the FDR's First Hundred Days,
127–28; pivotal role of congressional
legislation during FDR's New Deal,
125–29; standout congressional
members, 126–27; wartime (WWII)
shift in power from Congress to
FDR, 129–30
Nicaragua: arms sales to Iran to support
the Nicaragua Contras, 328. *See also*
Iran-Contra scandal
Nichols, Bill (D-AL), 271–78
Nields, John, 331
9/11 Commission, xx, 306–11; background, 306–7; politics and, 309–11;
reforming national intelligence,
307–9
Nixon, Richard (R-CA): actions taken
without congressional approval, 5;
Alger Hiss and, 234; all-volunteer

force and, 245–47, 253; base closures
and, 279; impoundment and, 147;
resignation of, 326–27, 338; secret
campaign contributions, 196; Vietnam War and, 257–58; War Powers
Resolution of 1973 and, 261–62;
Watergate, 37, 38, 263–64. *See also*
Watergate scandal
NLRB v. Jones, 6
No Child Left Behind (NCLB) act,
201–9; background, 201–3; compro-
mises, 207–8; four factions of federal
education policy, 205; George W.
Bush and bipartisan efforts, 203–7;
mixed results, 208–9; testing and
accountability measures, 205–8;
vouchers, 203, 205, 206. *See also*
Education reform
Nonmarital births: welfare reform and,
187. *See also* Welfare Reform Law of
1996
North Atlantic Treaty Organization
(NATO), 83–84; Long Term Defense
Program (LTDP), 103; Sam Nunn
(D-GA) and, 103–8
North, Oliver, 328, 331, 332, 333
Nuclear option (Senate), 16, 131, 133
Nunn-Lugar Act of 1991, 102, 110
Nunn, Sam (D-GA), xix, 9, 102–8, 290,
297, 299, 300; biographical sum-
mary, 102; deteriorating deterrence,
104–5; North Atlantic Treaty Organi-
zation (NATO) and, 103–8
Nye, Gerald P. (R-ND), 213, 217, 225

Obama, Barack, 316; Afghanistan and,
294; bypassing the Constitution, 4;
comments on campaign spending,
201; comparison to Clinton era,
183–84; deficit reduction negotiations with Boehner ("grand bargain"), 133, 149; Don't Ask, Don't
Tell Repeal Act of 2010, 300; FISA

About the Editors

MAXMILLIAN ANGERHOLZER III

Serves as the President & CEO of the Center for the Study of the Presidency & Congress (CSPC). He is also Senior Adviser and Corporate Secretary of the Richard Lounsbery Foundation, a philanthropic institution in Washington, D.C., which awards grants primarily in science and technology policy, education, international relations, and security. Mr. Angerholzer has served as the Special Assistant to the Vice Chairman of the Center for Strategic and International Studies (CSIS) in Washington, D.C. He holds a bachelor of arts (magna cum laude) in political science from the University of the South in Sewanee, Tennessee, and a master of arts from the George Washington University's Elliott School of International Affairs.

JAMES KITFIELD

Has written on national security, intelligence, and foreign policy issues for over two decades. Currently a contributing editor and formerly a senior correspondent at the *National Journal*, Mr. Kitfield is a three-time winner of the Gerald R. Ford Award for Distinguished Reporting on National Defense, a five-time winner of the Military Reporters and Editors Association award, and a recipient of the National Press Club's top prize for diplomatic correspondence. His many other awards include the Association of Former Intelligence Officers' Steward Alsop Media Excellence Award, and the German Marshall Fund's Peter R. Weitz Prize. A magna cum laude graduate of the

University of Georgia's Henry Grady School of Journalism, Kitfield is the author of two books, *War & Destiny* and *Prodigal Soldiers.*

CHRISTOPHER P. LU

During his long career in public service, Mr. Lu has served in all three branches of the federal government and is an expert on how policy gets made in Washington. On Capitol Hill, he was Deputy Chief Counsel for the House Oversight and Government Reform Committee, then Legislative Director and Acting Chief of Staff to then-Senator Obama. Following the 2008 Presidential election, Mr. Lu was Executive Director of the Presidential Transition Team. From 2009 to 2013, he was the White House Cabinet Secretary and Assistant to the President, and he is currently Deputy Secretary of the U.S. Department of Labor. A magna cum laude graduate of Princeton University and cum laude graduate of Harvard Law School, Mr. Lu also has worked as a law clerk to a federal court of appeals judge.

NORMAN ORNSTEIN

A Resident Scholar at the American Enterprise Institute, is a contributing editor and columnist for *National Journal* and *The Atlantic.* Named as one of 2012's Top 100 Global Thinkers by *Foreign Policy* magazine, Mr. Ornstein led a working group that helped shape the campaign finance reform law known as McCain-Feingold. His many books include *The Broken Branch: How Congress Is Failing America and How to Get It Back on Track*, and most recently, *It's Even Worse than It Looks: How the American Constitutional System Collided with the New Politics of Extremism*, a *New York Times* best seller. His vast experience includes positions over the last two decades at *USA Today, Roll Call,* the Pew Research Center for People and the Press, CBS News, and the Council of Foreign Relations.